1992

CONTEMPORARY
INDIAN TRADITION

The Smithsonian Institution gratefully acknowl-
edges a generous grant from the James Smithson
Society, and contributions from the Matsushita
Electric Corporation of America and the M. W.
Kellogg Company, in support of this publication.

We also wish to express our sincere appreciation to
the sponsors of the symposium on which this
volume is based:
Indian Advisory Committee, Festival of India
Department of Culture, Government of India
American Institute of Indian Studies
Ford Foundation
Northern Telecom International Limited
Communications Workers of America
Pfizer International Inc.
Philip Johnson

Richard Kurin was special consultant to the
volume editor.

CONTEMPORARY INDIAN TRADITION

Voices on Culture, Nature, and the Challenge of Change

EDITED BY CARLA M. BORDEN

Smithsonian Institution Press

Washington and London

Editor: Joanne Reams
Designer: Linda McKnight

Cover: *Speaking Street,* G. M. Sheikh, 1981, Roopan-
kar Museum of Fine Arts, Bhopal. Reproduced with
permission.

Library of Congress Cataloging-in-Publication Data
Contemporary Indian tradition.
    Includes index.
    1. India—Civilization—1947–   . 2. India—
Social conditions—1947–   . 3. Ecology—India.
I. Borden, Carla M.
DS428.2.C66 1988   954   88-6707
ISBN 0-87474-258-7

British Library Cataloging-in-Publication Data available
Manufactured in the United States of America
10 9 8 7 6 5 4 3 2 1

97 96 95 94 93 92 91 90 89

Table of Contents

Illustrations

PLATES

Lahiri Choudhury. Copyright D. K. Lahiri Choudhury, reproduced with permission.

FIGURE 19.2. Domesticated animals after a day's grazing in the forest. Photo: D. K. Lahiri Choudhury. Copyright D. K. Lahiri Choudhury, reproduced with permission.

FIGURE 19.3. India: Distribution of Elephants (1983).

FIGURE 19.4. A wild tusker in sub-Himalayan forest. Photo: D. K. Lahiri Choudhury. Copyright D. K. Lahiri Choudhury, reproduced with permission.

FIGURE 19.5. Desert in West Khasi Hills, Meghalaya. Photo: D. K. Lahiri Choudhury. Copyright D. K. Lahiri Choudhury, reproduced with permission.

FIGURES 19.6 and 19.7. Slash-and-burn cultivation. Photos: D. K. Lahiri Choudhury. Copyright D. K. Lahiri Choudhury, reproduced with permission.

FIGURE 19.8. A group of huts destroyed by a herd of elephants in northern Bengal. Photo: D. K. Lahiri Choudhury. Copyright D. K. Lahiri Choudhury, reproduced with permission.

FIGURE 19.9. Rogue *maknā* (tuskless male elephant) liquidated. Photo: D. K. Lahiri Choudhury. Copyright D. K. Lahiri Choudhury, reproduced with permission.

FIGURES 19.10. and 19.11. Masonry-sided elephant-proof ditches. Photos: D. K. Lahiri Choudhury. Copyright D. K. Lahiri Choudhury, reproduced with permission.

FIGURE 19.12. Elephants at their morning bath at Sonepur. Photo: D. K. Lahiri Choudhury. Copyright D. K. Lahiri Choudhury, reproduced with permission.

FIGURE 21.1. Architecture born out of rituals (Sun Temple at Modhera). Photo: Stein Doshi & Bhalla, Ahmedabad.

FIGURE 21.2. Lingaraj Temple at Bhubaneshwar. Reproduced from Percy Brown, *Indian Architecture* (Hindu and Buddhist Periods), by permission of the Publishers, D. B. Taraporevaia Sons & Co. Private Ltd.

FIGURE 21.3. A typical house, Jaipur. Photo: Stein Doshi & Bhalla, Ahmedabad.

FIGURE 21.4. A typical street entrance to a house, Jaipur. Photo: Stein Doshi & Bhalla, Ahmedabad.

FIGURE 21.5. Plan of Fatehpur Sikri. Reproduced from John D. Hoag, *Islamic Architecture,* by courtesy of Electa Editrice, Milan.

FIGURE 21.6. View of model showing courts and classrooms, Indian Institute of Management, Bangalore.

FIGURE 21.7. Linking corridor in Tirupati Temple complex. Photo: Stein Doshi & Bhalla, Ahmedabad.

FIGURE 21.8. Corridor, Indian Institute of Management, Bangalore. Photo: Stein Doshi & Bhalla, Ahmedabad.

FIGURE 21.9. Corridor, Indian Institute of Management, Bangalore. Photo: Stein Doshi & Bhalla, Ahmedabad.

FIGURE 21.10. Pataleshwar Temple, Pune. Photo: Stein Doshi & Bhalla, Ahmedabad.

FIGURE 21.11. Shikhara Temple at Khajuraho. Photo: Stein Doshi & Bhalla, Ahmedabad.

FIGURES 21.12. and 21.13. Sangath, views from across the garden and steps. Photos: Stein Doshi & Bhalla, Ahmedabad.

FIGURE 21.14. *Havelī* (large residence) in Jaisalmer, showing a separate skin for openings to the exterior and shading the main structure. Photo: Stein Doshi & Bhalla, Ahmedabad.

FIGURE 23.5. Belapur Housing, New Bombay. Photo: Joseph St. Anne, Bombay, reproduced with permission.

FIGURE 23.6. Mud house, Rajasthan. Photo: C. M. Correa, reproduced with permission.

FIGURE 23.7. People in pipe. Reproduced from Charles Correa, *The New Landscape* (Bombay: The Book Society of India, 1985), with permission of the author.

FIGURE 23.8. Mythic city. Photo: Joseph St. Anne, Bombay, reproduced with permission.

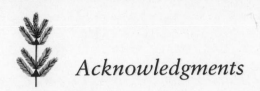

Acknowledgments

So very many individuals contributed to the work and pleasure of "The Canvas of Culture" symposium as well as the subsequent preparation of this volume, and I wish I could recognize all of them by name here. Whether they provided a needed clarification of fact, recommended a seminal book or article, greeted a weary traveler at an airport, or helped define the scope and purposes of the undertaking—and some people fit several descriptions—every one of them has my whole-hearted appreciation.

At one point in time Richard Kurin was so used to my calling him for advice that he could answer the phone "Hello, Borden" before even hearing my voice. Our talks about India and the ways it is studied, in the context of planning the symposium program and the numerous essays he reviewed, were always engrossing and illuminating. Extremely generous with his knowledge and opinions, he was a wonderful colleague and guide from start to finish.

The symposium and I would hardly have been set off in the direction we were, with the same commitment and momentum, except for Gieve Patel. While he was a fellow at the Woodrow Wilson International Center for Scholars in 1984, he happily brought to an end our search for a theme through which we could explore the kinds of concerns we thought we should. Then, for the next year, he continued to prompt, investigate, evaluate, and listen faithfully. His friendship helped turn a special assignment into an experience of growth, and that made an enormous difference.

Pupul Jayakar was symposium cochairperson in far more than name. Because of her involvement and interest we were able to make "The Canvas of Culture" a central event in the Festival of India and a memorable occasion for those who took part in it.

Francine Berkowitz's informed imagination and constant support on all levels were immeasurably important to the program and to me, as they have been to countless others with connections to India. I looked forward to opportunities to confer with A. K. Ramanujan on the symposium and the book; he was gracious and wise in his counsel and gently led me toward understanding when I needed it. Sunil Roy was a cherished and trusted source of ideas and assistance and played an active role in varied aspects of the symposium. Maureen Liebl performed complicated and vital tasks for Festival of India symposium organizers and participants with efficiency and resourcefulness, caring, and cheer. Niranjan Desai, who had responsibilities for the entire festival, facilitated our operations at critical stages. Nathan Glazer, Kapila Vatsyayan, Sylvia Gottwald, Barbara Ramusack, Rajmohan Gandhi, Michael Meister, Chidananda Dasgupta, Satish Gujral, and Brian Silver, along with many others I would have enjoyed knowing under any circumstances, significantly enriched the process and results, too. And how different my visits to India might have been if Pradeep Mehendiratta, his family, and the staff of the American Institute of Indian Studies had not looked after me so well I fortunately can only wonder.

At the Smithsonian, Ralph Rinzler deserves mention here, as do Diana Duke Duncan, Jeffrey LaRiche, Ed Bastian, and, of course, S. Dillon Ripley. And in my office, the director Wilton Dillon launched the planning, found funding, and enabled me to pursue my ambitions to their full extent; Jutta Lewis organized publicity and invitational events with her natural competence and grace; Becky Dodson worked eagerly behind the scenes. Helen Leavitt, Dorothy Richardson, and Ulrike Duenkelsbuehler also lent a welcome hand. Daniel Goodwin, Ruth Spiegel, Alan Carter, Linda McKnight, and Joanne Reams produced this volume for the Smithsonian Institution Press. Their skill and their enthusiasm for the project are reflected throughout.

Several people in addition to Richard Kurin offered their expertise and judgment for editing some of the papers, including my prologue: Michael Robinson, Mihir Bhatt, and Bill Lebovich, who each read a section's worth; Cristy West; Bruce Beehler; Michael Meister; Jeffrey LaRiche; Wilton Dillon; A. K. Ramanujan; Edith Levine; Mangalam Srinivasan; Manjula Kumar; Milton Singer; Barbara Rossi; and Ramu Gandhi. Scott Berger was of great help in checking references. Allen

Thrasher and Susan Oleksiw sifted through the entire manuscript for Indian-language words to put them in good order.

I am especially grateful to Ravi Dayal and Rukun Advani at Oxford University Press in New Delhi for their favorable response to our efforts to provide an Indian edition of this work.

Milton Singer, who was not able to attend the symposium, nevertheless was as engaged with the proceedings as anyone. The time, thought, information, and attentive encouragement he gave were a privilege to receive. In his foreword, he has added his own voice to those raised here.

Last but not least, the participants themselves influenced this program in all its facets. Each of them with whom I had the opportunity to spend any time provided valuable insights I tried to apply, or introduced me to colleagues, social settings, and works of art they knew I would learn from and enjoy. They were kind and open, even courageous. For the knowledge, sustenance, and satisfaction they have brought over the last several years, I am deeply grateful.

Plate 1.

Plate 1. Aerial view of Piazza
Pubblico, Siena.

Plate 2.

Plate 4.

Plate 2. Effeti del buon governo
in città (Effects of Good Government), *Ambrogio Lorenzetti,
1338–40.*

Plate 4. Storie della vita di Cristo
(Story of the Passion), *Duccio di
Buoninsegna, 1308–11.*

Plate 3.

Plate 3. St. Francis Bears Witness
to the Christian Faith before the
Sultan *(panel from an altarpiece),
Sassetta (or Stefano di Giovanni),
1437–44, wood. Reproduced by
courtesy of the Trustees, The
National Gallery, London.*

Plate 5.

Plate 6.

Plate 5. Woman at Her Toilet
Wringing Water from Her Hair,
Indian (Rajput, Punjab Hills),
Basohli, early eighteenth cen-
tury, watercolor on paper. Ross-
Coomaraswamy Collection,
17.2798. Courtesy, Museum of
Fine Arts, Boston.

Plate 6. Pabuji ka Phad, *scroll of*
heroic exploits of Pabuji, with nar-
rator and accompanying performer,
Rajasthan, contemporary.

Plate 7. Assassination of Indira Gandhi, *Ajit Chitrakar, 1985, narrative scroll from Mid-napur, West Bengal.*

Plate 8. Chakshudana Pata, *Dukhushyam Chitrakar, 1985.*

Plate 9.

Plate 9. Kin, *G. M. Sheikh, 1979.*

Plate 10.

Plate 10. Speaking Street, *G. M. Sheikh, 1981.*

Plate 11.

Plate 11. Revolving Routes, G. M.
Sheikh, 1981.

Plate 12.

Plate 12. Summer Diary, G. M.
Sheikh, 1985.

Plate 13.

*Plate 13. Untitled, Sudhir Pat-
wardhan, 1984, oil pastel on paper.
Source is first or second century A.D.
Butkara sculpture.*

Plate 14.

*Plate 14. Untitled, Sudhir Pat-
wardhan, 1984, oil pastel on paper.
Source is Mughal miniature, c. 1640.*

Plate 15.

Plate 16.

Plate 15. The ceremonial opening day of the Sonepur melā in 1978. In 1985, the same row of tuskers contained only five animals.

Plate 16. The house form conceived through tactile and visual sense (in village Sam in Rajasthan desert).

Plate 17. A study of Sangath campus.

Plate 18. Sangath, view from across the garden and steps.

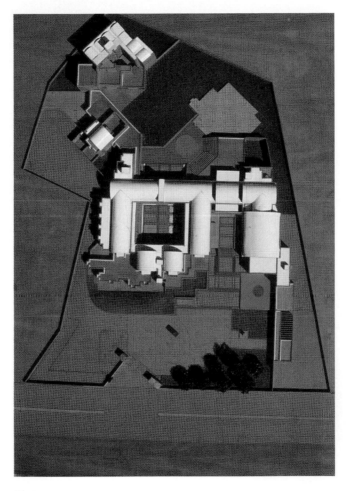

Plate 19.

*Plate 19. Model, Gandhi Labour
Institute, Ahmedabad.*

Plate 20. Roof terraces,
National Institute of
Immunology.

Plate 21. Cidade de Goa.

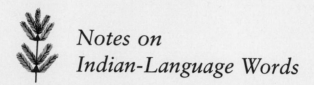

Notes on Indian-Language Words

Proper names appear in this volume without diacritics; we have generally kept the original spelling, except when another form of the name is more widely known in the West (e.g., we use Krishna rather than Krsna). Titles of Indic texts also have no diacritics but are italicized. Terms appear in italics and with diacritics (following the Library of Congress transliteration system), unless they have become familiar in English (e.g., purana). The endnotes and bibliographic references are presented for scholars who may wish to consult the sources, and so they are as precise as possible.

FOREWORD

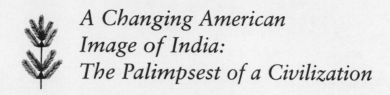

A Changing American Image of India: The Palimpsest of a Civilization

Milton Singer

The present book and the Smithsonian symposium on which it is based are notable in America's changing image of India. One might have expected that a major event in the 1985–86 Festival of India would celebrate the colorful folk arts and crafts, the great variety of people and languages, the elephants, tigers, and maharajas of the travel posters, and the great epics and myths that stirred Thoreau and Emerson. Many of these images, to be sure, were represented in various exhibitions and events of the Festival of India, and nowhere more vividly than in the demonstration of living arts and crafts called "Aditi: A Celebration of Life." These images are also given some form of representation in this book, but in a more ambivalent mood. The tiger and the elephant have become endangered species, the sacred rivers and groves are threatened by pollution and destruction, the myths and epics are being rediscovered in regional languages and variants, the folk arts and crafts are being modernized and commercialized. This is not meant to suggest that the old romantic image of India as the land of the fabulous and marvelous, of the ancient treasures of wisdom, has now been converted into the nineteenth-century stereotype of teeming millions of caste-ridden, superstitious, and starving people crowded off their lands and streets by sacred cows and monkeys.

The authors of these essays are obviously too well informed and critical to have embraced either the romantic image or the image of the white man's burden. It is not immediately apparent that their essays share a common image of India, as they do. In fact the diversity of their backgrounds, training, and professional careers would make such an outcome quite unexpected, and their essays tend to emphasize the diversity of India's traditions.

In view of the Smithsonian's participation in the development of recent American scholarship about India and Asia, it is not surprising that it should have been asked to host several of the Festival of India exhibitions and to organize the symposium that produced the present book. Nor is it surprising that some of the same scholars, both Indian and American, who have contributed to the establishment of Indian studies at American colleges and universities were also represented at the symposium. This book, however, was not designed as an anthology of specialized scholarship or as an introductory textbook on India, nor is it a random selection of articles about India. As the book's editor and the symposium's organizer, Carla Borden, explains in her prologue, she selected contributors who were likely to have some significant things to say about how contemporary India is rediscovering its cultural traditions and adapting them to the solution of present problems. A notable and distinctive feature of her selection is that it includes Indian writers, poets and playwrights, painters, journalists, and union organizers, architects, a museum director and designer, as well as some university professors, Indian and American, who specialize in academic disciplines relating to India. The interest, variety, and readability of the essays more than justify her selections.

In spite of the strong nonacademic representation among its contributors and the general audience for which the volume is intended, the portrait of India that emerges from the book bears a recognizable likeness to the portrait produced by academic scholarship and teaching. (For a sample of this scholarship, see the references by Brown, Cohn, Das, Dimmit and van Buitenen, Marriott, O'Flaherty, Singer, Singer and Cohn, Srinivas, and Vatsyayan.) This convergence may be due in part to the permeable boundaries between the academic and the nonacademic worlds and, to some extent, to the participation of some of the contributors in both worlds. But the resemblance between the two kinds of portraits, I would suggest, may also be explained by the essential similarity of the problems presented and the convergence of the solutions. The familiar story of the elephant and the six blind men's descriptions of it, an old Indian story, is a graphic parable about how a diversity of descriptions gets generated by taking different viewpoints. The story also assumes, however, that there is one and the same elephant for the six blind men to discover and describe.

One way of reading this book is as a selection of striking and apt illustrations of the symposium's organizing theme: rediscovery of the past as adaptation for the future. There is, however, another perspective from which to read the book, not incompatible with the first. That is the perspective of the student of the comparative study of civilizations who asks, how do the essays in this book help us to think about Indian civilization as a whole and the various parts that make it up?

In his lecture "Thinking About a Civilization," presented to a 1957 conference *Introducing India in Liberal Education* at the University of Chicago, Robert Redfield, the anthropologist, asked,

> Can the mind take hold of so large, complex, and changing a thing as a civilization? . . . To think of a civilization requires the making of choices: the rejection of something in favor of something else. The choices have to do with the content, the substantial characteristics, and also with the "fuzzy" limits of the civilization in time and space. The effort requires perspicacity of abstract comprehensiveness in event and fact, while responsible to event and fact for confirming, rejecting, or modifying the abstraction. It encounters the civilization as happenings through long time and as characteristics at any particular time, and meets the problem of combining, in alternation or in some synthesis, the cycle and the spirit of the civilization . . . : India as a limited number of regions characterized by soil, water, climate, and spatial relationships in which people have worked out their lives; India as a past succession of major events; India as predominating and persisting institutions, economic, political, or social; India as kinds of people speaking kinds of languages and following kinds of customs; India as philosophies, moralities, and religions. How much of this can be held in the mind? What of it can be combined? What new comprehensive ideas for characterizing India can be found (Redfield in Singer 1957, 10–11)?

Later in the same lecture, Redfield answered his questions by suggesting that one comprehensive conception of a civilization would be to think of it as a physical thing with physical properties of form, dimensions in space and time, and an interrelation of parts. Such a conception, he suggested, is a sort of scaffolding, or "three-dimensional diagram of the civilization, a product of my imagination as influenced by the physical bodies I know from common experience and of course as guided by what I learn of the civilization. I may think of it in reference to the designs or decorations of a textile, to the construction of an edifice, to a machine, or to a living organism" (ibid. 12).

The editor did not explicitly employ Redfield's conception of Indian civilization as an organizing principle for this book. Yet, interestingly, she did use the metaphor of "the canvas of culture" as the title for the symposium. Also interesting is the fact that at least two of the papers presented to the symposium used two of the physical models of Indian civilization mentioned by Redfield. Kapila Vatsyayan's paper "Canvas or Body Organism" developed the conception of Indian civilization as a living organism, not merely as an analogy or metaphor but as a living reality. That Surajit Sinha's paper presented a Redfieldian conceptual framework that relates tribal cultural traditions to those of peasant castes, and to urban classics, is less surprising, since Sinha was associated with Redfield's project in the 1950s at the University of Chicago. I should like in any case to comment briefly on some of the essays in this book from the perspective of Redfield's conception of a civilization, whether or not that conception is discussed by the authors.

INDIA'S DIVERSITY AND UNITY

Belonging to a generation somewhat older than most of the contributors to *Contemporary Indian Tradition*, I have the advantage (and disadvantage) of about thirty years' historical perspective on the subjects of the essays in this volume. Having listened to Prime Minister Jawaharlal Nehru speak to the Indian National Congress in January 1955 at Avadi near Madras about the "socialistic pattern of society" and also recalling his castigation in other speeches of the "fissiparous tendencies of casteism, linguism, and communalism," and his appeals for "emotional integration" of the nation, I was struck by the impression that none of the essays seems to worry about the problem of national unity and integration. The "fissiparous tendencies" may still be evident in Sikh separatism in Punjab, in tribal separatism in Assam, and in Hindu-Muslim communalism in Gujarat, but the violent acts they have generated are attributed by the authors to a modern, secular, central government's drive for homogeneity. The implied political solution seems to be pluralism and tolerance for diversity—linguistic, social, and religious, at local and regional levels as well as at the all-India level. Practically all the essays tend to echo this emphasis on diversity, although the essay by Veena Das gives it a most eloquent expression:

> It is imperative for us now to search for other models of pluralism
> within our own history and mythology, for images of the self and the
> other, of being and meaning, in order to develop them creatively. . . .
> What we are looking for is alternative designs for life based upon the
> recognition of difference. The quest for homogeneity and similarity—
> the premises for the idea of harmony in the modern world—ends up
> treating society as a mere "collection" of people. To my mind this has
> simply sanctioned increasing violence and the worship of death.

Das's tolerance for diversity draws the line at the ideology of the modern secular state and of Sikh, Muslim, Hindu, and Christian fundamentalist movements, which

> display antipathy to popular religious practices evolved through centuries of living together. . . . I am not advocating that we simply tolerate pluralism but that we try to find a theory in which differences and divisions may be celebrated as providing a design for life. Although the metaphor of purity is very dear to the Indian and has even been given a political context now, I may conclude by saying that complete purity is a condition of sterility. It is only on condition that one is willing to be polluted that creative communication becomes possible.

Das's plea for tolerance and celebration of diversity will strike a responsive chord in anyone who has been subjected to the coercive pressures of social conformity. Whether these pressures are primarily generated by the modern secular state and are oppressive and unjust, as she asserts, is an arguable proposition. She does not, in any case, propose pat and dogmatic solutions for this problem. Rather she calls for a constructive rethinking of how the question of variety has been viewed in Hindu culture, and how the traditional doctrines might be adapted to present and future needs. Her own discussion of the relations of polytheism to monotheism, of *dharma* and the ends of life, and of pilgrimage exemplify a thoughtful and creative approach to the task of reconciling orthodoxy with popular traditions, an approach that avoids the zealotry and violence of various brands of ideological purity.

Das sets herself a noble task, indeed, to which the present volume may be a prelude. While Indians work toward the day when more of the voices of the hitherto oppressed can be heard and become part of Indian history, what are some of the differences and divisions that need to be recognized and celebrated and, eventually, to be emotionally integrated into India's civilization? This book wisely does not attempt to make an exhaustive survey of such differences, but it does highlight some very important ones and embeds them in the historical contexts in which they have emerged or are now emerging. A few comments may help the general reader identify some underlying themes.

The diversity of religions and rituals, regional languages and literatures, local and regional theater, and folk arts and crafts is being recognized and celebrated in these essays. Even the great epics, long considered as the unifying core of Indian civilization, are rediscovered in the living oral tradition of the "ocean of stories." Most striking of all, Advaita Vedanta, the nondualist Indian philosophy best known in the West, is invoked to support a metaphysical and theological democratic pluralism that finds a spark of divinity and of creativity in everyone, even in Mark Twain and the late actor Peter Sellers. Ramchandra Gandhi's apt translation of Advaita philosophy into Mark Twain's vernacular English invites a reciprocal translation of the recent song "We Are the World" into the Advaita doctrine of the identity of the self and the world.

The essays on literature and the arts reflect very well Surajit Sinha's levels of cultural development—tribal, peasant, and urban—in reverse sequence: the classical Sanskrit texts and myths discussed by Wendy Doniger O'Flaherty, the rediscovery of classical Tamil texts described by A. K. Ramanujan, the regional folk theater and dance dramas that inspired the playwright Girish Karnad, and the "sea of skill" in the folk and tribal arts and crafts described by Rajeev Sethi, who brought forty craftspeople and two thousand artifacts to the impressive Festival of India exhibit, "Aditi."

O'Flaherty's discussion of Sanskrit classics challenges the popular Western conception of "classics" as eternal and universal texts. The most sacred Sanskrit texts, the Vedas, she points out, were also the most restricted, transmitted orally and guarded jealously by members of particular Brahman families who "owned" particular Vedas. In South India today, some Brahman families include in their names the name of the Veda the family was traditionally required to learn and transmit, although Sanskrit education, and even Vedic Sanskrit, is now available to wider groups. The great epics the *Mahabharata* and the *Ramayana* and the puranic myths, however, were from early times transmitted, as O'Flaherty notes, in writing as well as orally, in more fluid forms, and made accessible to wider audiences in regional languages through public recitals and dramatic and musical performances.

During a first stay in Madras City in 1954–55, I attended in and around the city so many performances using a great variety of cultural media, in which episodes from the epics and myths were recited, sung, danced, dramatized, ritualized, and filmed, with lithographs, sculptures, papier-mâché, colorful costumes, stage sets, and musical instruments, that I began to think of Indian culture as encapsulated in the multimedia enactments that I called "cultural performances." These performances became for me the minimum meaningful units of observation and the data for analyzing cultural changes and cultural continuities associated with the urbanization of both folk and classical cultural traditions.

Ramanujan's account of how some Tamil classics were rediscovered in the nineteenth century by a Tamil scholar through encounters with Hindu, Jain, and English Tamil scholars and communities dramatizes his observation that India has many traditions and many pasts, and that the past and present change each other. Himself a poet, translator, linguist, and folklorist, Ramanujan voices his personal ambivalence toward his Brahman Sanskrit legacy in his poem "Prayers to Lord Murugan." The prayers to Lord Murugan, Ramanujan explains, are antiprayers, using an old poem to make a new poem say some new (and surprising) things.

A similar ambivalence toward Sanskrit drama is expressed by the Indian playwright Girish Karnad as he reviews his search for indigenous Indian dramatic forms and finds a sense of energy and rich technical means in popular and folk theater. For him, as for the other artists, the past coexists with the present as a parallel form. The image of plural Indian traditions and plural worlds is most strikingly projected in the paper "Among Several Cultures and Times" by the Indian Muslim painter Gulam Mohammed Sheikh. In his case, visits to the Italian city of Siena and its Renaissance frescoes, and to the Indian paintings in the Victoria and Albert Museum in London, helped him to discover that the "rationale for structure [in Indian painting] did not lie in any principle of enclosure in an outer border or frame. . . . The painting is revealed in stages . . . , detail by detail. . . . What emerges in the end is an image of multiple visions, each in relation to as well as independent from the others." This discovery no doubt recalled to the painter the world of his childhood, in which he experienced "a close convergence of Hindu and Muslim rituals in family customs and ceremonies" and "prayed five times a day in the mosque, but . . . moved in the company of Jain and Brahman friends, including a priest, the rest of the time."

TRANSITIONS FROM A TRADITIONAL TO A MODERN SOCIETY

In India, the relation of the individual self to society and culture differs from the Western conception. The contrast was dramatically sketched in the paper "Models of Psychological Healing: Indian and Western" by Sudhir Kakar and is also referred to in some of the essays. An Indian psychoanalyst trained in the West and author of the influential book *The Inner World: A Psychoanalytic Study of Childhood and Society in India,* Kakar contrasts the modern Western individualistic assumptions about the goals and methods of psychotherapy with the traditional relational assumptions underlying psychotherapy and related healing practices in India. The expected presence of the patient's family, the greater reliance on silence and looking and less on talking, the stress on "surrender to powers beyond the individual" and on "harmonious integration with one's group" characterize the Indian approach, according to Kakar. "The Indian cultural orientation demands that the therapy be public and the ritual standard. The therapy requires a polyphonic social drama that attempts a ritual restoration of the dialogues, not only within the patient, but with the family, community, and its gods."

Although he does not use the therapeutic aphorisms, Kakar's contrast can be summed up in a contrast between Freud's aphorism "Where id was, there shall ego be" for Western psychotherapy and "Where ego was, there shall we, the family, be" for India.

The American psychoanalyst Alan Roland, who has lived and worked in India and Japan, has reported observations on psychotherapy in these countries that tend to agree with Kakar's. Roland has introduced the concepts of a "familial self" and a "we-self" to mark the distinctive features of Indian self-development (Roland 1982).

Kakar's contrast between Western and Indian psychotherapies would seem to confirm the French anthropologist Louis Dumont's now classic treatise *Homo Hierarchicus: The Caste System and Its Implications* (Dumont 1980 [1966]), in which Indian society is characterized as hierarchic and holistic, whereas Western society is portrayed as egalitarian and individualistic. For Dumont, however, this contrast is not a descriptive empirical generalization, at the level of concrete facts, but an ideal-typical construction to guide observation and interpretation of cultural ideologies and social norms. With this qualification, it becomes possible to reconcile Dumont's view of the Indian caste system with the more empirically oriented views of M. N. Srinivas, McKim Marriott, and others who have found a good deal of mobility and change in the caste system (Srinivas 1966; Marriott 1976).

It is in any case refreshing to note that the anthropologists at the symposium did not persist in their proverbial preoccupation with the Indian caste system, but instead concentrated on the more interesting and fruitful topics of the changing culture of agriculture, the contemporary Indian family in the city, gender and sex roles, and the Chipko popular environmental movement in the Himalayas. By doing so, they forged some important links to the social changes so impressively documented by nonanthropologists in the fields of folk arts and crafts, journalism, the organization of self-employed women, and ecology.

India is still often characterized as a "traditional" society and contrasted with the "modernity" of the West: This contrast needs a good deal of qualification, but its valid features refer to the great heritage of Indian civilization (over five thousand years) and the predominantly agricultural and rural character of its population (Brown 1966; 1972). In his essay "Transformations in the Culture of Agriculture," Arjun Appadurai makes an interesting application of the French theorists Foucault and Bourdieu to argue that in spite of the many modernizing changes in Indian farmers' way of life and ways of knowing that have been taking place in the last thirty years, many of the traditional ways remain useful and necessary, especially for the poorer farmers. The bullock cart, the leather water container, the use of animal manure, and the water diviner may become obsolete with the inroads of cash crops, chemical fertilizers, and electrified irrigation, but for a large proportion of farmers, Appadurai contends, the use of traditional techniques and folk knowledge remains critical for survival. He also suggests that the logic of commercialization in market time is changing the traditional rhythms of agricultural life and its social calendar, reinforcing the structure of inequality and domination of rural life.

Sylvia Vatuk's essay "Making New Homes in the City" complements Appadurai's by showing the ways in which the increasing migration to urban centers is changing the structure of the family and the position of the elderly. Although her essay does not support the generalizations that prevailed in the sociological literature until recently, about how urbanization and industrialization produced social disorganization, anomie, and extreme individualism, and in fact indicates that some of the traditional norms of the Indian joint family are still alive in the urban as well as the rural setting, her essay notes that "a great number of migrants come from the poorest segments of the rural population and enter the cities at the bottom of the urban hierarchy, most of them never to rise significantly within it." Under these circumstances, the institution of the family is subject to special stress and begins to show some of the symptoms of a "culture of poverty": family violence, abandonment of wives and children, and neglect of the aged.

Just as the essays by Appadurai and Vatuk highlight some of the problems of a transition from a traditional agricultural to a modern urban society, so do the Mandelbaum and Bhatt essays complement one another on the changes in the status of women. The custom of separating and veiling women, known in North India as purdah, shows several unexpected features according to Mandelbaum's survey. It is taken up by newly prosperous families as a matter of prestige, and relaxed in families of old wealth, and it may be more strictly enforced by Hindu than by Muslim families. An individual woman's observance or nonobservance of purdah is more than the isolable act of an autonomous individual; it reflects on the honor of both her natal and marital families, and in doing so it symbolizes their past achievements and their present positions and power.

In spite of its apparent cultural devaluation of women, the custom of purdah does not necessarily lower a girl's self-esteem, writes David Mandelbaum, because "Indian girls are assured of their worth by whom it really matters: by their mothers." Mandelbaum follows the Indian psychoanalyst Kakar in identifying this and the later sources of a woman's self-confidence in the family circle. Mandelbaum also suggests that this kind of self-confidence, along with education, prepares Indian women to participate in politics, professional careers, and even to become active feminists.

Ela Bhatt's essay "Organizing Self-Employed Women for Self-Reliance" provides evidence of women who do assume and perform social roles as self-sufficient self-employed workers, without "talk[ing] about their husbands and children." The story of how a textile union in the city of Ahmedabad was able to apply Gandhian methods to organize over twenty thousand self-employed women into a successful cooperative union is too dramatic to summarize. But the implications are important and obvious for an economy in which 6 percent of working women are employed in industrial organizations and 94 percent are self-employed. As Bhatt herself points out, her approach offers a way of organizing self-employed women into "a culture of self-employment" that makes use of the economic and political institutions of a modern society without destroying women's capacities to control the conditions of their work and the sources of their income.

It is interesting to observe that when I first visited India in 1954–55, and later in the 1960s, problems of economic development and planning were in the forefront of public discussion, problems about which American experts had much advice to offer, including such recommendations as that Indians should stop worshiping sacred cows and should acquire a Protestant ethic of work, hold fewer festivals, and get rid of the caste system.

Today Indian as well as Western economists are more sophisticated in their diagnoses and recognize that India and the Third World face some special problems of economic development.

One set of problems, not primarily or exclusively economic, to which some of the essays address themselves are those directly associated with the natural environment—not only the pollution of air and water by industrial wastes, but also the misuse of the natural resource base of land, trees, and water. The disappearing species of the elephant, the tiger, the fish in coastal waters are making obsolete those alluring images on the tourist posters. It is difficult to believe that the environmental movement in India began only in 1972, but, as one of the papers notes, it is an idea whose time has come. Judging from the levels of knowledge and dedication displayed in the essays, this is an area of dramatic effort and creative innovation. It is an effort not restricted to official bureaucratic channels. Grass-roots, popular movements have become active, as is documented by the essay on the Himalayan Chipko movement by Gerald Berreman, an anthropologist who has done first-hand field research in the region. The estimate that there may be as many as six thousand such movements in the country not only testifies to the intensity of public interest in the environmental problems but also gives promise that public support and funds may be forthcoming to deal with them. One hopes that S. Dillon Ripley's plea for a long-run perspective will be heeded.

INNOVATION AND CULTURAL TRADITIONS IN INDIAN CIVILIZATION

The essays on the reinterpretation of traditional architecture, which close the volume, recapitulate in a dramatic juxtaposition the theme of the entire symposium: rediscovery of the past as adaptation for the future. Three prizewinning Indian architects, each with Western training and experience, reflect on the relation of their constructions to traditional Indian architecture. Between them there is a continuum of deviations from the "international modern" style of such an architect as Le Corbusier, who was selected by Prime Minister Nehru to design Chandigarh, the capital of Punjab, in the 1950s. Only one of these architects, Raj Rewal, echoes the Le Corbusier idiom, when he advocates "reinterpretation of the past without embellishment." Yet even he sounds like a postmodernist when he writes "The search for symbolic values, which fulfill contemporary aspirations but carry relevant echoes of the past, assumes importance in the Nehru Pavilion."

Ironically, the architect who seems least sympathetic with Le Corbusier's modernism and functionalism is B. V. Doshi, who actually worked in Le Corbusier's Paris studio and also represented him in Chandigarh and Ahmedabad. Doshi regards modernism as a "measurement-oriented" intellectual approach, which falls short of the "holistic experience" that relates an individual's center to the physical and intellectual world and thus regains for him personal faith and identity and a sense of community—an experience reported lacking by the residents of Chandigarh. In a separately published interview ("Le Corbusier—Acrobat of Architecture"), Doshi gives an informative appreciation of Le Corbusier's personality and methods of work (Kagal 1986).

The architect Charles Correa, working in Bombay with its millions of squatters, was so impressed by their "incredibly inventive design solutions of color, form, and building" that he believes "it is not necessary for architects to design houses; people already have a rich heritage of constructing them." The architects' "real responsibility," he concludes, is to provide an urban context in which the popular design solutions are viable. "The architect . . . , instead of reinforcing the status quo, must be an agent who helps to invent the future."

In spite of such differences in their attitudes toward modern and postmodern architecture, these three architects agree on the values of such traditional Indian building devices as sunbreakers (*jālīs*), courtyards and terraces open to the sky, and the hierarchy of spaces that provide ambiguous transitions between public and private areas of activity and inactivity. Doshi in fact suggests the historical speculation that the isolation and sequencing of such spaces for ritual activity led to a definition of sacred space, as in temples, and eventually to a science of architecture.

The individual variations among architects in their attitudes toward tradition and innovation suggest that similar variations may be found among practitioners of other crafts, arts, and sciences. This possibility is indeed intimated by several essays in the book and is congruent with the emphasis on the diversity of Indian cultural traditions already noted.

Kartikeya Sarabhai's paper "Technology for Development: The Cultural Context" provides a guide for appropriate technology when he recommends that architects design international airports to take into account the fact that one person's air travel may mean twenty-five to thirty people at the airport rather than assume that only one person should come to fetch or to drop off a friend. His proposal for "centers of excellence" to evaluate, modify, develop, and transmit technology that is not only based on an understanding of modern science and technology, but also understands people and their customs, as well as the processes and goals of development, may yet show the West how to adapt modern science and technology for the benefit of people rather than the converse.

The editor reports that the theme for the Smithsonian symposium, the rediscovery of the past as adaptation for the future, suggested by an Indian, "seemed to touch the core, especially among artists but with philosophers, anthropologists, and some scientists as well. . . . It mattered a great deal." Non-Indian readers of this book would probably like to know why this theme struck such a responsive chord among Indians. Was it merely a revivalist or nostalgic response, or did it express some deeper feelings and understandings which Indians have about themselves and their civilization? As one of the symposium chairpersons, Pupul Jayakar, said at the symposium, "I have no understanding when we refer to a tradition of the past or a tradition of culture of the past. What exists today is tradition, is culture."

This may well be an understanding of cultural traditions that some anthropologists would share. Yet there are also anthropologists, especially in the United States, who would want to add that all culture and all cultural traditions are invented (see, e.g., Cohn in Hobsbawm and

Ranger 1983; Wagner 1975). If this is indeed so, then the relations of tradition to the past and to innovation become problematic and may be quite different in the case of Indian civilization from what they are in the case of American civilization. Prime Minister Nehru, in any case, suggested something of the distinctive Indian attitude toward the past when he used the metaphor of a palimpsest in his *Discovery of India:* "She was like some ancient palimpsest on which layer upon layer of thought and revery had been inscribed, and yet no succeeding layer had completely hidden or erased what had been written previously. All of these existed together in our conscious or subconscious selves, though we might not be aware of them. And they had gone to build up the complex and mysterious personality of India" (Nehru 1946, 47).

A related thought is expressed by Nehru in explaining why Indians travel abroad: "We in India do not have to go abroad in search of the Past and Distant. We have them here in abundance. If we go to foreign countries it is in search of the Present. That search is necessary, for isolation from it means backwardness and decay" (Nehru 1946, 578–79; cf. Singer 1980, 36–38).

Prime Minister Rajiv Gandhi, Nehru's grandson, may have been following his grandfather's example when he came to Washington to negotiate with President Reagan on the Science and Technology Initiative and to add new layers to the palimpsest of Indian civilization.

The Smithsonian symposium, at about the same time, also featured a full session entitled "The Interplay of Science, Technology, and Culture," as well as a closing morning session, "Intellectual Cooperation with India: Some Next Steps." Presentations at these sessions included papers such as "Innovation and Stagnation in Medieval Indian Astronomy" by David Pingree, an internationally recognized authority on Indian astronomy, astrology, and mathematics; "Forest, Field and Heaven: Three Perspectives on Science in Modern India" by Robert Anderson, a social anthropologist who has studied the sociology of science in India; and a paper by an Indian theoretical physicist at the University of Texas, Austin, who expressed some of an Indian scientist's intellectual and emotional struggles to return to his cultural traditions and yet have the courage to say "Science is what I seek; technology may follow": equally well, "Insight and happiness are what I want to recognize; let utility follow" (quoted from E. C. G. Sudarshan's paper "Global Aspects of Indian Culture").

Robert Redfield's seminal suggestion that the civilizations of China, the Middle East, Meso- and South America, South and Southeast Asia, and the West originated from the expansion and interaction of small communities and the systematization of their indigenous folk cultures into a great tradition ("orthogenetic change") as well as from the stimulus and borrowings of foreign cultures and civilizations ("heterogenetic change") has many far-reaching implications for thinking about intercultural relations and the processes of persistence and change in cultural traditions (Singer 1976). In the case of South Asia, there is archaeological evidence that the probable ancestors of Indian and Pakistani cultural traditions had their origins in the indigenous Indus civilization at Harappa and Mohenjo-Daro, whose development was also stimulated by the networks of trade from Mesopotamia and later from Iran (Possehl 1986). Whereas many histories of South Asia have tended to emphasize the foreign invasions and their successive political and cultural influences, other histories, on the contrary, have tended to emphasize the distinctive and persistent indigenous social and cultural traditions such as the caste system, the joint family, the sacredness of the cow, the belief in fate and transmigration, and their alleged resistance to change. The net result of these conflicting tendencies has been an image of South Asian civilizations as an ocean of stories drawn from ancient myths and legends washing over a few small islands of true history. In such an image there can be no innovation and historical change, for it has all happened before, including the changes. As Krishna tells Arjuna in the *Bhagavadgita*, he should not shrink from fighting in the war against his kinsmen because, from the God's omniscient viewpoint, the war has already been fought and the kinsmen have already been slain (van Buitenen 1981). The significance of the essays in this book is that they give us new insights into the cosmic mystery of how it is that the members of a "traditional" civilization can rediscover their pasts in the recurrent cycles of their history and yet invent new adaptations of their traditions for use in an indeterminate present and an open future.

When some successful Madras industrialists familiar with the Indian theory of the recurrent cycles of the ages, or yugas, insisted that the industrial progress India had made since 1947 was irreversible, it seemed to me that they were recognizing genuine innovations, some of which they themselves had invented while at the same time "traditionalizing" them, that is, assimilating these innovations to a persisting traditional culture. When, on the other hand, some community leaders in a New England town organized and advertised their annual Yankee Homecoming celebration as "Yankee City in Renaissance" and as "Progress through the Past," they seemed to think of themselves not as traditionalists but as pioneers dedicated to exploring the frontiers of the past (Singer 1977, 1987). But the Madras industrialists, the Yankee City community organizers, and the anthropologist were not taking a deity's omniscient point of view; they were expressing the values of their respective cultures, their personal experience and special training. For all, the coexistence of tradition and innovation was a possibility, a probable tendency, and an actuality in some cases (Singer 1980, 1987). They would probably all accept F. Champion Ward's concluding statement at the symposium about liberal education as applying to their respective fields:

> In every age the task of liberal education is to discern the future which the new generation confronts and to shape for that future a legacy appropriate to its deepest requirements. I submit that, in our time, that legacy must be drawn from a reservoir as wide and various as the human spirit and as deep as its most profound achievements. As this symposium draws to its close, let us hope that it and the Festival which is to follow will bring all of us closer to such a common legacy.

REFERENCES CITED

Brown, W. Norman
  1966   *Man in the Universe: Some Continuities in Indian Thought.* Berkeley and Los Angeles: University of California Press.

  1972   *The United States and India, Pakistan, Bangladesh.* Cambridge: Harvard University Press.

Cohn, Bernard S.
  1983   Representing Authority in Victorian India. In *The Invention of Tradition,* ed. E. Hobsbawm and T. O. Ranger. Cambridge: Cambridge University Press.

Das, Veena (ed.)
  1986   *The Word and the World: Fantasy, Symbol and Record.* New Delhi: Sage Publications, Inc.

Dimmit, Cornelia, and J. A. B. van Buitenen (eds. and trans.)
  1978   *Classical Hindu Mythology.* Philadelphia: Temple University Press.

Dumont, Louis
  1980   *Homo Hierarchicus: The Caste System and Its Implications.* Chicago: University of Chicago Press.

Kagal, Carmen (ed.)
  1986   Le Corbusier—Acrobat of Architecture. B. V. Doshi interviewed by Carmen Kagal. In *Vistāra:* The Architecture of India. The Festival of India, 204–14.

Kakar, Sudhir
  1978   *The Inner World: A Psychoanalytic Study of Childhood and
            Society in India.* Delhi: Oxford University Press.

Marriott, McKim
  1976   Hindu Transactions: Diversity without Dualism. In *Transaction
            and Meaning,* ed. B. Kapferer. Philadelphia: Institute for the
            Study of Human Issues.

Marriott, McKim (ed.)
  1955   *Village India.* Chicago: University of Chicago Press.

Nehru, Jawaharlal
  1946   *The Discovery of India.* New York: The John Day Co.

O'Flaherty, Wendy Doniger (ed.)
  1975   *Hindu Myths.* Harmondsworth: Penguin Books.

Possehl, Gregory L.
  1986   *Kuli: An Exploration of an Ancient Civilization in South Asia.*
            Durham: Carolina Academic Press.

Redfield, Robert
  1957   Thinking About a Civilization. In *Introducing India in Liberal
            Education,* ed. M. Singer. Chicago: University of Chicago Press.

Roland, Alan
  1982   Toward a Psychoanalytical Psychology of Hierarchical Rela-
            tionships in Hindu India. *Ethos* 10:232–53.

Singer, Milton
  [1972]   *When a Great Tradition Modernizes: An Anthropological
  1980   Introduction to Indian Civilization.* Chicago: University of
            Chicago Press.

  1976   Robert Redfield's Development of a Social Anthropology of
            Civilizations. In *American Anthropology, The Early Years,* ed. J.
            Murra. Minneapolis: West Publishing Co.

  1977   The Symbolic and Historic Structure of an American Identity.
            Ethos 5:428–54.

  1984   *Man's Glassy Essence: Explorations in Semiotic Anthropology.*
            Bloomington: Indiana University Press.

  1987   Yankee City in Renaissance. In *Dimensions of Social Life: Es-
            says in Honor of David Mandelbaum,* ed. P. Hockings. Berlin:
            Mouton de Gruyter.

Singer, Milton (ed.)

1959   *Traditional India: Structure and Change*. Austin: University of
        Texas Press.

1968   *Krishna: Myths, Rites, and Attitudes*. Chicago: University of
        Chicago Press.

Singer, Milton, and Bernard S. Cohn (eds.)

1968   *Structure and Change in Indian Society*. Chicago: Aldine.

Sinha, Surajit

1959   Tribal Cultures of Peninsular India as a Dimension of the Little
        Tradition. In *Traditional India*, ed. M. Singer.

Srinivas, M. N.

1976   *The Remembered Village*. Berkeley and Los Angeles: University
        of California Press.

1966   *Social Change in Modern India*. Berkeley and Los Angeles: Uni-
        versity of California Press.

van Buitenen, J. A. B. (ed. and trans.)

1981   *The Bhagavadgita in the Mahabharata*. A Bilingual Edition. Chi-
        cago: University of Chicago Press.

Vatsyayan, Kapila

1983   *The Square and the Circle in the Indian Arts*. New Delhi: Roli
        Books International.

Wagner, Roy W.

1975   *The Invention of Culture*. Englewood Cliffs: Prentice-Hall.

PROLOGUE

Designs

Carla M. Borden

I

This is, essentially, a personal book. Some one individual created the symposium on which it is based—like a piece of sculpture, if you will, from the resources in the environment and within the realm of her own—and edited the essays; that is certainly part of the explanation. But the main body of it consists in what the authors convey in their texts. "In India we must seek," Ramchandra Gandhi reminded us; the symposium as a reflection of India "[sought] to ask questions—questions which have no immediate answers or solutions but need to be held on the ground of mind, to be pursued relentlessly," Pupul Jayakar added. The contributors have undertaken the charge earnestly and honestly, if not with humor as well: for knowledge, harmony, and justice, a sustainable environment, a language for expression, models to follow and values to lead. Each in his or her own way, they respond to challenges and opportunities close to their lives. The experience they share—"deep experience," as Stella Kramrisch described—is often autobiographical and never only academic. In their inquiry too the Americans have some emotional stake.

The context that the Festival of India and the Smithsonian provided for this subjective look into contemporary India was a three-day symposium on the "rediscovery of the past as adaptation for the future." We had cast about for an appropriate perspective for some months; this one, brought to our attention by Gieve Patel, seemed to touch the core, especially among artists but with philosophers, anthropologists, and some scientists as well. If it was felt to be "tired" in certain circles, we found just the opposite; it mattered a great deal. In fact, I soon noticed that all I had to do was mention the word "rediscovery" to Indian consultants and prospective symposium participants, and then I could listen to most of them finish my thought.

What did we mean by "rediscovery of the past"? Time per se had relatively little to do with it, and nostalgia nothing at all. What was "past" might have originated long ago and still be functional or accessible—and so part of the present—like a building, a philosophy, a myth, a craft, a dramatic form, a pattern of interaction, a memory. It might be inactive, or forgotten, or discarded, for a whole range of reasons. We proposed to explore continuity and change in India from the inside, to mark the bringing to consciousness and conscious utilization of the past—which is multiple, spiritual, emotional, and empirical—for the sake of the present and the future. How did one wish to synthesize old and new—even East and West? In what ways could relearned or restructured truths be applied to defining goals for the individual and the community and to achieving them—and with what effects? Sacred groves are important not only for religious reasons but for water conservation and as gene banks. Some farmers today, recognizing that they must preserve the long-term biological diversity of their land, are turning to the reestablishment of sacred groves as part of the answer and drawing on elements of modern Western scientific resource management as well. In architecture and planning, acquaintance with historical and traditional forms has inspired among some practitioners a reinterpretation of building activity to incorporate practical respect for the environment and for cultural conditions along with modern techniques. The present grew from the past and, as the artists have described most explicitly in their essays, the two change one another.

One could cite cases of apparently similar processes at work in various kinds of societies. The anthropologist Theodore Schwartz wrote, "In my own work on long-term culture change in Manus, I have found that on each successive field trip (eight over the past 30 years) more and more of the old culture has returned, but with transformations, sometimes brought about through imperfect remembering, even by those who were alive when the old practices were still vital. . . . In memory they reshape the past to meet present needs so that both past and present change together."[1] Diego Rivera, according to one of the organizers of a Detroit Institute of Arts exhibition on the artist, "created a new esthetic for the Americas by combining pre-Columbian imagery and modern technology." Another curator commented, "He was a very individual artist all the way along, and . . . his Mexican style was a conscious choice made for a definite end. . . . He certainly wasn't continuing an indigenous tradition. . . . He, with his compatriots, made it up, inventing what we think of as the Mexican style by drawing together all sorts of things from his classical training as well as a love and admiration for Mexican art."[2] Closer to home, "Can this music [rock and roll] that once celebrated the urgency and immediacy of the moment race onward by looking backward? The positive view is that rock is once again recharging and replenishing itself by returning to its earliest, best impulses."[3]

The interest in knowing where a person or community has been to understand who one is and can become happened to presuppose a psychoanalytical bent on the organizers' part. (This also made focus less important than process and insight. We were not only looking at processes pertinent to India; we were trying to be part of them. And we were, in a sense, a gathering in search of a focus, out of which "contemporary Indian tradition" eventually emerged.[4]) Clearly, however, there are other possible approaches than the psychoanalytical, diverse cultural, political, philosophical beliefs, and scholarly interests that have guided these investigations.

India's political independence gave added impetus to the self-reflective impulse. There was a country's and an enormous population's future to shape. *The Discovery of India,* which Jawaharlal Nehru had published in 1946, is an instructive document in this regard. That so many of those symposium speakers selected for their engagement with the recovery and reformation of a viable identity are of an age to have matured in independent India can hardly be accidental. Other nationalist movements, aspiring to the creation of geopolitical entities or not, have been characterized by efforts to retrieve, revive, reinvent, and redefine elements of culture in a creative way, by a return to pride in roots, while looking ahead.[5] Although the experiences before and during colonial empire in what are now India and the United States were so vastly different—and the time elapsed since the date of national independence so many generations longer for us—the commemorations of the bicentennial of the U.S. Constitution and Bill of Rights beginning in 1987, and anticipation of the Columbus Quincentenary in 1992, have prompted serious self-examination and reevaluation of events and traditions.

Severe stresses and strains that have come to the fore in India since independence also account for probes into tradition where less violent, destructive alternatives might be discerned. Many of the symposium speakers have been struggling for society to accept such models as valid and indeed necessary for survival.

While I, because of my ignorance, am in no position to claim that great numbers of Indians do or do not concern themselves actively with "the rediscovery of the past as adaptation for the future" in their life and work, my appreciation of how widespread familiarity with it is in India has only grown.[6] It is not a novel or trivial phenomenon, nor is it, in this historical moment in India, passé. For these reasons, we anticipated that building our symposium around it would constitute a welcome challenge, a unique and promising opportunity for analysis and learning for everyone involved.

The decision to concentrate on contemporary India was one the Smithsonian as a whole made. Most of its major programs for the Festival of India—including the "Aditi" exhibition and the *melā* at the Festival of American Folklife—were celebrations of India today. We were further encouraged to follow the guidelines by the suggestion that the symposium might have some influence on directions that India scholarship in the United States could take. Here the arts component was crucial. Scholars such as A. K. Ramanujan had indicated that too little is known about contemporary Indian literature and art in the United States; too few recognize that there is much to know. Not many American writers have paid attention to Indian poetry, for example, and even in the academic community of Indianists the understanding and interest were reported to be limited. We could play a role in redressing the imbalance by featuring artists in a key festival program, and we tried hard to do so.

"The Canvas of Culture," the general rubric by which the symposium was known, was suggested by Rajeev Sethi. Each of the sessions could have been expanded into a separate symposium, but we saw special value in juxtaposing them, working them into a woven fabric of discussion. The relationships among the interconnected questions and observations then could be seen and explored; they might even produce fresh insights and suggest new frameworks for understanding and action. Sessions included practitioners in various fields, and we had asked all of them to speak to one another and to a wide audience. We chose a particular assortment of session topics to reflect the Smithsonian's multifaceted interest in India and to recognize areas in which especially fertile thinking and activity along the aforementioned lines are underway. The number of topics seemed unavoidable, given India's complexity, and the scope, we felt, also would permit a broader appreciation of Indian civilization than was available from any other single Washington program.[7] Since the Office of Interdisciplinary Studies was established at the Smithsonian (under a different name), it has specialized in generating and disseminating knowledge by fostering the cross-fertilization among fields of inquiry that occurs when diverse individuals are brought together to consider important themes and problems of modern civilization. The "canvas" was a natural metaphor, a rearticulation of a tradition.

I should note here, should it not be obvious from looking through this book and the symposium schedule in the appendix, that we did not hope to be, nor could we have hoped to have been, comprehensive or encyclopedic in presenting aspects of contemporary Indian life in three days or in one subsequent volume. The cloth has holes and loose threads around the edges. We offered points of view from people whose work has been thoughtful, influential, and provocative.

And so we return to the sources of the volume's personality. They are an extraordinary group. "Some of the best minds of India" was one assessment. Many Indian stars of different worlds found themselves face to face—like "'Frankenstein Meets Godzilla,'" another speaker volunteered—and together they generated a special radiance that is still bright. There also was an exceptional, if small, number of U.S. scholars of Indian culture who brought a complementary set of insights to the endeavor. The mix of Indians and Americans was of primary importance for the program, the festival, and institutions and individuals in India and the United States. The opportunity was an auspicious one for continuing and enhancing professional-level cooperation, for initiating and pursuing exchanges and discourse. A postsymposium panel discussion in fact was devoted to perpetuating the goals and achievements of the festival.

I have indicated that the symposium was not exclusively for scholars. The Smithsonian's unique position as a national research and educational institution made it possible and desirable for us to affect a general audience. It also was not exclusively *of* scholars. Since we were concerned with firsthand experience, practitioners and "activists"—who of course could be scholars, too—were integral to the program. If an architect, a painter, a union organizer, a policymaker would talk about his or her convictions, ideas, and work, as these apply to current situations, why should we not take advantage of the chance to hear from them directly?

The gathering was cause for considerable excitement and was greatly relished. According to many accounts, it may have been unprecedented, at least in scale. One speaker, who already had traveled to the United States twice in 1985 and was far from eager to make the trip again, nevertheless found the occasion "too tempting to miss." Despite the intensity of the schedule, participants wanted to hear one another's presentations. The encounters sparked some new connections, even among people who had known of one another before, and produced some concrete instances of collaboration. One guest, a professor at a major American university, reported finding much useful material at the symposium for his effort to create new methods of teaching South Asian studies. Another had not written an essay for ten years and was delighted to be "reintroduced to intellectual life." The presence of non-academics was often remarked upon and warmly applauded, and by no means only because they were fresh faces, new blood for regular conference-goers. A speaker was impressed with the way so many individuals from so many different fields, without comparing notes on their presentations beforehand, still seemed to "mesh." The meeting surprised some by its harmony. And it left one with the question, "Why don't we organize a forum like this in India?"

Naturally, not everything worked as we would have liked. Most regrettable were the inability of a few individuals to accept our invitation to speak and the lack of time for discussion at the sessions. But in this volume we can pick up where we left off, informing, engaging, searching, and enjoying. We hope, too, to continue lowering barriers between and within cultures, academic and lay, Indian and non-Indian.

Although particular people made the symposium and this book, it should be clear that they are not isolated from their cultures but are participants in them. Their personal perspective is at the same time a social one. The issues and transformations they explore—the presentations on the environment are a striking case in point—also bear strong connections to cultures beyond their own. However generalizable their experience may be, surely the complex of values, motivations, and imaginative responses expressed here can move us toward a deeper understanding of Indians and India, in evolving context.

A few more comments before I proceed. I was asked to elucidate in these introductory remarks the decision-making mechanisms that resulted in the choice of theme and speakers. On the latter score, despite a planning period that was relatively short, countless people suggested countless names, and opinions conflicted with one another often enough. I can add to what I have written above only that a notable proportion of advisers teach or were trained—or both—at the University of Chicago; I endeavored to be objective; I had to trust in my own experience and judgment; and Pupul Jayakar, chairperson of the Indian Advisory Committee for the Festival of India and cochairperson of the symposium, was extremely supportive in approving a large list of Indians whose airfare to the symposium the Government of India provided.

Our intention from the outset was to publish a book from the symposium. The series of publications by the Office of Interdisciplinary Studies consists of eleven volumes before the present one, with four more in process. I also fully expected, when I decided to see the project through to publication, that I would use the title of the symposium for the volume and include all of the presentations. The publisher and I agreed on a book, rather than proceedings; but after long scrutiny it became painfully evident to me that coherence in the book required shifts in the expectations. Some essays fit less well than others, not for any lack of perspicacity or sensitivity on the authors' parts; and then a new title was conceived to reflect better what the contributors actually said and meant. I profoundly regret any confusion, embarassment, or hurt I have caused by the omissions.

II

In his foreword, Milton Singer considers two ways to read this volume: as a selection of illustrations of the theme "rediscovery of the past as adaptation for the future"; and as a means toward constructing a conceptual framework for comprehending Indian civilization. The "canvas" metaphor reemerged there; Singer also introduced the image of a palimpsest, which Nehru had used. And then there is the body organism, a notion elaborated at the symposium by Kapila Vatsyayan and Veena Das that has strongly influenced the structure of the book.

> [India is] an integrated, self-structuring system[,] . . . always in movement and flux. . . . The being and the meaning is in the whole, for no part, no element is capable of degeneration [or] regeneration without the other. . . . The question to be asked is, is it a matter of rediscovery of the past for adaptation to the future [*sic*], or is it a question of understanding the organism which is still alive and capable of both normal degeneration and regeneration? (Vatsyayan)

I regard Vatsyayan's questions as complementary and very much connected (although I hesitate over the word *normal*). Nevertheless, though many of the essays included emphasize rediscovery as a tool for understanding and renewal, not every one does. Only looking at them in the context of a complex body of tradition, with elements coming and going and interacting, allowed me to encompass and represent them all. I could not separate form and content.

Veena Das's opening essay sets a tone for the volume and advances key concepts for analyzing the structure and character of Indian civilization and society: the body, unity in diversity, and a property of diversity that "it is not very concerned with boundaries; each group merges into other groups at its margins." Interestingly, at the very end of the volume two essays manifest the open-endedness of categories as well. Charles Correa describes the lack of clear definition between in-

door and outdoor spaces in Indian architecture ("Even when there are enclosing elements, they usually take the form of porous screens, so the skin is not only visually transparent, but air and breezes can move through."), and B. V. Doshi identifies qualities of ambiguity, transition, and rhythm that help built forms to generate holistic experiences. Such deliberate sequencing of elements in a design for a certain kind of response, and such permeability of boundaries in space and society—not to mention, in light of the symposium theme, in time—parallel, if they have not actually inspired, the organization of the volume. Some essays follow others for similarity, some for variation or contrast. The plan may be too subtle or artificial; it is in any event not neat, and I am glad for the authors' freedom that made it so. The essays by Wendy O'Flaherty, Rajeev Sethi, and Gerald Berreman particularly, with an integrity of their own, seemed to me best to end or begin sections, for there they direct, improve, and demonstrate the circulatory flow from one area of concentration to another. When one notes, for example, that Arjun Appadurai's and Madhav Gadgil's essays include discussion of religion, that all the "environment" essayists involve themselves with the social order, and that all the architects refer to sacred structures and/or religious values, the environment, social institutions, and aesthetics (the reason their essays conclude the volume), one realizes that not only the margins are fluid.

The essays affirm the interdependence of diverse forms of life and inanimate nature, of aspects of social life, of senses, of the supernatural. (Distinguishing the parts is nevertheless convenient, desirable under the circumstances of trying to communicate across cultures, realistic, and even practically and philosophically necessary. I shall say more on the subject in a moment.) Reading the essays either singly or in clusters, one is struck further by the dynamism of the relations between the parts. For A. K. Ramanujan, the past "changes as we attend to it" and transforms the present. All of Gulam Mohammed Sheikh's worlds—past and present, real and imagined, literary and visual, Muslim and Hindu, India and the West among them—are simultaneously in "dialectic interaction." Changes in biological and cultural diversity, Anil Agarwal asserts, are linked inextricably, as are journalism and the body politic, Aroon Purie records. The destruction of the environment in rural areas, detailed throughout Part 4 and in Gerald Berreman's essay, sends those people forced from their traditional means of livelihood to cities, where they need housing, which architects like Correa feel responsible to provide, and suffer new forms of intrafamilial stress, assessed by Sylvia Vatuk. "What is most characteristic about Indian civilization," observed Bernard Cohn, a symposium participant, "are processes by which diverse elements are related to one another to form the civilization."[8]

The nature of unity is profoundly important to many of the essayists—as it has been to me in working on this many-centered collection. To say that unity is organic, which we have so far, is to say that the whole is composed of dependent parts that through their various combined vital functions sustain the entity. Then what are the parts, what are their functions and connections, what happens when they deteriorate? Examination of these issues is the stuff of the book.

In summarizing how several of the essays take up these questions, I shall start with C. M. Naim's. Naim proposes that in Islam the whole—the consolidated community—has submerged the parts—individual Muslims; in the Indian political structure, the national government has retained more control than befits a democracy. To correct the latter situation, he recommends increasing the "arenas for democratic political action[,] . . . decentralization and diversification of the foci of power." But questioning the supremacy of the community, with the goal of giving Muslims rightful control over their own destinies, is a far more controversial matter, one must conclude. In order for Muslims to participate in and contribute to secular, democratic Indian society, they must "recognize that there is no one Muslim past, that, in fact, there are as many pasts as there are Muslims . . . [and take] full cognizance of their own diversity." The individual is the primary entity for democracy; we start with his distinctive social identity.

Veena Das also challenges the myth—or the norm—of undifferentiated solidarity, but on somewhat different grounds. Oneness is truth; and if it can only be supported by manyness, if the most fundamental question of Indian civilization is the relation between the one and the many, then not only is the need for variety basic but so are the ties and communication among the various religious and ethnic groups in India. Such assumptions have in effect been assaulted, however, by both modernizers and fundamentalists for whom unity and diversity are contradictory, unity being equated with homogeneity. As a result of their sway India is suffering violent conflicts that threaten to destroy it. What Das directs us to do, with utmost urgency, is to "search for . . . models of pluralism within [India's] own history and mythology, in order to develop them creatively[,] . . . [to search for] alternative designs for life based on the recognition of difference. . . . Differences [can] provide the basis of dependable, enduring relationships." For both Das and Naim, it seems to me, suppression of variety, even for the purpose of establishing a workable polity and a harmonious society in India, is at the least inexpedient, and at the most wrong.

Advaita (nonduality), the subject of Ramchandra Gandhi's presentation, raises the issue to a higher philosophical level from which self-distinctiveness as a goal in itself looks like vanity. "Tragedy lies in our regarding anything or anyone as 'other' than ourselves"; *advaita* "teaches that you cannot be reduced to your body, mind, society, history, or culture, . . . not even if these are a beautiful body, a clever mind, a prosperous society, an ancient and sophisticated history and culture." The "spirit of pluralism" requires aid from the philosophy of *advaita*. Universal in scale and democratic in application, *advaita*, according to Gandhi, is the hope of civilization on earth.

Wendy O'Flaherty does not attempt to grapple with the salvation of India or discuss power and politics, and she conveys, rather than a sense of crisis, one of accommodation in India. Truth there is multiple. "Indians may maintain a belief in several different, contradictory answers to the same question; they alter their definitions of reality in order to let such contradictions survive." Although "this sort of plurality is . . . a widely shared cultural assumption," O'Flaherty indicates that it is also a "still-debated open question." Of course, by its very nature, it would be. The challenge that is posed is to us in the West, to rethink our seemingly secure definitions of the bases of our culture—classics written and oral, and other forms of art such as painting and sculpture—through illuminating comparison with Indian tradition.

Ela Bhatt presents the facts that in India 89 percent of working people and 94 percent of working women are self-employed. Poor though they so often are, they contribute a great deal to the economy. Yet their interests and rights as economic agents have been neglected, because of gender bias but also because of a granting of domain to a culture of work patterned after industrialized Western countries. The rationale for the Self-Employed Women's Association Bhatt founded is to make this substantial population visible, make them count in labor laws and policies, and enable them to become individually and collectively self-reliant, in attitude and income. The trade union assumes a different role, with the emphasis given to relationships among workers who are outside of organized industry. The society must be open and true to its real self; the system must evolve to include and acknowledge all its parts.

Girish Karnad's plays draw on Indian history, myth, and legends, on Western dramatic forms, on contemporary politics, on conventions and techniques of traditional popular theater, and on emotional need and intellectual curiosity, transforming them for integrated artistic expression. And when Chandrakala Devi, a housewife we meet in Rajeev Sethi's essay who made sculpture at the "Aditi" exhibition, walks, "art walks with me," she says. Being and creating become the same.

The dramatic progress in agricultural production in India since independence has entailed changes in the contents of agricultural knowledge farmers possess. "Not only is new knowledge [especially of technology] obvious, but older knowledge is rapidly disappearing," Arjun Appadurai explains, "and knowledge lost is choice foregone." The farmers with fewest assets are at greatest risk of not being able to make ends meet; "while the new kinds of knowledge are (uncertain) roads to wealth, the older kinds provide the surest way of surviving from day to day in many parts of India." There is a transformation as well of farmers' traditional way of knowing, not, according to Appadurai's research, "accompanied by a widely shared and perceived increase in well-being for the communities whose mental life is being transformed." Sethi also addresses issues of obsolescence: loss of reliable markets for traditional products, loss of pride in traditional skills, the "breakdown of kinship structures and interaction patterns [that] has seriously challenged the tradition of oral instruction" to transmit and preserve these skills. Berreman insists that village life in the Himalayas "is dangerously impaired, its continuation even jeopardized," under conditions created by "development" activities. In D. K. Lahiri Choudhury's essay, as in others, we face the situation of species in danger of extinction. What is to be conserved or salvaged, how, why, and for whom? If fragmented vision has posed these threats to the continuity of ways of life—or to life itself—a more systemic view may help both the parts and the whole to adapt.

It is plain that the organism falters, and we may wish for more evidence from some essayists that the supports and therapy they prescribe in faith will set things aright. "I don't think the answer lies in not recognizing conflicts," Anil Agarwal wrote me. "It lies in finding ways of conflict resolution that are humane, which integrate more and alienate less. . . . Saying this, however, is much easier than doing it." Happily, other essayists report that balance may be restored, with constant efforts required to maintain it, and movement does occur in the desired direction.

One might shape yet another mold for the book and fill it with primary material on India's intellectuals. The product would be true to the organizers' intentions. My impression is that such material, and this much of it together, is not readily found elsewhere in print. The facts and opinions that compose the analyses are both fresh and known to different audiences, and are occasionally difficult to distinguish from one another. In any event, they are important in their own right, so inviting the scholar and layperson to further interpretation and research.

At the risk of incurring the attention of the *New Yorker,* or of confusing readers with too many possible approaches to the essays—even though they are related and are in no way intended to dictate understanding—

there is one more metaphor I would like to insert. It should come as no surprise to readers who have followed my train of exposition up to this point. Indra's net, a Kegon Buddhist concept,

> which significantly bears the name of one of the major deities of old India, is to be visualized—meditated upon—as stretching throughout the entire universe: its vertical extension represents time; its horizontal, space. At every point where the net's threads interconnect, one imagines a crystal bead symbolizing an individual existence. Each one of the innumerable individual crystal beads reflects on its surface not only every other bead in the net but every reflection of every other bead, thus creating numberless, endless reflections of each other while forming one complete and total *whole*.[9]

I have no wish to violate this symbol by applying it to a book, but I find invoking it hard to resist. I have alluded to many reflections so far: the permeable boundaries first. Gieve Patel's discussion of Sudhir Patwardhan's drawings includes the comment that in them "there is a quiet shuttling between the tenses, or unexpected combinations of them, an intimation of an existence with fluid boundaries." Indeed, not only are images of themes projected in every direction, but even their descriptions bounce off one another.

> The counterbalancing of different structural systems, along with constantly changing floor configurations and the skewing of the dormitory block from the right-angle geometry of the [Gandhi Labour I]nstitute's building, are natural reflexes much like our constant inhaling and exhaling. (Doshi)

> [Siena] is built on hills; lanes radiating from a piazza each widen and close at intervals like the movements of people using them. The uphill route of streets corresponds to rising breath released as one reaches small open squares on the way, while return downhill is quick and sudden for an ecstatic gasp at the wondrous sight of the shell-like great piazza. . . . (Sheikh)

> Later, when I saw murals in Shekhawati all over the high mansions of a street, it became clear that the physical movement of the viewer was essential in grasping their scale and structure. . . . In Shekhawati the painting is revealed in stages as one walks through the street, detail by detail; images grow over windows and doors in an open-ended structure linked by these details. Both painting and its perception required improvisation . . . the painter and the viewer effected upon the space. Reading of a picture in time has many equivalents. . . . (Sheikh)

The ambiguous, open-ended character of the built form starts to reveal itself right at the entrance, which makes one wonder about where to move and how to reach the sanctum. In achieving a destination, there are many ways to go. You can find your own space, in your own time, through your own movement. And the space has to be something beyond just a structure; it has to be a book, to reach different people and give them the kind of information they need at certain points of time and space. (Doshi)

"A Guide to Lord Murugan" tells where to go and how to find Murugan. (Ramanujan)

The very metaphor of Indra's net might be said to be reflected in a thought by Veena Das: "The pilgrim center is precious not because it is unique but because, like a crystal, it reflects other spaces."

If the quotations above appear to demonstrate a lack of originality, just saying the same thing, we might look at them more closely. Certain beliefs and assumptions, certain traditions, pervade Indian culture; others, and bodies of knowledge, may be more particular and localized. Members of the culture evoke and adapt a heritage sometimes unevenly shared, at different times, to create meaning and direction, to realize well-being. The selections and combinations reveal distinctive patterns of thought and feeling. The repetitions breed awareness and familiarity and, through them, better chances for insight.

Some reflections shadow or block one another out. Caste is an evil, but it also can be a resource. The past can be dangerous and coercive, and tradition repressive; they release and enhance creative energy as well. Several essayists claim that rural villagers have a traditionally conservationist relationship with nature, yet one of them qualifies this position. Are women the leaders and foundation of Chipko, the famous grass-roots organization in the Himalayas, or do men and women play equal roles? According to most views expressed here, the government deserves only serious blame, not credit or confidence, for the state of the environment, but there are some dissenting voices.

To enumerate each recurring idea and its interpretation in various contexts in the prologue would involve more patience than I or readers need summon. The index includes many of them; all seem worth tracking—even such apparitions as that Sheikh's life and Naim's challenge fulfill one another (the two happen not to have met before the symposium), or that a traditional cluster of houses Raj Rewal uses as a model, in which "the identity of the individual unit is partially submerged," has its social-psychological counterpart in the "relational" view of the self and society.

For editorial reasons, some of the symposium presentations do not appear as essays in this volume. This section is devoted to them. Of high repute, and long study and practice in their fields, the speakers had a great deal to say on subjects of interest. Through excerpts from their talks plus brief commentary, I hope I can represent them in some appropriate fashion.

Obviously, I have found validity, inspiration, and methodological advantage in "unity in diversity" as a guiding principle. That limits are and should be set on what kinds of differences such a system will tolerate is a matter receiving some attention in the foreword (see Milton Singer's remarks on "India's Diversity and Unity," especially on Veena Das's essay) and in the papers. And it comes to the fore in a discussion of science. Is science simply modern and Western, as some contend; can it only be transferred to other cultures? Or can traditional values coexist with, interact with, and enrich the pursuit of science in India and elsewhere? In the case of ecology, as Madhav Gadgil describes so well—and perhaps in applied science more widely—synthesis is possible and fruitful, although achieving it requires open-mindedness. However, when we turn to theoretical science in India, we encounter signs of an unresolved conflict between the two schools of thought. The followers of each seemed to regard the other's position as illegitimate, and I could not coax them into a dialogue. "Science," said Nathan Glazer, chairman of the "Interplay of Science, Technology, and Culture" session, "was a basis of that power which permitted the West to dominate the East. The East is now free of this political domination. It needs to grow and be effective in science and technology to be truly independent, but it also wants to restore and strengthen its distinctive cultures, its distinctive and distinguished past, which is another mark of independence. And one may wonder, are the two aims compatible? Is there any distinctive national achievement in science?"

One marker at the intersection of science and culture is psychotherapy. Psychoanalyst and scholar Sudhir Kakar compared psychotherapeutic practices in the East and West and the human models underlying them, stressing the differences between them while recognizing that the models are not mutually exclusive. Since many of the essayists cite Kakar, and Singer explains Kakar's central arguments in the foreword, I will not repeat them.[10] However, Kakar's symposium paper suggests two other ideas that bear especially on this volume and invite consideration. One is distinguishing the patterns, theories, and institutions that are universal or constant from those that are specific to a culture, as well as observing the ways concepts and models can be relativized to make them more responsive to different kinds of human experience. (Development is prominent among those discussed in the book.) The other has to do with effecting change in the Indian context. Not all change is good, desired, or controllable from within, and change is inherent in India, as it is elsewhere; I refer to the kind of deliberate, creative change the essayists propose and have accomplished. In illustrating a temple healing ritual, Kakar states that success is achieved when the "normal cosmic order" is reestablished and the patient accepts "old values and old authorities. . . . Faith and surrender to powers beyond the individual are better than individual effort and struggle[;] . . . the source of human strengths lies in harmonious integration with one's group, in the individual's affirmation of the community's values . . . , in his or her obedience to the community's gods, and in his cherishing of its traditions." Yet the vision of a better society does arise, and one can be inside and outside in some fortuitous measure to claim new possibilities.

Kartikeya Sarabhai, director of the Centre for Environment Education at the Nehru Foundation for Development in Ahmedabad, shared with the symposium audience a joke about a zoology student who went into a laboratory and found that a container of spiders was open. "Shouldn't we get a lid," the student asked his professor, "so the spiders won't escape?" "Don't worry," the professor replied, "they are Indian spiders. If one tries to climb out, the others will pull him down." The educational system instituted by the British shoulders more than a little responsibility for such an anti-enterprising ethos, but needed reform in that area is part of a larger effort.

> The colonial attitude manifests itself through making people imitators. Technology is looked upon in terms of finished products rather than as a tool. Products developed in very different contexts are copied rather than modified or developed afresh using modern materials, processes, and ideas suitable to our own cultural and economic milieu. . . . The receiver has to be stronger than the technology to be received, otherwise technology can destroy cultures. . . . The identification and building up of such receivers of technology is, therefore, a very crucial part of the development process. . . . The ability to select has three requirements: an understanding of science and technology in the particular field, an understanding of India, its people and culture, and an understanding of the processes and needs of development. . . . In India, sensitivity to culture must also mean an awareness of the resources of that culture. The country is very richly endowed with a population that has the necessary skills for development as well as knowledge and wisdom imparted through an oral storytelling tradition. If a knowledge of modern science and

technology were spread through such a storytelling technique, illiteracy would not be a barrier. The innovative among the rural population could then act as the selectors and modifiers of modern technology for their economic and social benefit, integrated with their mode of life.

Sarabhai and his organization have worked to further these ends.

David Pingree, professor of the history of mathematics and of classics at Brown University and author of numerous books and articles in these disciplines, reviewed the history of medieval Indian astronomy in an exploration of how it "managed to be both innovative and stagnant at the same time. . . . The basic elements of Indian mathematical astronomy came from the West in several stages," beginning in the late fifth or early fourth century B.C., and Indian astronomers improved and advanced scientific ideas they received from ancient Babylonia and Greece. "In trigonometry and analemmas the Indians were the teachers of the Arabs, and ultimately of the West"; their "most brilliant achievement was their discovery, without a knowledge of the calculus, of the misnamed 'Gregory's Series' for π and of the power series of Sines, Cosines, and Tangents"—rediscovered in Europe several centuries later, after they had been forgotten in India. Modern astronomy in India developed in the mid-nineteenth century, again through influence from the West. The stagnation in the earlier period was a product in the first place of the pragmatism of medieval Indian astronomy. Seeing "its function to be the development of methods of solving the problems encountered in preparing the annual calendar, in predicting eclipses, in casting horoscopes . . . [and] satisfying the society for which it performed these functions, [it] conceived of no other questions as ones it ought to attempt to answer." If the origin of knowledge is believed to lie in revelation, then the basic theoretical assumptions informing the astronomers' work, such as the structure of the universe, would be ipso facto correct. In the second place, the educational system concentrated on rote learning in a very circumscribed environment, usually the family, with the result that knowledge did not grow easily and its communication was extremely limited. The values and methods of modern science, which have been adopted in India, are different; still, cultural expectations and traditions, though they also have changed, affect the conduct of science everywhere.

The two other presentations at the session focused on the nexus between science and culture in contemporary India. In an allegorical style, E. C. G. Sudarshan, a physicist affiliated with the Center for Particle Theory at the University of Texas at Austin and the Institute of Mathematical Sciences in Madras, illustrated some striking affinities between physics and classical "global" (or holistic) Indian philosophy. Among them were concepts of time, space, causality, substance and process, and experiment and experience that both utilize to explain the universe. His conclusion:

> We have had many people talk passionately, scientifically, clinically about the destruction of the environment: but the greater tragedy is the destruction of the environment for total experience, isolation of science from tradition by limiting the purview of science. Going about it this way . . . not excellent science emerges, too selfish and sterile to generate its own technology, too limited in scope to produce joy in the heart and a song on the lips. The scientist gets isolated from his culture and his people and becomes less of a person for being a scientist. . . . I do not think that in the long run there is any possibility except to return to tradition. . . . Tradition is in the present and so is the future. In fact, that which is true is forever new. . . . Tradition does not allow [the] possibility of simply negating all that one has grown up with, all that one is growing up with, without due examination. . . . One must put the same searchlight on tradition as . . . [on] contemporary science and technology.

In his reflections on forestry, agriculture, and physics, Robert Anderson, an anthropologist who has done much research on the techniques and cultures of science, quoted a young Indian theoretical astrophysicist struggling with questions Anderson had heard from Indian scientists more than twenty years earlier: "Why have our best institutes so far failed to reach the standard of the best Western institutes? What can we do to change the situation? If we want to practice science, then is it essential to stay abroad, or shall we be able to continue our research activities even if we go back to India? . . . How can one acquire the proper psychological gestalt for full scientific creativity?"[11] The "unresolved conflict," Anderson's phrase, is the contest between harmony and invention, which shapes perceptions even among scientists about the proper scope and role of the sciences, as well as the sciences' relations to their subject matter and with one another.[12]

Surajit Sinha, director and professor of sociology and anthropology, Centre for Studies in Social Sciences, Calcutta, and Jyotindra Jain, senior director of the Crafts Museum in New Delhi, dealt with discovering the past through the vitality of traditions, with preservation, and with diversity. Jain contended that the written puranic literature assumed to be the original source of myths, rituals, and art forms in India is not necessarily so at all. Recounting myths, legends, and rituals of the goddess and the buffalo in Gujarat, he indicated that orally transmitted regional forms have existed independently in their local cultural contexts, in some cases predating the Sanskrit versions, and at a later stage acquired links with the puranic tradition. Variations in the Sanskrit literature itself were the expression of multiple traditions of myths prevalent in different regions and periods. "Every myth and its version is an authentic and complete entity by itself . . . [and] the antiquity of certain myths and ritual practices can be [demonstrated by] their centrality within the given society's structure of beliefs and practices. . . . Some of the contemporary survivals of ancient traditions can contribute formidably to our understanding of the nature and characteristics of past institutions and practices."

"According to the 1981 census," Sinha reported, "there are 577 Scheduled Tribes in India comprising about eight percent of our population." These tribal groups have a vigor and a moral and environmental grounding that should be preserved themselves and also could serve as guideposts in the "modern and post-modern phases of restructuring . . . Indian civilization." Since independence, the "dominant national stance . . . has been development and integration with the mainstream." But tribal leaders, rather than advocating absorption of tribal groups into the caste system, feel "that the only way to achieve real status today is to accept the constitutional protective cover of tribal identity"—in other words, through ethnic solidarity movements (which ingeniously recreate and reinterpret tribal traditions), to "accentuate boundaries"—"and to gain access to modern skills through formal education." The task of "working out a universal framework of social relations and a world view at the national level" that Sinha envisions then calls for following a model in India different from the "mainstream-sidestream" or "core-periphery" one. A distinguished Naga political leader articulated such a model: "a great river within which many streams are 'concurrently flowing' to give shape to the body politic of a new nation."

Whereas Sinha spoke of social and cultural creativity within tribes and in the civilization as a whole, past, present, and future, Haku Shah portrayed the creative energy he believes resides in every person. Scholar of folk and tribal arts and crafts, Shah sees the creative act as the essence of life, the celebration of life, a source of joy for the creator and the observer, a moment of self-awareness and sharing with the universe. One need not worry about cultivating an Indian identity in art; if the "effort of a creative act is sincere enough," it will automatically be present. Poverty does not inhibit creativity either. On the other hand, "outside forces" like the family and the school can and do stifle the creative process. They "have their norms for measuring creativity.

When a man tries to express a little which is pure in himself, these forces sit down to evaluate his expression and mar his growth. . . . They preach, and their 'sermons' are shallow and mediocre. . . . They start 'teaching' in a manner in which the teacher engulfs the student rather than making him free." Shah himself stands as an exemplar of facilitating, liberating intervention. "Ganesh," a street singer, came often to the Shahs' house in Ahmedabad. One day Shah asked him to draw, and despite "Ganesh"'s initial reluctance he took the pen and paper he was offered. In the several years since, his work has become fantastic, reflecting meticulous observation and great concentration, "will and intuition," and voluntary devotion to this newfound creative pursuit. "He sees himself in everything. . . . For him his drawings are real." See Figure 1, *The Wedding of the Ants*.

The last word shall belong to Kapila Vatsyayan, a leading figure in the arts, scholar, and Secretary of the new Indira Gandhi National Centre for Arts in New Delhi. She wrote in extensive detail about the terms by which one should understand India—its own terms, "native categories," "indigenous classifications . . . which are relevant to the tradi-

Figure 1. The Wedding of the Ants, *"Ganesh."*

tion, have been relevant, and will continue to be relevant." A single case is "*śāstra*," usually translated as "theory," but in it "empiricism, pragmatism, and applicability are inherent"; it is not the opposite of "practice." "To look at the Indian tradition we must look at the concepts that a culture evolves to look at itself." She proceeded to explain how six pairs of terms are used in the arts, social sciences, and other disciplines, referring to the primary textual sources in which the Indian world view is embodied. She also posited that "the body and the body organism . . . is the most fundamental paradigm . . . in this culture, . . . used both as a metaphor and reality, both as something which is physical and metaphysical. . . . It takes us into the attitude of the Indian towards senses, . . . mind, and soul. . . . The outer and the inner, the external and internal, the seen and unseen . . . are all parts of a whole. . . . Fluidity and transubstantiation of one category into the other [including matter and energy], at the level of both concept and form, [is] inevitable."[13]

IV

During a first trip to India for purposes of planning the symposium, I spent an evening with Satish Gujral, a prominent artist who also has designed the award-winning Belgian Embassy in New Delhi and the University of Goa. He made a distinction between Indian contemporary art and contemporary Indian art—and although I was not quite sure what he meant when he said it, I knew the idea was important. To understand what is Indian, and how processes at work in the world in our lifetimes impinge on, and can be adapted to, what is Indian, turns out to apply to all the areas this volume covers. In a 1986 article on architecture, William J. R. Curtis, a British architectural critic and historian, named the idea "authentic regionalism."

> There is certainly a mood gathering momentum which rejects the glib reproduction of international formulae and which seeks out continuities with local traditions. No doubt this reflects a spirit of increasing self-confidence in the Third World after colonial occupation, but is also part of a wider reaction against simplistic models of modernisation. At its worst it may degenerate into a skin-deep instant history in which ersatz images of the vernacular are combined with pastiches of national cultural stereotypes. At its best regionalism penetrates to the generating principles and symbolic substructures of the past[,] then transforms these into forms that are right for the changing social order of the present. It is a matter of sensing beneath the surface

memories, myths and aspirations that give a society coherence and energy, and then providing these with an authentic expression.[14]

"The specifics of the history, metaphysics, and geography of India compel a version [of modernity] which has to be different and unique," Ashok Vajpeyi stated at the symposium. "Narrow revivalism" and "parochial nationalism" are ideologies no one espoused to attain it. But then how to be modern, traditional, and true to one's own temperament at the same time, an Indian poet asked?[15] If the coexistence and expression of the three is the goal—in the arts, in addressing genuine needs that are environmental, political, social, spiritual, and moral, and in determining India's relationships with the rest of the world—then the challenge the essayists accept is in finding the means. With hope and vigor, they strive for mastery, and a more creative order.

A generation-plus of voices of India, and some of America (they may not be part of India, but India is part of them), have been kept waiting for too long.

NOTES

1. Personal correspondence from Theodore Schwartz to Wilton Dillon, 6 May 1984. It seems worth noting that Papua New Guinea became independent in 1975.

2. Both citations from Leslie Bennetts, "Retrospective of Diego Rivera Work Celebrates the Artist's Centennial," *New York Times*, 1 June 1986, 61.

3. Don McLeese, review of *Rock of Ages*, *New York Times Book Review*, 28 December 1986, 3.

4. *Contemporary* is a more neutral and inclusive word than *modern*; that is why I have used it. For analyses of modernity and tradition, see, for example, Lloyd I. Rudolph and Susanne Hoeber Rudolph, *The Modernity of Tradition: Political Development in India* (Chicago: University of Chicago Press, 1984) and Milton Singer, *When a Great Tradition Modernizes: An Anthropological Approach to Indian Civilization* (Chicago: University of Chicago Press, [1972]1980).

5. "It is unnecessary to emphasize anything as familiar as the importance of history, tradition, and memory to successful nationalism" (Henry Steele Commager, *The Search for a Usable Past* [New York: Alfred A. Knopf, 1967], 4). On the role of language in nationalism in India, R. Parthasarathy wrote,

"Whenever a people feel impotent under foreign rule, or find themselves threatened by economic, political or ideological aggression, it is to their language that they turn, transforming it into an instrument of freedom. The partition of Bengal in 1905 was one such occasion when Indians rediscovered the emotional importance of their languages in helping them to establish their national identity and self-respect. Language confers a sense of identity that nothing else does. It is to language that we must turn to discover a people's Weltanschauung" ("Subramania Bharati: The Poet of Tamil Resurgence" [Paper presented at the Center for Asian Studies, University of Texas at Austin, 1984], 10).

6. See, for example, an editorial in *India Today*: "How do you make a people in transition conscious of their roots? How important are these roots? . . . Any civilization in control of the process of change preserves its past and uses it to give meaning to the present, even shape its future. Japan has done it. . . . What has been left behind was whole; what we have now are broken parts of something new" (*India Today,* 15 December 1986, 5). Or "the motivating drive behind the Festivals of India staged abroad, like the one now being staged in Delhi, needs to be appreciated for what it is: a carefully planned and executed effort to promote a new, modern idea of Indianness and indeed a novel idea of modern India" (*India News,* 1 December 1986, 7, from the *Times of India*).

7. "What are you doing," a tourist asked one of the symposium participants in a Smithsonian elevator, pointing to his name tag, "canvassing culture?"

8. Bernard S. Cohn, "India as a Racial, Linguistic, and Cultural Area," in *Introducing India in Liberal Education*, ed. Milton Singer (Chicago: University of Chicago Press, 1957), 51.

9. Nancy Wilson Ross, *Buddhism: A Way of Life and Thought* (New York: Alfred A. Knopf, 1980), 54. I am indebted to Cristy West for telling me about this concept and referring me to Ross's book.

10. They are more fully expounded in Kakar's *Shamans, Mystics and Doctors: A Psychological Inquiry into India and Its Healing Traditions* (New York: Alfred A. Knopf, 1982) and "Psychoanalysis and Non-Western Cultures," *International Review of Psychoanalysis* 12, no. 4 (1985): 441–48, for example.

11. Arnab Rai Choudhuri, "Practicing Western Science Outside the West: Personal Observations on Problems and Prospect" (Remarks delivered in Chicago, 1984), cited by Anderson.

12. See Anderson's "Cultivating Science as Cultural Policy in India," *Pacific Affairs* (Spring 1983).

13. This theme is further developed in Vatsyayan, *The Square and the Circle in the Indian Arts* (New Delhi: Roli Books International, 1983).

14. William J. R. Curtis, "Towards an Authentic Regionalism," *Mimar* 19 (January–March 1986):80. See also Curtis' "Architecture moderne, racines indiennes: Raj Rewal," in *Raj Rewal* (Paris: Electa Moniteur, no date), 18: "On se permet de parler d'une 'architecture moderne indienne' qui comprend la modernité et la tradition, l'artisanat et la mécanisation, l'ornementation et la rigeur formelle et intellectuelle."

15. Nissim Ezekiel in remarks presented at the Conference on Indian Literature, University of Chicago, 17–20 April 1986. Managing any two was easy enough, he said; achieving all of them was an intractable problem. Other writers at the conference—Nirmal Verma, U. R. Ananthamurthy, and Ayyappa Paniker—echoed Ezekiel's dilemma.

PART 1

Being and Meaning

CHAPTER 1

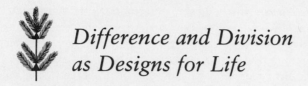

Difference and Division as Designs for Life

Veena Das

Indian society is inundated today with images of death and violence. In the last few years there has been an escalation of conflict that has polarized religious communities, castes, and agrarian classes, and the great numbers of people who are anguished over this do not seem to find any language for expression. Why are we experiencing the sense of crisis that threatens to destroy our moral fabric? Does it represent the pangs of a dying society—one, as many feel, that is now held together only by the violence of the state, which has had to intervene between these opposing groups? Or are we suffering through the throes of a society being reborn? How shall we address these urgent questions?

The Indian Constitution provides a framework within which the rights of individuals as well as the relationships between social groups are expected to be regulated and negotiated within the overarching conception of a neutral, secular state. According to this theory of state, which relies heavily upon the "commonsense" of Western social sciences, modernization of society leads to a "secular," "scientific" at-

This paper has been written for a concerned but popular audience. I have, therefore, dispensed with the usual scholarly apparatus of footnotes and references. It is also a paper written with the pain and sorrow of someone who sees a way of life disappearing and thus makes no pretense toward value neutrality. I wish to record my thanks to Carla Borden for the thoughtful questions she raised on many of the issues.

titude to life. Loyalties to one's religion, caste, region—in short, all those loyalties we often designate as "primordial loyalties"—become privatized, so that the state can dispense with them in establishing a relationship with its citizens. Instead, it is clear that religion, caste, and regional considerations have gained in importance in the country's political life. This fact may be seen in Muslim fundamentalists successfully agitating against the right of the Supreme Court to interpret the Shariat law to provide relief to a divorced, aged Muslim woman; in members of the Sikh community who had lived in harmony with their Hindu neighbors for centuries now finding it necessary to reinterpret their history in order to give themselves a separate identity; in Hindus organizing into militant communities for the "release" of various sacred places that, given the cultural geography of India, are also sacred to the Muslims. Regardless of whether the demands made by such movements are in themselves good or bad, let us note that the only answer modernists can offer to them is to substitute national, secular symbols for religious ones—and this is not an answer at all. In the case of the third example I cited, a museumlike approach to religion is hardly likely to satisfy those for whom religious belief is not simply a matter of aesthetics. Transforming sacred sites over which Hindus and Muslims are in conflict into national monuments, as has been suggested, ignores the sentiments of both Hindus and Muslims about the sacred nature of these sites.

It seems to me that in the whole nationalist endeavor to transform Indian society, we have paid scant attention to the manner in which our past, in its essence, could be adapted for the future. It is imperative for us now to search for other models of pluralism within our own history and mythology, for images of the self and the other, of being and meaning, in order to develop them creatively. It is not frozen metaphors that we seek from our past, nor exotic myths and rituals that bear no relation to life whatsoever. What we are looking for is alternative designs for life based upon the recognition of difference. The quest for homogeneity and similarity—the premises for the idea of harmony in the modern world—ends up by treating society as a mere "collection" of people. To my mind this has simply sanctioned increasing violence and the worship of death.

"Unity in diversity" is almost a cliché in discussions on Indian society, mouthed so often in political rhetoric that it has become an empty phrase upon which few seriously reflect. In my understanding, the fundamental question of Indian civilization is this very relation between the one and the many.

One of the most celebrated Hindu creation myths of the puranic period is the story of Purusha, the primeval man who offered his body as a sacrifice. From this sacrificial body the world was created: His eyes became the sun and the moon, his breath the wind; from his mouth came the Brahmans, from his arms the Kshatriyas; his stomach became the Vaisyas and his feet the Sudras. The question of the one and the many was posed as the problem of the relation between the body of one Purusha and the "many" encountered in the physical and social world. Later, in the devotional schools of Hinduism that flourished in the period A.D. 600–900, the problem became the relation between the one God who is true being without form (*nirākār*) and the many forms in which gods and goddesses appear in myths and rituals. None of these discussions reduced unity to homogeneity.

In considering variety as an expression of human creativity, to discover the conceptual resources of a worldview in which differences provide the basis of dependable, enduring relationships, I will take up three particular subjects: the structuring of the world of gods; the social order of *varṇa* (caste) and *puruṣārtha* (aims of life); and finally pilgrimage as an example of the meeting of the sacred and the social.

ONE GOD OR MANY

The structuring of the divine in Hinduism, from the early sacrificial cult of the Vedas to the later mythological elaborations given to gods and goddesses in the puranic literature, has been named polytheism. It ought to be noted, though, that "polytheism" could not be easily translated into Sanskrit or any of the regional languages, and that the tension between polytheism, on the one hand, and the monotheistic and monistic views of the more "spiritual" texts such as the Upanishads and the Vedanta, on the other, was not of the same order as in religions of Semitic origin.

The critiques of Hinduism that were developed in the eighteenth and nineteenth centuries by missionaries included scathing attacks on the polytheistic beliefs of Hindus. A well-known nineteenth-century Anglican bishop in Calcutta, Bishop Whitehead, interpreted the belief in many gods and goddesses as a sign of the Hindus' readiness to be converted, and he could not see any spirituality in these gods and goddesses. (He even remarked that the Goddess Kali carried about her objects that would be more suited to the pockets of an English schoolboy.) Such critiques were accepted, established, and internalized among the Indian elite, especially the Hindu reformers, who came to view monotheism and polytheism as opposed and unequal rather than as having a relation of creative complementarity. Swami Dayanand

Saraswati, founder of the Arya Samaj (Aryan Society), attributed the proliferation of deities in Hinduism to the greed of the Brahmans who used the simplicity of the peasants to exploit them through religious mystification. He sought to rediscover in Hinduism the one dominant God, Isvara, and to banish all other gods and their representations. The *Satyartha Prakash,* the sacred text of the Arya Samaj, tried to give the Vedas the authority of canonical texts. In the Hindu tradition, forms of knowledge that were held to be eternal and valid for all times and those that were unstable and could adapt to changed circumstances were both vitally important—without assuming that the distinction between them could be reduced to that of sacred and secular—but the reformers were unable to comprehend the texts' relationship of singularity and plurality in these terms. Thus, they strove to recreate a Hinduism that, although virulently opposed to Anglican Christianity, ironically reproduced all its categories: a single, all-powerful God, even though he was clearly not the God of history; one singular and authoritative scripture; a parish; a congregational space; and contributions of the devotee as a means of maintaining religious bureaucracy rather than as offerings to the divine.

The reformers also tried to apply Christian and Islamic models in dealing with popular traditions. Christianity and Islam went as conquering religions to many areas of the world and found themselves in conflict with the popular pietistic movements they encountered. Although the authors of texts such as the *dharmaśāstra*s had laid out rules of conduct so that even the king was enjoined to respect local custom, and the relation between the orthodox tradition and popular traditions should not have been so uneasy in Hinduism, we find in the writings of Raja Rammohun Roy, Dayanand Saraswati, and other Hindu reformers bitter assaults on popular Hinduism.

The dominant schools of philosophy of religion have posited a connection between the variety of human ephemeral desires and the creation of many gods in religions of non-Semitic origins, as well as a link between the movement toward monotheism and spiritual progress; and so it is no wonder that when these ideas on the superiority of monotheism as a giant step forward in human history came to India in the colonial context, they wielded great power over the imagination of the Hindu elite of the nineteenth century and influenced their interpretation of the ancient texts.

If we wish to understand the creative role of desire, we shall have to first reinstate it to its proper place in the conduct of human life. In the Hindu view, there is something rather than nothing because of God's desire to create; the human desire to create is seen as contiguous to God's desire. In the sacrificial cult of the Vedas, for instance, not human sin but human desire is seen as the root of a religious and ethical life. What transcends and regulates desire is the movement from desire for worldly objects to desire for heaven. Thus we find the apparent contradiction that desire for the world becomes the foundation for desire to renounce the world; only one who has felt such a desire to renounce worldly passions could be the true subject of sacrificial rituals. *Svargakāmo yajeta*—"May he perform sacrifice who is desirous of heaven." This injunction points to a worldview in which desire, instead of interfering with true spirituality, becomes the means through which human beings can recognize their own contiguity to the divine.

Whereas contemporary scholars of the history or phenomenology of religions are not explicit in their criticism of polytheism, they often define polytheistic universes in such a way that the beliefs they encounter there are treated as magical or exotic. Rarely do they grant the possibility that human relations with divinity in monotheism and polytheism are not irreconcilably or even really different, or that the latter view of life may be able to provide a critique of the dominant monotheistic traditions of Islam and Christianity.

Rather than asking how Christianity or Islam may help us to discover monotheistic trends within Hinduism, we may ask whether humankind has lost anything in its march toward monotheism. The need for variety is basic to human existence. It is worth remarking that even in religions in which the oneness of God is the fundamental ethical premise, this need for variety has asserted itself in the particularization of one or another aspect of God by the process of "marking" or mediating. The jealous face of God has to be complemented by a loving face. Local madonnas are endowed with special powers of healing. There is the concept of trinity within Christianity, which was always suspected of polytheistic tendencies by Muslims. In Islam itself there is a proliferation of saints as the religion spread around the world and absorbed diverse local customs.

To the Syrian Christians of Malabar, the divinity of Christ is expressed in his being the Son of his Father, but his humanity—the meaning of his life from the human point of view—is best comprehended through his relation to his mother. Although references to Mary in the Gospels may be few, popular imagination has created legends and songs around her. Susan Visvanathan, who has recently recorded many songs that old women in this region remember, shows how women formed a special link with the Mater and her festivals. Opposition to the place given to these festivals in traditional Syrian rituals, which is now being strengthened in the church hierarchies in Malabar, not only represents an attack on the religious needs of women but also on a feminine perspective toward the life of the Christ.

If the religion of a people is maintained as much by the piety of its ordinary believers as by the learning of its elite, then we would have to consider the above expressions as legitimate, and as providing humankind with important visions. That they have often been suppressed on the grounds that they constituted departures from the singular, orthodox tradition may be read within the context of power rather than of truth.

Hinduism teaches us that there is no contradiction between belief in one and belief in many. In the story of Purusha, which illustrates this beautifully, his fantasy body is not, significantly, the perfect body, the body made whole, but the mutilated body of a sacrificial victim whose different members are scattered over the universe and all compose it. The manyness of groups that form the social order does not contradict but holds the oneness of Purusha.

Every social order has a fantasy body behind it. In the medieval world it was the body of the king, and his installation included rituals by which different parts of the earth could be brought into a symbiotic relationship with his body. In the modern world, we have created a new fantasy body corresponding to the body politic, in which the connecting links between individual and community, society and state, and the person and the cosmos are yet to be fully understood. The image of the social order that the story of Purusha celebrates is under great stress. The process of the Semitization and transformation of Hinduism that began with Swami Dayanand Saraswati is now so dangerously complete that instead of the open character of its categories, its recognition that oneness can only be supported by manyness, we have religious leaders who urge us to become "one," to eliminate all our differences and to purge ourselves of those very influences from the variety in our environment that are the living proof of our spiritual hospitality to the rest of the world. In this context, it becomes imperative that we take our heritage seriously, to rehabilitate the legitimacy of variety and speak for the creativeness of human desire rather than of order based upon repressive law.

DIFFERENCE AND DIVISION IN THE SOCIAL WORLD

Increasing population, the penetration of markets in rural areas, and the emergence of new forms of inequality have led to great conflict over shrinking resources, manifested in a steady escalation of violence and atrocities against lower castes and tribal groups in many regions in India. The modernists, who find it axiomatic that our institutions of state and market are liberating whereas "primordial loyalties" are enslaving, attribute the conflicts to the caste ideology itself; they see the state with its legal apparatus as the agency through which such aberrations may be remedied and look to a common civil code as the basis for building secure nationhood. I want to suggest the opposite here: that a creative transformation of some of the assumptions of the ideology of caste may, in fact, help us to deal with the aberrations of the modern state.

If caste ideology was experienced as enslaving by lower castes, the modern state also has been experienced as a hostile force. The process by which the state and the market were given sole legitimate claim to law and reason, preempting traditional institutions such as religion, tribe, or caste, was begun by the British. In establishing the "rule of law" and through it the "good society," the colonial powers clearly had to dismantle other forms of authority or redefine them so that they would become "nonrational" and subordinate, and the modern Indian state inherited some of these functions. Its rights extend to the enactment of laws pertaining to marriage, sexuality, divorce, adoption, and inheritance, that is, to control over the individual in every aspect of life, so that the state becomes the arbiter of relations within the family or between the sexes. Many groups resist these rights as intrusive and as compromising their identity as religious communities within a secular state.

Modern legal systems also apply the language of property to most of the relations between humans and resources, creating problems that cannot be solved easily. In many parts of India tribal groups did not have any concept of immovable property. They believed that land was given by God for human use and that transactions between people could not alienate them from the fruits of the land. A person was thus free to set up a house anywhere within the tribal territory, to hunt within it, or to use the products of the forest on which the tribals' modes of life depended. With the encroachment of the market, tribals' land was "bought" by others. From the point of view of the tribe, what was being transacted through the "sale" was the right to use; from the point of view of the buyer, it was "ownership" that was at issue.

I am not proposing that various tribal groups in India be preserved as museum pieces or that we deny the right to these groups to live as historical beings, to adapt their forms of life in accordance with the changes they perceive in the wider system. Nor do I think that one can wish away the existence of markets or of modern nation-states. I am simply trying to point out that the modern state and its functions must be submitted to critical analysis, especially in matters of marital and sexual relations, and that the concept of law itself might be enriched if we could develop new legal languages for relations that are defined in terms other than those of individual ownership and possession. To create forms of nationhood and state more responsive to our own historical experience, we should have the courage to experiment with our heritage.

In this endeavor some of the principles of *varṇadharma* and *puruṣārtha* may perhaps play a role. The *dharmaśāstra*s, for instance, cited above, spoke not only of the law that could be enacted, interpreted, or applied by the king, but also of the customs evolved by various groups living within the territory of the king in the context of their own lives. The king did not have the right to enact laws that would contradict the immemorial right of a group to live according to its customs. The attempt to provide unity through the king's law was balanced by the recognition that rules evolve in the context of forms of life and cannot be replaced from above.

The legitimacy of the nation-state has historically rested on its claims to a more universal morality than that of primordial groups such as caste and tribe. But there is another notion of morality I want to present, which is based upon my reflections on the theory of *puruṣārtha*, the four ends of life that a person may pursue. These four ends are *dharma, artha, kāma,* and *mokṣa,* roughly translated as a proper code of conduct, pursuit of instrumental ends, pursuit of desire, and renunciation. Although these four ends of human existence are part of a scheme, the good life may be considered one in which *kāma* is pursued only to the extent that it does not conflict with *artha,* and *artha* only to the extent that it does not conflict with the pursuit of *dharma. Dharma* is defined as not only the code of conduct for an individual or a group but also as a constitutive system in which the right relations between people and nature, between different social groups, and also between people and gods are preserved: a moment in the system as well as the transcendental value of the system. *Mokṣa,* is opposed to the other three ends and is usually reserved for the last stage of a person's life, when he or she has renounced the social world and is engaged in austerities for the release of the soul.

In this view morality is universal in that the laws governing human existence are particular to the person who is exhorted to follow his or her *dharma,* according to his or her *svabhāva* (nature). When the *dharma* of an individual is equated with the *dharma* of his or her caste or marital position, as is often the case, the law can easily become the predetermined *telos* into which the individual fits. But if we can purge *dharma* of its tendency to predetermined *telos* and modify it to deny order based on coercion, I believe that it can provide a foundation for thinking about individual creativity and variety in relation to a system of law. In such a formulation, law would not be a set of rules to be applied to all in a mechanistic fashion by a superior authority but rather would embody a recognition that groups and individuals have a right to discover their own modes of being and to devise the rules that are to govern their existence. It is not my argument that modes of being evolved by individuals or groups cannot be subjected to criticism, for very often the notion of justice for the group may be at the cost of justice to the individual. However, the criticism must be communicative in nature, not imperative. In the case of tribal groups mentioned earlier, whose ideas about property may be at variance with the individualistic notions evolved in the context of market relations, it seems necessary that modern legal languages grapple with the problem of common property. To do that, as Chatrapati Singh and others have been arguing, the state needs to enter into a dialogue with such groups and develop a cooperative morality that can be the basis of communicative action.

What would be the nature of moral judgments in this kind of system? I am reminded here of the image of Lord Krishna, in the role of the charioteer of Arjuna, the warrior hero of the *Mahabharata*. When Arjuna could not bring himself to wage a war that Krishna considered righteous, Krishna stood by him as a friend, accepting Arjuna's fears and yet exhorting him to follow his *dharma* as a Kshatriya. Krishna does not appear here as a judge, separating the faithful from the damned, nor does he hand out rewards and punishments. In such a model of friendship, questions arising from the need of human beings for variety and for a recognition of differences may be dialogically related to the need for order. An imposition of a "rule of law" based on homogeneity and singularity seems opposed to the principles of social and cosmic order that we have tried to develop in these two sections.

THE PILGRIMAGE AS THE MODEL FOR INTEGRATION

My third subject, pilgrimage (defined as a journey to a sacred site), has special meaning to me, because through it the message of harmony in difference was communicated to a vast majority of Hindus who did not have access to the learned texts of their tradition.

The anthropological definition of pilgrimage specifies it as a space of liminality, or antistructure. The sacred site is one that is spatially distant but spiritually near. There are many kinds of pilgrim sites recorded in Hindu tradition: Some are founded by the sojourns of gods on earth, others are established as living emblems of the powers of various sages or commemorate events in the lives of good people. However, one characteristic is common to all of them. When the devotee reaches the pilgrim site, after having endured many hardships, he or she is subtly reminded that this is not the sacred center, the end of the journey, but rather the beginning of another spiritual journey, for the particular pilgrim site is linked by a series of images and symbols with other sacred spaces. Let me again proceed by example.

One of the holiest shrines of the Hindus is Kedarnath, situated in the Himalayas. The pilgrim lovingly carries clarified butter from home to apply to the body of Siva (who is present in the form of a rock in a dark cave), in order to give it strength. The priest then recites the following story. Once Siva was being pursued by Arjuna, who had acquired celestial weapons. In order to escape from Arjuna, Siva assumed the form of a buffalo, which incidentally is also the form of the famous demon Mahishasura. Arjuna's brother Bhima recognized Siva nevertheless, and even as Siva was fleeing, Arjuna cut his buffalo body into several pieces. The places where these parts fell came to be regarded as holy shrines. Hence, even as one embraces the mutilated body of Siva in the cave, one is transported by the narrative to other places, other times, and to the secret connections between gods and heroes and between gods and demons. The mythic idea of the sacrificial death of god is hardly unique to Hinduism. It might be necessary to remind ourselves, however, that the pilgrim center is precious not because it is unique but because, like a crystal, it reflects other spaces.

The pilgrim site of Dwarka in Gujarat is different in nature from Kedarnath. Here, rather than the sacrificed body of god to be healed by the pilgrim's love, one sees the splendid body of Krishna, the king of Dwarka, in his palace. Having offered obeisance, the pilgrim is told to take a ferry to Beta Dwarka temple palace, which is situated on an island in the sea. One of the many stories about why there are two Dwarkas relates that the original was on the island, but because of a poor Brahman devotee of Krishna who had become so weakened by age that he could not swim to the temple every day, Krishna decided to move to the shore rather than give his devotee pain; his image was one day found there and a new temple was established. Here is a hint that the true Dwarka lies in the heart of the devotee. Confirmation came to me on a recent visit when the priest said, "So you think you have seen Dwarka. But the real Dwarka was a city under the sea. Only the pure can see it reflected in their heart as a clean mirror reflects an image."

The city of Dwarka, the abode of the adult Krishna, already presumes the existence of Braj, where Krishna spent his childhood as a carefree cowherd. Why is the childhood of Krishna located in a space so removed from his adulthood? I cannot help but think that Indian society uses the metaphor of spatial distance to draw attention from one to the other, to the necessity of placing one segment of life in the context of another, one part of the body in the context of its totality, and every life in the context of the totality of other lives.

It is ironic that the very nature of pilgrimage that elaborates the rich notion of connections and communication, of looking from the self to the other, should now provide in modern India the context for bitter conflicts between Hindus and Muslims. It is the language of exclusion, power, and hatred that is coming to dominate discussions on pilgrimage today, not the language of interconnection, inclusion, and love. I am certain it will be pointed out to me that the establishment of Muslim sacred sites on preexisting Hindu sites was not an act of love. I can only reply that whatever the origins of these sites, the devotion of common people made them symbols of mutuality and common concern. The attempt to untie the knots in which history has bound the various religious and ethnic groups in India can only cause conflict and sterility. Instead we may discover from our medieval history the means to live together in diversity and make India the spiritual home of all those ideas that are under attack from fundamentalists and purists.

In the introduction to this paper I stated that the search for homogeneity leads to violence. One of the features of the kind of diversity I have been describing is that it is not very concerned with boundaries; each group merges into other groups at its margins. The nature of social groups in India as well as the study of their prescriptive norms supports this view. Yet social entities in India, under the influence of fundamentalist movements or the ideology of the modern state, are trying to reinvent a tradition that would establish their boundaries on the grounds of similarity and negate all interconnections and communication between them. Fundamentalist movements in Islam now deny the creativity of Sufi cults that experimented with Hindu symbols; Sikh fundamentalists are engaged in remaking a history in which the position of Sikhism as a mediating philosophy through which the differences between Hinduism and Islam could be given a language is completely rejected; and Hinduism, as I have shown, is also transformed to such an extent that it shies away from openness and seeks to be monolithic. All of these fundamentalist movements, including those within Christianity, display antipathy to popular religious practices evolved through centuries of living together. When blurring of boundaries becomes so hard to tolerate, and homogeneity is the ideal, then it is necessary to eliminate those who confuse distinctions by the use of violence. This would explain why tribal groups living on the borders of India and Burma, for instance, have had to endure such prolonged hostility; the idea of groups that both belong and do not belong to the country has no place in the modern state structure. It seems to me that unless these trends can be reversed, we will have failed in our civilizational responsibility toward India. We must look again at structures of significance in relation to the sacred, to adapt the conceptual models in such a way that they do not become instruments for inferiorizing certain traditions and those who live by them. I am not advocating that we simply tolerate pluralism but that we try to find a theory in which differences and divisions may be celebrated as providing a design for life. Although the metaphor of purity is very dear to the Indian and has even been given a political context now, I may conclude by saying that complete purity is a condition of sterility. It is only on condition that one is willing to be polluted that creative communication becomes possible.

CHAPTER 2

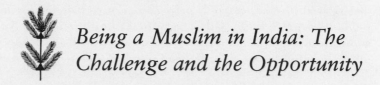

Being a Muslim in India: The Challenge and the Opportunity

C. M. Naim

"The Muslims of India . . . face what is a radically new and profound problem; namely how to live with others as equals. This is unprecedented; it has never arisen before in the whole history of Islam" (Smith 1959, 289). So wrote Wilfred Cantwell Smith, perhaps the most perceptive Western scholar of Islam in South Asia, in his book *Islam in Modern History,* first published in 1957 and still of great relevance. He also observed, a few pages earlier: "The question of political power and social organization, so central to Islam, has in the past always been considered in yes-or-no terms. Muslims have either had political power or they have not. *Never before have they shared it with others*" (ibid., 287). (Emphasis original.)

Smith's statements reflect his analysis of how Muslims have viewed their history in accordance with their conviction that "[Islam's] purpose includes the structuring of a social community, the organization of the Muslim group into a closed body obedient to the Law." "It is this conception," Smith continues, "that seems finally to be proving itself inept in India" (ibid., 288). He decries some of the consequences of that view and does not seem to share it entirely. However, when he underscores his point by characterizing the Muslims in China and black Africa as being not free, or when he argues that the Muslims of the Soviet Union "are a minority within a vast non-Muslim domain [,] [b]ut they are not joint rulers[;] they do not participate in the choice and responsibility of the course of events" (ibid.), he is not merely betraying a personal preference for Western-style democracies. He is also revealing greater affinity with the way most Muslims of India have ideally tended to view themselves: an undifferentiated, consolidated community, either wielding power as a communal group or not at all.

Group or communal identity has indeed been of paramount importance to the Muslims, as can be seen in the fact that the beginning of serial time in Muslim history is marked by the moment of the emergence of a separate Muslim commuity in Medina. The religious experiences of the Prophet were of two kinds, the mediated revelation of the Word of God—the *wahy*—and the unmediated, direct experience of the proximity of God at the end of the Prophet's "celestial journey"—the *mi'rāj*. The pivotal status of the first for the whole of Islam is obvious, while the second not only places Muhammad in a unique position as compared with other Muslim prophets but also has tremendous significance for Sufistic or mystical Islam. Instead of using either of these events as a starting point, though, 'Umar, the second Caliph, chose the year of the *hijrah*, the emigration of Muhammad from Mecca, which led to the emergence of a separate, cohesive community of believers in Medina. That moment was perceived as an absolute breaking away from any space-time relationship with the past and as the beginning of a new life that is explicitly the life of the community.

The importance given to the self-image of a consolidated community and the community-forming role of the Prophet is further reflected in the fact that though all Muslims, including learned scholars of religion (the ulama), grant validity to the concept of *kashf*—the unmediated, direct inspiration of humankind from God—they have never willingly tolerated any such inspiration that also led to the formation of a separate community within Islam. This can be seen—within the context of South Asia—in the persecution of the messianic Mahdavis[1] in the fifteenth century and in the harsh treatment meted out to the followers of Mirza Ghulam Ahmad in Pakistan more recently.[2] Although far apart in time and ideas, the two victimized groups share one common feature: They attempted to create a distinct community of believers within the general body of Islam. It appears as if the finality of Muhammad as a prophet is not merely with regard to the matter of *wahy* or revelation; rather, it also includes community formation. We can say that the original community of believers, as it took form in Medina through the temporal actions of the Prophet, has become a kind of metacommunity for all Muslims for all times. In its normative role it has completely overshadowed the experience of Islam in Mecca (which makes one wonder what the shape of Islam would have been if the Prophet had met with immediate success in Mecca). Simultaneously, the history of that community in Medina, as that community became more consolidated and more powerful, has served as a kind of metahistory, from which must emanate the dynamics of all subsequent, serial histories. Needless to say, this emphasis on the primacy of the community has been at the cost of the significance of the individual.

In this century, with regard to the Muslims of South Asia, the pervasive power of that view of history could be seen in the popularity of the Khilafat movement[3] as well as in the success of the Pakistan movement, which, paradoxically enough, was led by a nonreligious, modernist leader who had opposed the earlier movement. One also can justifiably argue that the same view of community and history was behind the attitude of the Pakistani and Indian Muslims who opposed the subsequent establishment of Bangladesh (see Naim 1975, 27–37).

It could be seen as well in the way most of the more traditional, piety-minded Muslim leaders chose to respond to the emergent situation in India in 1947. One group, the so-called nationalist ulama, conceived of the future constitution of a free India as a contract between the Muslim community of India and the non-Muslim others, much in the manner of the contract that the Prophet had made with the Jews of Medina.[4] In doing so, they overlooked two things: first, that in the original contract the Prophet had the ultimate authority; second, and more important, that the original contract was between groups, whereas the Constitution of India was a contract between the individual and the state. The result was that these learned people supported a secular polity based on adult franchise within which they nevertheless wished the Muslims to act as a consolidated group.[5]

Then there were absolutists of another kind, the members of the Jama'at-i-Islami,[6] who believed then, and continue to believe now, that the Muslims in India should be a "protected minority": in other words, a kind of *dhimmī*[7] in Hindu India. Their leader, Maulana Maudoodi, advised the Hindus of India in May 1947 "to study the lives and teachings of Ramachandra, Krishnaji, Buddha, Guru Nanak, and other sages." "Please study," he said, "the *Vedas, Puranas, Shastras* and other books. If you cull out any divine guidance from these, we would request you to base your constitution on this guidance. We would request you to treat us exactly on the lines of the teachings of your religion. We would raise no objections" (cited in Hassnain 1968, 51–52). Some years later, when pressed on the latter point in Pakistan, he declared that he would not mind if the Hindus applied the laws of Manu to the Muslims of India and treated them as worse than outcasts.[8]

Fortunately, the Constituent Assembly of India did not oblige Maulana Maudoodi, nor, for that matter, did it enter into a contract with the "nationalist" ulama. Instead, the Indian Constitution set into motion in India two historical processes of the modern age, democracy and secularism.

That brings us back to the radical problem, as phrased by Smith, that the Muslims face in India: how to live with others as equals. If the preceding discussion of the twin concepts of community and history has even some validity, it must be evident that any "rediscovery of the past as adaptation for the future" is not likely to help much. If the Indian Constitution does not wish to treat the Muslims as _dhimmīs_, and if, as is generally believed, the Muslims of India have never in the past had to share power with others, how can they now use their past to adapt themselves for a democratic and secular future? Is there no choice for them but to reject their past?

I believe the answer is yes—with one qualification. What is imperative is not that they reject the past out of hand—which could be well-nigh impossible—but that they recognize that there is no one Muslim past, that, in fact, there are as many pasts as there are Muslims. The so-called Islamic past is but an abstraction, constructed by and useful to those who traditionally have made exclusive claims to hold power. How integral this abstraction is to the question of power can be seen in the fact that Muslim modernists of the League variety, conservative ulama of assorted kinds, even sympathetic Western observers, not to mention the Orientalists, all seem to come up with almost the same, monolithic, undifferentiated Islam. When Smith wrote "Muslims have either had political power or they have not," he tacitly meant only those Muslims who could in the past hold exclusive power and did. Likewise, his statement "_Never before have they shared [power] with others_," no matter how much hedged with exceptions, turns our attention away from the reality that, in all the centuries of "Islamic" history in India, a very large number of Muslims have always had to share _powerlessness_ with others. It is not in the mythology of one thousand years of exclusive power but in the centuries of shared degrees of powerlessness, or what Ashis Nandy more elegantly calls "one thousand years of conflicted but meaningful neighborliness," that the Muslims of India can expect to find guidance for the kind of power sharing proposed by Indian democracy. In full cognizance of their own diversity, they must turn not to some single, monolithic abstraction but to the concreteness of their own maximally differentiated pasts.

It follows, of course, that like the Muslims of India the non-Muslims of India also have a multitude of pasts. To think otherwise, to postulate a single, undifferentiated past for all the non-Muslims, would be intellectually dishonest, no matter how ideal or even pragmatic it may seem. It would also be disastrous for India at the present time, when it is beset with communal violence. To my mind, only individuals have real pasts; groups do not. Groups, at best, have aggregates, or, at worst, abstractions. Abstractions can only too easily become coercive, particularly when the nature and motives of the people who construct such abstractions are lost sight of by those who subsequently want to use them for their own innocent purposes. To understand this last point, we need only remind ourselves of the disastrous Khilafat movement, which was supposed to bring the Muslim masses into the nationalist movement and create greater communal harmony but ended up doing exactly the opposite.

Let us now turn to what I feel is the challenge and the opportunity before the Muslims of India, namely to gain individually creative awareness of the diversity of their pasts and thus break out from under the hegemony of that vision of a monolithic, communal past that has been and still is being used—by their leaders as well as by their detractors—to deny them control of their own individual destinies. No doubt that is easier said than done. Any effort on these lines would be fanatically opposed by the religious orthodoxy—as in the recent controversy concerning the maintenance rights of divorced women—while the modernist, bourgeois leadership already has repeatedly shown its predilection for a separate, consolidated Muslim polity. Then there is another acute problem.

The Indian national polity is still in the process of creating a viable and equitable balance between provincial autonomy and central authority, between regional identities and the national identity—the former stressing diversity over unity, the latter unity over diversity. This is indeed a critical aspect of that endless process called nation building. However, it makes the task before the Muslims of India rather more difficult. At present, Muslim minds are being coerced on the one hand by the votaries of a monolithic Islam, and on the other by the proponents of the so-called Indian mainstream. My belief in the many pasts of the Muslims and my understanding of the present political scene suggest that there exists a third choice: The Muslims of India, after transcending their communal exclusivity, should instead recognize and strengthen their local and regional orientation. They should do so not out of any expedience—though the expediency of avoiding violent conflict is manifestly there—but because that orientation already exists in the specificity of their diverse pasts, even if it is not consciously recognized and thus made vital and functional as is the case with their non-Muslim compatriots.

Indian Muslims, or for that matter all South Asian Muslims, differentiate themselves from the Muslims of other nations, say, the Arabs, and one may presume that isolating those differentiating features would lead to a discovery of their Indianness. But South Asian Muslims also differentiate among themselves, and, as the emergence of Bangladesh tells us, such differences are of much greater import for the people involved than any abstracted Muslim, or even Indian Muslim, identity—particularly so when the context is of power and hegemony, whether social, cultural, or economic. Our recognition of many pasts, we should remember, entails not merely a horizontal, territorially defined differentiation, but also a vertical differentiation within any smaller unit.

This assertion of the diverse regional orientations by the Muslims of India will also contribute to the enhancement of democracy in the country. The political crisis facing India today does not arise out of any failure of secularism, even though the secularization of the society has not kept pace with its politicization. The bigger cause is that the process of democratization—that is, the devolution of power from the largest construct, the state, to the smallest actual unit, the individual—has not only not kept pace with the tremendous rise in the political expectations of the Indian people but has in fact slowed down. Simultaneously, the arenas for democratic political action have declined both in number and in kind. And even in the arenas that exist, one saw not too long ago the imposition of a single political will. This slowing down and diminution will have to be reversed. The future of democracy in India lies in the decentralization and diversification of the foci of power, and Indian Muslims will not be able to play their rightful role in that future if they fail to remove themselves from the concept of a consolidated Muslim polity emanating from a single Muslim past.

Being a Muslim in India is at the same time a challenge and an opportunity: to become functionally alive in the developing, secular democracy. I suggest that a way to meet that challenge is for the Muslims to discover their own individual, highly differentiated pasts and only then to engage in making aggregates of them, first at the local and regional levels, and later at the national level. I submit that there is no one Muslim or even Indian Muslim past, or for that matter even a single Indian past. Such constructs are only abstractions, and not entirely neutral. In the process of discovering the past, as we move from the individual to increasingly larger units, the quantum of abstraction increases as does the potential for the past to become restrictive. I also submit that those who seek to discover the past exist in certain objective political conditions, as did the creators of that past which is being rediscovered. If those conditions—past and present—are overlooked in the rediscovery process, then that abstract past can also become concretely coercive.

NOTES

1. The Mahdavis were the followers of Sayyid Ahmad of Jaunpur (1443–1504), the self-proclaimed *mahdī* or promised reformer at the end of the first Muslim millennium. Within a short period they formed small communities all over India, but orthodox religious leaders, hand in hand with the Sur and the Mughal state power, prevailed over them. There are, however, still some Mahdavi groups in Hyderabad and Gujarat. See Ikram 1975b, 24–32.

2. Mirza Ghulam Ahmad of Qadian (1837–1908) declared himself a messiah and a *mahdī* in 1891 and claimed to be divinely inspired (Ikram 1975a, 177–87). His followers the Ahmadis (also called the Qadianis, after Ahmad's birthplace), remarkable for their missionary zeal, are found in largest numbers in Pakistan, India, and some African countries. They have frequently been persecuted in Pakistan, where in 1974 the National Assembly declared them non-Muslims. The assembly accused them of not believing in the finality of Muhammad as a prophet, a charge that has been denied by a large number of Ahmadis.

3. When at the end of World War I the defeated Turks were forced to withdraw from their Arab and other non-Turk colonies, the Muslims of British India sought to protect the temporal and religious powers of the Ottoman caliph, claiming that the proposed dissolution of the Ottoman Empire would be an attack on Islam. They did so in the face of rising Arab nationalism and Turkish republicanism, and they were led in this movement by a strange triumvirate: Maulana Abdul Bari, a traditional scholar and sufi; Muhammad Ali, a graduate of Aligarh and Oxford; and Mohandas K. Gandhi, who thought that by helping the Muslims of India at what they considered to be a critical moment in their history he could win their friendship for the greater cause of Indian nationalism. Eventually, the Arabs gained their freedom and the Turks got rid of the caliphate, while the so-called Khilafat movement failed to create even a lasting political alliance between the Hindus and the Muslims. In fact, its immediate consequences were a number of extremely violent communal incidents and a consolidation of Muslim nationalist aspirations opposed to Indian nationalism. See Minault 1982.

4. Smith 1959, 285. In a footnote on page 287, Smith points out: "In the case of the Madinah Jews with whom the original *mu'āhadah* [contract] was established, power was not really shared; it was an agreement for each community to live its own life, rather than for the two to participate in constructing a life in common." Also see Friedman 1976, 181–211, particularly page 186, where one dissenting leader is mentioned as urging the Muslims to abandon the way of life in Medina—"sovereignty and self-rule"—in favor of the Meccan way "which is one of suffering and in which the most conspicuous qualities are endurance, reliance on Allah, truth and moral integrity."

5. Much the same thinking, though not so extremely expressed, is even now evident in the opposition of the Majlis-i-Mushawarat and other Muslim organizations in India to any legislative reform in the Muslim Personal Law.

6. An organization and movement started in 1941 by Sayyid Abu-l-A'la Maudoodi (1903–79). "[Maudoodi] would appear to be much the most systematic thinker of modern Islam. . . . He presents Islam as a system, one that long ago provided mankind with set answers to all its problems, rather than as a faith in which God provides mankind anew each morning the riches whereby it may answer them itself" [Smith 1959, 236]. Also see Sayeed 1957, 59–68.

7. "According to Muslim canon law on the conquest of a non-Muslim country by Muslims, the population which does not embrace Islam and which is not enslaved is guaranteed life, liberty and, in a modified sense, property. They are, therefore, called ahl al-dhimma, 'People of the convenant or obligation', or simply al-dhimma or dhimmīs" ("DHIMMA," Shorter Encyclopaedia of Islam [Leiden: E. J. Brill, 1961], 75).

8. "I should have no objection even if the Muslims of India were treated in [a Hindu] form of Government as Shudras and Malishes and Manu's laws were applied to them, depriving them of all share in the Government and the rights of a citizen" [quoted in Hassnain 1968, 52]. Maulana Maudoodi's statement was made before a commission of enquiry set up by the Government of Pakistan to look into the anti-Ahmadi riots of 1953.

REFERENCES CITED

Friedman, Yohannan
  1976   The Jam'iyyat Al-'Ulamā'-I Hind in the Wake of Partition. Asian and African Studies (Jerusalem) 11, no. 2.

Hassnain, S. E.
  1968   Indian Muslims: Challenge and Opportunity. Bombay: Lalvani Publishing House.

Ikram, Shaikh Muhammad
  1975a   Mauj-i-Kauthar. Ninth reprint. Lahore: Idarah-i-Saqafat-i-Islamiyya.

  1975b   Rūd-i-Kauthar. Sixth reprint. Lahore: Idarah-i-Saquafat-i-Islamiyya.

Minault, Gail
  1982   The Khilafat Movement. New York: Columbia University Press.

Naim, C. M.
    1975   Muslim Press in India and the Bangladesh Crisis. *Quest* (Bombay) 94 (March–April): 27–37.

Sayeed, Khalid B.
    1957   The *Jama'at-i-Islami* Movement in Pakistan. *Pacific Affairs* (New York) 30:59–68.

Smith, Wilfred Cantwell
    1959   *Islam in Modern History*. New York: The New American Library.

CHAPTER 3

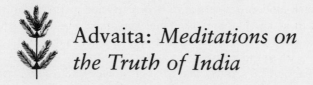

Advaita: *Meditations on the Truth of India*

Ramchandra Gandhi

I

Ramchandra Gandhi: Professor Kramrisch, friends. I don't have a written paper, and I really can't pretend that this is entirely because of my vehement fondness for the oral tradition of India.

I was not able to write a paper for an audience I did not know, and I did not make the attempt also because I wanted my presentation to be a spontaneous response to this very special celebration of India in America.*

Let us begin with a piece of purana, sacred mythology, from America. I believe Mark Twain was very sad one day and somebody asked him why he was so sad, and he said he suddenly remembered something that happened in childhood to him and his twin brother. They were being given a bath by their mother in a tub and one of them drowned. The world thought it was his brother who had drowned. Actually it was he, Mark Twain, who had drowned.

Now, that is pure Advaita, quintessential nonduality. Mark Twain is not here trying to suggest merely that he loved his brother, that he missed him very much. With deadly seriousness (don't forget he is a humorist) he is identifying himself not merely *with,* but *as,* the drowned child. Pure Advaita.

---

*This spontaneity is sought to be preserved in the edited and augmented form of the original presentation that follows.

Examples can be multiplied of stories, of realization, of insight, to show that Advaita, nonduality, is a universal, and not a culture-specific, discovery. This is not surprising because Advaita is the ultimate *democratic* discovery that all beings are essentially Being, a discovery or rediscovery of self-knowledge that everyone everywhere can attain. And yet, and yet, it is distinctively in India that this discovery is sanctified, supported continuously, and honored by revelation and civilization, all the way from the earliest Upanishadic testaments such as the *Isopanisad* down to such modern revivifications of revelation as the authoritative utterances of a sage like Shri Ramana Maharshi. The shepherding of Advaita by India and of India by Advaita is what makes Advaita the distinctive truth of India.

I realize, by God's grace, that the reason we Hindus don't chop off the heads of our *jñānīs*, sages, or crucify them, is not because we are necessarily better men and women, no! We are not! *Śruti,* revelation, prevents us from this crime against truth, because it declares that in self-realization there is no blasphemy in the utterance "I am Brahman, Godhead," because in self-realization I am not *other* than anything, I am one with the essence of all, with the "I" of all. Self-realization is not self-glorification; beatitude is not blasphemy. There is here ground for humility and not only pride.

This is an oral presentation, and the oral tradition is also a listening tradition, so I was listening to the speakers before me, and let me say how moved I was by Naim Sahib's presentation and how sensitive I thought his account was of the dilemma of the Indian Muslim.

However, I do think that it is not only at the level of *bhāvanā,* feeling, that Hindus and Muslims ought to be brothers and sisters, but also at the level of deep theological inquiry that is as much a part of the Islamic heritage as it is of the Hindu heritage.

Let me tell you a story from the life of Ramana Maharshi, the sage who at the age of sixteen extracted the truth and gift of immortality from the jaws of the fear of death in a dramatic, uninstructed, half-hour exercise of existential inquiry in the manner of the legendary Naciketas of the *Kathopanisad.**

Not long after this singular feat of self-realization, Ramana is summoned to Arunacala, Tamil Nadu's most sacred hill, to commune with his divine Father, Siva, I suspect rather in the way Jesus as a boy was led to Jerusalem. Part of the journey had to be covered by train. Ramana,

---

*An Upanishad (confidential or intimate instruction) of great antiquity and authority, which tells of the boy Naciketas's self-realizing discipleship of Death itself, and of Death's unexpected offer of immortality to all fearless and ceaseless spiritual seeking.

lost in *samādhi,* spiritual absorption, would have failed to get off at the right station had he not been alerted by a fellow passenger, a *maulvī,* Islamic theologian, who, legend has it, mysteriously disappeared after performing this crucial service to humanity.

In this story of the good *maulvī* and Ramana I read the secret solicitude of Islam for Advaita and, indeed, its need for it. Urgent theological venturesomeness in Islamic thought can hardly find a more hospitable environment than India.

Naim Sahib, I think we ought to pool all our Advaitin philosophical and spiritual resources in India—Hindu, Buddhist, Jain, Muslim, Christian, tribal, independent, visiting American, all kinds. There might then be some hope of founding brotherhood and sisterhood more securely than on feelings alone, which we know can be very irrational.

Aristotle was a great philosopher, but I think he made two very great mistakes. Two, however, is not such a large number when it comes to mistakes that philosophers make, so this remark is not a condemnation of Aristotle.

Aristotle made the first mistake when he suggested that people were rational animals; and I think he made the second mistake when he suggested that they were social animals. People are both rational and irrational, utterly simultaneously, embarrassingly simultaneously, and they are both social and solitary, again simultaneously.

But at all times, a person is a *sikh,* a seeker after the essence of things, the absolute and common ground of all that is or can be, an Advaitin, in lucidity and even in darkness, in saintliness as well as in criminality. How few Sikhs and Hindus know that the word "*sikh*" is colloquial for "*śiṣya,*" that is, pupil, seeker! Etymology is the hope of Punjab.

Refreshed by our rich philosophical tradition, and reassured by the continuity of our history, we must once again perform in India today the philosophical task that India and Greece performed in antiquity, the task of restoring in rigor and realization a sense of wonder to human self-consciousness, without which the adventure of civilization on earth cannot be saved. Without wonder there is no love, and without love we risk the annihilation of life on earth. India and Advaita can help transform the wretchedness of humanity's egoistic self-love into wondrous saving self-realization.

From Mark Twain let us turn in tribute to Peter Sellers, with whom, also, all of us died recently.

In the film *The Party,* this great comedian does the part of an Indian immigrant in Britain. A scene shows Sellers trying to gatecrash a party, symbolizing, I suppose, the desire of many of us to force our entry into the modern world, the twenty-first century, etc. A doorman stops Sellers with the sarcastic words, "Who do you think you are?" In his inimitable accent—I wish I could imitate that Indian accent—Sellers retorts, "In India we don't *think* who we are. We *know* who we are."

Ramana Maharshi would have loved Peter Sellers. Without humor there is no Advaita.

Solemn nonduality is about the most dualistic thing you can imagine, like Queen Victoria, if I may say so with apologies to Margaret Thatcher.

Why is slapstick so abidingly funny? Because it rests in the truth of Advaita. Advaita teaches that you cannot be reduced to your body, mind, society, history, or culture, not even if these are a beautiful body, a clever mind, a prosperous society, an ancient and sophisticated history and culture. Nor are you their owner. You are their trustee, in the Gandhian sense of that word whose application extends way beyond economic organization.* It is comical vanity to think that you are the owner of your body, mind, etc., a falsehood liable to bring you tumbling down at the first encounter with adversity and acquisitiveness, in the way the banana peel brings down the fat man in the circus act. If the idiot figure—as in Dostoevsky—can represent the exceptionality of a Christ's saintliness, the clown figure can represent the singularity of the wisdom of a Shri Ramana. Minorities image and thus hold in trust the absolute minority, that is, *oneness,* of God.

A philosophy, such as Advaita, that can explicate humor is very probably true. If it can also illumine tragedy, it *must* be true. And Advaita does indeed do so. Tragedy is not mistaking mother for wife and father for foe; presumably a computer could reduce the chances of that sort of error to negligibility. Tragedy lies in our regarding anything or anyone as "other" than ourselves, in failing to see ourselves as infinitely many-centered self-consciousness. A favorite illustration of tragedy in Advaitin literature is a woman looking everywhere for the necklace she thinks she has lost, but which in reality is round her neck all the time. Contrary to a widespread view held in modern literary circles both Indian and Western, Indian thought is quite well equipped conceptually to understand the notion of tragedy. A deeper reading of Sophocles in Advaitin terms is possible and demands to be made—perhaps by a Peter Brook and a possible future Indian cinema and stage not only obsessed with but also illumined by the *Mahabharata* and by the tragic beauty of classical Greek civilization.

---

*In his economic thought Mahatma Gandhi emphasized the need for going beyond the idea of individual or collective ownership of the means of production to the idea of holding these in *trust* for others, a suggestive idea demanding philosophical and sociological extension.

I share Veena Das's scepticism about monotheism's claims to superiority over polytheism within the framework of dualistic thought. If God is *other* than what I essentially am, if God is wholly other than what I essentially am, then it is not self-evident that the single God of monotheism is preferable to polytheism's plurality of the divine. Today God in singularity may be on my side, but not necessarily also tomorrow. It's either him or me, so I might think, as Judas may have thought, and I might kill him. Nietzsche talked about the murder of God, and he *meant* just that. Many theologians are inclined to say, oh, he didn't quite mean that, he was a nice chap, you know, he meant only that the old notion of God is dead.

I think that's a grave injustice to Nietzsche, to his tragic honesty. If God is wholly other than me, I might honor him today, but such is the thought even of a little bit of ontological otherness that I might grow suspicious of him and I might wait and wait and wait and get at him, kill him because it is me or him. An Advaitin reading of Nietzsche throws a flood of light on the murder of Christ and on the theological bases of atheism. Dualistic monotheism is neither morally nor metaphysically superior to polytheism. Unless it is aided by Advaita, the spirit of pluralism in the world today is likely very deeply to bury the idea of God.

Advaita can restore to the idea of God its proper dimension of singularity without monotheistic hegemonism. If you conceive of God in the Advaitin spirit as not being essentially other than yourself, and if you conceive of him in the freedom of the spirit as pure self-consciousness without form, then you have to conceive of him as one. There isn't a plurality of formlessness. But if you choose to conceive of him as with form, concrete or abstract, plurality is unavoidable. Polytheism is the necessity that the idiom of form imposes. It is not a failure of morality or theology.

Outside Advaita, your monotheism is as vulnerable to murder, to misunderstanding, to misrepresentation, to corruption, as polytheism—probably more so, because in polytheism there is surely a greater variety of possible approaches to God, greater democratic freedom.

But no, outside nonduality, I would not vote for polytheism against monotheism or the other way around. I wouldn't, not even in this democratic age, I wouldn't do that.

One way of looking at Christ from India is this: Here was an *advaita-jñānī*—incarnate self-realization—thrown up by a tradition that was (and continues to be) hostile to Advaita, a fact and a feat that reinforce the truth of Advaita. And an *advaita-jñānī*, mind you, is the highest form of manifestation of Godhead. So it isn't that when we say this in India, of Jesus Christ, that he was an *advaita-jñānī*, we are withholding from him some higher status: no, not at all. We ascribe to him the highest possible spiritual status, of self-realization. But not to him alone, of course.

Now, given that, the murder of Christ becomes—at least to me, a lover of Jesus—clear. It is very likely that Jesus taught not only that he and the Father are one, but also, identically with the teaching of the Upanishads, that *all* were in essence one with the Father. Most of his contemporaries were morally and spiritually unequal to this Advaitin challenge and connived at his killing, fearing God in him dualistically— murderously, as it happened. Mainstream Christianity's continuing suspiciousness of Advaita is a continuing crucifixion of Christ. Oedipus prophesies the fate of dualism.

India is a trustee, not the owner, of Advaita. We honor the Buddha and the Christ, no less Mark Twain and Peter Sellers.

II

We are all supposed to be up against materialism. What is materialism? Let me offer a definition of materialism from the Advaitin point of view, from the point of view of nonduality. Materialism is the basic bad news that whatever ultimate reality might be, it ain't you. It is not you.

I remember as a schoolboy I used to be reasonably bright, or so I thought. After examinations I would go up to the teacher hoping that she might give me the good news that I had got the highest marks. But from her expression I would know that whoever had got the highest marks, it was not me.

Basic bad news. Materialism is the basic bad news that whatever ultimate reality might be, whether conceived dialectically, historically, theologically, psychologically, anthropologically, any way you like, it is not *you*, and that's terrible bad news. You might say that's not bad news at all, because if I am not ultimate reality, I don't have to look after the universe, it's somebody else's job! Aside from the lack of enterprise that attitude reflects, how do you know that this somebody else or something else—ultimate reality—will look after you abidingly if he or she were not you, essentially? And all this quite apart from the fact— hard to repress in a democratic age—that you haven't got the first prize, the highest honors. Spoilsport schoolboy thought this, but there is truth in it.

Idealism is would-be antimaterialism, but it is mostly cast in a dualistic mold and turns out to be a form of materialism as defined above, an embarrassment that ought to help idealism shed its sanctimonious self-image.

Dualistic idealism is dualistic theism in its most powerful form, and this is materialism because dualistic theism's God—omnipotent, omniscient, and other things—is not me, is not the core of me, not the essence of me, and constitutes the kind of irreducible *otherness* in relation to self-consciousness that is the hallmark of materialism, from Greek atomism down to the establishmentarian voice of modern science. (The esotericism of contemporary physics, not yet adequately philosophically examined, is a possible exception to this generalization.)

I think in the world today the really big battle is between dualistic materialism and the camouflaged materialism that is dualistic idealism: the battle between the Soviet Union and the United States, ideologically speaking. And in this battle—I decided to speak honestly here—I believe that the Soviet Union has an edge over America. (Basic bad news, huh?)

Shall I tell you why? Dualistic materialism is able to extract a terrific price from its adherents because it teaches the essential unreality of consciousness and self-consciousness, dismissing them as epiphenomena, a euphemism for essential unreality. This is false belief, of course, but it facilitates a degree of surrender to the system (give yourselves over to the revolution, because your "selves" are unreal anyway) that is not matched by what dualistic idealism is able to coax out of *its* adherents, because of the absence in its cultural milieus of a dominant theory of the epiphenomenality of consciousness. I hope American dualistic idealism will not espouse that theory to match dualistic materialism's power of extracting loyalty from human beings. The Indian hope is that both systems would renounce dualism and embrace the Advaitin view of the many-centeredness of self-consciousness, self-same in humanity and other forms of life and nature, not excluding so-called nothingness, moving thus closer to ecological and aboriginal modes of thought and life and bidding goodbye to expansionism, ideological and political and economic, which is what lies at the back of the world crisis today. Modern Indian society and governments may often not adequately or at all articulate or exemplify this hope of Advaita, but surviving traditional Indian metaphysical sensibility and resurgent Indian spirituality emphatically do.

On the question of the significance of aboriginal religious thought and ritual in India and its relationship to Hinduism, I would like to point out that Hinduism is the most elaborate conceptual articulation of aboriginal truth that humanity possesses. Whatever the current estrangements between mainstream Indian society and aboriginal Indians, the fact remains that Indian civilization alone among the major civilizations of the world has been philosophically and spiritually hospitable to aboriginal consciousness and forms of life, never traditionally threatening these theologically or ecologically. The coherence of supremely iconoclastic and abstract Advaita and image worship, which is the essence of Hinduism, is also the deep structure of aboriginal life and thought.

It is a matter of great pride for India that the aboriginal peoples of America have acquired the name "Indians" by an accident of navigation that may well have been also a design of providence—the linguistic *līlā,* play, of God. The chief of the Stoney Indians once said to my brother, "We are Stoney Indians, you are Phoney Indians."

When Indians deny Advaita and aboriginality, they are indeed phoney.

A great price is demanded by Advaita, the price of giving up what traditional Indian philosophical anthropology calls *dehātmavāda,* the powerful and prestigious idea that I am only this body, that I am only this form. I am all forms conceivable, and also essentially formless. And you. I am you. (I am vast, I contain multitudes, as Whitman sang, almost echoing Krishna in the *Gita.*)

That reminds me of a trying classroom situation in which I once found myself some years ago in Hyderabad, when I had to confront an unexpected taunt a student of mine threw at me. The student was of Marxist persuasion, and I was going on and on about Advaita, alas not nearly as eloquently as I am doing here.

The young Marxist said, "Professor, it is all very well for you to say that you are me and so on. *I* am hungry, *you* eat. *You* are me." By the grace of God I said, "You are wrong, friend. I have two stomachs, and my hunger will not be appeased until your stomach is also full."

The doctrine that we have many bodies, many forms, is a profound doctrine. Remember what Paramahamsa* Sri Ramakrishna said when he was dying of cancer? He was dying of cancer of the throat, he couldn't drink even a drop of water, and some of his more doubting disciples said—all *jñānī*s and *paramahaṃsa*s have doubting disciples, devil's advocates—they said, "O Master, why don't you ask your Mother (Divine Mother, Kali) to heal your throat?"

The Master was of course on very intimate terms with the Divine Mother, and he agreed to call on her. He went into *samādhi,* contemplative ecstasy, and presumably had a heart-to-heart chat with Kali about incurable cancer of the throat. As he came out of *samādhi,* the disciples impatiently asked what she had to say. Ramakrishna matter-

---

*"Supreme Swan," highest spiritual status conferred by tradition on a sage who unerringly discriminates between reality and illusion, even as the swans of mythology separate adulterating water from milk.

of-factly reported that the Divine Mother was most compassionate and had graciously said, "Ramakrishna, you have millions of other throats for drinking, why do you worry about this one diseased throat here?"

This is a tremendous story, pure Advaita.

A final quick sketch of a proof of Advaita. The opposite of Advaita is duality, otherness. All men are others, not brothers, says dualism. And otherness goes with the idea of the sovereignty of causality, with the thought of causality's insatiable hunger for otherness, for devouring something other than itself, for manipulating, modifying, conquering something other than itself.

If otherness were the truth of the nature of things, causality would reign supreme without a single exception. Embarrassingly and logically fatally for dualism, however, causality abdicates its supposed sovereignty in human communication, in our speaking to one another.

I am speaking to you now, and I am not speaking to you at the top of my voice, I am not trying to prove merely that I have the causal power of producing noises that you will be compelled to hear. I am communicating with you, and although that does involve indicating to you the power, causal power, that I have over you of producing unignorable noises, it also involves indicating to you simultaneously my substantial renunciation of such power, causality's self-limitation in successful communication. The exhibition of self-limiting causal power is the very heart of communication, discernible when we speak, when we write finite sentences, when we make finite speeches, although I can see the chairperson becoming very, very sceptical about the finitude of my speech. If you were essentially other than myself, my causal power in relation to you would be effective or ineffective, but it could never be self-limiting, it could never amount to communication as opposed to coercion. But we do communicate with each other! Therefore, I am not essentially other than yourself. I am you; Advaita is true.

Advaita demands celebration as the *śruti*-sustained, continuously revealed truth of India and the nature of things, and especially from India it demands pioneering exemplification and the most dedicated discipline of humility, of which I have been a poor example today. Thank you very much for your patience and supportiveness; it has been a privilege talking to you.

CHAPTER 4

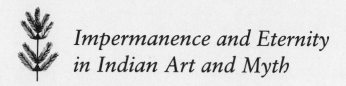

Impermanence and Eternity in Indian Art and Myth

Wendy Doniger O'Flaherty

The classics of India challenge our assumptions about the inevitable distinctions between written and oral texts. In India, we encounter more oral traditions than written ones, and more fluid traditions than frozen ones. But more than that; we find a reversal of the assumed link between what is written and fixed, on the one hand, and what is oral and fluid, on the other. Let us for the moment define a classic in a rather broad sense, as a work of art (particularly, but not necessarily, a work of literature) that comes to be accepted by a tradition over a great period of time as embodying what is good and true. We in the West pride ourselves on our classics, and that pride is based upon two different but related assumptions: that our classics are in a sense eternal—forever fixed, frozen in the amber of carefully preserved written documents—and that they provide a shared communal base for all educated members of our culture. The Indian examples to follow, however, show us that both of these assumptions are not true of classics in general, and we will find that they are not even exactly true of our own classics.

THE PAGE AND THE STAGE IN THE WEST

Let us begin by looking more closely at our first assumption about our own classics and take the works of Homer and Shakespeare as paradigmatic classics, which surely no one will object to. Homer, we now know, was one—perhaps the last one—in a series of poets who improvised constantly in reworking the great themes that they had inherited. Of course, Homer used these sources to compose his *own* poem. Shakespeare, too, had such sources as Holinshead's *Chronicles,* Plutarch's *Lives,* and Homer himself (perhaps in the original Greek, perhaps in Chapman's translation), though Shakespeare used these sources with even greater freedom than Homer used his. Although it is true that the texts of Homer and Shakespeare did become frozen not long after they were composed, and that they have remained frozen in manuscript form for many centuries, preserved by cultures in which the oral tradition was officially dead and buried, it is also true that each generation has been inspired differently by these classics and retranslated them: Homer became reincarnated in Virgil and Dante in one sense, and in Chapman, Pope, and Lattimore in another. It may even be, as has been suggested, that the very defining characteristic of a classic is that it is a work that must be retranslated by each new generation. Still, the *core* of meaning is preserved, even when the words of the translations change. Classics define themselves as being tied to a fixed core in the distant past, but the ties that bind the classic to its past are different in the East and in the West. Our "tradition" of the classics, including Homer, was lost for centuries and only discovered, and self-consciously recreated, at the time of the Renaissance; the Sanskrit tradition in India, as we shall see, was continuous, unbroken for over three thousand years—a contrast that makes us realize how wrong we are when we think that we have "always" had our classics.

The ways in which our written classics continue to change, then, include written retranslation and reinterpretation. But even more radical are the changes that occur through performance. A different Hamlet was reborn in David Garrick, in John Barrymore, in John Gielgud, in Laurence Olivier, to say nothing of the ways in which the play as a whole was transformed in the hands of each innovative director—and I refer not to any gimmicks of costumes and sets (setting the battle of Agincourt in the French fields of World War II, or the *Merchant of Venice* in a Victorian marketplace, or *Hamlet* in a gang of Hell's Angels), but to genuine reinterpretations of the play itself. It is also significant that when these classics are transformed in performance, we experience them as a group, sitting together in the darkened theater; this shared moment is an important source of our belief that the plays of Sophocles or of Shakespeare or of Tennessee Williams are our classics. Thus even our "written" classics are in fact experienced, in their most important form, orally. So much for our own fixed, written classics.

Let us turn now to our second major assumption, that what makes our classics our classics is the fact that they are shared by all educated members of our community. This assumption is unfounded: we do not know our own classics. Even in the good old days (*in illo tempore,* as Mircea Eliade would have put it), when everyone who mattered was able not only to read Greek but to translate editorials from *The Times* of London into Greek prose—even then, the paradox of the classics was that they *excluded* rather than included people. The classics were the texts that *we* knew and *they* didn't—they being hoi polloi, the great unwashed. The classics defined a tiny elite who in turn defined the Community as consisting of themselves. Nowadays, of course, even that arrogant self-deception has been shattered. Only a tiny percentage of Americans read Homer in English translation, let alone in Greek, and it is Dick Tracy and "Dallas" that provide what shared culture we have.

These two examples are particularly apt, I think, because they belong to the genre of the serial, a Western parallel to the never-ending chain of stories that is taken up, link by link, night after night, by village storytellers in India. When Dickens published his novels in serial form, the English-speaking world would hang upon the next installment; it is said that when a ship docked in New York carrying the latest chapters of *The Old Curiosity Shop,* the crowd on shore cried out to those on board, "What's happened to Nell? Is she still alive?" Serials present the experience of a common world, since everyone is reading or watching the same episode at the same time. Something of this function of the true series was carried on, for a while, by the sagas written by English and American novelists—Galsworthy's *Forsyte Saga,* Faulkner's Scopes novels, even Howard Fast's *Lavette Saga.* Today, this shared subtext exists primarily in soap operas on television. Yet we pride ourselves on having one of the highest literacy rates in the world. So much for the shared, communal base of our Western classics.

ORAL AND WRITTEN PRESERVATION IN THE EAST

India has two sorts of Sanskrit classics, typified by two great texts, the *Rg Veda* and the *Mahabharata.* The *Rg Veda* is a massive collection of hymns, a text of over 350,000 words (as long as the *Iliad* and *Odyssey* combined) that was preserved orally for over three thousand years; and the great Sanskrit epic, the *Mahabharata,* is a text of over 3 million words (almost ten times as long as the *Rg Veda*) that was preserved orally and in manuscript form for over two thousand years. The relationship between orality and fluidity in these texts is the reverse of what one might expect if one simply extrapolated from what we think we know of Western classics.

The *Rg Veda* was preserved orally even when the Indians had used writing for centuries (used it as the writers of Linear B used their script, for everyday things like laundry lists and IOUs). But they refused to preserve the *Rg Veda* in writing because it was a sacred magic text, whose power must not fall into the wrong hands. Unbelievers and infidels, untouchables and women, were forbidden to learn Sanskrit, the sacred language, because they might defile or injure the magic power of the words; if the sacred chants were to be spoken by such people, it was believed, the words would be polluted like milk contained in the skin of a dog.[1] The text was, therefore, memorized in such a way that no physical traces of it could be found, much as a coded espionage message would be memorized and then destroyed (eaten, perhaps—orally destroyed) before it could fall into the hands of the enemy. This exclusively oral preservation also ensured that the *Rg Veda* could not be misused even in the right hands: You couldn't take the *Rg Veda* down off the shelf in a library, for you had to read it in the company of a wise teacher or guru, who would make sure that you were not injured by its power, as the sorcerer's apprentice was injured when he meddled with magic he did not understand.

Now, one might suppose that a text preserved orally in this way would be subject to steadily encroaching inaccuracy and unreliability, that the message would become increasing garbled like the message in a game of "telephone"; but one would be wrong. For the same sacredness that made it necessary to preserve the *Rg Veda* orally rather than in writing also demanded that it be preserved with meticulous accuracy. The *Rg Veda* is regarded as a revealed text, seen in a vision or "heard" (*śruti*) by the human seers to whom the gods dictated it. And one does not play fast and loose with revelation. When Friedrich Max Müller finally edited and published the *Rg Veda* in the middle of the nineteenth century, he asked a Brahman in Calcutta to recite it for him in Sanskrit, and a Brahman in Madras, and a Brahman in Bombay (each of the three spoke a different vernacular language); and each of them said every syllable of the entire text exactly the same as the other two said it. There are no variant readings of the *Rg Veda,* no critical editions or textual apparatus. Just the *Rg Veda.* So much for the inevitable fluidity of oral texts.

Correspondingly, the expected fixity of written texts dissolves when we look at the second sort of Sanskrit classic, typified by the epic *Mahabharata.* Although the epic was preserved both orally and in manuscript, it is so extremely fluid that there is no single *Mahabharata*; there are hundreds of *Mahabharata*s—hundreds of different manuscripts and innumerable oral versions. The *Mahabharata* is not contained in a text; the story is there to be picked up and found, to be claimed like a piece of uncultivated land, salvaged as anonymous treasure from the ocean of story; it is constantly retold and rewritten both in Sanskrit and in vernaculars.[2] A. K. Ramanujan has remarked that no Indian ever hears the *Mahabharata* for the first time[3]; Alf Hiltebeitel has described it as "a work in progress"[4]; and Milton Singer has seen it as a literature that "does not belong in a book."[5] The *Mahabharata* itself describes itself as unlimited in both time and space: "Poets have told it before, and are telling it now, and will tell it. . . . What is here is found elsewhere, but what is *not* here is nowhere else."[6] In contrast with the divine *Rg Veda* that was "heard" (*śruti*), the *Mahabharata* is regarded as entirely humanly made, "remembered" (*smrti*) and reconstructed differently by all of its many authors in the long line of literary descent from its first, human author. There is a soi-disant critical edition of the *Mahabharata*, with an apparatus of "interpolations" longer than the text itself, but it has not been able to defend its claim to sit alone on the throne of the Ur-text. For the *Mahabharata* grows out of the oral tradition and then grows back into the oral tradition; it flickers back and forth between Sanskrit manuscripts and village storytellers, each adding new bits to the old story, constantly reinterpreting it.

Once we begin to distinguish between texts that were (or that we think may have been) *composed* orally (in contrast with those that may have been composed in writing), those that were *preserved* orally (in contrast with those preserved in manuscript), and those that were traditionally *performed* orally, we begin to glimpse the complexity of the problem.[7] For written and oral texts have both fluid and fixed forms.[8]

Our shifting textual sands shift still more when we distinguish between the use of the inside and the outside of written texts. To use the inside means to use the text in a fluid way, as one might use an oral text: to interrupt the recitation in order to ask about the meaning, to write a commentary, to choose only appropriate passages to recite on a particular occasion; but to use the outside of the text means to use it in a rigid way, to read or recite it without necessarily knowing its meaning at all, to recite it without any care for the choice of an appropriate passage. Indeed, the "outside" of the text may be used even more rigidly: The book may be set down but never opened, making a silent statement about status or community; or the whole text may be recited from beginning to end so fast that no one can possibly understand it, as a way of gaining merit.[9]

Thus, just as the oral tradition of the *Rg Veda* is frozen, the so-called manuscript tradition of the *Mahabharata* is hopelessly fluid. Indeed, Indians have long been aware of the constant interaction between oral and written traditions of the *Mahabharata*. They explain that when Vyasa, the author of the *Mahabharata*, was ready to fix it in writing, he summoned as his scribe the elephant-headed god Ganesa, patron of intellectuals and merchants. (In doing this, Vyasa was reversing the roles that had been played by gods and mortals in the redaction of the *Rg Veda,* where gods had dictated the text to mortals, who inscribed it only in their memories.) Ganesa agreed to take Vyasa's dictation, but only on condition that Vyasa would not lag behind and keep Ganesa waiting for the next line; Vyasa in turn stipulated that Ganesa must not write down anything he did not understand. When, in the course of work, the divine amanuensis seemed to be getting ahead of the mortal author, Vyasa would quickly throw in a "knot" that would make Ganesa pause for a moment. This accounts for the many scribal errors, corrupted lines, and linguistic stumbling blocks in the manuscript tradition of the great epic.[10] The curse of Ganesa torments every scholar who works on a combined oral–written tradition. It is ironic, I think, that the passage narrating the dictation by Vyasa to Ganesa is the very first one that the critical edition relegates to an appendix—indeed, to an appendix to an appendix; the passage that accounts for the irregularities in the epic resulting from its dual oral–written status is rejected as just such an irregularity or "knot." So much for the inevitable fixity of the written tradition.[11]

In India, many people are illiterate; but we are certainly wrong if we assume that illiteracy is an indication of cultural deprivation. The oral tradition has made it possible for millions of Indian villagers to be richly, deeply familiar with their own classics. When printing began to make texts of the *Ramayana* widely available in India, both in Sanskrit and in vernacular translations, this did in fact lead to an increase in private study of the epic, but it also led to a great increase in the practice of public recitations of the *Ramayana,* attended by great crowds of literate people who experienced in the oral presentation something different from what they experienced in reading it silently at home.[12]

THE FLUIDITY OF TRUTH

The fluidity of the Indian oral–written tradition is in part merely one aspect of the more general fluidity of Indian attitudes to *all* kinds of truth. There is no Ur-text, for there is no Ur-reality. Indians may maintain a belief in several different, contradictory answers to the same question; they alter their definitions of reality in order to let such contradictions survive.[13] All truths being multiple, it is not surprising that the true version of any story is also multiple. In Sanskrit texts, the bard may recite a myth in a certain way, only to be interrupted by someone in the audience to whom the tale is being recited (an audience that is built into the text), who argues, "We heard it differently." When the person in the audience tells that second version, the bard replies, "That is true, too, but your version happened in a different world-era"—or, in some stories, "in a different rebirth."[14] That is, the same event happens over and over again, but it may not happen in exactly the same way each time; and each happening is true.

A wonderful example of the degree to which this sort of plurality is both a widely shared cultural assumption and a still-debated open question is the manner in which the Jains told the story of the end of the *Mahabharata*:

> The great Jaina sage Hemacandra went about lecturing to great crowds, telling them, among other things, that the Pāṇḍavas, the heroes of the *Mahābhārata*, had become Jaina monks at the end of their lives. Upon learning of this, the Brahmins of that city complained to the king, pointing out that in Vyāsa's *Mahābhārata*, the Pāṇḍavas died in the Himālayas, after propitiating Śiva. "But these Jainas," they continued, "who are actually Śūdras, since they have abandoned the true works of the Purāṇas, babble things about the Pāṇḍavas which are contrary to the *smṛtis*." The king summoned Hemacandra, who said, "That the Pāṇḍavas renounced the world as Jaina monks has been said in our scriptures, and it is equally true that their sojourn in the Himālayas has been described in the *Mahābhārata*. But we do not know whether the Pāṇḍavas in our scriptures are the same as those in Vyāsa's work, or indeed by still other authors in different works.[15]

The king, who keeps insisting on his duty to remain impartial, ends by praising the open-minded Jain over the exclusive Brahmans.

In the West, we tend to think of art as permanent, perhaps as the only permanent thing there is; as Homer tells us, when everything else perishes, the story, the *kleos,* the myth, is all that remains. Indeed, Helen argues that the only purpose she can see in certain of her deeds (such as having run off with a no-good man like Paris) is that people in the future will make songs about them.[16] Storytelling is the only way that we know to ward off death; if only we could tell stories forever, like Scheherazade, we would never die at all. Western civilization tends to embalm the written word, to accord enduring status to physical incarnations of art. Our libraries are full of books, our museums full of paintings, and these books and paintings are often the only surviving traces of lost civilization.

In India, by contrast, neither books nor paintings are assumed to have that sort of permanence. Material art there is fluid. As we have seen, it is the spoken word, not the written word, that is eternal; sacred literature is eternal in being handed down first from God to mortals and then from one mortal to another (the infinite *paramparā*), just as the individual soul survives in eternity by being handed over from one body to another. This analogy has deep roots in Indian civilization. The authors of the *Rg Veda,* the invading Indo-Aryans, highly valued their freedom and feared any constraint; they wandered constantly and restlessly, always in search of new grazing land for their horses, never staying in one place long enough to build any lasting dwelling. Although later they settled in cities, the old wanderlust never disappeared, and spiritual leaders, both Buddhist and Hindu, soon began to desert the cities and to abandon their material goods, to wander about as mendicants or to live in the forests, away from the constraints of civilization. The city became a metaphor for the body, the perishable prison of the eternal soul, the trap laid by material life (*saṃsāra*); what the soul sought was freedom, *mokṣa.*[17]

Given this cultural background, it is not surprising that the physical incarnations of art and literature are neither valued nor trusted in India; impermanence is the very nature of *saṃsāra,* the material world. Books are eaten by white ants or rotted away by the wet heat of the monsoon, and the secular literature that is preserved orally lasts no longer than the mind that knows it. Painting, too, is not always intended to last. The women painters of Mithila use vivid natural colors that soon fade. "For the artists, this impermanence is unimportant—the paintings are not meant to last. The *act* of painting is seen as more important than the form it takes, and elaborately produced marriage sketches may be cast off after use, to be eaten by mice or even used to light fires. Frescoes on courtyard walls often fall victim to rain, whitewash, or the playing of children."[18]

Nowadays, many Indian artists have caught our taste for preservation; they come here to learn from our artists and conservators techniques to preserve their work.[19] Indeed, there must have been Indian artists long ago who wished to preserve their work, for though the earliest religious monuments in India were carved in wood that decayed, sculptors very soon decided to build more lasting temples in stone; stone temples and stupas dating from the pre-Christian era imitate woodcarving techniques, transferred (clumsily, at first) to the more enduring medium. These permanent art forms, however, sacred and secular, have existed side by side with the transient forms, just as frozen *śruti* existed side by side with fluid *smṛti.*

Indian sacred art, in particular, is often purposely consigned to the realm of the ephemeral in order to prevent its profanation, with much the same logic that prevented the preservation of the *Rg Veda* in writing. When great Vedic sacrifices are performed, involving many priests and lasting for many days, large and elaborate ritual enclosures are constructed of bamboo and thatch; at the end of the sacrifice, these enclosures—which have become dangerously charged with sacred power—are burned to the ground.[20] In many domestic celebrations, intricate designs are traced in rice powder on the immaculate floors and courtyards of houses, and after the ceremony these are blurred and smudged into oblivion by the bare feet of the family. The material traces of ritual art must vanish in order that the mental traces may remain intact forever. It is as if a choice were made, somewhat like the choice that one makes when viewing a beautiful scene in a foreign land: If one photographs it, one has preserved it (more or less) forever, but the act of photographing it may interfere not only with the full experience of it at the moment but with one's own power to preserve it in memory. Many people in India do not wish to be photographed, for they believe that the preserved image of themselves somehow drains a fraction of their life force or soul. Oscar Wilde toyed with this idea in his novel about Dorian Gray, whose portrait aged while he did not—until the portrait was destroyed.

For the festival of Durgapuja in Bengal, hundreds of more-than-life-sized papier-mâché statues of the Goddess Durga are made and beautifully decorated; at the end of the week-long celebration, the statues are carried down to the Ganges in torchlight parades at night and cast into the dark waters. The word used to describe this dismissal or throwing out of the statue is *visarjana,* cognate with *visarga,* the word used to describe the emission of the universe—that is, its creation—by Brahma. In this sense, all fabricated things come into true existence only by being thrown out, or thrown away; only when the body is shed is the soul set free. One word for art in India is *māyā,* often translated as illusion. And the world of *māyā* is the world of matter (*prakṛti*), of rebirth (*saṃsāra*), which is impermanent; against it the Hindus contrast the world of truth, of ultimate reality (*brahman*), of spirit (*puruṣa*), of release (*mokṣa*), which is eternal.[21]

THE SURVIVAL OF MYTH

Of all literary forms, drama best reproduces the effects of myth, most powerfully through the catharsis of the tragic drama, but also in the surreal humor of great comedy. In our day, drama (or film) often takes the place of the communal ritual that was a frequent (though certainly not inevitable) complement to the traditional myth. Drama built upon archetypes functions as the enactment of a myth.

Hindu literature is self-conscious about the relationship between myth and life as it is manifest in myths that are enacted in the theater. The use of aesthetic experience in salvation was the subject of much discussion; by seeing, and therefore participating in, the enactment of the myth of Krishna, one was led unconsciously into the proper stance of the devotee. Moreover, the viewer was not merely inspired to decide what role in the cosmic drama he or she wished to play (mother, lover, brother, or friend of Krishna); one was inspired to discover what role one *was* playing, had been playing all along, without knowing it.[22] Alf Hiltebeitel has beautifully described the way the real world gradually absorbs the stage in Indian religious performances: "The nightlong dramas, acted out on a small patch of ground beneath petromax lanterns, are finally unravelled at dawn on a stage that grows with the morning light to include first the surrounding outlines of village trees and buildings and then, in effect, the familiar world of the day."[23]

Hindi films still perform the function of mythology for Indian society. Sudhir Kakar has interpreted popular Hindi film "as a collective fantasy containing unconscious material and hidden wishes of a vast number of people. . . . Hindi films may be unreal in a rational sense, but they are certainly not untrue. . . . [They] are modern versions of certain old and familiar myths."[24] This is more literally true of Indian films than it is even of our own films, for Hindi films are often rather lurid reenactments of the sacred stories, with matinee idols playing the parts of the gods. In India, even where people do still tell the old stories in the traditional way, films began to usurp the position of myths. It is not, therefore, as one might have thought on the basis of the Western situation, that myths flee from their classical shrines when these crash down under the assault of modern, materialistic can(n)ons, and find refuge in the cool, dark halls of cinema. No, even when the temple is still standing, the myths find another, supplementary home in the medium of film. As a mythological analysis of a film such as *Karz* demonstrates, old archetypes never die; they just lurk quietly in the background of the sets of Hindi films.[25]

Indeed, where mythological themes are culturally so omnipresent as they are in India, it is particularly easy for a sophisticated filmmaker to select such themes as elements in a film and to feel instinctively that they will magnify the image that he wishes to project, literally, to a mass audience. One film, *Santoshi Ma,* told the story of a goddess named Santoshi Ma; the film became so popular that the cult of the goddess spread throughout India. In R. K. Narayan's novel *Mr. Sampath,* a filmmaker decided to reenact a story of the destruction of Kama, the god of erotic love, by Siva, the god of yogis; and the actors playing the parts are swept up helplessly into a parallel reenactment of the story in their private lives.[26] Clearly films, like the legitimate theater, present a modern instance of that impermanent swinging door through which myth and reality eternally pass one another.

And the myths survive in other modern avatars: the Indian version of our own Classic Comics (*Amar Chitra Katha,* "Immortal Picture Stories") presents the ancient Hindu classics in a strangely Westernized but still recognizably Indian form. Although these comics are ostensibly written for children, many adults read them; and for some, they provide the only remaining source of the classical mythology. And there are other, even more unlikely cartoons in which the myths live on. Hindus who may not know from the *Rg Veda* or the *Mahabharata* the story of the aged sage Cyavana, who was rejuvenated so that he could marry a beautiful young girl,[27] may know the story from another source: newspaper advertisements for a patent medicine called Cyavan-Pras ("Cyavana-Food"). The ad begins with a Sanskrit verse that can be translated thus: "This is the story of the Cyavana food that the sage Cyavana ate; even though he was worn out with old age, he became a joy to the eyes of women." The verse is followed by a series of cartoon illustrations with descriptions below them, in English, telling the story of Cyavana. This "rejuvenating tonic," containing gooseberry, is said to be the one that the Asvins, the divine physicians, gave to the old sage: "Thus Cyavana was blessed with the special yoga and having consumed it he became a full-grown youth pleasing to the eyes of the women. Kottakkal Arya Vaidya Sala manufactures this potent tonic prescribed by the Divine Physicians in the traditional and conventional manner with scrupulous care and attention."

One way or another, through oral or written exposure, Indians know their myths so well that the retelling of the myths takes on the function of communion rather than communication. People listen to stories not merely to learn something new (communication) but to re-live, together, the stories that they already know, stories about themselves (communion).[28] In reading written classics, one expects and demands surprises; but it is characteristic of oral classics that the audience takes pleasure in predicting what will happen and satisfaction in seeing it happen.[29] No one who has been asked by a young child to tell for the umpteenth time "the story about the time when I fell into the lake" will ever preface a tale with the disclaimer of "stop me if you've heard this one before." And no one who has been corrected by a child in the retelling of a tale ("No, no, it was the *first* little pig who built his house of straw, not the *second*.") will try to "improve" on an old favorite with new variations.

In the West, as in India, many children's books function as classics, and as myths, in a way that no other works do. For these books provide a shared culture, as we give our children the books that we loved when we were children. Here is the one universal *paramparā* or unbroken lineage of transmission in our world. And in addition to this shared content, there is the shared form of the transmission, the performance of the classics: Reading aloud to children is for many people the only moment when the oral element of the mythological traditions is still actively preserved.

In India, as in the West, children are the key to the preservation of the world of myth. For India, too, is under pressure from the mobs of rationalists and modernizers to demythologize. True, the plays reenacting the lives of Krishna and Rama are still celebrated even in many highly urbanized settings, and people still travel from the cities to the country to see performances in their traditional settings. But as people move from the villages to the cities, the professional storytellers—those who present the dance dramas of the myths or recite the long epics, in Sanskrit or in the vernacular of the district—lose part of their audience. And even more threatening than the possibility that the particular craft of the storytellers will die out is the undeniable fact that, already, the *contexts* for storytelling are fast dying out—the occasions when stories are told, the moments of quiet work at the loom or during the mending of nets, the long winter evenings around the fire. But children are a safeguard against this loss, too; for however busy one may be, working in a factory or at an office desk, there still comes a moment when food is prepared and eaten, when children are washed and made ready for bed. And there, as here, a small voice will say, "Tell me a story."

Children in India represent the only form of *physical* permanence, the eternal chain of rebirths in an infinity of bodies (the chain of *saṃsāra*, the world of matter and marriage and mating), in contrast with (and often at the sacrifice of) the setting free (*mokṣa*) of the immortal soul. We see our physical selves preserved in the bodies of our children; and we see our mythical selves preserved in their memories. For many—all but those who achieve Release—this is the only eternity there is. As the Hindu lawbook put it, "You beget children, and that's your immortality, O mortal."[30]

NOTES

1. For this and other definitions of people beyond the Aryan pale in ancient India, see Wendy Doniger O'Flaherty, "The Origins of Heresy in Hindu Mythology," *History of Religions* 10 (May 1971): 271–333; and "The

Image of the Heretic in the Gupta Purāṇas," in *Essays on Gupta Culture*, ed. Bardwell L. Smith (New Delhi: Motilal Banarsidass, 1983), 107–28.

2. Wendy Doniger O'Flaherty, *Dreams, Illusion, and Other Realities* (Chicago: University of Chicago Press, 1984), 129–32.

3. Personal communication from A. K. Ramanujan, cited in O'Flaherty, *Dreams*, 130.

4. Alf Hiltebeitel, *The Ritual of Battle* (Ithaca: Cornell University Press, 1976), 14–15.

5. Milton Singer, *When a Great Tradition Modernizes* (Chicago: University of Chicago Press, 1972), 75–76.

6. *Mahābhārata* (critical edition, Poona: Bhandarkar Oriental Research Institute, 1033–60), 1.1.23 and 1.56.34.

7. V. Narayana Rao, in a comment made at the Conference on the Purāṇas, Madison, Wisconsin, 3 August 1985.

8. A. K. Ramanujan, comment made at the Conference on the Purāṇas, Madison, Wisconsin, 3 August 1985.

9. Philip Lutgendorf, "The Life of a Text: Tulsīdās's *Rāmacaritamānasa* in Performance" (Ph.D. diss., University of Chicago, 1985), 81.

10. *Mahābhārata*, appendix 1, #1, verses interpolated after line 30.

11. My argument here contradicts much of what Jack Goody says about writing and orality in *The Domestication of the Savage Mind*.

12. Lutgendorf, "The life of a text," 121.

13. O'Flaherty, *Dreams*, 10–11, 187–89; Wendy Doniger O'Flaherty, *Śiva: The Erotic Ascetic* (New York: Oxford University Press, 1973; 1981), 4–11, 33–39.

14. O'Flaherty, *Śiva*, 19, citing *Śiva Purāṇa* 4.27.23–24; cf. *Rāmāyaṇa* (Baroda: Oriental Institute, 1960–75), 7.4.3–4 and 7.16.44.

15. Padmanabh Jaini, "Jaina Purāṇas: A Purāṇic Counter Tradition" (Paper presented at the Conference on the Purāṇas, Madison, Wisconsin, 1–4 August 1985), 66–71. Citing a sermon by Hemadri, in Prabhācandra's *Prabhāvacarita*, ed. Jinavijaya Muni, Singhi Jain Series, 13 (1940), 187–88.

16. Homer, *Iliad*, 6.358.

17. O'Flaherty, *Dreams*, 268–79.

18. O'Flaherty, *Dreams*, 293, citing Yves Vequaud, "The Colors of Devotion," *Portfolio* (February–March 1980): 62–63.

19. Personal communication from Rick Asher and Carla Borden.

20. Frits Staal, *Agnicayana: The Vedic Ritual of the Fire Altar* (Berkeley: Asian Humanities Press, 1983), 689.

21. O'Flaherty, *Dreams*, 11–13.

22. Rūpagosvāmin's *Bhaktirasāmṛtasindhu* 2.27, cited by David L. Haberman, "Imitating the Masters: Problems in Incongruency," *Journal of the American Academy of Religion* (March 1985): 41–50. See also the discussion in Wendy Doniger O'Flaherty, *Women, Androgynes, and Other Mythical Beasts* (Chicago: University of Chicago Press, 1981), 87–88, and cf. also *Bhāgavata Purāṇa* (Bombay: Venkatesvara, 1832), 3.25.34.

23. Alf Hiltebeitel, "Purāṇas and the *Mahābhārata*: Their Relationship in Classical and Folk Genres" (Paper presented at the Conference on the Purāṇas, Madison, Wisconsin, 1–4 August 1985), 11.

24. Sudhir Kakar, "The Ties that Bind: Family Relationships in the Mythology of Hindi Cinema," *India International Quarterly* 8 (March 1980): 11–22.

25. Wendy Doniger O'Flaherty, "The Mythological in Disguise: An Analysis of *Karz*," *India International Quarterly* 8 (March 1980): 23–30.

26. R. K. Narayan, *Mr. Sampath* (London: Eyre and Spottiswoode, 1949).

27. *Ṛg Veda* (London: Oxford University Press, 1890–92), 8.1.30–34; *Mahābhārata* 3.122–23; cited by O'Flaherty, *Śiva*, 57–61.

28. V. Narayana Rao, private conversation, cited in O'Flaherty, *Dreams*, 129–30.

29. V. Narayana Rao, remarks made at the Conference on the Purāṇas, Madison, Wisconsin, 1–4 August 1985.

30. Āpastamba, *Dharmasūtra* (Bombay: Venkatesvara, 1892), 2.9.24.1; cited by O'Flaherty, *Śiva*, 76.

PART 2

"The Presence of the Past":
Artists Speak

CHAPTER 5

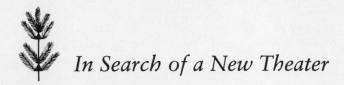

In Search of a New Theater

Girish Karnad

My generation was the first to come of age after India became independent of British rule. It therefore had to face a situation in which tensions implicit until then had come out in the open and demanded to be resolved without apologia or self-justification: tensions between the cultural past of the country and its colonial past, between the attractions of Western modes of thought and our own traditions, and finally between the various visions of the future that opened up once the common cause of political freedom was achieved. This is the historical context that gave rise to my plays and those of my contemporaries.

I was twenty-one when I received a scholarship to go to England for further studies. It is difficult to explain to a Western audience—or even to a modern Indian audience—the traumas created by this event. Going abroad was a much rarer occurrence in those days; besides, I came from a large, close-knit family and was the first member of the family ever to go abroad. My parents were worried lest I decide to settle down outside India, and even for me, though there was no need for an immediate decision, the terrible choice was implicit in the very act of going away. Should I at the end of my studies return home for the sake of my family, my people, and my country, even at the risk of my abilities and training not being fully utilized in what seemed a stifling, claustrophobic atmosphere, or should I rise above such parochial considerations and go where the world drew me?

While still preparing for the trip, amidst the intense emotional turmoil, I found myself writing a play. This took me by surprise, for I had fancied myself a poet, had written poetry through my teens, and had trained myself to write in English, in preparation for the conquest of the West. But here I was writing a play and in Kannada, too, the language spoken by a few million people in South India, the language of my childhood. A greater surprise was the theme of the play, for it was taken from ancient Indian mythology from which I had believed myself alienated.

The story of King Yayati that I used occurs in the *Mahabharata*. The king, for a moral transgression he has committed, is cursed to old age in the prime of life. Distraught at losing his youth, he approaches his son, pleading with him to lend him his youth in exchange for old age. The son accepts the exchange and the curse, and thus becomes old, older than his father.* But the old age brings no knowledge, no self-realization, only the senselessness of a punishment meted out for an act in which he had not even participated. The father is left to face the consequences of shirking responsibility for his own actions.

While I was writing the play, I saw it only as an escape from my stressful situation. But looking back, I am amazed at how precisely the myth reflected my anxieties at that moment, my resentment at all those who seemed to demand that I sacrifice my future. By the time I had finished working on *Yayati*—during the three weeks it took the ship to reach England and in the lonely cloisters of the university—the myth had enabled me to articulate to myself a set of values that I had been unable to arrive at rationally. Whether to return home finally seemed the most minor of issues; the myth had nailed me to my past.

Oddly enough the play owed its form not to the innumerable mythological plays I had been brought up on, and which had partly kept these myths alive for me, but to Western playwrights whom until then I had only read in print: Anouilh (his *Antigone* particularly) and also Sartre, O'Neill, and the Greeks. That is, at the most intense moment of self-expression, while my past had come to my aid with a ready-made narrative within which I could contain and explore my insecurities, there had been no dramatic structure in my own tradition to which I could relate myself.

One of the first plays of postindependence India to use myth to make a contemporary statement was Dharma Vir Bharati's *Andha Yug* ("The Blind Age"). The play is about the aftermath of the Kurukshetra

---

*In the *Mahabharata*, King Yayati has five sons; after the elder four refuse their father, the youngest yields to his entreaty.

War, which forms the climax of the epic *Mahabharata*. The entire epic is in fact a buildup to this great confrontation between Good and Evil, in which God himself participated in the form of Lord Krishna. It was during this war that Krishna expounded the *Bhagavadgita,* a discourse on the ethics of action and knowledge that has exercised the most profound influence on Indian thought through the ages. Yet this fratricidal war left in its wake nothing but desolation and a sense of futility. No "new world" emerged from the wholesale massacre of the youth of the country. Arjuna, the hero, became impotent. Lord Krishna himself meekly accepted a curse and died an absurd death. In his play, Bharati used the myth to give voice to the sense of horror and despair felt in India in the wake of the partition of the country and the communal bloodbaths that accompanied it.

Although later Satyadev Dubey's production proved that it was genuine theater, *Andha Yug* was actually written for the radio, as a play for voices. It was as if, at the time of conceiving the play, the playwright could imagine no stage on which to place it.

Indeed this contradiction haunts most contemporary playwrighting and theater in India. Even to arrive at the heart of one's own mythology, the writer has to follow signposts planted by the West, a paradoxical situation for a culture in which the earliest *extant* play was written in A.D. 200! The explanation lies in the fact that what is called "modern Indian theater" was started by a group of people who adopted "cultural amnesia" as a deliberate strategy. It originated in the second half of the nineteenth century in three cities, Bombay, Calcutta, and Madras. None of these seaports built by the British for their maritime trade had an Indian past of its own, a history independent of the British. These places had developed an Indian middle class that in all outward respects aspired to "look" like its British counterpart. The social values of this class were shaped by the English education it had received and by the need to work with the British in trade and administration.

Inevitably the theater it created imitated the British theater of the times, as presented by visiting troupes from England. Several new concepts were introduced, two of which altered the nature of Indian theater. One was the separation of the audience from the stage by the proscenium, underscoring the fact that what was being presented was a spectacle free of any ritualistic associations and which therefore expected no direct participation by the audience in it; and the other was the idea of pure entertainment, whose success would be measured entirely in terms of immediate financial returns and the run of the play.

Until the nineteenth century, the audience had never been expected to pay to see a show. Theater had depended upon patronage—of kings, ministers, local feudatories, or temples. With the myth-based story line already familiar to the audience, the shape and success of a performance depended on how the actors improvised with the given narrative material each time they came on stage. Actors did not rehearse a play so much as train for particular kinds of roles, a system still followed today in folk and traditional theater forms. The principle here is the same as in North Indian classical music, where the musician aims to reveal unexpected delights even within the strictly regulated contours of a raga, by continual improvisation. It is the variability, the unpredictable potential of each performance that is its attraction. The audience accepts the risk.

With the new theater, in conformity with the prevailing laissez-faire philosophy, risk became the producer's responsibility, the factor determining the company's investment policy. The audience paid in cash to see a show guaranteed as a "success" and in return received as much entertainment as could be competitively fitted within the price of a ticket. A performance became a carefully packaged commodity, to be sold in endless identical replications.*

The proscenium and the box office proclaimed a new philosophy of the theater: secularism—but a commercially viable secularism.

The secularism was partly necessitated by the ethnic heterogeneity of the new entrepreneurial class. In Bombay, for instance, the enterprises were financed by the Parsis, who spoke Gujarati. But the commonly understood language was Urdu, popularized by the Muslim chieftains who had ruled over most of India since the sixteenth century. Naturally many of the writers employed by the Parsi theater were Muslim. And the audience was largely Hindu!

The consequences of this secularism were that every character on stage, whether a Hindu deity or a Muslim legendary hero, was alienated from its true religious or cultural moorings; and myths and legends, emptied of meaning, were reshaped into tightly constructed melodramas with thundering curtain lines and a searing climax. Unlike traditional performances, which spread out in a slow, leisurely fashion, these plays demanded total attention, but only at the level of plot. Incident was all. Even in companies run entirely by Hindus, the basic attitude was dictated by this Parsi model.

There was, however, a far more important reason for the superficiality of the fare. The audience that patronized the Parsi theater professed values it made no effort to realize in ordinary life. Whereas in

---

*Interestingly, although in Bombay ticketing of shows was the logical result of bringing theater within the free market economy, in Bengal, where the Anglophile landed gentry had immediately made theater their exclusive privilege, ticketing was the means by which this privilege was attacked and the form made accessible to the middle class.

public it accepted the Western bourgeois notions of secularism, egalitarianism, and individual merit, at home it remained committed to the traditional loyalties of caste, family, and religion. Only a society honest enough to face squarely the implications of this division within itself could have produced meaningful drama out of it. But as the new bourgeoisie claimed to be ashamed of the domestic life-style to which it nevertheless adhered tenaciously, the theater certainly would never be allowed to acknowledge and project these contradictions.

It is possible to argue, as Ashis Nandy has done, that this inner division was not psychologically harmful at all but was a deliberate strategy adopted by this class to ensure that its personality was not totally absorbed and thereby destroyed by the colonial culture. What-ever the case, the effect on drama was to render it sterile. Despite its enormous success as spectacle over nearly seventy years, the Parsi the-ater produced no drama of any consequence.

With the advent of "talking" films in the 1930s, the Parsi theater collapsed without a fight. In the West, movies diminished the impor-tance of theater but did not destroy it. In India, professional theater was virtually decimated by the film industry, which had learned most of its tricks from the theater and could dish out the made-to-order entertain-ment on a scale much larger than the theater could afford and at cheaper rates. India has not seen a professional theater of the same proportions since.

In the process of settling down, the Parsi theater had absorbed several features of traditional or folk performing arts, such as music, mime, and comic interludes. In Maharashtra, for instance, where this theater flourished and continues to survive, its greatest contribution was in the field of music, in the form of a rich and varied body of theater songs. However, to my generation of playwrights, reacting against memories of the Parsi stage in its decadence, music and dance seemed irrelevant to genuine drama. The only legacy left to us then was a lumbering, antiquated style of staging.

Yet there was no other urban tradition to look to, and in my second play, having concluded that Anouilh and Co. were not enough, I tried to make use of the Parsi stagecraft. This time the play was historical and therefore, perhaps inevitably, had a Muslim subject. (I say inevitably, for the Hindus have almost no tradition of history: the Hindu mind, with its belief in the cycle of births and deaths, has found little reason to chronicle or glamorize any particular historical period. Still, indepen-dence had made history suddenly important to us; we were acutely conscious of living in a historically important era. Indian history as written by the British was automatically suspect. The Marxist approach offered a more attractive alternative but in fact seemed unable to come to terms with Indian realities. Even today Marxist ideologues are lost when confronted with native categories like caste. It was the Muslims who first introduced history as a positive concept in Indian thought, and the only genuinely Indian methodology available to us for analyzing history was that developed by the Muslim historians in India.)

My subject was the life of Muhammed Tughlaq, a fourteenth-century sultan of Delhi, certainly the most brilliant individual ever to ascend the throne of Delhi and also one of the biggest failures. After a reign distinguished for policies that today seem farsighted to the point of genius, but which in their day earned him the title "Muhammed the Mad," the sultan ended his career in bloodshed and political chaos. In a sense, the play reflected the slow disillusionment my generation felt with the new politics of independent India: the gradual erosion of the ethical norms that had guided the movement for independence, and the coming to terms with cynicism and realpolitik.

The stagecraft of the Parsi model demanded a mechanical succession of alternating *shallow* and *deep* scenes. The shallow scenes were played in the foreground of the stage with a painted curtain—normally depicting a street—as the backdrop. These scenes were reserved for the "lower class" characters with prominence given to comedy. They served as *link* scenes in the development of the plot, but the main purpose was to keep the audience engaged while the deep scenes, which showed interiors of palaces, royal parks, and other such visually opulent sets, were being changed or decorated. The important characters rarely appeared in the street scenes, and in the deep scenes the lower classes strictly kept their place.

The spatial division was ideal to show the gulf between the rulers and the ruled, between the mysterious inner chambers of power politics and the open, public areas of those affected by it. But as I wrote *Tughlaq*, I found it increasingly difficult to maintain the accepted balance between these two regions. Writing in an unprecedented situation where the mass populace was exercising political franchise, in however clumsy a fashion, for the first time in its history, I found the shallow scenes bulging with an energy hard to control. The regions ultimately developed their own logic. The deep scenes became emptier as the play progressed, and in the last scene, the "comic lead" did the unconventional—he appeared in the deep scene, on a par with the protagonist himself. This violation of traditionally sacred spatial hierarchy, I decided—since there was little I could do about it—was the result of the anarchy which climaxed Tughlaq's times and seemed poised to engulf my own.

(An aside: Whatever the fond theories of their creators, plays often develop their own independent existence. In his brilliant production of

Tughlaq, E. Alkazi ignored my half-hearted tribute to the Parsi theater and placed the action on the ramparts of the Old Fort at Delhi; and it worked very well.)

Another school of drama had arisen in the 1930s, at the height of the struggle for national independence. When social reform was acknowledged as a goal next only to independence in importance, a group of "realistic" playwrights had challenged the emptiness and vapidity of Parsi drama. The contemporary concerns of these playwrights gave their work an immediacy and a sharp edge lacking in the earlier theater, and a few plays of great power were written. While trying to awaken their audience to the humiliation of political enslavement, many of these new playwrights made a coruscating analysis of the ills that had eaten into Indian society. This was essentially the playwright's theater; the plays were presented by amateur or semiprofessional groups and were mostly directed by the playwrights themselves. Unlike in the Parsi theater, where a hard-headed financial logic was the guide, here the writers, the actors, and the audience were all united by a genuine idealism. They created a movement, if not a theater, for the times.

Although its form aimed at being realistic, it must be pointed out at once that this drama concentrated on only a small corner of the vast canvas explored by Western realistic theater.

The door banged by Nora in *The Doll's House* did not merely announce feminist rebellion against social slavery. It summed up what was to be the main theme of Western realistic drama over the next hundred years: a person's need to be seen as an individual, as an entity valuable in itself, independent of family and social circumstance. Indian realism, however, could not progress beyond analyses of social problems, for in India, despite the large urban population, there really has never been a bourgeoisie with its faith in individualism as the ultimate value. "Westernization" notwithstanding, Indians define themselves in terms of their relationships to the other members of their family, caste, or class. They are defined by the role they have to play. In Sudhir Kakar's words, they see themselves in "relational" terms in their social context, and they naturally extend the same references to theater as well.

Let me give an example. A few years ago Arthur Miller's *A View from the Bridge* was presented in Madras. Eddie Carbone, the play's protagonist, is an Italian dockworker. He is a good man, but tragedy is brought about by his incestuous passion for his orphaned niece. He harbors two young, illegal Italian immigrants in his house, one of whom falls in love with the niece. Consumed by jealousy, Eddie breaks his code of honor, betrays the immigrants to the authorities, and is killed by one of them.

The audience watching the play in Madras was English educated, familiar with Western literature. Many of them frequently went abroad and had a living contact with the Western way of life. The production was a success. But most of the audience entirely missed the element of incest in the play; rather, they chose to ignore it as an unnecessary adjunct to an otherwise perfectly rational tale. Eddie was his niece's guardian, a surrogate father, and it was only right that he should be interested in her welfare. You certainly could not blame him for trying to safeguard her future. On the contrary, the illegal immigrants emerged as unsympathetic, for they had betrayed their host's confidence by seducing the niece's affections.

Even apart from consideration of social roles that led the Madras audience to write its own *A View from the Bridge,* Eddie Carbone perfectly fits an Indian archetype: the father figure aggressing toward its offspring. Our mythology is replete with parental figures demanding sacrifices from their children—as in my own *Yayati*; Eddie's position was not one in which the Indian audience was likely to find any tragic flaw.

To get back to realistic theater, its great improvement over the Parsi theater was that it took itself seriously both as art and as an instrument of social change. Yet it remained saddled with the European model. Bernard Shaw became its presiding deity. The proscenium continued, only now the grand spectacles gave way to the *interior set* with the invisible fourth wall. And that three-walled living room succinctly defined the basic limitation of this school of writing.

From Ibsen to Albee, the living room has symbolized all that is valuable to the Western bourgeoisie. It is one's refuge from the sociopolitical forces raging in the world outside, as well as the battleground where values essential to one's individuality are fought out and defended. But nothing of consequence ever happens or is supposed to happen in an Indian living room! It is the no-man's-land, the empty, almost defensive front the family presents to the world outside.

Space in a traditional home is ordered according to the caste hierarchy as well as the hierarchies within the family. Whether a person is permitted inside the compound, allowed as far as the outer verandah, or admitted into the living room depends on his or her caste and social status. And it is in the interior of the house, in the kitchen, in the room where the gods are kept, or in the backyard, where family problems are tackled, or allowed to fester, and where the women can have a say. Thus the living room as the location of dramatic action made nonsense of the very social problems the playwright set out to analyze, by distorting the caste dimensions as well as the position of women in the family.

How could these playwrights have so misunderstood the geography of their own homes? The three-walled living room was a symptom of a much more serious malaise: The conceptual tools they were using to analyze India's problems were as secondhand and unrealistic as the European parlor. The writers were young, angry, and in a hurry. The concepts defined for them by their English educators were new and refreshing and seemed rational. If the tools didn't quite fit the shifting ambiguities of social life, reality could be adjusted to fit these attractive imports. It may also be said that the refusal to go beyond the living room exactly mirrored the reluctance of these Westernized, upper-caste writers to go to the heart of the issues they were presenting.

To my generation, a hundred crowded years of urban theater seemed to have left almost nothing to hang on to, to take off from. And where was one to begin again? Perhaps by looking at our audience again, by trying to understand what experience this audience expected to receive from theater? This at least partly meant looking again at the traditional forms that had been ignored by the Parsi theater. The attempt, let me hasten to add, was not to find and reuse forms that had worked successfully in some other cultural context. The hope, rather, was to discover whether there was a structure of expectations—and conventions—about entertainment underlying these forms from which one could learn.

The most obvious starting point should have been the Sanskrit theater. *Sakuntala* and *Mrcchakatika,* two Sanskrit masterpieces, had been presented successfully on the Marathi stage in the early part of this century. Recently, Ratan Thiyam, K. N. Panicker, and Vijaya Mehta have brought Sanskrit plays alive again for today's audience. But no modern playwright has claimed, or shown in his work, any allegiance to Sanskrit sensibility. Sanskrit drama assumed a specific social setting, a steady, well-ordered universe in which everyone from the gods to the meanest mortals was in his or her allotted slot. Even in its heyday, it was an elitist phenomenon, confined to a restricted group of wealthy and educated courtiers, remote from the general populace.

Along with this court theater there had existed other, more popular forms—more flexible, varying in their emphasis on formal purity. The exact relationship between Sanskrit theater and these popular forms is of course difficult to determine. Sanskrit was not a language spoken in the homes; it was the language of courtly, literary, and philosophical discourse. The popular forms, on the other hand, used the natural languages of the people. Further, most of these languages came into their own as vehicles for artistic expression only around A.D. 1000, by which time Sanskrit literature—particularly drama—was already moribund. Even the aesthetics of these two theater traditions differed. Sanskrit drama underplayed action and emphasized mood. It avoided scenes that unduly excited the audience. The popular forms wallowed in battles and hard-won marriages, blood and thunder. The biggest hurdle from our perspective is that unlike in Sanskrit, in which plays were written as independent works of art, this class of performing arts eschewed written texts and depended on improvisation within limits prescribed by their separate conventions, making it difficult to trace their historical growth. But in India, as other chapters in this volume point out, the past is not totally lost; it coexists with the present as a parallel flow. A rich variety of regional theater forms still exist, with a continuous history stretching over centuries, though through these centuries they have undoubtedly undergone changes and even mutilations.

For the first two decades after independence, how traditional forms could be utilized to revitalize our own work in the urban context was a ceaseless topic of argument among theater people. The poet Vallathol had given a new identity to Kathakali, Shivaram Karanth a new lease on life to Yakshagana. Habib Tanvir has gone to areas in which the traditional troupes operate, taking with him his urban discipline. He has taught, lived, worked, and toured with the local troupes and evolved through them a work that is rich, vital, and meaningful.

But what were we, basically city-dwellers, to do with this stream? What did the entire paraphernalia of theatrical devices, half-curtains, masks, improvisation, music, and mime mean?

I remember that the idea of my play *Hayavadana* started crystallizing in my head right in the middle of an argument with B. V. Karanth (who ultimately produced the play) about the meaning of masks in Indian theater and theater's relationship to music. The play is based on a story from a collection of tales called the *Kathasaritsagara* and the further development of this story by Thomas Mann in "The Transposed Heads."

A young woman is traveling with her insecure and jealous husband and his rather attractive friend. The husband, suspecting his wife's loyalties, goes to a temple of Goddess Kali and beheads himself. The friend finds the body and, terrified that he will be accused of having murdered the man for the sake of his wife, in turn beheads himself. When the woman, afraid of the scandal that is bound to follow, prepares to kill herself, too, the goddess takes pity and comes to her aid. The woman has only to rejoin the heads to the bodies and the goddess will bring them back to life. The woman follows the instructions, the men come back to life—except that in her confusion she has mixed up the heads. The story ends with the question: Who is now the real husband, the one with the husband's head or the one with his body?

The answer given in the *Kathasaritsagara* is: Since the head represents the man, the person with the husband's head is the husband.

Mann brings his relentless logic to bear upon this solution. If the head is the determining limb, then the body should change to fit the head. At the end of Mann's version, the bodies have changed again and adjusted themselves to the heads so perfectly that the men are physically exactly as they were at the beginning. We are back to square one; the problem remains unsolved.

As I said, the story initially interested me for the scope it gave for the use of masks and music. Western theater has developed a contrast between the *face* and the *mask*—the real inner person and the exterior one presents, or wishes to present, to the world outside. But in Indian traditional theater, the mask is only the face "writ large"; since a character represents not a complex psychological entity but an ethical archetype, the mask merely presents in enlarged detail its essential moral nature. (This is why characters in *Hayavadana* have no real names. The heroine is called Padmini after one of the six types into which Vatsyayana classified all women. Her husband is Devadatta, a formal mode of addressing a stranger. His friend is Kapila, simply "the dark one.") Music—usually percussion—then further distances the action, placing it in the realm of the mythical and the elemental.

The decision to use masks led me to question the theme itself in greater depth. All theatrical performances in India begin with worship of Ganesa, the god who ensures successful completion of any endeavor. According to mythology, Ganesa was beheaded by Siva, his father, who had failed to recognize his own son (another aggressive father!). The damage was repaired by substituting an elephant's head, since the original head could not be found. Ganesa is often represented onstage by a young boy wearing the elephant mask, who then is worshiped as the incarnation of the god himself.

Ganesa's mask then says nothing about his nature. It is a mask, pure and simple. Right at the start of the play, my theory about masks was getting subverted. But the elephant head also questioned the basic assumption behind the original riddle: that the head represents the thinking part of the person, the intellect.

It seemed unfair, however, to challenge the thesis of the riddle by using a god. God, after all, is beyond human logic, indeed beyond human comprehension itself. The dialectic had to grow out of grosser ground, and I sensed a third being hovering in the spaces between the divine and the human, a horse-headed man. The play *Hayavadana*, meaning "the one with a horse's head," is named after this character. The story of this horse-headed man, who wants to shed the horse's head and become human, provides the outer panel—as in a mural—within which the tale of the two friends is framed. Hayavadana, too, goes to the same Goddess Kali and wins a boon from her that he should become complete. Logic takes over. The head is the person: Hayavadana becomes a complete horse. The central logic of the tale remains intact, while its basic premise is denied.

The energy of folk theater comes from the fact that although it seems to uphold traditional values, it also has the means of questioning these values, of making them literally stand on their head. The various conventions—the chorus, the masks, the seemingly unrelated comic episodes, the mixing of human and nonhuman worlds—permit the simultaneous presentation of alternative points of view, of alternative attitudes to the central problem. To use a phrase from Bertolt Brecht, these conventions then allow for "complex seeing." And it must be admitted that Brecht's influence, received mainly through his writings and without the benefit of his theatrical productions, went some way in making us realize what could be done with the design of traditional theater. The theatrical conventions Brecht was reacting against—character as a psychological construct providing a focus for emotional identification, the willing-suspension-of-disbelief syndrome, the notion of a unified spectacle—were never a part of the traditional Indian theater. There was therefore no question of arriving at an "alienation" effect by using Brechtian artifice. What he did was to sensitize us to the potentialities of nonnaturalistic techniques available in our own theater.

How invigorating this legacy of traditional theater has proved for Indian theater can be illustrated by two other plays, which appeared soon after *Hayavadana*. In his *Ghashiram Kotwal,* Tendulkar uses Dasavatara, a traditional semiclassical form, to investigate a contemporary political problem, the emergence of "demons" in public life. These demons are initially created by political leaders for the purposes of their own power games but ultimately go out of control and threaten to destroy their own creators. It is a theme recurrent in Indian mythology: the demon made indestructible by the boon of gods and then turning on the gods themselves. (A decade after the play was written, in Punjab, Sant Bhindranwale and Mrs. Indira Gandhi seemed to be reenacting the theme in real life in horrifying detail.)

The central theatrical device in the play is the use of about a dozen singers who start conventionally enough as a chorus. But as the play progresses, they become the human curtain alternately hiding the action and revealing bits of it as in a peep show. From neutral commentators, they slide into the roles of voyeurs who enjoy the degeneration they condemn, of courtiers who perpetrate atrocities, and of the populace that suffers the harrassment. In the final scene the demon is ritually destroyed, torn limb from limb; the city is exorcised, and the now-purified stage is filled with revelers led by the politician who initially created the demon.

In Jabbar Patel's production, music and dance become the instru-

ments of comment and analysis. Ritualistic movements turn impercepti-
bly into an orgy or a political procession; the music by Bhaskar Chan-
davarkar, based on traditional devotional tunes, continually turns upon
itself, sometimes indulgently, sometimes critically. Unexpected breaks
jangle the nerves of the audience. There is no explicit political analysis,
but the matrix of the myth and the ironic use of Dasavatara drive the
point home.

Unlike most Indian playwrights writing today, Chandrasekhar
Kambar does not come from an urban background. As he was born and
brought up in the country, there is no self-consciousness in his use of
Bayalata, a secular folk form of his region. He draws upon the rich
resources of popular speech and folklore with an effortlessness that
conceals a rare sophistication of sensibility and technique. He is a poet
at ease with the ballad, and his approach to poetry on stage is through
the ballad rather than the lyric; the imagery is the action, the metaphors
serve to resonate the narrative at different levels of meaning.

Jokumaraswamy starts with a fertility rite in honor of the phallic
deity Jokumara, who is worshiped in the form of a snake gourd and
then consumed by those desirous of bearing children. The basic situations as well as the music are all traditional, in the sense that they are set
pieces, familiar in Bayalata drama. The impotent chieftain's virgin wife
feeds the snake gourd by mistake to the village rake and has a child by
him. The rake's death at the hands of the chieftain's men is a kind of
gang rape-cum-fertility offering. The chieftain himself is literally left
holding a baby he cannot disown.

Through this semicomic tale, Kambar makes a very Brechtian statement about the right of the peasants to the land on which they work
virtually as serfs for an absentee landlord. But the analysis goes beyond
this rather obvious political manifesto to a complex exploration in
action of political power as a compensation for sexual inadequacy, of
philandering as a psychosexual equivalent of anarchism, which can be
controlled by love and responsibility. By working out the psychological, social, and political implications of the concept of virility, the
play brings out the ambigious nature of the very fertility rite it had set
out to celebrate.

It must be admitted that the popularity of traditional forms on the
urban stage has much to do with the technical freedom they offer the
director. Music, mime, and exotic imagery open up vast opportunities
for colorful improvisation, which nevertheless can—and alas! all too
often does—degenerate into self-indulgence. So far, however, the benefits have far outweighed the shortcomings, and our past—or, if you
prefer, our parallel if ignored present—has provided a source of energy
that will keep at least some of us going for quite a while.

CHAPTER 6

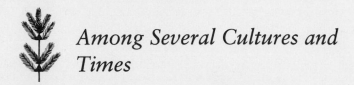

Among *Several Cultures and Times*

Gulam Mohammed Sheikh

Living in India means living simultaneously in several cultures and
times. One often walks into "medieval" situations, and runs into
"primitive" people. The past exists as a living entity alongside the
present, each illuminating and sustaining the other.

As times and cultures converge, the citadels of purism explode.
Traditional and modern, private and public, the inside and outside
continually telescope and reunite. The kaleidoscopic flux of images
engages me to construe structures in the process of being created.

Like the many-eyed and many-armed archetype of an Indian
child, soiled with multiple visions, I draw my energy from the source.
(Catalog, "Place for People," Bombay and New Delhi, 1981)

This was written in response to a prevalent view of one world—one
culture and a singular notion of time taught to us as a philosophy of life.
As applied to painting, this view meant working in one mode at a
time, figurative or abstract, and one genre, naturalistic or surrealistic,
"Indian" or "modern," whichever one to be expressly shorn of stains of
other arts or aspects of life that would pollute its purity. In addition, art
practice aspired to the ideal of a "masterpiece" fixed in a frame and
exclusive of the context to which it belonged. Any combination of
alternatives had to be harmonized: that is to say, one diffused in the
service of the other to singularize the experience, for otherwise it would

lead to a schism, a dilemma, split vision, schizophrenia. *Eclectic* was a bad word.

The world as it came to me, however, came almost invariably manifold, plural or at least dual in form. In art, painting came in the company of poetry and images from life lived, from other times, from painting, sometimes from literature, and often from nowhere, emerging together through scribbled drawings and words. The multiplicity and simultaneity of these worlds filled me with a sense of being part of them all. Attempts to define the experience in singular terms have left me uneasy and restless; absence of rejected worlds has haunted me throughout.

In childhood I saw a close convergence of Hindu and Muslim rituals in family customs and ceremonies; indeed names of kin could belong to either tradition. Under the strict gaze of my father, I prayed five times a day in the mosque, but I moved in the company of Jain and Brahman friends, including a priest, the rest of the time. It was a daily routine to recite the Koran in the morning at home and learn Sanskrit at school in the afternoon. My town, Wadhwan Camp (renamed Surendranagar after independence), was a nineteenth-century extension of a far older Wadhwan (believed to be ancient Vardhamanapuri). Frequenting the Birdwood Library[1] and Irish missionary hospital in town was as usual as visiting the twelfth-century Ranakdevi temple, step-wells, or shrine of Gebanshah Pir[2] by tramway in the adjoining Wadhwan. In our lane we faced a massive wall and would have been orphaned without it. It was at once barrier and link—however invisible, the world beyond it was just as much a part of our life—and the communities on either side lived in a dual world of isolation and unison.

The meaning of reality was larger than even these worlds; I believed when my father spoke of white genies springing across the riverbed in a single leap or when friends described stones rolling from one end of the *maidan* (green) to the other on their own in the early hours of the morning. Standing alone on the old iron bridge as the aged clock tower ticked, I visualized angels whirling above trees of the graveyard as Japanese planes flew over them at the end of the Second World War. The vision of the procession of Gebanshah Pir in the backyard of our little house at midnight is as clear and vivid in my mind as the long hours spent in the hot, burning afternoons of summer.

Art that fed my mind was equally polymorphic: The unbelievable scenery and fictitious mansions my brother painted in sweeping strokes on glass were akin to popular pictures from Nathdwara (Figure 6.1)[3]; a wash painting[4] my drawing teacher showed me represented a domestic scene in a romantic style; a staid watercolor landscape in academic mode, made by an English amateur my Anglo-Indian geography teacher

Figure 6.1. Idyllic landscape, Nathdwara, Rajasthan, contemporary.

asked me to emulate, came from yet another world. Most powerful in their effect were the large and lurid cinema hoardings (billboards) and dreamy damsels of popular periodicals in which photographic image was recast in various collages with blaring colors. Against these, the practice of drawing an oleander branch in a ceramic vase at school was infinitely dreary (and put me off all oleander branches and vases for the rest of my life), and the matter-of-fact illustrations in school textbooks, which we disfigured with a vengeance at every available opportunity, were equally dreadful. So when I painted landscapes of unvisited sites and seductive belles or picture-stories for a wall journal* I edited with a poet-teacher friend, images from these different worlds tumbled out in one form or another.

I reached Baroda in 1955 for formal education in art. Here works of great artists and epochs traditional and contemporary, Eastern as well as Western, took me by storm, pushing all I had brought from home into a remote private corner of mind. Michelangelos and Picassos in the art history classes (and glimpses of Sienese murals and Indian miniatures) opened hundreds of windows, although our souls and hearts were tied to the abstracts of Soulages, Kline, and others, which jumped out of the pages of international art journals. Indeed, swept up in the

---

*Hand-drawn, hand-written periodical.

high tide of "modern art," the motto was to be here in the moment of the day; the entire stockpile of earlier traditions was left ashore or in the oblivion of art history. Under the impact of that brief period of unabating excitement when life meant eating and drinking art—even sleeping on it and sparing it for others[5]—I looked for my own personal expression. But it was difficult to find a clear spot in the shadows of "masters" and peers, and the only alternative was to snuff them out. In the search for a singular image, I devised (initially under the influence of M. F. Husain) a whinnying white horse in chase or isolation, perched on the horizon between dark expanses of earth and sky, harnessed to a tonga or, more often, free of associations of specific time and place. I painted these elements over and over again in different combinations (while writing anguished poems with ennui in rambling free verse) until the reductive process led to repetitions as the emotional surge subsided. Most of the paintings seemed to be haunted by images that stood outside the frames.

It was at this stage that I left for an England going through the last lap of the Pop and the heyday of the Minimal at the Royal College of Art in London, the nerve center of the avant-garde in the early- and mid-1960s in England. Much as I remained unconvinced of the surface culture of art and its insinuations, I tried both prevalent modes and effects (complete with photographic collage and color-stripes with masking tape, etc.) to get them out of my system and mixed them with the expressionist simulation of paint I was familiar with. This was my first—albeit unconscious and unsuccessful—attempt to play with multiple imagery and form. In the end, however, the short-term device of the collage formula left me in yet another aimless limbo.

It appeared to many of us then that after the marathon of movements in the arena of art, painting was breathing its last. Curiously enough, the ephemeral form of film seemed to be the most vital creative alternative of the day, and Fellini and Buñuel presided over the eclipse of painting. Perhaps the rootlessness caused by the cult of internationalism coincided with the flickering substance of the film image. Cinema in that period tried to appropriate effects of painting—thus assisting in the process of pushing art into other blind alleys of non-art, anti-art, and similar variations for a decade or so. Disillusioned by the art of the day and with a heart full of void I looked to the Flemish, the early Italians, to Piero della Francesca at the National Gallery, and to the Indian miniatures at the Victoria and Albert Museum. Going back to "moderns" of earlier days, Magritte drew me close for devastating myths of the real and the unreal, much like Fellini in *8 1/2*; Morandi's little drawings and etchings for the love of the unprofound scenery of his local Bologna; Beckmann for the frightening images of violence and the enigma of the unknown.

A visit to Italy was a revelation of sorts; it unlocked deep and unsatiated reserves of responses to the early Renaissance, especially the Sienese and Piero della Francesca. Looking at the works of Ambrogio Lorenzetti, Sassetta, and Duccio revived faith in painting once again. Painting, for the Sienese, was an act of love offered with tenderness, humility, and passionate conviction. Every surface of paint simmered with a feeling of touch, with the result that walls in paintings smelled of human warmth. I discovered how this came to be in the provincial town of Siena. The city is built on hills; lanes radiating from a piazza each widen and close at intervals like the movements of people using them. The uphill route of streets corresponds to rising breath released as one reaches small open squares on the way, while return downhill is quick and sudden for an ecstatic gasp at the wondrous sight of the shell-like great piazza, large as a lake and touched by the shadowy arm of the Palazzo Pubblico campanile (Plate 1). Lorenzetti's cityscape *Effects of Good Government* (Plate 2) has passages of the experience of walking through Siena. Not painted as a static scene of a city observed from a window, it opens gradually from one end of the wall as one scans the secret nooks and corners, lanes, byroads, rooftops, and the distant cathedral, through the viewer's own movements. Such paintings, done much before the illusionism of the Renaissance overran the intimate realism of this provincial terrain, apparently do not conform to the rationales of Palladian perspective. In Sassetta (Plate 3), color is not tainted by the intervention of cast shadows[6]; its luminosity is heightened by a saturation of hues in the absence of dramatic effects of light and dark. Probably this was a result of color perceived in clear daylight rather than indoors, as seems to have been the convention since the Renaissance, when manipulation of source of light and play of shadows became the nucleus of pictorial form. Duccio was all light. Deeply entrenched in the spirit of the Gospel narrative, scenes of his *Maestà* polyptych run as folios to be read in different orders as golden skies and pink-orange grounds lead across episodic borders of frames (Plate 4). Moreover, Duccio's *Story of the Passion* is set in his hometown Siena, and his Christ may well have been modeled in the likeness of a kinsman.

Much of the Indian painting I saw in the Victoria and Albert Museum (initially through a direct passage from the Painting School of the Royal College to the museum's cafeteria, and later in prolonged savorings in the company of Robert Skelton) and elsewhere was strikingly close to the experiences of looking at early Renaissance pictures. The Jaipur, Bundi, and Kishengarh Krishna images were identifiably set in

Figure 6.2. Exterior of the house of Sawantram Chokha, Shekhawati, Rajasthan, nineteenth century.

specific time and locale in costume, postures, and countenance. The world of Mewar, Malwa, and Basohli was timebound yet timeless. Space was construed as a buoyant expanse of "flat" color rippling with proximate and distant views and images alternating (Plate 5). Color was derived from light and air, aromas and sounds, rather than describing complexions and surface tints of objects. Cast shadows had no place here—even night scenes were "moon-drenched"[7] or full of visibilities. In fact it was rare to find paintings made for sight alone: Each simmered with reference to other senses and arts of literature, music, or drama. Based on music, the Ragamala paintings retained their sparkling visual tenor and flowed with candid, melodious nuances. Indeed there was hardly anything singular in traditional Indian painting. Landscape that the Kota,[8] the Kangra,[9] and the Mughal artists painted was made of the forests and treks they traversed on foot; it opened along the routes following the itinerary of images. Elsewhere images were read like, or in the company of, words in books, in different directions and combinations. Later, when I saw murals in Shekhawati[10] all over the high mansions of a street (Figure 6.2), it became clear that the physical movement of the viewer was essential in grasping their scale and structure. As in

Gulam Mohammed Sheikh

Figure 6.3. Amra Killing Traitorous Spy and Freeing Hamza, *folio from the* Hamza Nama, *1562–77.*

many Indian paintings, the rationale for structure did not lie in any principle of enclosure in an outer border or frame. In Shekhawati the painting is revealed in stages as one walks through the street, detail by detail; images grow over windows and doors in an open-ended structure linked by these details. Both painting and its perception required improvisation (as in music) the painter and the viewer effected upon the space. Reading of a picture in time has many equivalents, more prominent among them being scrolls. In Bengal, the *paṭa* (scroll) painter, the Patua, unrolls the highly animated images in succession while reciting the story; in Rajasthan, often a woman performer dances with a lamp lighting the episode sung about by the narrator (Plate 6). The tales of Bengali *paṭa*s belong to different cultures and times: from the traditional Chandimangal[11] and Manasa[12] stories for Hindus to Satta Pir[13] for Muslims and the "creation story" for the tribal Santhals, or stories of the assassination of Indira Gandhi and life in Calcutta for a more "modern" audience (Plates 7 and 8).

For multiplicity of image and form, the *Hamza Nama* has no parallel (Figure 6.3). About a hundred artists (including calligraphers, gilders, and binders) worked over a period of fifteen years (1562–1577) during the reign of Akbar to illustrate Persian tales of a rebel who is often identified with the uncle of the Prophet. Despite their Islamic origin and belonging to a powerful pictorial tradition, Hamza stories are not painted in the Islamic world but are totally set in the Indian context, with local flora and fauna, sultanate architecture, and dramatis personae derived from a variety of racial types. They also hint at the overlapping characters of Hamza and the charismatic emperor Akbar. Painted on cloth lined with paper, the story was read from the back while the picture was held to the audience. The format of the pictures is a category apart; not small enough to be miniatures nor as large as murals, the approximately 2 1/2-by-2-foot pictures cannot be rolled as scrolls either because of their lining. The painters included recruits from various parts of India who worked under the supervision of two Persian masters Akbar's father Humayun had brought to India. Introduced to Flemish prints at a later stage, they used all modes and methods known to them—Persian and a variety of Indian and European—often working collectively on a single folio incorporating vegetation, figures, architecture, even drawing and coloring by different hands.

The collective nature of the work does not result in a cacophonic collage, for each artist consciously shares hand and heart with the other. What emerges in the end is an image of multiple visions, each in relation to as well as independent from the others. For instance, the tenor of loud faience patterns matches the animated intensity of figures, keeping the spatial planes alive with resilient tensions. The boundless

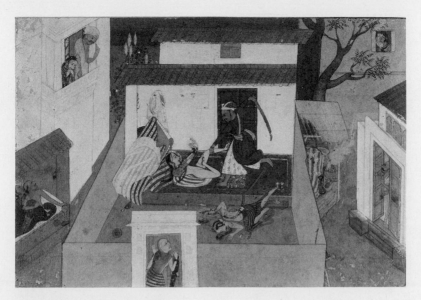

Figure 6.4. Crime Passionel, *Gangaram, Bikaner, Rajasthan, c. 1745, opaque watercolor on paper.*

energy of the pictures often explodes through the borders. This reveals in some respects a quality of life—of living together of communities, each with a definite view of the world in dialectic interaction with the other. Difference is not a sign of disorder or disunity. In painting, individual vision is not an exclusive, private preserve; it shines more in sharing than in separation.

Hamza Nama also reveals another vital dimension of Indian art, rarely acknowledged: the portrayal of the physical reality of life in India. Along with the archetypal Indian crowds in movement, it uncovers aspects of brutality and violence both latent and explicit, often in vivid, gory details. More evidence is forthcoming of the Indian artist's concern for the sordid realities of the place and time he lived in. The horrific realism of the murder scene by Gangaram (Figure 6.4)[14] shatters the myth of idealism the traditional Indian artist is saddled with.

Returning to India and visiting my hometown, I saw accretions of time past still alive in interaction with elements of change, unharmonized yet vital. Much of what I had left behind came back to me, the childhood strangely in the company of new images. Somewhere the luminosity of Sassetta's interiors overlapped with the procession of

Figure 6.5. Returning Home after a Long Absence, *G. M. Sheikh, 1969–73.*

Gebanshah Pir, and moving along the overused streets and repeatedly touched walls brought recollections of the streets of Siena Ambrogio had painted. Painting and life images exchanged places.

My hands and eyes were full of these worlds. It was a *multiverse* of sorts. And I decided to use it all. I felt it would be impoverishing, unreal, and artificial to give up anything—even, out of a sense of guilt, oil painting and the kind of naturalism I was taught at school, for they had now become part of my life experience. I would rather add them to my bag of tricks than discard them. And I have said it all in the first person because I feel that every act of painting or writing is in some respects an attempt in autobiography, revealing you in your past while simultaneously projecting what you are in the present. It allows you to step out of your skin to look at the self and the world you belong to from inside and outside.

Figure 6.6. About Waiting and Wandering, *G. M. Sheikh, 1981.*

In *Returning Home after a Long Absence* (Figure 6.5), I used the community ghetto against a wall tall enough to distance it from the factory that lay beyond, angels and prophet from a famous Persian miniature, mother's portrait from a photograph. This was followed by a series of walls and the redolent vegetation I would see at the edge of town that made me imagine things as a child. Into *Kin* (Plate 9), I brought people related to me and the environment I knew, or created

Figure 6.7. City for Sale, *G. M. Sheikh, 1981–84.*

from what I knew. But it was with *About Waiting and Wandering* (Figure 6.6) that I set off on a journey mixing space and time in a spinning structure. *Speaking Street* (Plate 10) has a claustrophobic enclosure relieved by a little window where a woman lies on a charpoy, and it makes allusions to local beliefs that dogs can perceive angels even though they do not cast shadows. In *Revolving Routes* (Plate 11), there are the world of childhood (on the top left) and the Baroda home, part of the British residency (on the top right), and below it the college where I teach, along with "quotes" of images of Brueghel, Balthus, Mughal miniatures, and Baroda street and city images, and on the bottom left a speaking tree with heads of friends and teachers. The largest painting, *City for Sale* (Figure 6.7), is set in Baroda against the backdrop of communal riots, which threaten to rip the city apart. The psychic brutalization manifests itself in violence and absurdities—like the Hindi cinema.

What preoccupies me now is the epic trajectory of time and space. In the *Mahabharata* or *Kathasaritsagara*,[15] stories run within stories at several levels, each connected yet independent. In the most recent series of paintings, images of my worlds, rather than flowing into each other in fluid space, now hop over sectioned areas. The latest deals with horizontal panels on a vertical plane spilling into each other (Plate 12). And where they do not, a man bores a hole to see into the heart of another man in the panel below.

Gulam Mohammed Sheikh

NOTES

1. Named after the British Indologist George Birdwood.

2. Muslim saint whose shrines are all over Gujarat.

3. Center of pilgrimage of Vaishnava sect where idyllic landscapes are sold as souvenirs along with ritual images of the deity Shrinathji.

4. Technique of painting evolved by turn-of-the-century Bengali artists after Japanese ink drawing, using washes of watercolor to create misty effects.

5. Borrowed (with apologies) from the following translation by Arun Kolatkar of the Marathi saint-poet Janabai's poem:

> I eat god
> I drink god
> I sleep on god . . .
> God is within
> God is without and moreover
> There is god to spare.

Vrishchik 1 (September–October 1970), ed. Gulam Sheikh and Bhupen Khakhar, Baroda.

6. Timothy Hyman characterizes pre- and post-Renaissance as arts of light and shadow, respectively. Cast shadows did not appeal to most art of the world, including Indian. Having known Europeans through illusionistic pictures, the Chinese expected them to have their bodies divided into dark and light complexions.

7. Phrase borrowed from W. G. Archer, *Rajput Miniatures from the Collection of Edwin Binney, 3d* (Portland, Oregon: Portland Art Museum, 1968), 26.

8. School of painting in Rajasthan known for hunting scenes.

9. School of painting in the Punjab Hills renowned for its delicate sensibility.

10. Part of Rajasthan adjacent to Jaipur where numerous mansions belonging to mercantile communities were painted in the eighteenth and nineteenth centuries.

11. Painted scrolls illustrating stories of the mother goddess Chandi, the snake goddess Manasa, and a Muslim saint, respectively.

12. Ibid.

13. Ibid.

14. See Stuart Cary Welch, *India: Art and Culture* 1300–1900 (New York: Metropolitan Museum of Art, 1985), 252 and 375.

15. Original compiled in Sanskrit by Somadeva in 1063–81, based on traditions dating back to the first century B.C. (Somadeva Bhatta, *The Katha Sarit Sagara: or, Ocean of the Streams of Story*. Translated by C. H. Tawney. 2d ed. 2 vols. [Delhi: Munshiram Manoharlal, 1968]. This is an abridged version; the full text in translation is *The Ocean of Story*. [London: C. J. Sawyer Ltd., 1924–28].)

CHAPTER 7

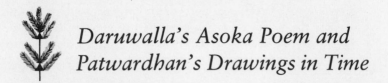

Daruwalla's Asoka Poem and Patwardhan's Drawings in Time

Gieve Patel

I have chosen to discuss details from the work of two contemporaries, the poet Keki Daruwalla and the painter Sudhir Patwardhan. Both are fairly prolific. Yet, by setting aside the full body of their work and selecting a narrower focus, I hope to gain a little in sharpness and clarity. In the case of Keki Daruwalla, I shall examine one poem mainly, "The King Speaks to the Scribe," as a successful example of transposition of the past to illuminate a present and a future need; and in the case of Sudhir Patwardhan, a series of drawings that experiment with time.

Keki Daruwalla, a senior official in the Indian Police Service, has worked for many years in the heartland of the Indo-Gangetic plain. The harshness that characterizes much of his poetry is derived from a temperament that is racked by the suffering it sees all around, but that cannot allow personal squeamishness to obscure a full and detailed viewing of any given situation, however painful it may be. By the corresponding inner logic of this poetry, Nature itself is seen as a thing of impassive and reckless beauty.

When such a poet comes upon a need to articulate the feeling of mercy in the face of dreadful violence, how will he go about it? It is apparent that Daruwalla could find no contemporary imagery or incident that would be sufficiently rich, true, and complex to contain this new urge. Efforts to grapple with traditional Hindu and Muslim religious lore as a possible lever to lift him out of contemporary horror were to my mind only relatively successful. This poet had to go back to the third century B.C. to look into Emperor Asoka's conversion to Buddhism soon after he had won a bloody victory over his enemies at the battle of Kalinga.*

"The King Speaks to the Scribe" is a monologue. Asoka speaks to his scribe Kartikeya and explains to him the nature of his new beliefs. He instructs him how to word his message and tells him that it should be carved in rock in different parts of his kingdom, so that all who read it may join their emperor in this great change of heart. In keeping with his largely democratic vision, the emperor also directs his scribe to carve the edict** in simple language—the language of the people, not that of the court.

Note that Asoka in the third century B.C. is aware of what we today call the problem of displaced persons—the tearing away of people from their loved ones and the drifting apart of populations, the inevitable effect of war that is almost a greater misery than death and slaughter. Daruwalla picks up this theme from the edicts and gives it a special place in his poem.

And note, too, the reference to the tribals, aboriginal folk who live in the forests and who are in an uneasy relationship to the mainstream life of the country. They were clearly a constant source of trouble to Asoka's administration. In his edicts, he offers them special amnesty, albeit worded in language that indicates how much they were outsiders then, as indeed they still are today.

The King Speaks to the Scribe***
(Third Century B.C.)

First Kartikeya, there's no pride involved,
nor humility; understand this. I speak
of atonement, that is, if blood can ever
be wiped away with words. We will engrave

---

*For further information on Asoka, see Vincent A. Smith, *Asoka, the Buddhist Emperor of India* (Clarendon, Texas: Oxford Press at Clarendon, 1920); Amulyachandra Sen, *Asoka's Edicts* (Calcutta: Indian Publicity Society, 1956); Beni Madhab Barua, *Asoka and His Inscriptions* (Calcutta: New Age Publishers Ltd., 1946).

**Asoka's inscriptions, often referred to as edicts, are for the most part reflections, sermons, and declarations of his ideals, aspirations, and acts of piety and duty. Ed.

***Keki Daruwalla, "The King Speaks to the Scribe," from *The Keeper of the Dead* (New Delhi: Oxford University Press, 1982). Reprinted with permission.

this message on volcanic rock, right here
where the earth still reeks of slaughter.
A hundred thousand courted death, mind you.
The battlefield stank so that heaven
had to hold a cloth to its nose. I trod
this plain, dark and glutinous with gore,
my chariot-wheels squelching in the bloody mire.

Nothing stands now between them and destruction,
neither moat nor bridge nor hut nor door-leaf.
No lighted tapers call them to their village.
It is to them that you will speak, or rather
I will speak through you. So don't enunciate
the law of piety, no aphorisms
which say that good is difficult and sin easy.
And no palaver about two peafowl
and just one antelope roasting in my kitchen
instead of an entire hecatomb as in
my father's days. There may be huts where
they have nothing to burn on the hearth-fires.
Spare me the shame. And no taboos, please,
forbidding the caponing of roosters
or drinking of spiritous liquors,
the castration of bulls and rams and
the branding of horses. So listen with care,
Kartikeya, and I will tell you what to write.

First talk about the sorrows of conquest
and other miseries attendant on
enslavement. In all lands live Brahmins,
anchorites and householders, each enmeshed
in the outer skin of relationships,
that network of duty and herd impulse
through which each charts his particular furrow.
And the sword falls on such people and their
children are blighted,,while the affection
of their friends remains undiminished.

Daruwalla's Asoka Poem and Patwardhan's Drawings   123

Mark that, don't talk merely of rapine and slaughter
but also of separation from loved ones.

And about my sorrow what will you say?
How will you touch that weed-ridden lake-floor
of my despair and keep from drowning?
Say simply that of all the people killed
or captured, if the thousandth part were to
suffer as before, the pain would overwhelm me.
Tell them I have abjured pride, the lowest
can abuse me now and I shall not answer.
Let the dust of humility cover my head.
Even the tribals, dark and bullet-headed,
the blubber-skinned, the ones from whom our demons
and *yakshas** have borrowed their faces,
I invite to my fold. Let them turn from crime
and their aboriginal ways and they will not suffer.

Cut deeper than the cuts of my sword
so that even as moss covers the letters
they are visible. Write whatever
you chance on. Don't look for-a white-quartz boulder.
Anything will do, a mass of trap rock
or just a stone sheet. And the language simple,
something the forest folk can understand.
I am not speaking to kings, to Antiyoka
and Maga or Alikasudra. And no
high-flown language. I am not here
to appease gods. Even they must be ignored
for a while and their altar-fires turn cold.
Men don't have enough fuel to burn their dead.

Mind you, Kartikeya, between me and them is blood.
Your words will have to reach across to them
like a tide of black oxen crossing a ford.

---

*Sometimes benevolent, sometimes malevolent spirits.

A special point of interest: Daruwalla has Asoka instructing Kartikeya as much on what he should *not* say as on what he should. In one of these instructions, the modern poet alters the sense of the original Asokan edict for a specific purpose. The poem says

> And no palaver about two peafowl
> and just one antelope roasting in my kitchen
> instead of an entire hecatomb as in
> my father's days.

In contrast, the original edict says

> Formerly, in the kitchen of His Sacred and Gracious Majesty the
> King, each day many hundred thousands of living creatures were
> slaughtered to make curries. But now, when this scripture of the Law
> is being written, only three living creatures are daily slaughtered for
> curry, to wit, two peacocks and one antelope—the antelope, however,
> not invariably. Even those three living creatures shall not be slaugh-
> tered in future.

The tone of Asoka's statements, which are believed to have come directly from himself and not through intermediary speech writers, is
confessional and exhorting. And at least one thesis states that he was
fond of antelope and peacock meats, that in this edict he admits as
much, and freely indicates that giving these up entirely will entail a
struggle, though he intends ultimately to do so. Daruwalla, however,
has *his* Asoka say, "no palaver about all this, do not make too much of
this reform, do not trumpet it about, there are serious enough other
things to think of," reminding us again that he is not in this poem
primarily concerned with giving us a critique of the historical Asoka.
Rather, through this movement back into history, he is drawing a critique of today's rulers; and by inverting Asoka's original edict he draws
attention to the propensity of contemporary statesmen for bruiting
about their very few and slight worthy acts to the listening world.

And this is the moment for me to reiterate how important this
poem is for us today, how each apparently archaic reference points to a
problem we are living with—be it political publicity and propaganda,
war refugees, the conflict of majority with tribal populations, or the
search for a language and for ideas that could reach the remotest and
most deprived persons.

Our appreciation of this poem would not be complete without some
idea of Daruwalla's earlier work. I have already mentioned its uncom-

promising harshness, which is brave and truthful. Here are two quotations.

From "The Ghaghra in Spate," describing an annual flooding of one of the north Indian rivers:

> And through the village*
> the Ghaghra steers her course
> thatch and dung turn to river-scum
> a buffalo floats over to the rooftop
> where the men are stranded
> Three days of hunger, and her udders
> turn red-rimmed and swollen
> > with milk-extortion
>
> Children have spirit enough in them
> to cheer the rescue boats
> the men are still-life subjects
> > oozing wet looks
> They don't rave or curse
> For they know the river's slang, her argot
> no one sends prayers to a wasted sky
> for prayers are parabolic
> they will come down with a plop anyway.

A second quotation, this time from the poem "Death by Burial" (A mob attacks a group of bandits with lathis, tough wooden staves. The bandits in this case happen to be untouchables, which gives the Hindu and Muslim populations of the village a rare opportunity for unanimity.):

> there is nothing much to distinguish**
> one lathi blow from another
> The same inverted back, the same arc through the air
> the curve consummated on the cowering body
> and beneath the raining blows
> > a swarm of limbs
> > twisting like tentacles

---

*Keki Daruwalla, "The Ghaghra In Spate," from *Under Orion* (Calcutta: Writers Workshop, 1970). Reprinted with permission.
**Keki Daruwalla, "Death by Burial," from *Under Orion* (Calcutta: Writers Workshop, 1970). Reprinted with permission.

Both these extracts are from Daruwalla's first collection of verse, *Under Orion*. In subsequent works he attempts again and again to extricate himself from the nightmares he has observed and sees as recurrent. In the Asoka poem he finds not just the subject matter he is looking for, but a tone, a measure, of calming, of distancing. He is able to take several lines straight from the edicts and use them in his modern poem, though the rest of the poem works by evocation and even, as we saw, by some displacement of the original text. But he *can* use these lines almost verbatim because the ideals of rulership Asoka was struggling with are relevant and unrealized by us two thousand years after his death.

Daruwalla's poem is hardly devoid of violent imagery; indeed it would have been false had it been so. But once this violence is fully experienced, the entire cup of it is drained, and the poet emerges, with the emperor, on the side of remorse and recompense.

Viewers of contemporary painting in India have reacted to Sudhir Patwardhan's depictions of common people and the urban and small-town environment with immediate recognition and identification. In his earlier paintings, a rich emotionality deriving from the artist's own psyche fuses with the subjects in the painting. In later works, the artist has practiced an intentional distancing, so that his subjects may be allowed to express their own life and vigor, with as little directive from the artist himself as is possible.

I have chosen not to deal with the paintings but with a set of recent drawings that are speculative, in many senses of that word, and exist on the knife-edge of successful achievement.

At some point, three or four years ago, the artist began work on heads of contemporary persons, in pencil and in pastel media. The starting point often was the recapturing of some detail of a person seen within the last few days: a carpenter whose shop the artist passes on his way to work (Patwardhan, incidentally, is a radiologist), the eggseller who comes to the door daily, some "typical" person, like a spruce and well-groomed South Indian youth. All these heads are grounded in immediate reality.

Soon the focus began to alter. The heads acquired unexpected identities in time. Using a Butkara wood carving from the second century A.D. as source material, Patwardhan preserved the wooden quality in his drawing (Plate 13). However, the drawing intends that the man be seen as flesh and blood, too.

A head isolated from a crowd scene in a Mughal miniature is almost literally transposed, except that the costume carries a slight suggestion of futuristic design (Plate 14); another head has Florentine headgear, and a face mask used by Jain monks even today (Figure 7.1);

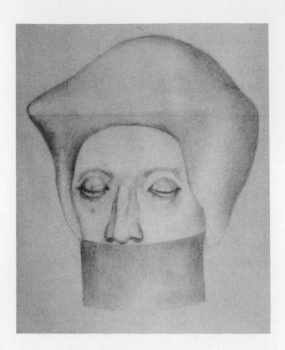

*Figure 7.1. Untitled,
Sudhir Patwardhan,
1983, pencil on paper.
Sources are seventeenth-
century Flemish paint-
ing and contemporary.*

Vermeer's *Maid Pouring Milk* is given a Jain face mask, too! The tenses of past, present, and future begin slowly to lose their rigid, encapsulated boundaries. Finally, two sets of isolated eyes gaze away deprived of context—an act of looking from one undefined dimension into another (Figure 7.2).

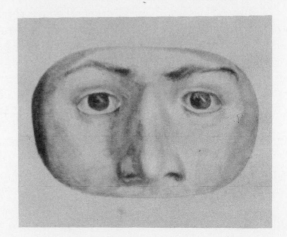

*Figure 7.2. Untitled,
Sudhir Patwardhan,
1983, pencil on paper.*

I said earlier that I find these drawings speculative. I favor that description of them—it covers the notion of a gamble, and has a philosophical overtone as well. A gamble is not guaranteed to succeed, and the element of risk is certainly paramount in these drawings. The dangers of slipping into a masquerade pageant—or into a facile time-machine fantasy—are very real. I believe Patwardhan has avoided these pitfalls. In the Butkara and Mughal heads, there is the slightest movement away from the originals, the smallest suggestion of something not being quite what it appears to be. And then as Patwardhan proceeds, he consistently avoids extravagance, in face or costumery. There is a quiet shuttling between the tenses, or unexpected combinations of them, an intimation of an existence with fluid boundaries.

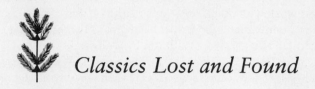

CHAPTER 8

Classics Lost and Found

A. K. Ramanujan

Just as our biological past lives in the physical body, our social and cultural past lives in the many cultural bodies we inherit—our languages, arts, religions, and life-cycle rites. In this short paper, I wish to talk about some of the relations between the past and the present in India, especially through literature, and about the ways the present and the past transform one another, of which discovery is only one.

I shall begin with two anecdotes of fieldwork as parables for the kinds of changes that occur, then describe the way certain Tamil classics were (re)discovered in the nineteenth century, and end with an example of how a modern poet makes use of his traditions.

A friend of mine, a student of American Indian languages, had made it his business to preserve those that were dying. One of the languages had only a single speaker left, a poor, very old, very toothless but spirited woman. My friend found some money for his fieldwork, brought the woman to the University of California in Los Angeles where he worked, and anxiously began recording her, studying her language syllable by syllable, consonant by consonant, for months. He paid her a small fee every week and she saved it carefully. She had for years dreamed of getting herself some dentures, and now that she had the money, she went and bought a full set of teeth. And as soon as she did so, a whole new set of dental consonants emerged in the language. The sound structure of the language appeared now in a new light. It was like restoring a painting. The past, like other cultural constructions, changes as we attend to it.

The second anecdote shows, in a somewhat different way, that the observer, the discoverer, the historian, the collector soon becomes a part of what he works with. Murray Emeneau, the eminent American linguist, studied the language and collected the songs of the Todas, a pastoral tribe in the Nilgiri Hills in South India, in the early 1950s (Emeneau 1971). When he visited the tribe again a few years later to continue his work with them, to his great surprise they sang to him new songs about a white man who had collected songs among them several years earlier. He had created a tradition by studying it.

The past is another country, as the saying goes. With the past, too, one adds oneself to it as one studies it. One is changed by it and the past itself is changed by one's study of it.

Sometimes a piece of the past comes alive in the present, becomes relevant, even seditious, because it seems to provide powerful instances for something forbidden or censored in the present. *Hamlet* in Poland (see Jan Kott's *Shakespeare, Our Contemporary*), or Shakespeare's own history plays in Elizabethan England, dramatizing problems and fears of succession; or the film *Ivan the Terrible* in Russia; or the epic *Ramayana* all over India (and outside, in Indonesia, Thailand, etc.), conveying political messages, and in contemporary India Tendulkar's Marathi play *Gashiram Kotwal,* or Girish Karnad's *Tughlaq* in Kannada—all are instances of artists using episodes from past history to comment on the present. They give new meanings to the past in the present.

I myself got a glimpse of how immediate and dangerous the past could be when I visited northern Sri Lanka in 1983, just after the troubles between the Tamils and the Sinhalese majority had erupted.

I was speaking to a Tamil audience innocently about classical Tamil poetry. When I came to talk about the old war poems, especially the elegies on dead warriors, I choked on them. I couldn't read them to the Tamil audience in Jaffna. Several Tamil insurgents had been killed in the region recently, and I remembered suddenly in the middle of this somewhat academic presentation that they had been adolescents, their beards still soft, like the young warrior in this ancient poem:

> O heart*
> sorrowing
> for this lad

---

*A. K. Ramanujan, "O heart," from *Poems of Love and War*. Copyright © 1985 Columbia University Press. By permission.

once scared of a stick
lifted in mock anger
when he refused
a drink of milk,

    now
not content with killing
war elephants
with spotted trunks,

this son
of the strong man who fell yesterday

seems unaware of the arrow
in his wound,

his head of hair is plumed
like a horse's,

he has fallen
on his shield,

his beard is still soft.[1]

One of over two thousand poems composed by five hundred poets collected in eight anthologies about two millennia ago, this could have been written (with some changes in detail) yesterday. In a culture like the Indian, the past does not pass. It keeps on providing paradigms and ironies for the present, or at least that's the way it seems.

The classical Tamil tradition, such as the poem above represents, was not always known to the Tamils themselves, or actively present to them. In the eighteenth century, Hindu scholars, devout worshipers of Siva and Vishnu, did not wish to read so-called nonreligious poems and would not teach them to their pupils. The epics *Cilappatikaram* and *Manimekalai* were non-Hindu; the latter was clearly Buddhist. So, even the finest Tamil scholars of the time ignored these breathtaking epics and the anthologies of early Tamil; most didn't even suspect their existence and gave their nights and days to religious and grammatical texts, many of which were of minor importance.

The story of the rediscovery of these great classical texts in the nineteenth century is a dramatic one. Even the factual account sounds like a parable and works like a paradigm for the way "a great tradition modernizes."[2]

The name of U. V. Saminata Aiyar (1855–1942)[3] became a legend in his own lifetime among students of Tamil. A young man of vast learning, he met, almost by chance, a liberal-minded *munsif* (civil judge), Ramasami Mudaliyar, in a temple town called Kumbakonam. In his autobiography,[4] Aiyar recalls that day as a Thursday, the twenty-first of October, 1880, and dedicates a whole chapter to this fateful meeting, for it was no less, for him and for Tamil culture.

The *munsif*, who had just been transferred to the small town, asked Aiyar what he had studied and under whom. Aiyar mentioned his well-known mentor and listed all the grammars and religious texts and puranas and commentaries he had labored over and learned by heart. The judge was not impressed. "Is that all? What is the use? Have you studied the old texts?" He mentioned some. Aiyar, one of the most erudite and thoroughgoing of Tamil scholars, had never heard of them.

The judge later brought out a handwritten copy of an old poem and asked Aiyar to take it home. The judge told him how he had long ago studied a small part of it in a textbook compiled by a Eurasian of English descent, Rev. Henry Bower, and he could not now make much sense of the whole text. The English language, English-educated Indians like Mudaliyar, and English people are important forces in the discovery of the Indian past. Indology is an invention and gift of Western scholarship, an ambiguous gift according to some (see Said 1978).

Aiyar was confident he could read anything in the Tamil of any period. Yet he found that, with all his learning, he could not understand much of the manuscript. It was a lesson in humility. He knew the words but they seemed to mean something he couldn't guess at. He didn't know the stories. Familiar names referred to unfamiliar characters. He read what he could to the judge, and they struggled with it together for six months. He had by now gathered that it was not a Hindu text at all, but a Jain text, the *Civakacintamani*, and he began to make inquiries about it.

A friend told him one day that there was a Jain community a few streets away from where Aiyar lived. Why not go there and find out whether anyone in that community knew the text? So they went to visit a rich and influential Jain gentleman. Even as they entered the house, Aiyar noticed mango leaves and decorations on the door frame, signs of a happy ritual occasion. He asked the gentleman, "Did you have a special feast or holiday today?" The Jain gentleman replied, "No, sir, we were reading this sacred text, the *Civakacintamani,* for the past six months with our teacher. We finished it today. So we are celebrating the end of our reading with a happy ceremony." This entire community knew the text that Aiyar had been laboring over for months. They revered it and lovingly studied it as their forebears had done in earlier times.

Such incidents brought home to Aiyar, as they bring home to us, that Indian tradition is not a single street or a one-way street but consists of many connected streets and neighborhoods like that town itself. Interlocking and coexistent though they are, people of one neighborhood may have never stepped into another. India does not have one past, but many pasts.

Aiyar's little excursion into this fascinating, ever-available but never-entered neighborhood was an eye-opener. He now recognized what he didn't know, even after years of studying with great Tamil teachers, going from guru to guru in search of classics. He decided to master the Jain text, edit it, and publish it, even though he didn't belong to the Jain community. He traveled in his spare time seeking copies of the text and found twenty-three of them, four of which were complete. By working on this text and collating the copies, solving the puzzles they set, he taught himself to become a superb editor and commentator, one of the first of his kind. While he was engaged in this self-education and cultural discovery, everything was grist for his mill. For instance, he once saw an English Bible in an acquaintance's home, and, leafing through it (he didn't have enough English to read it), he learned of the concept of concordances, which he used creatively in all his later work.

Aiyar also discovered to his astonishment that once before, in the sixteenth century, another Brahman scholar had done something very similar. As Aiyar began to look into the commentaries, he found two works by Naccinarkkiniyar, the first skimpy, and the second full and detailed. When he asked his new-found Jain friends about them, they told him the legend they all knew, one that must have seemed like reverse déjà vu to Aiyar. Naccinarkkiniyar had first written a commentary on the *Civakacintamani* on his own, but the Jains of the time had said in response to it, "You don't understand a thing about this text or the Jain tradition." He had taken their criticism to heart, gone to a Jain village, and passed himself off as a Jain to do fieldwork as anthropologists do these days. After a period of this kind of learning, he wrote a new commentary, full of well-earned detail.

Now the text had to be rediscovered again in the nineteenth century and seen in a new light by Aiyar. There is a mythic precedent for this process, too: The Vedas were stolen by a demon and carried off into the ocean, and Lord Vishnu himself had to take on the avatar of a boar, enter the ocean, destroy this demon—the demon of Time truly—and retrieve the Vedas.[5]

Naccinarkkiniyar's commentary on the *Civakacintamani* quoted several texts and authors for whom he gave no names, and this made Aiyar realize that there were many more classical Tamil texts to be found. He devoted the rest of his long life to roaming the villages, rummaging in private attics and the storerooms of monasteries, unearthing, editing, and printing them. In fact, soon after he had discovered the *Civakacintamani,* he returned to the monastery where he had studied for years, and he discovered there a second copy complete with commentary; it had been hand-copied carefully by his own teacher, Minakshisundaram Pillai, who had never mentioned it to his prize pupil. He also found a neglected bundle of palm-leaf manuscripts in a corner, thrown together in a basket, and they were the Eight Anthologies of classical Tamil, from which I have quoted above the elegy on the young warrior.

When texts were no longer rare manuscripts that were physically owned by certain people but were copied from palm-leaf manuscripts onto paper, and especially when they were put into print, the relationships between authors and audiences were revolutionized. There is of course much more to say about the sociology of knowledge than this—and I have done so elsewhere (Ramanujan 1985).

Because of the lifework of scholars like Aiyar and his contemporaries,[6] the "Tamil Renaissance" became possible, and a "great tradition modernized." But modernity, itself a new attitude to history and tradition, with a new kind of pride in the past, also discovers and includes the Indian past, through new techniques of discovery and through a juxtaposition of "the pastness of the past" and its "presence." As Denis Hudson observes, "[Madras] city's most modern institutions use symbols of Tamil Nadu's most ancient past [especially literary ones]. Maxims from a Tamil text on ethics of the fifth or sixth century are painted near the driver's seat of public buses. A statue of the heroine of a fifth century epic stands on the thoroughfare on Marina Beach near the University of Madras. Poems of ancient Tamil bards are standard subjects of college syllabi. The names of kings and heroes of the classical literature are the names of contemporary politicians" (Hudson 1981).

Translators like George Hart and me, almost a century after Aiyar's fateful meeting with the *munsif,* are now reading and translating the Tamil classics (Ramanujan 1967 and 1985; Hart 1980). The word *translate,* as you know, is only Latin for the Greek word *metaphor.* Both mean "carry across."

People usually praise translators for their labor of love. I must say, though, that one translates not just out of love, but also out of envy of the past masters, in order to appropriate and repossess the wonderful classical poems—and, of course, ultimately to publish them in one's own name. A medieval Sanskrit epigram about the past says, "If you have not read the ancients, how can you write? If you *have* read the ancients, why do you write?" One cuts through that dilemma by translating the past. Translation then participates in our dream of making out of a historical past a contemporary past, creating out of the so-called linear sequential order of history a simultaneous order, an active presence.

One of the early texts Aiyar edited was a poem of the sixth century (circa), the first long devotional or bhakti poem to appear in any Indian language, the first religious text to appear in any native tongue—till then, religious texts had been composed only in Sanskrit. The text was *Tirumurukarruppatai,* a "Guide to Lord Murugan." It tells where to go and how to find Murugan, an ancient Dravidian god with six faces, twelve eyes, and twelve hands, a Dionysian god of fertility, joy, youth, beauty, love, war, and travel. He is worshiped in six famous hilltop shrines in Tamil Nadu; the poem, too, has six parts, as the devotee's human body has six *cakra*s or vital centers. The poem, the country with its six shrines, the god of six faces, and the devotee's body all correspond to (or with) one another.

The very day Aiyar finished editing this poem and closed the books, as it were, he saw, right outside his window, a devotee of Murugan with a *kāvaḍi,* a bamboo frame with peacock feathers that his worshipers carry on their heads. The devotee was singing a section of this sixth-century poem, *Tirumurukarruppatai.* Aiyar says he felt blessed by that good omen. In this instance, and in other realms as well, the past the scholar was just discovering was already present to others in the culture, always had been. The scholar was editing only the written text of a poem well known and much loved in the oral recitative tradition.

For its form, *Tirumurukarruppatai* depends on an even older Tamil poetic genre, the war poems (*puram,* or "exterior" poems)—especially the so-called Guide Poems (*ārruppaṭai*), where one poet guides a poorer colleague toward a patron who would recognize his talent and reward him handsomely. In the Murugan poem, the old secular relation between poet and patron has been transposed into the relation between devotee and god. I shall quote here just one section from "Murugan: His Places":

Where goats are slaughtered,*
where grains of fine rice are offered
    in several pots with flowers,
and His cock-banner is raised
in the festival of festivals
for many towns around;

wherever devotees praise
and move His heart;

where His spear-bearing shamans
set up yards
for their frenzy dance;

and in forests, parks,
lovely islets in rivers,
streams, pools, certain spots
    like four-way crossroads, meeting places,
cadamba oaks in first flower;

in assemblies under the main tree
and in town halls;

in sacred pillars;

and in the awesome vast temple
where the daughter of the hill tribe
worships

raising a banner with His splendid bird on it,
patting white mustard seed into ghee,
chanting wordlessly her special chants,
bowing
and scattering flowers,
wearing two cloths
    different in color and kind,

---

*A. K. Ramanujan, "Murugan: His Places," from *Poems of Love and War*. Copyright ©
1985 Columbia University Press. By permission.

A. K. Ramanujan

threads of crimson on her wrists,
scattering parched grain
and offering soft white rice
 mixed with the blood
 of strong fattened large-footed rams
in small offerings in several dishes,
sprinkling sandal fragrances
with yellow turmeric,
cutting together red oleander
 and big cool garlands
and letting them hang,

 blessing the towns
  on the rich hill-slopes,
 offering the sweet smoke of incense,
 singing *kuṟiñci** songs
  while the roar of waterfalls
  mixes with the music of instruments,
 spreading red flowers,
 spreading fearful blood-smeared millet,

 where the daughter of the hill tribe
 sounds Murugan's favorite instruments
 and offers worship to Murugan
 till He arrives
 and comes into her
 to terrify enemies and deniers:

 in that place then
 they sing till the dancing yards echo,
 they blow all the horns at once,
 ring all the crooked bells,
 bless His elephant
  with a peacock-shield on his forehead
 who never runs from battle.

---

*Songs of the hillside landscape presided over by Murugan.

There
the suppliants offer worship,

    ask and ask
    as if to ask is to be given already.

    He dwells in all such places
    and I speak what I truly know.

Nakkiranar
Tirumurukarruppatai: 6[7]

In 1967, Fred Clothey, now a professor of religion at the University of Pittsburgh, studied Murugan, his temples, icons, and texts, and wrote a dissertation for us at Chicago.[8] I was one of his readers, and as I worked with his chapters—I was in Madras that year—a series of prayers formed themselves in my head. The prayers were addressed to Murugan, with many references to the iconography and history I was steeped in, and also to the sixth-century poem that Aiyar, among others, had edited. I will close, somewhat immodestly, with these prayers (Ramanujan 1971, 57–62). My poem, too, talks about some Indian attitudes to the Indian past, with which I was somewhat despondently preoccupied at the time. I had felt that Sanskrit itself and all that it represented had become an absence, at best a crippling and not an enabling presence, that the future needed a new past. Many things have changed since then and so have I. But the mood, the relation to what the God Murugan means, is a real one, and I hope it speaks not only for me.

Tirumurukarruppatai is a poem of faith and strength; mine is one of lack and self-doubt, in which it is like some other religious poems (e.g., some Virasaiva poems) that I had translated. These prayers are antiprayers; they use an old poem in a well-known genre to make a new poem to say new things. The past works through the present as the present reworks the past.

Prayers to Lord Murugan *

I

Lord of new arrivals
lovers and rivals:

---

arrive
at once with cockfight and banner-
dance till on this and the next three
hills

women's hands and the garlands
on the chests of men will turn like
chariotwheels

O where are the cockscombs and where
the beaks glinting with new knives
at crossroads

when will orange banners burn
among blue trumpet flowers and the shade
of trees

waiting for lightnings?

2

Twelve etched arrowheads
for eyes and six unforeseen
faces, and you were not
embarrassed.

Unlike other gods
you found work
for every face,
and made
eyes at only one
woman. And your arms
are like faces with proper
names.

3

Lord of green
growing things, give us
a hand

in our fight
with the fruit fly.
Tell us,

will the red flower ever
come to the branches
of the blueprint

city?

4

Lord of great changes and small
cells: exchange our painted grey
pottery

for iron copper the leap of stone horses
our yellow grass and lily seed
for rams'

flesh and scarlet rice for the carnivals
on rivers O dawn of nightmare virgins
bring us

your white-haired witches who wear
three colors even in sleep.

5

Lord of the spoor of the tigress,
outside our town hyenas
and civet cats live
on the kills of leopards
and tigers

too weak to finish what's begun.
Rajahs stand in photographs
over ninefoot silken tigresses
that sycophants have shot.
Sleeping under country fans

hearts are worm cans
turning over continually
for the great shadows
of fish in the open
waters.

We eat legends and leavings,
remember the ivory, the apes,
the peacocks we sent in the Bible
to Solomon, the medicines for smallpox,
the similes

for muslin: wavering snakeskins,
a cloud of steam.
Ever-rehearsing astronauts,
we purify and return
our urine

to the circling body
and burn our faeces
for fuel to reach the moon
through the sky behind
the navel.

6

Master of red bloodstains,
our blood is brown;
our collars white.

Other lives and sixty-
four rumored arts
tingle,

pins and needles
at amputees' fingertips
in phantom muscle.

7

Lord of the twelve right hands
why are we your mirror men
with the two left hands

capable only of casting
reflections? Lord
of faces,

find us the face
we lost early
this morning.

8

Lord of headlines,
help us read
the small print.

Lord of the sixth sense,
give us back
our five senses.

Lord of solutions,
teach us to dissolve
and not to drown.

9

Deliver us O presence
from proxies
and absences

from sanskrit and the mythologies
of night and the several
roundtable mornings

of London and return
the future to what
it was.

A. K. Ramanujan

10

Lord, return us.
Bring us back
to a litter

of six new pigs in a slum
and a sudden quarter
of harvest.

Lord of the last-born
give us
birth.

11

Lord of lost travellers,
find us. Hunt us
down.

Lord of answers,
cure us at once
of prayers.

NOTES

1. Ramanujan, *Poems of Love and War*, 165.

2. Reference to Milton Singer, *When a Great Tradition Modernizes: An Anthropological Approach to Indian Civilization* ([1972]1980).

3. For earlier discussions of this remarkable scholar's work and the "Tamil Renaissance," see Ramanujan 1970; Zvelebil 1973; Hudson 1981; Ramanujan 1985.

4. *En Carittiram* ("My History"), abridged by Ki. Va. Jagannatan (Madras: Tyagaraja Vilasam, 1958); for an English translation, see S. K. Guruswamy, *The Story of My Life* (Madras: U. V. Caminataiyar Library, 1980). Denis Hudson, above, has a very readable translation of the relevant chapter.

5. I was reminded of this myth by V. Narayana Rao.

6. Two older scholars before Aiyar ought to be mentioned: Arumuka Navalar (1822–79) and C. V. Damodaram Pillai (1832–1901).

7. Ramanujan, *Poems of Love and War*, 215.

8. The dissertation later became a book: Fred W. Clothey, *The Many Faces of Murukan: The History and Meaning of a South Indian God* (The Hague: Mouton Publishers, 1978).

REFERENCES CITED

Emeneau, Murray B.
  1971   *Toda Songs*. Oxford: Clarendon Press.

Hart, George L.
  1980   *Poets of the Tamil Anthologies*. Princeton: Princeton University Press.

Hudson, Denis
  1981   Renaissance in the Life of Saminata Aiyar, a Tamil Scholar. *Comparative Civilizations Review* 7 (Fall 1981).

Kott, Jan
  1964   *Shakespeare, Our Contemporary*. Garden City, New York: Doubleday.

Ramanujan, A. K.
  1967   *The Interior Landscape*. Bloomington: Indiana University Press.

  1970   Language and Social Change: The Tamil Example. *Transition in South Asia: Problems of Modernization*, Robert I. Crane, ed. Monograph and Occasional Papers Series, Monograph No. 9. Durham: Duke University Program on Comparative Studies on Southern Asia.

  1971   *Relations*. London: Oxford University Press.

  1985   *Poems of Love and War*. New York: Columbia University Press.

Said, Edward
  1978   *Orientalism*. New York: Random House.

Zvelebil, Kamil V.
  1973   *The Smile of Murugan, On Tamil Literature of South India*. Leiden: E. J. Brill.

PART 3

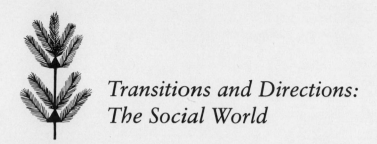

Transitions and Directions:
The Social World

CHAPTER 9

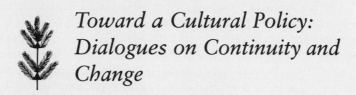

Toward a Cultural Policy: Dialogues on Continuity and Change

Rajeev Sethi

"Aditi: A Celebration of Life," a Festival of India exhibition I conceived and designed, brought two thousand contemporary and ancient artifacts with forty craftspeople and performers to the Smithsonian Institution in Washington, D.C. Singing in one of the "Aditi" galleries, Phool Mala Devi, a Baul woman, saw the housewives of Mithila paint on the walls of the exhibition. One day she decided to rest her *iktārā** and asked me for some rice powder; and then she herself painted a great maze on a platform by a showcase containing the mother goddesses. Her diagram was the *alpaṇā*** of the mother goddess Shasti; Phool Mala called it the protective womb of the mother and drew it as she would on a yielding earth. From generation to generation all over the subcontinent, housewives have acquired the concentration to make auspicious diagrams for protection, abundance, and celebration in varied traditions of floor painting.

Seeing the Baul woman's unexpected participation, I became excited for several reasons—the beauty of the symbol itself, the untouched faith it reflected in the magic evoked by the diagram, and the ease with which it was rendered and recalled. Furthermore, the diagram was

---

*One-stringed instrument.
**Floor drawing of a woman from Bengal.

identical to other ancient designs, such as a stone maze found in Cornwall, England, and stamped medallions from Knossos, Crete, whose purpose or meaning has been long forgotten. But their similarity to her *alpaṇā* did not impress Phool Mala. "The people in England and Crete must have something new now," she said, adding, "We also forget and then we make up something new. But sometimes it comes back when we need it."

Can the age of such easy recall last much longer, though? What will the loss of rituals and customs mean? When the breakdown of kinship structures and interaction patterns has seriously challenged the tradition of oral instruction, how and what do we proceed to preserve, and for whom? And beyond conservation, where do we focus our efforts to turn development into an advantage for the traditional artisan and his or her community?

The potter has stopped making some votives because there is no longer a felt need to propitiate certain deities linked with diseases that are now extinct. Good! The worship of Shitala Mata, the goddess of smallpox, will change as she takes on different functions in the context of modern medicine.

Women who sang the most telling songs on the way to the well, sharing the day's happenings with each other, have now merely to open a faucet in their homes. Again good! The water pot designed to be carried on the waist or the head becomes less useful and requires redesigning. But how does the energy so enshrined in the songs of the women find a new vehicle for its expression? Young men and women continue to sing; however, most of the film music that is so popular, it seems to me, cannot equip them as well to handle personal or community relationships as did some of their own songs and ballads, now slipping from memory.

The women of Haryana, as in other areas of the north, celebrate Ahoi Asthmi, a festival for the health, safety, and long life of progeny that involves the making of wall reliefs and drawings with the help of children. During the ceremony special stories are told, foods cooked, worship performed—and each ritual reflects the delicate interplay of social roles. Now the housewives buy printed sheets of the ritual drawings from the bazaars, stick them on distempered walls, and offer perfunctory prayers. When walls are made of concrete, it is easier not to mess about with mud or paint. Hardly anyone still knows the content and context of the faith. Why go on? "We just do it because it has been done by the ancestors—my mother would have remembered the reasons. We only believe." Would your daughter continue to do the same, even if she doesn't know or care about the meaning of the ritual?

"Maybe, but she is now educated, and you educated people don't need all this."

Over the centuries every major influence that has come our way has been accommodated, with a measure of caution and concern. The arrival of the Aryans, the visit of Alexander, journeys on the silk route, the rise and decline of the Mughal Empire, the colonial rule of the British, the impact of the media and modern technology—all these have left us a grafted tree with exotic flowers at the end of each branch. Perhaps what we today call "Indian" is not only that which is worthy of becoming old, but also that which exudes an ephemeral fragrance. Change is inherent; it is a barometer of people's awarenesses, resources, and values at any given time. The real relevance of the old values is in the inspiration they provide for the present. We do not worship the past for the sake of history.

The deterioration of tradition occurs when those who pursue traditional skills for a living do not receive the rewards they need—psychic and material—to support themselves. People studying the traditional arts seem to get more recognition than those practicing them, and the practice is not always considered modern or economically fruitful even by the artists and their community. But there is no doubt in my mind that the art will survive only as long as the artist does. The imaginative skill of artisans shows the nature of insight that leads to the process of renewal, of growth, of progress from the old tools to the new.

The moment of fusion between skill and insight occurs in the traditional craftsperson's and artist's mind much as it would in that of an artist any place, any time; their creative process can be as private, detached, and anonymous as it can be community based—and their point of view as contemporary as, if not the same as, that of a "modern" painter explaining his or her work.

For example, in "Aditi" one met Chandrakala Devi, an extraordinary housewife, who created an entire tableau of sculpture that had little to do with her traditional memory and much to do with her skill for making grain jars. Wife of a railway inspector, she does not have a house whose walls and floors she could decorate as the season or rituals commanded. Instead she spends a lot of her time on the train. Once, while in the latrine and with all the movement within her and without, she suddenly saw the whole wall of the toilet come alive with vivid images of the *Mahabharata*. She concluded that if this sacred experience could happen to her in a toilet, she could have the experience anywhere at all. Now she says there is no need for her to wait for that moment when making, being, expressing become the same. "When I walk," she says, "art walks with me." Fine lines between art and craft disappear with Chandrakala.

During the past fifteen years, I have been deeply involved in the setting up and organization of a cooperative of itinerant performers. These artists—jugglers, acrobats, magicians, balladeers, and puppeteers—are today being bandied about the world as the living repository of our ancient traditions, earning a great name for India. In this role, I brought them to "Aditi." At the same time that they are praised abroad, however, they are the victims at home of the colonial and shortsighted Bombay Beggary Act of 1954; "soliciting alms through any pretence" such as singing, dancing, and juggling is seen as tantamount to beggary. For years, they have been hounded by the police, bundled off into poor homes, and ignored by cultural institutions.

It is very important to examine the roots of their arts again, to fortify ourselves with connections and meanings we may have forgotten, and to instill pride in a people who suffer from a debilitating sense that their skills are of no use any longer. But can this even be begun when the artists have no roof over their heads? And what comes afterwards? The real issue in this age of industry and flux is the survival of an environment that nurtures the irreplaceable inheritance of time-honored skills.

The reason to focus on crafts is twofold: skilled work is the most eloquent visual manifestation of a culture's inherent character, and it gainfully employs a vast and crucial sector of people. It has become increasingly apparent to development planners that agricultural advances alone cannot be a panacea for rural unemployment.

However, craft traditions are more vulnerable than they have ever been, and the craft world in India is presently caught up in a state of indecision. In the past thirty years, traditional skills and forms flourished as various handcrafted products found a growing clientele in national elite markets and abroad. The interest in both Western and Indian markets for ethnic and exotic bric-a-brac inevitably declined, whereupon the craft traders quickly tried to move into a Western design ethos without a proper understanding of the skills and technology necessary to enter this new market. Likewise, work commissioned by foreign designers in India (very rarely acknowledged as being "made in India") often lacks the spirit of innovation. A rash of sequined razzmatazz on Seventh Avenue only caters to the image of India as a fad. This increasing dependence on alien design and marketing intervention has raised pertinent queries on the future of India's crafts as a socioeconomic expression of and for an indigenous people. Spread over a large country and isolated in various skill pockets, craftspeople are producing fewer items for regional and local consumers. Although some crafts historically have been molded around and occasionally initiated by the requirements of nonlocal patrons, others have been altered and debased through outside influence to such a point that they have lost their ritual significance for a local community. There is clearly a need, therefore, to create a resurgence of interest in India's abundant skills that is both serious and consistent, with appropriate inputs from the West, and taking great care in the introduction of new ideas and patterns in the process.

Although official or scholarly patronage—or lack of it—and expanding markets can distract the artist, alternatively they can energize, leading to innovation and an extension of the tradition. There are as many variables as there are craftspeople and circumstances.

The potters of Chinar today make terracotta Mickey Mouses and Donald Ducks for tourists, exactly as the people of Mithila now produce pictures on paper by the dozen for a large, undiscerning clientele. But it is also true that the newfound material comfort and status earned through such diversification give these craftspeople the opportunity to seek out and savor continuity with a traditional medium. In Mithila, more women find more time to paint and have more freedom to experiment with new themes and material, and even men (previously unthinkable) have taken to the brush. Traditional sculptors, who used to go from place to place making temples and palaces, are not better off today breaking stones for roads, switching professions completely, or living in abject poverty—but the example of Kesaria Ram from Uttar Pradesh, working in his own village backyard to carve a supremely designed outdoor divan for Mario Bellini, indicates another possible choice.

Too narrow a view of tradition can limit growth. For instance, the stigma of untouchability upon a caste of people who work with leather has led to the discontinuation of work by several thousand leather craftspeople. Although current economic pressure is leading others of more "respected" castes to take up this heretofore unacceptable profession, tradition must be bent to both technical and cultural ends for social mobility to be realized: evolving better technologies in the flaying and curing of hides in the cottage sector, designing practical new footwear to meet the farmer's changing requirements, explaining the advantages of wearing a leather shoe instead of a plastic one, and enhancing pride in the shoemakers' profession. Better working conditions, organized marketing, and new ideas will infuse a sense of direction for the future.

The influence of the mass media to convert culture into a leisure activity profoundly affects the way people perceive and express themselves. With the rural population often intimidated by this urban view of culture, village craftspeople need now more than ever to have the right perspective reinforced. Must hand products imitate factory- or mill-made alternatives? In the name of intermediate technology and decentralization of production, do we have to perpetuate inefficiency and a poor product? What is the relationship of quality, function, and form? What has been the role of traditional ornamentation? Does a television set ingeniously woven on the edge of a sari drape as well on the bend of a woman's shoulder as does a paisley? Where does identity converge with innovation? The craftspeople themselves will have to address such questions before there can be any hope of success.

Not only are some skills being transformed in an unwholesome fashion, but others are fast disappearing as, not unexpectedly, products on which they have been perfected over the ages have themselves become obsolete. However, if in today's village there is little use for large washing basins in terracotta, can the same skill to turn and fire large-sized pottery be applied to making irrigation pipes? If necessary, can the potters' market be expanded, albeit minutely, by asking them to produce large pots, planters, and floor and wall tiles for city and suburban homes? Will new designs support the effort to train additional craftspeople?

Traditional methods of converting a variety of material through the patience, economics, and versatility of handwork can readily be applied to the production of a multitude of objects that fit into contemporary life-styles, and many of these skills are capable of sustaining the imagination of creative designers anywhere in the world. The evolution of a design for a traditional handicraft is wholly dependent on a dialogue between the maker and the consumers over a period of time. Saleable products emerge from the craftsperson's understanding of the market and the consumers' communication of their felt needs and tastes. In the industrial age the bridge between the producer and the consumers is rarely interpersonal, and the traditional craftsperson has to seek others' help to interpret the demands of consumers who are often strangers in faraway lands. Although history is replete with such precedents, the role of a designer today as an interpreter or catalyst of modified or new form is crucial.

To begin designing for a new product, the first step would be to systematically collect and study the usage of product forms that are currently retailed. It would also help to record and reproduce those that have lately disappeared but are within feasible recall of manufacture and to study existing tools and raw materials that might be used in inventive ways.

The second step would be to find a satisfactory, up-to-date method of disseminating information and exchanging ideas. In ancient India, a system of interdependent guilds provided the structure through which much-needed information about craft collectives and technologies could be spread with customary speed and clarity—by word of mouth—to organize production. The guilds also served as a sort of alphabet; different combinations of letters were used by the creator or consumer who desired a new effect.

Today, in order to invigorate the development of skills, to develop a whole range of new prototypes that would explore and demonstrate the vast vocabulary of handicraft skills for new markets, and to improve communications and production, we need a designer-oriented national directory of crafts that would be accessible to the people who need it most. This ought to include names of craftspeople and entrepreneurs and other information that would inspire and guide concerted action in the field. The Festival of India in the United Kingdom, the United States, and France offered the first opportunity to begin work in this direction, and we do not intend to lose the momentum gained in the preparation of its major craft exhibitions.

As proposed, Shilpa Sagar, "the sea of skill," would collate data and provide scope for interaction among craftspeople and designers, most of whom seem now to be working in separate grooves. Information would be classified under craft usage, choice of basic materials, and primary skills in a modern system of information storage and retrieval. Swift and ready access to such a system by designers, craftspeople, and producers within the country and from abroad would facilitate finding out what can be made where and by whom and at what cost.

Finally, much innovative work is called for to organize management at all levels and streamline production procedures.

The vitality of India's traditional crafts stems from the fact that they are a part of a living culture with an exciting potential for growth. Patronage and guidance on the scale envisioned are intended to stimulate research, sharing of technology, imaginative experimentation, and on-the-job training in both India and the West. The effects on trade, it is hoped, will be direct, and the effort that includes "Aditi," "The Golden Eye" exhibition at the Cooper Hewitt Museum, and a national directory of crafts, appreciating craftspeople as a valuable resource, will create the base for a muscular infrastructure of commercial enterprise. Without this we cannot hope to place the most gainful benefits at the doorstep of the craftspeople's workshops.

Surely any effort that leads to the survival of a heritage that is endangered by indiscriminating industrialization cannot remain an issue of only national concern.

CHAPTER 10

The Changing Social Role
of Journalism in India

Aroon Purie

A basic fact of journalism is that its state inevitably reflects the character of society. In order to understand the changing social role of journalism in India in the past few decades, it is necessary to take a brief look at India itself. And that is a daunting task. So much has happened in the country and to the country in a short span of thirty-eight years.

Change in India is special because it means change in the lives of 750 million people, almost a fifth of the world's population crowded into merely one-fortieth of its land. Such is the diversity of the land and its people that generalizations become self-defeating. It is almost as if everything you say about India is true, and its opposite is also true, or almost true.

India is a country of paradox, contradiction, and contrast. With greater heterogeneity than the continent of Europe, it is still one country. Occupying several centuries at once, it is an ancient civilization but a young country, a predominantly agricultural economy that is also the world's fifteenth largest industrial power, in some senses like a horse-cart being drawn by a locomotive. It is the world's largest democracy but one ruled by a single family for all but a few years of its history. It is a secular country blighted with the world's worst communal violence; a country where the noble goals and rights of equality, liberty, and justice are enshrined in the constitution but where the brutalization of citizens is commonplace; a country with the world's third largest pool of skilled workers but afflicted by massive unemployment of the educated. The list is endless.

India is experiencing uneven development, rapidly rising literacy, politicization of the masses, and an explosion of expectations. It is attempting to achieve within decades transitions that the more developed societies of today took centuries to accomplish. And unlike them, it is doing so in the context of universal suffrage and a full-bodied democracy. The result is a society that is divisive, contentious, faction-ridden, endlessly noisy—as former American ambassador to India, John Kenneth Galbraith, described, a "functioning anarchy." Yet with all our diversity and massive poverty, we have found a stable system of government that reflects the growing aspirations of the people. In the whole developing world, there is no other democracy that holds such a promise of viability.

The same promise applies to the Indian media, too. Abe Rosenthal of the *New York Times* tellingly refers to a poor Indian peasant in a village near Delhi who confidently criticizes the prime minister and the government and merrily gives his name and address, not afraid that these could go into print. "Where else could that happen . . . [?] In China, in Eastern Europe, in the Soviet Union, the very idea of listening to such questions—let alone answering them—would strike terror. They could not be asked or answered in most of Asia, in almost all the Middle East or Africa or in many countries of Latin America."[1] Rosenthal's observation underlines not only the fact that a free press exists in India but also that its value is understood and appreciated by a vast majority of our people, even if they cannot even read and write. There is no doubt that the free press in India, with all its faults and failures, is the keystone of India's democracy. And it is so because the press in India has basically lived up to the expectations of an inherently liberal and free society.

Despite serious handicaps such as a shortage of newsprint, widespread illiteracy, and poor purchasing power, the press in India has grown numerically as well as qualitatively. Today India has six times as many publications as it had in 1952, and five times as much circulation, although the population has barely doubled in the same period. The phenomenal rise in circulation has been even more pronounced in the regional, vernacular press than in the more prestigious and high-visibility English-language press. How many countries in the world can boast of newspapers published in eighty-five languages or as many as 1,595 journals devoted to philosophy and religion? Over 20,000 publications with a combined circulation of about fifty million crowd the Indian newsstands, and more than 700 new ones are added every year. In fact, 30 of these publications, which include some of the most prominent newspapers in the country, were started more than one hundred years ago. Whereas most cities in the United States would have 1 or 2 newspapers, Delhi alone has 8 dailies, and Bombay 14. As both an institution and an industry, the press in India is in much better shape today than ten years ago, something that cannot be said of many of India's other institutions.

So what is the role of the press in such a country? Whether a poor country needs or can afford a free press is a frequently debated question. It is often argued that bread is more important to a starving man than free speech, and that a free, belligerent press spreads cynicism, impedes the development process, and renders governance difficult in countries that are difficult to govern anyway. The right answer to this question, though, is that the poor man needs a free press more than his rich neighbor. If you are educated, aware, and have money, you would have the means to look after your interests. But when most of the people are impoverished, illiterate, and inarticulate, the press has a special responsibility to take over the role of spokesman for people of all classes, not just its middle-class audience, to act as a bridge between the government and the governed, to prevent social explosions that can threaten the polity, to document the reality in the country. One example of the Indian press doing this occurred three years ago, when a group of quacks claiming to be eye surgeons operated on a large number of people in the state of Rajasthan, blinding them in the process. They could be brought to book only because of prompt media disclosures that led to an indignant public outcry. In the United States, media or no media, the victims would have gone to the courts on their own and claimed heavy compensation.

Another dramatic illustration of the role of the press in a country like India comes from Professor Amartya Sen, the distinguished economist. In his lecture, "Food Battles: Conflicts in the Access to Food," he says that "India has not had a famine since independence. Given the nature of Indian politics and society, it is not likely that India can have a famine even in years of great food problems. The Government cannot but afford to take prompt action where large-scale starvation threatens. Newspapers play an important role in this, in making the facts known and forcing the challenge to be faced." He contrasts the Indian case with that of China, which suffered a major famine from 1959 to 1961, after the failure of what was called the Great Leap Forward, in which between 16.3 and 23 million avoidable deaths occurred. There was little knowledge of these conditions within China at the time, although many rumors spread abroad. The terrible facts have been officially acknowledged only very recently, by a regime that is critical of the past leadership. The irony of this, according to Professor Sen, is that the Chinese poor are much better fed in a normal year than their Indian counterparts.[2]

It cannot be overemphasized that in a poor, developing society, it is the function of the press to focus attention on the condition of the majority and keep vigil on behalf of those without the ability to protect themselves. There are not enough institutions in existence in India that can voice the concerns of the unorganized, often gullible masses. And when the voice of the press was muzzled, during the Emergency of 1975–77, Mrs. Gandhi quickly lost touch with the public mood, so that she received a sound drubbing in the elections that followed. Somewhat ironically, it was the censorship of the Emergency and the accompanying wholesale attack on the rights and liberties of every citizen in the land that drove home how deeply ingrained the traditions of democracy and a free press were and made both journalists and readers fundamentally aware of the role of the press. Had there been no censorship, thousands of people would not have been sterilized in a grotesquely mistaken zealousness for family planning, and many thousands fewer of the urban poor would have been uprooted from their shanty homes and dumped outside city limits because they were an eyesore.

The role of the press in India can be specially defined in another way, too: in relation to the other institutions in the country. First, the vast radio and television networks in India are owned and controlled by the government, so that free opinion is not aired, and reportage is restricted mainly to official pronouncements. Therefore, the fundamental functions of a free press devolve even more on the privately owned print media.

Second, the press in any free society exists in a symbiotic relationship with the body politic: the legislature, judiciary, and the executive. To the extent that these institutions are healthy and vibrant, the functioning of the press is confined largely to its traditional role of reporting and interpreting events. But if they are ineffective, or on the decline, journalism has an extra obligation. It has to buttress, strengthen, and aid the functioning of these other institutions that help to make for a free society.

In India, Parliament has seen the Congress party enjoying a steamroller majority for most of the last three decades and more. This did not matter too much in the early years, when stalwart parliamentarians thrown up by the long years of the freedom struggle kept the government on its toes, and when an enlightened prime minister like Jawaharlal Nehru did not try to use his majority to stifle voices of criticism. Over the years, however, conditions have changed. Parliament has been progressively packed with people of less distinction, inner-party democracy within the Congress party has virtually faded away, the sittings of the two houses of Parliament have become steadily briefer and the debate during these sittings less meaningful. Today, instead of the press following Parliament, Parliament takes its lead from the press. Many of the great disclosures of official corruption and abuse in the past decade were first printed by the press, and subsequently raised in Parliament by opposition M.P.'s who pressed the government to explain.

The symbiotic relationship of the press and other institutions of a democratic polity is particularly relevant in the case of the judiciary. In India, the press and the courts have supported each other when under pressure from the executive. The courts struck down a government attempt to regulate the price at which papers could be sold, and the press was severely critical of the government when it departed from the tradition of appointing the senior-most judge of the Supreme Court to the post of chief justice and instead appointed a handpicked judge. At the same time, the doctrine of a "committed" judiciary—that is, committed to an ideology rather than unaligned—was publicly aired by government spokesmen. The press led the fight against this pernicious doctrine, and it has in practice been abandoned in recent years, though other threats to the independence of the judiciary continue to surface.

The social role of the press has expanded significantly in yet another manner that concerns the judiciary. In a system plagued by injustices of every hue, and where the ordinary laws of the land are habitually ignored or violated by the organs of the state themselves, the press has focused attention on how child workers are branded by their employers, how women are bought and sold in the flesh trade, how people are detained indefinitely in prison without being brought to trial, and how the ministers in a state government do not pay the workers on their farms the officially prescribed minimum wages. Such reportage has energized the courts, enlarged the role of the judiciary, and given rise to what is now called in India public interest litigation. Any citizen, including the newspaper reporter, can write a letter to the Supreme Court on, say, a civil rights issue, and the court will intervene and question the executive. Inevitably, then, the frontiers of justice have been pushed forward in a frequently unjust society.

In many senses, therefore, the social role of journalism goes beyond what the purist in a stable, developed society would assign to the profession. And if journalism has to help preserve and strengthen public institutions, it also has to be a catalyst for change. Exposure per se is often of not as much help as it would be in a society with more articulate public opinion, or in a system that was as responsive as it should be. Very often, then, a journalist has to assume the role of social activist, moving courts against injustice that the government conveniently chooses to ignore. The simple fact is that there is more wrong than right in India. Politics are sordid, the bureaucracy is riddled with corruption, police brutality is considered a cliché, academic institutions are faction ridden, and the arts are bedeviled with more politicking than exists in politics. As the well-known British Broadcasting Corporation correspondent Mark Tully said when receiving an award for his reportage on India: "I am lucky to be in India, which is a place where award-winning stories happen."[3]

When a monotonous recital of failures and social evils in investigative stories can lead to readers losing interest after a period of time, the tendency would be to reason: "We know what is wrong with society. But what can be done about it?" Therefore pontificating in generalities in the comment columns should give way to following issues through with good reportage. For instance, one of the perennial stories in the Indian press concerns the delay in the courts, with heartrending accounts of the human cost involved. But a journalist in a country like India should not leave it at that, expecting public consciousness to take care of redressal; he needs to examine the procedures of the lower courts and in the process of investigation suggest ways in which these can be changed so that they become a matter of public debate. The journalist cannot be satisfied with reporting what is happening but must also say what should happen—churning out ideas and brainstorming the mind of the nation. And these additional responsibilities have to be discharged in an environment where the journalist has fewer sources of information than in the more open societies.

The call for a socially responsible press can prove a double-edged sword, for the term is subject to varying interpretations by people with different objectives, some of them in conflict with the ideal of a free press. Because the national opposition has often had a thin presence in Parliament, opposition leaders see the press as a valuable forum and would describe the media's social responsibility as one of carrying out an endless tirade against the government, taking on the mantle of a perpetual adversary, irrespective of the context. For the rulers themselves, the definition has varied from Nehru's outpourings of Jeffersonian liberalism to Mrs. Gandhi's changing moods that launched her on a campaign to demolish the press during the Emergency and made her extremely distrustful of the media in her second reign, when she tended to condemn any critical reference as being antinational.

Although democratic rule came forty years ago, and limited self-governance a decade before that, the history of the free press in India dates back more than a century. A study of this history, of the legacy and tradition that the modern Indian press can draw on, shows how from the start the press combined reportage with larger social purpose. It also shows how journalism gradually changed after independence, going through several stages of transition to emerge in its present form.

The Indian journalist is fortunate in that the foundations of the profession were laid by the leaders of the national freedom movement, who turned journalism into a peaceful yet lethal weapon of attack on colonial rule. Although an incipient nationalist press grew in stature as it fought with the British, taking the freedom struggle to the masses on the one hand and to the outside world on the other, the real birth of the press in India more or less coincided, significantly, with the creation of the Congress party, which was later to become synonymous with the freedom movement. One of the earliest nationalist newspapers was *Kesari,* formed by the militant Congress leader Bal Gangadhar Tilak in Bombay in January 1881. Inaugurating his newspaper, Tilak emphasized the traditional role of the press, which was to be vigilant about public affairs. He said, "The writing in this newspaper will be in accordance with the name given to it (*Kesari* or Lion). The continuous use of the journalist's pen has the same utility as the lights on the streets at night and the night-watch by the policeman. We, therefore, intend to write about how government officials perform their function with complete impartiality and without fear."[4]

From the early part of the twentieth century till independence in 1947, the most decisive driving force behind all change in India and also its press was Mahatma Gandhi. He regarded the press as a means to awaken the masses to agitate against the British Raj, and soon his two journals, *Young India* and *Harijan,* became powerful instruments in the freedom campaign, as well as for the spread of his ideas and philosophy. The Indian press in general mushroomed and became politicized. Journalism became a mission rather than a vocation and drew not only Gandhi and Tilak but Nehru, Subhas Chandra Bose, and practically all the great leaders of the freedom struggle.

Their firsthand experience meant that when they took over the reins of the country, they knew how significant a free press was in the kind of democratic system they wanted. For Nehru, the growth of a self-respecting, free press was as important as his industrial dream, and he soon initiated regular contact with the national press. His philosophy was implicit in his famous statement, "I would rather have a completely free press with all the dangers involved in the wrong use of that freedom than a suppressed or regulated one."[5]

National independence in 1947 marked a watershed for the Indian press. For all but a handful of the newspapers, owned by British interests, the task before this had been simple: fight for the national cause.

Everyone knew who was the hero, and who the villain. This period has often been accurately described as the "viewspaper phase" in India media history, when the job of the journalist was to be a part of the national movement, and when (as a wag remarked) it was a mark of patriotism to write bad English.

After 1947, the Congress party was no longer a national movement but a political party, and the great heroes of the freedom struggle had become the masters of India's destiny. The press had to choose a role for itself, and it found itself on the horns of a dilemma. Could it suddenly turn against the people whom it had extolled till the other day?

Inevitably, the press was expected to be socially responsible and, in the words of the first Press Commission, should help "secure and protect a social order in which justice . . . social, economic and political" would prevail. And indeed in those early years there was more consensus and cooperation in evidence than confrontation and criticism, with a great deal of acceptance of the policies, development objectives, and good intentions of the government. Most news consisted of what the government did or promised to do. Every speech made by Nehru was front-page news, if not the day's lead story.

The leading lights of the press establishment were sceptical of, if not opposed to, Nehru's neutralism in foreign policy, his emphasis on state ownership of industry, and his experiment in economic planning. But although Nehru did not mind criticism, the press in that era hardly ever tested his patience; such criticism as appeared was confined to a relatively benign ideological plane.

Some of the acquiescence of the press in fact contributed to Nehru's subsequent downfall. There was more reportage of his global aspirations as a world statesman than of the reality on the ground; the gross unpreparedness of the defense forces, which later led to a disastrous border war with China, was never even looked at; and when the country underwent a major reorganization with the creation of states based on the language of the region, the press supported a trend that has often been regretted since because it helped foster subnational identities.

If this cooperation with the government marked a fundamental change for the press, there were other transitions in evidence as well. In the first decade or two after independence, journalism ceased to be a mission; however, it did not quite become a profession. Journalists were underpaid, publications were run on tight budgets, little money was spent on traveling out into the country to get the news as it related to people, and government handouts became the daily bread of the journalist who drifted into the field for want of anything else to do. Journalists were not media stars except for a couple of well-known editors, and these editors saw their role essentially as writing the ponderous editorial or the well-rounded analytical piece rather than as leading teams that produced the news in the best manner possible.

These were also the years when what was derisively called the "jute press" dominated the scene. On the industrial horizon, in its newfound zeal for fair allocation of resources, the government gave birth to the licenses raj. The big newspapers were invariably owned by business magnates with substantial interests in a host of industries, ranging from engineering goods to textiles and jute. These industrialists looked at their newspapers as fringe operations, involving little money but giving them prestige and a certain clout with a government that had the power to grant licenses for industrial projects. Some of the magnates had financed the Congress party during the freedom struggle, and continued to do so after independence. It was a cozy relationship, and it did not make for very adventurous journalism.

There were the scandals, of course: The prime minister's special assistant became controversial and had to leave, a finance minister was forced to resign following revelations of his links with a fraudulent businessman, and a commission of inquiry was appointed to go into the charges of corruption against the chief minister of Punjab. But in these and other instances, the press merely followed the lead taken by members of Parliament, with perhaps the most vocal of them being, ironically enough, Nehru's son-in-law and Rajiv Gandhi's father, Feroze Gandhi of the Congress party.

Press criticism did acquire a new bite with the loss of the border war with China in 1962, when Nehru's policy of friendship with China stood exposed and a determined attack on Defense Minister V. K. Krishna Menon led ultimately to his resignation from the cabinet. Nehru emerged from all this a weaker man, the numerous charges of corruption tainted the reputation of his government, and the press began to play an increasingly strident role as the voice of public criticism and, in some measure, of public disillusionment, especially as developmental goals proved hard to attain.

Still, there was a continuing willingness on the part of the press to lean on the government, to be patronized by it. The national news agencies earned most of their revenue from clients that were various agencies of the government, and even press barons expected the government to build up the Fourth Estate as a strong pillar of democracy. Journalists were given subsidized housing, laws were enacted to give them better wages, and numerous publications survived on the strength of government advertising. Some of all this was well intentioned, but the help extended by the government also created dependence. And a web of visible and invisible strings bound newspapers and their employees to the centers of power. Such a phenomenon may take place in any democracy but is more likely in India, where political power commands more deference than any other power and where the hand of government is manifest in more ways than in the openly free enterprise societies.

The real divorce between the press and government came not in Nehru's administration, but during the rule of his daughter, Mrs. Gandhi. Even at the time she came into office, in 1966, she had an uneasy perception of the role of the press and frequently wondered how much freedom the press should have "in a country like India, fighting poverty, backwardness, ignorance, disease and superstition." Her doubts hardened as she took the country through a series of controversial measures, including the splitting of the Congress party as part of a bitter power game, a host of nationalizations of industries and banks, the abolition of the privy purses of Indian princes, and much else; as the press in those days was predominantly right wing, it took a critical approach to the whole range of changes. For the first time since independence, a government was constantly under attack from the press. The *Statesman* of Calcutta expressed grave doubts over the government's policy on Bangladesh, and B. G. Verghese, editor of the *Hindustan Times,* sent a correspondent to Uttar Pradesh to expose the fraud of Mrs. Gandhi's laying foundation stones in a wilderness for announced hospitals, bridges, and other projects with no sign of the projects coming up. He also openly questioned the accession of the Himalayan state of Sikkim by India, promptly earning him the tag of being antinational and the sack from the paper's proprietor, a jute magnate. (Verghese had at the same time been attempting serious developmental journalism; his paper adopted a village near Delhi, for example, to study over a period of time the changes that were taking place in the lives of the villagers.) Verghese and his kind of crusading journalism became trendsetters, and for the first time in the history of the Indian press there was widespread public outcry at the dismissal of an editor.

Mrs. Gandhi had started out as an insecure prime minister—with the press not exactly doing anything to reassure her. But when she had come to terms with the politics of the victory in Bangladesh, she began to consider the press more and more an institution of nuisance value. In such a situation the adversary relationship was bound to grow, and it did. Polarization and hostility increased, and the final break came with the Emergency that she imposed in June 1975. This marked the ultimate watershed in Indian journalism, its moment of truth.

Mrs. Gandhi bludgeoned the press with a ferocity that was far out of proportion to its power. The government cut off electricity to newspaper offices; obstinate papers found that the censors did not clear copy till after the morning delivery boys were out on their rounds; openly defiant journalists were arrested; and quotations from Mahatma

Gandhi's writings of forty years earlier were banned. Boardroom coups were manipulated to take control of inconvenient newspapers. This was a new experience for a community of journalists used to a by and large benign relationship with the government. All of a sudden, they were being asked to take on the entire machinery of the Indian state, and an autocratic and arrogant one at that. On balance they failed this litmus test, caving in tamely.

Most newspapers increased space allocation for sports pages or filled up the columns with soft features. Local officials often summoned senior correspondents of the major papers and gave them long, pointless handouts with instructions to publish them verbatim, grammatical errors and all. Flaying the national press for this timidity, an opposition leader later said, "You were asked to bend, but you crawled."[6]

Fortunately, there were honorable exceptions. The *Indian Express* and the *Statesman,* two major national dailies, stood up to the challenge to some extent and willingly paid the price for their "belligerence." Even more commendable was the case of many small journals and newspapers that fought alongside, perhaps with even greater fury. There was *Himmat,* a weekly edited by Rajmohan Gandhi, Mahatma Gandhi's grandson, and *Freedom First,* another small periodical from Bombay with no great financial backing.

In the process of testing the media's mettle, the Emergency created postindependence India's first media heroes. A rash of post-Emergency books were written by journalists, and those who had had a creditable record under adversity became household names. Meanwhile, those who did not sat in embarrassed silence, dreading the equivalent of the question, "And what did *you* do in the Great War, Grandpa?" For the Indian journalist, the Emergency was his first Great War.

It was also a time when illusions were shattered and perceptions permanently altered. Journalists rediscovered their role and importance (why else would the government have attacked them with such vehemence?); citizens, sensitized by the general assault on their rights, formed civil liberties groups that have acted in tandem with the press ever since; and the readers themselves realized that the absence of a free press meant a denial of their own right to know. Nobody could take anything for granted any more. This was one permanent gain of that bleak period.

The press, which had endlessly debated its freedom and rarely exercised it, began to flex its muscles.

The lifting of censorship after the Emergency caused a fresh hunger for news, journalism attracted a new kind of practitioner, and these led to the birth of a more vibrant press. The age of magazines had come, and journalism in India experienced an excitement that was heady for both the writer and the reader.

Leading this renaissance was *India Today,* a fortnightly newsmagazine launched in December 1975. With an initial print run of 5,000, it limped along till the end of the Emergency in March 1977, when the circulation was 10,000. But by the end of the year, that figure rose to 50,000, and today it is 325,000, making it the most widely circulated English-language magazine in the country.* Others followed—like *Sunday,* with a young, highly motivated staff—offering a different approach, an irreverent unconcern for journalistic precedent, racy writing styles, a desire to find news among people rather than within the government, and a higher level of professionalism. New printing technology resulted in better-looking pages, and new publishers offered enterprising journalists an option and a mobility they did not have before, at higher wages. Universities across the country introduced journalism courses, and the profession acquired a new glamor.

The new breed of journalism has produced several memorable stories. One reporter located children scampering around an army firing range, collecting stray bits of shell and metal that could be sold to make a living; in the effort to get pickings they ignored all safety warnings, thus often getting shot. Another reporter took money from his office and bought a woman in the flesh market of Madhya Pradesh to show that the business flourished. And numerous others reported on the rape of women in police custody, the burning of newly married wives by husbands who wanted more dowry, and so on.

This revitalized scene now strengthens journalism in several ways. A plurality of publications and proprietors means a more competitive market for news; so even if one publication is put down or toes the line, another one raises its head. It also gives journalists greater mobility, which makes for greater independence of action when there is pressure from the top. But in essence, what lay behind the plurality was the arrival of a new kind of journalist on the scene.

Tom Wicker, the *New York Times* columnist, emphasized the importance of the practitioner of journalism when he said: "The press in any democratic country with a free press is not really an institution so much as a diverse collection of human beings and organizations going about the business with different purposes, in different ways with different consequences, all operating under the loosest rules that are open to different interpretations. Therefore, how the press performs its social

---

*A Hindi edition was launched in 1986. Ed.

role depends a great deal on these diverse individuals and organizations." In post-Emergency India, it was the rise of a new set of individuals and organizations that took the press to today's vantage point.

The people entering the field have had a wider educational base and a more liberal outlook and were not conditioned and cramped by the usual copyboy route into journalism. Avoiding the traditional "for the record" style of merely reporting the news, they gave Indian journalism a new depth and dimension. Issues, rather than being merely reported, were analyzed and put into broader perspective, thus leading to extensive and nationwide debates. Increasingly, the subjects journalists covered were subjects of common concern—not just massacres or floods, but the process of development as well. In a most significant about-turn, they also have succeeded in getting rid of some of their chronic and rightly criticized obsession with politics, and it is indeed outside the realm of politics that the most profound change in the Indian media has taken place since.

In the West, the advent of television made the newspapers change. In India, where television is state run and unenterprising, this job has been performed by the newsmagazines. Newspapers are trying to narrow the lead of the newsmagazines, venturing into territories that were alien to them earlier, creating posts in civil rights, development, and rural reporting. Back in the 1960s, when Indian agriculture was undergoing a radical transformation because of the green revolution, few newspapers took the trouble to dispatch correspondents into the farming interior to report on the nature and complexities of the change. Very little at all was written about the green revolution in our press till it was right there in our midst and there was not enough space in the warehouses to store the grain. The crowning irony was the reproduction, by a leading newspaper chain, of an article on the impact of the green revolution in Punjab originally published in the *Los Angeles Times*. But in 1984, just a suggestion that eastern Uttar Pradesh, agriculturally one of the most backward parts of the country, was beginning a green revolution of sorts was enough to send a whole battery of journalists swarming over the place. The story made front-page headlines and even hit the cover of some magazines. There has been equally exhaustive coverage of the attempts at increasing milk supply, through a "white" revolution.

Other media successes of the past decade include the enormous publicity given to the effort of the hill populations of Uttar Pradesh to save their forests from being auctioned off to timber contractors, the focusing of attention on the building of a dam in the Silent Valley in Kerala, which would destroy a rare habitat of numerous species of animals and birds (eventually Mrs. Gandhi herself intervened to get the project scrapped), and the repeated reports of police killing people in fake encounters.

To sum up in historical terms, if the first decade in independent India was a period for somnolence, the 1960s saw a partial awakening and politicization of the press. The post-Emergency era brought professionalism, the most significant change of all.

One problem the urban-based English-language press is conscious of is that although it is able to come up with exposés, thanks to its better resources and reach, it is not capable of adequate follow-up at the grassroots level. Here the vernacular press does better. The Second Press Commission, in a study conducted in June–July 1981, found that eighty-one vernacular dailies in Bengal, Karnataka, and Kerala were quite regularly reporting on development and socioeconomic issues in the villages. The villager in India is aware of the press now. Even farm machinery and fertilizer are often advertised in the newspapers.

The exponents of the growing feminist movement in India have made their viewpoint felt in the world of journalism. In the last decade, women have entered the profession in large numbers. The dailies run weekly columns on women's problems and rights, a very recent phenomenon in Indian journalism. A monthly journal called *Manushi* also has earned a reputation for itself in international feminist circles.

Inescapably, however, the Indian press has realized that with its growing clout it has also become more prone to broadsides from the government and physical threats from extremist organizations. The increasing exposure to situations of terrorism is also a new professional hazard for the journalist. In Punjab, where a man called Jarnail Singh Bhindranwale ran a state within the state for over two years, there were at least two occasions when journalists covering the Punjab scene had a close brush with death at the hands of Bhindranwale's men.

But this is the price of power, and modern Indian journalists seem to have the courage to pay it. What should cause worry is the danger from within. Sectional loyalties surface quite easily in a country as polyglot as India, and with the press's rapid growth has come a tendency toward tribalization. If Hindus are battling with Muslims, or high castes are trying to attack low castes in society, the press has the vital duty of staying absolutely neutral. In some situations of this kind in recent years, newspapers have ceased to be impartial observers and have become virtually active participants. If the trend persists, this could become a reason for riotous mobs turning on newspapers. Happily so far, however, it must be said to the credit of the Indian press that it has been constantly thinking of self-correction. Professionalism also means accountability and introspection.

The second danger, trivialization of the kind we see in the Western press today, which results in sensationalism and headlines such as "Headless Body Found in Topless Bar," is relatively distant in India. To avoid it is doubly important because the printed word has great sanctity in India; and with both the radio and television controlled by the government, it is the print media that will be tested for its credibility and reliability.

The press in India thus has a manifold social responsibility, much greater than that of its counterparts in a developed country like the United States, where free speech is protected by such laws as the First Amendment and the Freedom of Information Act. In a society like India, economic growth could fail to keep pace with the rising aspirations of common people, so that they would then be tempted to follow the "beggar my neighbor" policy, leading to social tension. This perpetual threat gives the press a special obligation: while it protects its freedom and grows in strength and quality, it has to sift the genuine needs of various sections of society from the mass of demands and aspirations and then articulate them effectively.

And that brings us to where it all begins, to the first law of journalism, that the press is a mirror of society. An expanding consumerist economy, rising literacy, increasing plurality, and the decline in the vitality of other democratic institutions have produced a press that is growing handsomely in circulation and in significance. Add to this a commitment to free speech that has been tempered over a century and the existence of a courageous, enterprising breed of journalists, and there can be no doubt that the press will continue to grow in its role of holding a mirror to Indian society, helping it change for the better and strengthening democracy. That is as happy a thought as a journalist can have anywhere in the world.

NOTES

1. A. M. Rosenthal, "India's Gift: The Discovery of Each Day," *New York Times Magazine,* 7 October 1984, 61.

2. Prof. Amartya Sen, delivering the Twelfth Coromondel Lecture, 13 December 1982.

3. Mark Tully, remarks upon receipt of the Dimbleby Award in London for his reportage on Bhopal, 1985.

4. The lead article appeared in the first issue of *Kesari* on January 4, 1881. It has been paraphrased in J. Natarajan, *History of Indian Journalism* (New Delhi: The Publications Division, 1955), 110.

5. Nehru addressing the Newspaper Editors Conference, 3 December 1950.

6. L. K. Advani, president of the Bharatiya Janata party, on the Emergency.

CHAPTER 11

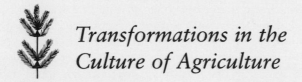

Transformations in the Culture of Agriculture

Arjun Appadurai

In the four decades since independence, agricultural production in India has made enormous strides. Progress can be measured in the amount of foodgrains produced, in the varieties of new technologies in use, and in institutions for credit, marketing, and irrigation. But there are two kinds of price to be paid for such progress. The first, about which much has been written, involves the fragmentation of landholdings, the deepening divisions between rural classes, and the pressure on farmers to migrate to cities. Local security systems such as the *jajmānī* system, a set of moral, ritual, and economic bonds between patrons (often land controllers) and clients (often agricultural laborers), also have been weakened in the face of increased commercialization of land, labor, and agricultural products.[1]

The consequence of these changes is that there is less sense than ever before of any sort of *moral economy* (Scott 1976) in which dependent agriculturalists can rely on the goodwill of their rural superiors in hard times. I have elsewhere characterized this shift in terms of the changing relationship between *enfranchisement* and *entitlement* in rural India, a change that gives poorer persons a wider voice in the conduct of public life but fewer claims upon subsistence in local economic systems (Appadurai 1984a).

The second kind of price for progress is less often discussed. This price is paid in the realm of culture, and it is what I wish to discuss, with a few examples, in this essay. I will also make some observations about the relationship between these two kinds of prices.

Agriculture is usually seen as a particular way of exploiting the environment through a specific technology and against a specific ecological backdrop. But agriculture is also a way of life. By this I do not simply mean that farmers, like the rest of us, have customs and habits, conventions and norms, but that farmers in India possess certain kinds of knowledge and that they are also heirs to a certain way of knowing. Such knowledge, and such a way of knowing, constitute the core of any particular culture of agriculture. I distinguish between what farmers know and how they know (between knowledge and epistemology) not only because this is an empirically appropriate distinction but also because it allows us to analyze important changes in the culture of agriculture of India.

What farmers know covers a great deal of ground, only a small part of which I can touch on here. Their knowledge is ecological, technological, biological, and sociological. Furthermore, such labels, products of relatively recent domain separation in the scientific vocabularies of the West, only weakly convey the structure of agricultural knowledge in places like India, where these domains are not so separated and where knowledge of water, animals, soil, persons, deities, crops, markets, and manure form part of an interacting whole. However, this knowledge is not canonical, abstract, synoptic, or evenly shared; it is unevenly shared, tied to specifics of place, time, and circumstance, and not often systematic. It is a knowledge of and for *practice,* a term I use in the sense of Pierre Bourdieu (1977) to refer to action that is culturally organized, oriented to results, and reproductive of social forms. Farmers are not pandits, and agricultural knowledge is not, in crucial ways, any sort of *śāstra.* Like other folk knowledges, it is context tied, linguistically idiosyncratic, partially articulate, and formalized by the outsider only at the risk of serious misrepresentation.

Yet complex and rich as it is, the archive of what farmers know can be established, in any particular region or community, at least in rough outline. It is a complicated fabric of theories about the soil, the climate and other natural forces, the cultigens, the animals, the social groups, and the government. These theories, which are not always easy to elicit, underlie opinions, expectations, and fears about a variety of day-to-day phenomena such as matters of health and sickness, financial trouble and well-being, and ritual obligations and plans. They also underlie the search for what we may call information (in contrast with knowledge); such information may concern rainfall, the likelihood of casual employment during the next day or the next week, the current prices for market crops in distant places. Closer still to the surface, there is the search for news: news of friends, relatives, happenings in the nearby town, visitors to the village, impending marriages, and so forth. Not only is what farmers know a structurally complicated archive, it is also phenomenologically complex, for it involves subtle shifts from theory to opinion to information to news, though these types of knowledge are progressively less enduring.

If you are a landless laborer, you are not likely to know a great deal about the financing of a twenty-five thousand rupee well, and if you are a 2-acre subsistence farmer, you are not likely to know very much about the cultivation requirements of sugarcane. But variations in temperament, curiosity, and reflectiveness can sometimes counteract the political economy of knowledge, so that a very poor but curious and reflective laborer may penetrate the knowledge that is normally restricted to wealthy and entrepreneurial farmers. In short, even though the edifice of agricultural knowledge is elaborate, part of its complexity lies in the fact that it is not an evenly shared, standardized corpus.

In the last century, and especially in the last thirty years or so, there have been some amazingly rapid shifts in the contents of agricultural knowledge. Farmers (or at least some farmers) know things about irrigation, about fertilizers, about new crops and new varieties of old crops, about tools and techniques, that would have been difficult for them to imagine in the past. Acquisition of new knowledge has always occurred in rural history, but there is good reason to suppose that the pace of change in such knowledge has been greatly accelerated in recent times, for reasons that need not be restated here. Whereas in the past such knowledge worked slowly, through mechanisms of observation and imitation, it comes today through the media, through agricultural colleges, and through public and private development agencies. The most dramatic changes have been in the domain of technology (in the narrow sense). Here, not only is new knowledge obvious, but older knowledge is rapidly disappearing as well. I will mention only three examples of such loss of knowledge, taken from my own field experience in a village in Pune District, Maharashtra State. The ethnographical specifics in the rest of this essay also draw on this experience, but in my general statements I have tried to stick to more widely recognizable phenomena.[2]

Very soon, knowledge of how to construct, maintain, and efficiently operate nonmotorized wells will become obsolete, just as knowledge about leather water containers has already largely vanished because of their replacement by metal water containers in wells. Why should we worry about the loss of this particular sort of knowledge? After all, it might be claimed, animal-powered traditional wells belong to an inefficient and rapidly disappearing way of farming, and it is likely (as well as desirable) that more and more farmers will acquire shares in motorized wells or in larger, modern systems of water distribution. Is it not simply urban romanticism about rural life to regret the passing of such knowledge?

The fact of the matter is that in many dry parts of rural India, like Maharashtra, a significant number of farmers still eke out their subsistence on the edge of commercial agriculture by their access to bullock-drawn well water. For them the understanding of the requirements and uses of such wells is by no means irrelevant. Secondly, for many farmers, participating in the ownership of electric motors for well water is a risky matter, partly because partnerships in such wells sometimes fail, or, due to economic exigencies, shares in such wells have to be sold (see Appadurai 1984b). In these cases, those without access to, and knowledge of, traditional techniques could be pushed out of the market in cash crops (which require irrigation) completely. This will make the ups and downs of farm fortunes sharper in the current transitional milieu. Thus, until there is universal and reliable access to electric power for wells, knowledge of bullock-drawn well water ought not to be pushed into obsolescence. Finally, insofar as bullock-powered wells often involve bullock-sharing systems, which draw poorer farmers into partnership arrangements, the elimination of these systems means also the end of certain forms of cooperation among these farmers. Again, until it is perfectly clear that all farmers operate in a world in which household autonomy is a safe and satisfying mode of organizing subsistence, such changes are risky ways of eating into social capital, particularly for poorer farmers.

As for the shift from leather to metal water containers, the argument is simpler. Farmers are inexorably pushed toward greater reliance on large-scale markets, regional price fluctuations, and uncertainties in supply. If ever there is a major change in prices for metal goods, a great many poorer farmers are likely to find themselves deeper in debt in order to afford metal water containers. In addition, since the making of leather water containers was an important occupational entitlement of the lowest leather-working castes, this shift pushes them into metropolitan markets for their goods and services, thus further compromising the integrity of rural economies.

With the increased dependence on industrially produced fertilizers, even among small farmers, detailed knowledge about how best to use animal manure for agricultural production will become restricted to an older generation and will then disappear. Again, why should we care? First, because in such complex traditional ecosystems, with their delicate relationships between the soil, fertilizer, agricultural productivity, costs of farming, and relative local self-sufficiency, there is ample evidence that animal manure can be extremely effective when available. The problem in the part of Maharashtra in which I worked is that in the last serious period of drought, in 1972, a great many cattle were sold, and local cattle populations have never returned to prior levels. When this situation is combined with the heavy pressure on farmers from government, agribusiness, and outside experts to shift to industrial fertilizers, we can see why farmers, even smaller ones, might be tempted to abandon the use of animal manure and the knowledge of the guidelines traditionally associated with its use. Among many farmers, the pressure to generate sizable short-term cash incomes (to meet subsistence needs that can increasingly be met only with cash) leads to overuse of chemical fertilizers, with disastrous long-term effects on the soil. Farmers are losing the capability to fall back on a technology that might, in certain circumstances, be best for them and their fields. Knowledge lost, in the case of agricultural techniques, is choice foregone.

As reliance on government geologists and other modern experts for locating subsurface water sources increases, there is going to be reduced demand for the services of water diviners. In rural Maharashtra, such individuals, known as *pānhāḍī*, are frequently called upon in the course of decisions to locate new wells. Whatever the objective virtues of their systems for divining the location of subsurface water (and I, for one, am quite open on this question), they serve an important role in contemporary decisions to sink wells. Sinking a new well, in the parts of rural Maharashtra with which I am familiar, is a costly, risky, and time-consuming process. It involves the commitment of a large and indefinite amount of family time for the supervision of whoever does the actual work, the taking on of debts to banks or cooperatives, and often the contracting of partnership ties with other local farmers. Given the nature of the costs and the potential benefits, it is a major decision and one attended with considerable anxiety. A crucial part of the decision is the question of where to locate the well. Farmers themselves have projections, based on village understandings, the location of other wells (old and new), and the advice of friends and neighbors, about where there is likely to be a good vein. Government geologists, who use Western scientific techniques and instruments, have a different conception of the water table and of the optimal places for a well on any given plot of land. So far, farmers are able to reach what they regard as reliable decisions in this crucial matter by triangulating these three kinds of knowledge and then arriving at a choice that best conforms with the predictions of either two or all three. As the expertise of water diviners disappears, it is not just that we lose an important traditional eco-technical skill. We also lose one component in a process that allows farmers to make a complex decision using multiple diagnoses. Here again, a loss in knowledge is a curtailment in epistemological multiplicity and choice.

What is true of material technologies is less true of ecological knowledge. Farmers' knowledge about rainfall, soil, and water as natural systems seems to have survived in many parts of India, but it is only a matter of time before reliance on radio, television, and other metropolitan forms of expertise pushes indigenous knowledge increasingly out of the picture. What is most resilient, of course, is knowledge about people, deities, cosmological happenings, and ritual calendars and rhythms. In this area the fabric of traditional rural knowledge seems to have been least affected. Still, since knowledge, especially in rural settings, is not tightly compartmentalized, the archive as a whole will probably begin to be structurally transformed, although it is difficult to say how or when.

I have spoken so far about the content or archive of agricultural knowledge. In this regard, I have suggested, change is fairly rapid and fairly extensive. But what about the traditional way of knowing, traditional rural epistemology? Here the picture is very complicated, but on the whole I believe change is slower. In order to make my case, I need to say a little more about what I mean by farmers' way of knowing.

Any community is culturally distinctive not only because it knows something distinctive but also because it has a distinctive epistemological style. This epistemological style has several dimensions; of particular importance are: (1) typical modes for assessing certain classes of phenomena, that is, modes of analysis; (2) typical ways in which knowledge is shared or distributed in the community, that is, the political economy of expertise in that community; and (3) the strategic relationship between sectors of knowledge, itself the result of a specific epistemological posture that determines, in any particular community, what kind of knowledge is regarded as prior to what other. Let me give some examples of each of these aspects of epistemological style from my own field experience.

In the matter of *modes of analysis,* I wish to refer to a longer paper I have written on the subject of rural terminologies of measurement.[3] Using material from Maharashtra, I suggested that the difference between contemporary Western terminologies of measurement and their non-Western, rural counterparts was not simply a difference in vocabularies, calling for care in translation. Rather, rural terminologies of measurement reveal assumptions about the relationship between number and quantity, the relationship between measures and standards, the acceptability of approximation over precision, and the centrality of social negotiation to measurement, which are fundamentally divergent from the abstract, context-free, precise norms to which contemporary scientific systems aspire. Thus, when farmers assess the extent of their lands, their yields, their local populations and subpopulations, their needs, and many other things, they do so in terms that are not just superficially different from our own but that also contain and reflect a very different understanding of what measurement is all about.

One illustration of this important difference will have to suffice here. Farmers engaged in growing onions (largely for the market) often have to buy onion seedlings from other farmers. When the purchase of these seedlings is negotiated, it is done in terms of a measure called a *vāphā*, a roughly standardized bed in which such seedlings are planted. The buyer bids a certain sum for a particular *vāphā* (or set of *vāphā*) of seedlings, and then there may be a counteroffer by the seller, and then a final resolution. Although this may look like standard haggling over the price (i.e., the value) of a clear-cut amount of something, it is rather negotiation over the amount itself, expressed in the idiom of price. Since these beds vary in size and shape, and since the number of seedlings in them has to be guessed at visually, what in effect the buyer and seller are bargaining over is their respective estimates of quantity, using the measure of price offers and counteroffers. Such relationships between quantity estimates, approximation, and value characterize many other sorts of activities in rural Maharashtra.

Yet, in a world increasingly defined by money, by markets, and by externally calibrated instruments of measurement such as clocks, calendars, and measuring tapes, a very different mode of measuring is becoming relevant to more and more contexts in rural life. This new mode is characterized by precise and context-free instruments of measure, nonnegotiable results of acts of measurement, and a generalized replacement of approximation by precision. Signs of this shift are everywhere, though the traditional mode of measuring is still the norm. But farmers who operate with cash flows, who work in industrial or quasi-industrial settings, and who respond to bureaucratic requirements in the search for cash, credit, electricity, or health needs must learn new ways to measure their world, or at least to express their estimates of things. Again this sort of erosion of traditional modes of analysis is not just unfortunate in itself; but to the degree that farmers' incorporation into larger systems of interaction and modes of thought is neither pleasant nor freely chosen, its accompanying epistemological costs must, in principle, be deemed high.

As regards the *political economy of expertise*, my thoughts are more tentative. I have already suggested that the archive of agricultural knowledge is not evenly distributed within any rural community. But this is not a sufficiently historical view. The fact is that it is possible to postulate a growing unevenness in the distribution of agricultural knowledge, both within and across specific agricultural communities and regions. The intensification of agriculture has among its many consequences one that involves specialization. Increasingly, there are crops (such as sugarcane) that demand that plots permanently be given over to them, and regions that are constrained to specialize in this or that crop because of market pressures and opportunities. There are farmers who specialize in this or that crop. The crudest example of this last factor is that, in more and more communities, there is a clear gap between wealthier farmers whose lands are largely or completely given over to commercial crops and farmers whose small plots are devoted mainly to subsistence crops.

Of course, this growing differentation does not have direct implications for the distribution of knowledge, since poorer farmers often work on the commercial plots of richer farmers, and richer farmers maintain portions of their land for subsistence crops so as to be free of the vagaries of the market. Yet there is no doubt that knowledge of agricultural operations is now more intricately shared, especially in regard to the overall strategic handling of livelihood. Wealthier farmers today speak the language of risk, of investment, of capital, and of planning in ways that reflect directly their exposure to, and interest in, the discourse of fertilizer companies, bank officials, large agricultural traders, and development experts, both public and private. Poorer farmers, by contrast, though they will occasionally speak of *bhāṇḍval* (capital), *naphā-toṭā* (profit and loss), and so on, are not competent users of the language of agricultural entrepreneurship.

These linguistic variations reflect deeper and subtler variations in how knowledge is shared. It seems clear that, over the long historical run, there is less and less, at the level of knowledge, of what Anthony Wallace called the replication of uniformity or Durkheim would have called mechanical solidarity; and more and more of what Wallace called the organization of diversity and Durkheim would have called organic solidarity (Wallace 1974; Durkheim 1964). In short, farmers increasingly know what they know in a piecemeal manner, consonant with technical and environmental segmentation as well as with social and economic stratification. Rural communities increasingly are held together because of differences—rather than through similarities—in what various persons and groups know about the conduct of agriculture. Needless to say, such unevenness can and does reinforce structures of inequality and domination in rural India. Although this tendency too is not yet ascendant, its direction is clear: It is toward that division of epistemological labor that characterizes complex modern communities the world over.

The strategic *relationship between sectors of knowledge* is the hardest aspect of the epistemological style of rural communities to pin down, but it is perhaps the most important. In any given epistemological universe, some things frame others, some things are regarded as less questionable than others, and some issues and perspectives color the way others are apprehended, discussed, and acted upon. It is this aspect of any particular system of knowing and speaking that Michel Foucault sought to capture in his idea of a discursive formation (see, for example, Foucault 1982).

One major shift that is underway in the discursive formation of rural India, again based on my fieldwork in Maharashtra, concerns the experience and handling of the temporal dimension of rural experience. Time is a central resource in all agricultural communities, and India is no exception. Time is experienced as the ongoing interaction of several kinds of rhythms and periodicities, cosmological, ecological, ritual, and economic. The timing of agricultural decisions reflects complex negotiations and compromises between these various kinds of periodicities, and I have elsewhere argued that poorer farmers are at a specific kind of disadvantage in the distribution of time as an agricultural resource.[4]

But I want here to make a more general point. Although it appears that in the past ritual and ecological periodicities set the rhythms of production, consumption, and reproduction and defined the framework of knowledge and belief within which production goals were established and pursued, this practical and epistemological priority is in the process of being reversed. Increasingly, time itself is subject to the overwhelming pressure of the marketplace and the logic of commercialization. That is, more and more of the rhythm of agricultural life is set by the labor, cash, and climatic needs of commercial crops, affecting not only wealthier farmers who are massively tied to markets in agricultural commodities, but also poorer farmers who provide the labor and part of the clientele for the products of this intensification and commercialization of agriculture. Although my observation is impressionistic, it seems to be the case that the logic of market time is beginning to increasingly crowd a limited social calendar, govern the pace of life, and leave ritual and ecological periodicities in a somewhat more marginalized role.

Let me briefly explain what I mean. The main commercial crops in part of western Maharashtra are sugarcane, onions, and peas, and most of the farmers tend to have at least a small amount of their total acreage under some of these crops. In general, the cash crops have been inserted into a cropping cycle previously dominated by the cultivation of sorghum and millet in two long seasons (monsoon and winter), with a low-activity hot season between them. In this situation, not only was there greater temporal slack during the year but also each crop did not make intense, precise, and frequent demands on the time of farmers. Although subsistence cropping in millet-growing areas does require certain key operations to be performed at certain times, both the length of the seasons and their internal activity structure leave considerable temporal flexibility. This does not pertain once major cash crops arrive on the scene, especially onions, peas, and, to some degree, sugarcane. The cultivation cycles for the commercial crops crosscut the preexisting calendar cycles, which, for most farmers, require room for the basic subsistence crops and also stretch considerably into the hot season, which was previously a slack period. Furthermore, the vegetable cash crops typically require more intense and carefully timed bursts of weeding, watering, and fertilizing. Finally, their own cycles of planting and harvesting frequently overlap with each other, as well as with those of the main subsistence crops. As a result, especially for farmers who are not self-reliant in terms of family labor, much of the year is a scramble to juggle the cycles of these various crops. As crop seasonalities begin to jostle each other and crowd the time available to many farmers, other periodicities frequently become subordinated to them. Marriage celebrations are frequently timed not solely by reference to auspicious moments, as determined by the Hindu almanac, but also must yield to the agricultural schedules of the principal families. Pilgrimages once undertaken with great liberality must now be handled more circumspectly, either by going shorter distances, by staying away fewer days, or by leaving key members of the work force behind. Major village festivals and rituals no longer seem to genuinely set the pace and structure of the rural calendar but rather to be islands of cosmological stability amidst an increasingly hurried flow of production-related activities. (This cosmological stability cannot indefinitely survive these changed circumstances.) Even at the microscopic level, women frequently find themselves performing important ritual tasks on the run: while rushing to work on someone's fields, on the way to get water or firewood, or tending the family goats or sheep.[5] In sum, the traditional interactive rhythm of ritual and ecological periodicities is now increasingly penetrated and framed by the requirements of labor, energy, cash, and demand associated with the commercialization of agriculture. This is not just an incipient shift in the way people set their clocks and use their time, but also a shift in the way they talk about their lives and experience the flow of time, insofar as we can tell by looking at what they say as well as what they do. This shift, as well, looks as if it is not likely to be reversed.

The farmers of Maharashtra are not passive victims of the changes occurring in their agricultural world. However, here, as in other matters, they are not uniformly reflective about the causes, nor are they uniformly resourceful about how best to cope with new circumstances. In general, they find it difficult to avoid the ideological pressure (from government, city dwellers, agribusiness interests, and agricultural colleges) to turn themselves into progressive and modern (*ādhunik*) farmers. For those who are able to make the leap from mere subsistence to entrepreneurial farming (even on a small scale), such progressive ideology is meaningful and consistent with their success. For the poorer farmers, though, there is a painful contradiction between this modern image and the reality of their lives, in which just ensuring the water, labor, and credit to forestall disaster requires great initiative and energy. What it takes to achieve a reliable foothold in the world of commercial agriculture is not something that any farmer can easily discover and put into practice.

For all the variations among these farmers, their relationship to the changes that have been discussed in this paper is alike in two ways. They are all aware that the forces affecting their villages lie in systems of production, consumption, exchange, and politics that far transcend their immediate environments. They are also all engaged in vigorous, even frantic, efforts to master these changes. For the richer farmers, these efforts constitute the life-style of rural entrepreneurship; for the poorer ones trying to combine subsistence farming with small investments in commercial farming, they constitute a new form of subsistence agriculture.

Insofar as both richer and poorer farmers conduct a significant part of their agricultural work on poor soil, with few modernized tools, with unreliable water, and with an eye to ensuring adequate subsistence in grains and vegetables, much of their traditional knowledge is more critical to them than ever. But it is useful less as a bank to draw on for creative adaptations to new circumstances than as a secure framework from which to make forays into the risks, worries, and unknowns of the world of commercialized farming. Although the new kinds of knowledge are (uncertain) roads to wealth, the older kinds provide the surest way of surviving from day to day in many parts of rural India.

There is obviously no simple way to assess (especially in a quantitatively satisfactory manner) whether the sorts of changes I have described in the culture of agriculture in regions of India are to be regarded as constituting a net loss or a net gain. In part, such an assessment requires a debate about the meaning of cultural conservation that lies beyond the scope of this essay.[6] But let me end with two suggestions on this issue.

First, in my discussion of the content (or archive) of agricultural knowledge, I have tried to propose that there are specific reasons for regretting the loss of particular pieces of knowledge. In regard to the transformation of traditional agricultural epistemologies, one can certainly argue that the only valid justification for the wholesale violation and transformation of a traditional way of knowing is if it is accompanied by a widely shared and perceived increase in well-being for the communities whose mental life is being transformed. At least in those parts of rural India with which I am familiar, there is no evidence for such a positive change in general well-being. Indeed, from the point of view of smaller farmers, there is considerable evidence that they have to run faster and scramble harder just to maintain the level of living to which they were previously accustomed. Rural women of the poorer classes appear to pay the heaviest price, in terms of their health, energy, and morale, for the transformation of Indian rural life.

What this means in the broader perspective of the rediscovery of the past as adaptation for the future is not that we should become guardians of a bygone way of thinking, nostalgic for some past rural golden age. Instead, because the transformations we are looking at are part and parcel of a large, even inexorable, set of changes in Indian rural life, it means that we cannot examine the pros and cons of conservation in this domain of culture without examining the costs and benefits of change in the political economy of agriculture as a whole.

NOTES

An earlier (and shorter) version of this essay was presented at the Smithsonian Institution in June 1985. I am grateful to participants at that gathering whose comments and suggestions helped to clarify my argument. I am also grateful to Carla Borden for her own comments and queries on an earlier draft, which also have helped me to sharpen this statement.

1. Although the exact degree to which the *jajmānī* system functioned as a sort of insurance system for poorer rural folk during periods of crisis is not clear, it does appear that such security as it represented is being rapidly undermined as land controllers increasingly turn to regional labor markets to meet their needs, and agrarian laborers are forced to widen their own alternatives to patron-centered modes of livelihood.

2. This essay is based on fieldwork conducted in Maharashtra in 1981–82,

with support from the American Institute of Indian Studies, the National Science Foundation, and the Social Science Research Council. It draws mainly on a collection of essays, now in preparation, called *Improvisation and Experience in an Agricultural Society*. Some of these essays are referred to below.

3. This essay, "The Terminology of Measurement in Rural Maharashtra," has also served as the starting point for a project supported by the Joint Committee on South Asia of the American Council of Learned Societies and the Social Science Research Council, which will eventually lead to an edited collection of essays by scholars from several disciplines on agricultural discourse in South Asia.

4. I have explored this theme more extensively in the essay "Time and Timing in an Agricultural Society," which will be included in the collection referred to in note 2.

5. The phenomenological situation of poorer rural women is discussed at greater length in an essay entitled "Dietary Improvisation in an Agricultural Society" by this author, which will appear in a collection of essays on diet and domestic structure being edited by Anne Sharman, Ellen Messer, Janet Theophano, and Karen Curtis.

6. The problem of conservation is dealt with somewhat more fully in Appadurai, "Technology and the Reproduction of Values in Western India," in *Development and Technological Transformation: Alternative Approaches*, S. Marglin and F. Marglin, eds. (Tokyo: United Nations University, forthcoming).

REFERENCES CITED

Appadurai, Arjun
  1984a   How Moral Is South Asia's Economy: A Review Essay. *Journal of Asian Studies* 43, no. 3: 481–97.

  1984b   Wells in Western India: Irrigation and Cooperation in an Agricultural Society. *Expedition* 26(3): 3–14.

Bourdieu, Pierre
  1977   *Outline of a Theory of Practice*. Cambridge, England: Cambridge University Press.

Durkheim, Émile
  1964   *The Division of Labor in Society*. New York: The Free Press. (French original, 1893)

Foucault, Michel
1982   *The Archaeology of Knowlege and the Discourse on Language.*
New York: Pantheon Books.

Scott, James C.
1976   *The Moral Economy of the Peasant: Rebellion and Subsistence in Southeast Asia.* New Haven: Yale University Press.

Wallace, Anthony F. C.
1974   *Culture and Personality.* New York: Random House.

CHAPTER 12

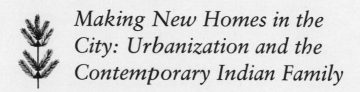 *Making New Homes in the City: Urbanization and the Contemporary Indian Family*

Sylvia Vatuk

The growth of Indian cities, both by natural increase and by the movement of individuals and families from rural to urban areas, constitutes one of the most dramatic social transitions occurring in India in recent decades. Although still a largely rural country, with over 76 percent of the population living in places of under 5,000 inhabitants and of predominantly agricultural livelihood, India has 12 cities of over 1 million inhabitants and more than 150 cities of over 100,000. By international standards, the rate of urbanization—in the sense of the increase in the relative proportion of urban to rural population—has been relatively slow in India. That proportion rose from approximately 16 percent in 1951 to a still modest 23.3 percent in 1981. But in absolute terms, the scale of urban growth has been enormous. The urban population is increasing at a considerably more rapid rate than the population of the country as a whole and has doubled in size within the space of twenty years. In 1981, almost 160 million Indians lived in places defined as *urban* by the Census of India, and of these 42 million lived in the 12 largest metropolitan centers.[1]

Migration from rural to urban areas is responsible for a large part of this urban population growth (Bose 1973; de Souza 1978). Although patterns and causes of urban migration differ by region, by social stratum within a region, and by city of destination as well, rural migrants by and large come to the city seeking better economic opportunities than exist for them at home. And despite the prevalence in India's cities of widespread unemployment and underemployment, and severe shortages of adequate housing, water supplies, and sanitation facilities, these places nevertheless serve as destinations of promise, for both the rural poor and the upwardly mobile rural elite (see, for example, Singh and de Souza 1980; Connell et al. 1976; Zachariah 1968).

One of the central questions for those concerned with the social impact of urbanization is how it changes the structure of the family and other primary social groups characteristic of the small, face-to-face communities from which rural migrants come. This issue was of great importance to social critics and scholars in Europe and America in the late nineteenth and early twentieth centuries. At that time, the predominant tendency was to see urbanization as a generally disruptive, disorganizing, and personally alienating force. In the literature of Western sociology, discussions of the nature of urban life and of the impact of urbanization upon migrants from rural areas often emphasize such points as the impersonality of social relations within the city, the fragility, shallowness, and temporary quality of interpersonal contacts, and the lack of an effective moral community that can set standards for behavior and enforce them.[2] On the family specifically, the literature stresses such processes as the rise of individualism, the decline of family loyalty and mutual responsibility, the fragmentation of extended kinship units, and the undermining of the stability of the marriage bond, upon which the existence of the traditional family unit depends (see, for example, Goode 1963).

In recent years, this image of the consequences of urbanization for family life has been modified somewhat, as research findings from American and European cities alike have revealed the extent of persistence of meaningful interpersonal relationships, neighborhood cohesion, and strong family ties, even under today's conditions of extensive social and geographic mobility.[3] At the same time, however, the tendency to view with some pessimism the fate of the urban family has carried over into the thinking of many Western scholars as they contemplate the probable social consequences of the current urban transformation in developing countries, such as India (see Goode 1963).

But pessimism on this score is not so readily apparent in the thinking of most Indians about the future of their own family system. Outsiders in India are continually engaged in discussions about social and cultural differences between their own country and that of their hosts. Regardless of the social class or education level of those raising the subject, a common theme in the comparisons offered is the relative closeness of Indian family ties—in contrast to those perceived to exist in the West—and the greater degree to which Indians take seriously their obligations to aid and comfort members of their family and other kin in time of need, particularly in old age, even when the fulfillment of such obligations can only be accomplished at the price of considerable self-sacrifice. No thoughtful Indian observer of the contemporary urban scene would totally overlook or belittle the fact that the institution of the family is vulnerable to the impact of social and economic transformations currently underway in that country; nevertheless, the outside observer gains the distinct impression of widespread confidence that the fundamental cultural basis of Indian family life is strong enough not only to withstand the dramatic social transitions that are occurring and will continue to occur in the society at large but also to contribute positively to the form that these transitions ultimately take. This way of thinking about the future of the contemporary Indian urban family ought not be quickly dismissed as ill-founded complacency, it seems to me, but should be considered very seriously. I shall endeavor to do this here, by exploring the roots of such an attitude, showing how old patterns and values are adapted to the needs and demands of new circumstances, and assessing the extent to which confidence in the survival of the Indian family is well placed.

When Indians speak of the family, they speak not of an individual couple with their children, but rather of a potentially much larger group of closely related men, their wives, and their children, sharing property, work, food, and love among them.[4] The men in this family ideally own some kind of productive property in common: land, tools of a trade, a shop or business. All of its members are thought of as contributing their labor—according to sex, age, and special ability—to the common endeavor, each expecting to have his or her individual needs met from the common store or purse, whose disbursements are under the management of a senior man or woman of the family. If some work outside for wages or a salary, or in a business activity separate from that of the rest of the family, their earnings ought properly to be pooled—entirely or at least in large part—in the common family budget and shared among all, in the same way as are the products of cooperative effort on a family "estate." Harmony within the group is striven to be maintained by means of a clear and generally agreed-upon hierarchy of seniority, by respect for elders, and a complementary concern for and nurturance of the welfare and happiness of the young. Members of a family are expected as a matter of course to place the interests of the group above their personal desires—or, better phrased, to regard the good of the family as coterminous with their own best interests and priorities.[5]

In the Indian conception of family, it is thought best for the members not only to share their property, their labor, and their consumption, but also to live together under a single roof. If circumstances dictate that some members must live apart—as long as they do so not in rejection of family bonds, but in furtherance of them—the family may continue to be regarded as an undivided unit and to operate in most respects in much the same way as if all occupied a common residence.

Families organized as cooperative economic and residential units are clearly well suited to the labor and other requirements of landowning peasant farmers. Indeed, similar family structures have been observed in agricultural societies around the world (Goldschmidt and Kunkel 1971). Such families also are in a good position to pursue certain kinds of business or trade in urban as well as rural settings. Roles in a productive enterprise can be assigned to members of a family according to their particular talents, and individuals can be selected for special training or assignments according to the needs of the firm at any given time. The trustworthiness of key employees is assured by family loyalty, and flexibility and adaptiveness to changing circumstances can be readily achieved.[6] The advantages are less obvious in the case of families that own little or no land or other productive resources. For those who must work for wages in the fields of others, or who are engaged in service or artisan occupations for which productive capital is limited to a few simple tools, a man and wife, possibly together with their minor children, form an effective and sufficient work team. The savings created by joint living and group preparation and consumption of food may not outweigh the costs of interpersonal conflict, competition, and tension. Since people in circumstances like these make up by far the majority of India's rural and urban populations, it is to be expected that the number of families actually attaining under one roof the potential size and complexity envisioned in the foregoing conception of the family must always have been relatively small. Demographic factors also militate against the large, multigenerational, extended family household becoming a predominant or even a common phenomenon. Most couples, under the mortality conditions existing in India until recent decades, would not succeed in raising more than one or two sons to adulthood, and few in the past lived to see the birth of great-grand-children. Most families, in fact, even in premodern times, would be unable to resist indefinitely the consequences of interpersonal tensions and conflicts of interest that are inevitable in real-life families structured in this way. Thus at some point there is a formal partition of family property and the establishment of two or more separate new families—each of which again strives toward the attainment and perpetuation of the larger family as a harmonious, cooperating, coresidential unit.[7]

Despite the actual stresses and strains of daily family life, the notion that a proper family is one that includes more than simply a married couple and their children pervades the thinking of Indians at all social levels and in all kinds of particular circumstances. The idea that when a young man marries he ought to remain with his parents and be joined in their household by the wife they have selected for him is likewise widely shared. This is the case even in those regions or social strata in which it is generally acknowledged that, in practice, such arrangements rarely survive more than a year or two beyond the wedding. The conviction that it is an able-bodied son's most sacred duty to take on the responsibility of his aged parents' support is also taken as axiomatic, even by those who, because of extreme poverty, must someday make the painful decision to feed the coming generation rather than repay their debt of life to the former.

It has been estimated that at least half of the observed growth of Indian cities over the past decades has been due to migration from rural areas. Let me begin, then, to talk about the family in the context of the migration process. It should be noted from the start that, in India, migration to the city involves primarily young adults and, for most regions of the country, predominantly males. This latter fact is reflected in the sex ratios of Indian cities, especially those located in the north and central regions, some of which have as few as six to eight women for every ten men (Bose 1973; Connell et al. 1976). An obvious implication of this migration pattern is that a significant proportion of recent migrants—and many of longer standing as well—are living not only apart from their own families but outside of a family setting altogether. However, many of those who come to the cities as unattached men join an existing household of relatives upon their arrival, or are assisted by relatives to find accommodations close by so that they can enjoy some of the advantages of regular interaction with kin.

A typical pattern in the move to the city is for a young single or recently married man to migrate in search of work or educational opportunities, leaving other family members—including wife and children, if any—in the rural home. Rarely is such a move an individual undertaking, nor is it typically seen as an opportunity to start a new, independent life. The decision for the move is, in the most usual instance, a family decision: The young man is *sent* to seek the family's fortune, rather than *leaving* the family to seek his own. Furthermore, the young man typically travels to the city—literally and figuratively—along routes trodden earlier by other family members, relatives, fellow villagers, or caste members. The way has very likely been prepared in advance: a place to stay and a promising job or small business venture lined up. It is quite clear from studies of urban migrants at all socioeconomic levels in India that a pattern of chain migration is the rule. Those who migrate choose cities where others of their kin and acquaintance network have gone before, even if these places are at a far greater distance than other cities toward which they might have headed. They then tend to settle in neighborhoods of the city, and to enter employment in occupations or in particular industries or firms, where others of their own kin group, or at least of their own caste and/or rural locality, are already established. Such migration is thus facilitated in more than one respect by family and other primary social ties. Rather than involving a break with the family and with other face-to-face relationships, urban migration and the subsequent adaptation to urban life typically *use* the family and kin and village networks as indispensible aids in accomplishing these processes (see, for example, Rowe 1973; Vatuk 1972).

Once the migrant has arrived in the city, it is rare for him to allow connections with the family to lapse. Whatever economic stratum he may occupy, it is expected that he will live as frugally as he can in order to save money to send to his family regularly, or on special occasions when funds are needed, as for the marriage expenses of a sister, a brother's or nephew's school fees, the repair of the family home, or the installation of a water pump. He will typically visit the village as often as possible, and at the minimum attempt to be present there for major holidays and ceremonials and at times of emergency. He will try to take leave from his job during the harvest season, if the family owns agricultural land. And he will surely be called upon after a time to make efforts—as people earlier did for him—to facilitate the migration of others to the city.

If the migrant has come with his wife, or if she has been permitted by the family to join him later in the city, his new household may soon require most of the man's earnings for its own maintenance, and remittances to the village will be reduced. But at this stage as well, the notion that the migrant household is merely a branch or outpost of the larger, rural-based family tends to persist. Efforts on the migrant's part to fulfill at least some of his obligations for the aid and support of other family members are rarely abandoned altogether, however meager his resources, unless he is totally destitute himself. Even if a man has no cash to send, he may be able to help by taking in other relatives or family members on a temporary or permanent basis. Eventually he may expect to accommodate his aging parents—or one widowed parent no longer able to fend for him or herself in the village home.

The flow of goods and services between the urban and rural households of such a family is of course not only in one direction. When the family in the village is engaged in cultivation, the migrant will certainly receive some quantities of grain, clarified butter, or other foodstuffs to supplement his diet, as long as the rural household has anything to spare from its own requirements. His children who live with him in the city will be welcome in the village home during school vacations or when recovering from illness, so that they may benefit from the fresh air of the countryside and the love of their kin there. In these and other ways, the family as an idea and as an ongoing social entity endures in its essentials, though distance separates some of its members.

Yet it cannot be denied that physical separation takes its toll on family relationships. Authority patterns within the larger family inevitably weaken as sons become accustomed to operating in the new milieu without the guidance or direction of the older generation. Daughters-in-law become accustomed to running their own household and chafe at the close supervision exercised by their husband's mother when they return for visits to the village. Standards of behavior and ways of spending leisure time differ between city and village. Women experience enhanced freedom of movement in the city, away from the watchful eyes of the mother-in-law and other senior village women, and often begin to question the necessity for observing in their stricter forms the female modesty practices current in the rural setting from which they have come. Married couples find in their separation from the larger family either an opportunity for growing intimacy and closeness, or conditions in which latent tensions and incompatibility, no longer cushioned by the perpetual presence of others, begin to lead to serious marital conflict and confrontation. The supervision of children becomes a heavier and more taxing burden, particularly for women. No longer does a mother have other closely related women in the same household or nearby with whom she can share child-raising responsibilities. It is difficult to monitor the associations and activities of the young, especially of young boys, who can escape with ease the eyes of those to whom they are known, and it is problematic to socialize children to adhere to parental values in those crowded and physically substandard shantytown areas of the major Indian cities where high proportions of the poorer rural migrants perforce settle upon their arrival in the city. The heterogeneous urban environment often seems threatening under such circumstances.

For those somewhat better off in the urban economic system, the new emphasis upon education requires parents, and especially mothers, to develop new skills in order to satisfactorily monitor their children's progress in school. Because of the structure of the urban workday and the nature of male employment activities, most fathers who hold formal-sector jobs are not able to train their sons to follow in their own occupational footsteps. In the poorer sectors of the population, the necessity for women as well as men to enter gainful employment, typically in marginal, irregular, informal-sector activities that offer little remuneration, means a general lack of supervision for much of the day for children beyond the nursing stage, and the early assumption by older children, particularly girls, of household and child-care responsibilities for younger siblings. In spite of aspirations for the education of children, they, too, are commonly pushed into income-generating activities at an early age. These are only some random examples of the kinds of adjustment problems faced by newly urbanizing families within their own household unit and vis-à-vis the larger family of which, in some respects at least, they continue to consider themselves a part.

In the observations I have made thus far, I have not attempted to deal systematically with the issue of the socioeconomic heterogeneity of Indian migrants or of the cities to which they come. In rural India, communities are of course highly stratified, in terms of caste, economic status, and in other respects as well. In the cities, economic differentials are intensified and their range broadened, so that one finds vast extremes of wealth and poverty. Those in the former category, and even those who live a relatively secure and comfortable existence, make up a very small proportion of the urban population. Although I have tried to speak of the "typical" urban migrant, it should not be forgotten that a great number of migrants come from the poorest segments of the rural population and enter the cities at the bottom of the urban hierarchy as well, most of them never to rise significantly within it.

The problem of measuring the extent of poverty in urban India is immense, technically as well as methodologically. Various estimates, most using some arbitrary income level as a poverty line, are available and suggest that the proportion of urban inhabitants living in poverty is as high as 50 percent on the average for all cities and considerably higher in some (see Dandekar and Rath 1971). But it has to be stressed that a large additional segment of the urban population, though having incomes above the very low official minimums, are nevertheless also living under conditions of extreme economic distress. A significant proportion of the poor consists of rural migrants or first-generation descendants of such migrants. For these people, however much they desire to maintain the priority of bonds of mutual caring and interdependence, the institution of the family is subject to special stress. Increasingly, observers of the urban poor report the incidence of such manifestations of family disorganization as family violence, abandonment by men of wives and children, and neglect of the aged.[8]

A key source of pride in the Indian family system is the provision it makes for the care of the aged within the home setting. Policy makers and social scientists in India until very recently have given little or no attention to the question of whether urbanization and other "modernizing" forces may be undermining this established system of old-age security. The failure to perceive the elderly as a population at special risk within the modern social context is consistent with the overall confidence in the strength and resilience of the traditional Indian family that I have alluded to earlier. But it is related to other factors as well: the relatively small proportion of the total population currently in the elderly age group and the large number of other social problems placing demands on limited public and private resources.

People sixty years of age and older in India constituted in 1981 only 6.2 percent of the total population—not much when one compares it with the situation in the United States and other Western industrialized countries. However, this 6.2 percent amounts to over forty-two million people.[9] The elderly are somewhat more heavily represented in rural than in urban areas in India, as a consequence of the fact that migration to cities involves primarily young adults. Furthermore, there is some return migration from urban to rural areas of old people who have spent their working lives in the city but prefer to pass their later years in more familiar and congenial surroundings. The aged left behind in the wake of the urbanization process, or returning to villages and leaving their children to earn in the city, face obvious problems of adjustment, living as they often must without the close presence of those who by rights should be their source of comfort and attention in their declining years. Even when the decision to send a son to the city has been made by the parents themselves, and even when the migrating young man has every intention and makes every effort to send some money home, his physical absence cannot but present difficulties for his elderly parents. But it is not only those left behind by city-bound children who are affected by the urban transition. Within the cities, the aged are especially vulnerable to the changing social conditions and changing culture of the family. Ironically, their special vulnerability arises in part out of strains that have always been present in the Indian family system as it is culturally constituted.

Every family system must provide for the smooth transfer of responsibility and control from one generation to the next. In India, such provision is embedded in the conceptualization of the individual life course as a series of stages (*āśramas*), each with its appropriate social role and mode of conduct. The central stage of life in this scheme is that of the householder—the married adult in his or her active years. In this period a man and woman are sexually active and economically productive; they concern themselves with family and community affairs. When their sons marry and begin to have children of their own, a couple ideally should turn over management of the household to the younger generation and enter another stage of life, in which they withdraw from worldly endeavors and devote themselves increasingly to spiritual matters. In this model, the notion that the parent-child relationship involves long-term reciprocity is central. A son takes on the burden of the family and of his parents' support in repayment of their nurturance of him in infancy and childhood. The parents, during their years as householders, earn the right to expect, and even demand, shelter, attentive care, and deference from their offspring. They depend upon their son and his wife to provide for their needs in later years. But this is not considered the dependence of the weak and helpless. Older persons perceive themselves as having handed over household responsibility of their own free will at an appropriate point in life, in order to rest and receive their rightful due from those they have cared for during the preceding years (see, for example, Prabhu 1963; Vatuk 1980).

Although the conceptualization of this life transition makes it possible, in theory, for aging to be welcomed as a respite from the more onerous aspects of adulthood, the transition for many individuals is not so easily accomplished in practice. As they age, men and women frequently experience difficulty giving up control over family resources and the activities of family members and find it hard to maintain harmonious interpersonal relationships with sons and daughters-in-law. The problem of keeping a sense of self-esteem in the face of their declining ability to contribute materially to the family's subsistence is in practice a difficult one. Urban migration and the conditions of urban living—especially for the majority, those who are poor and living in crowded housing—create an environment in which the underlying tensions between the generations, inherent in the family system under the best of circumstances, fester and eventually break into confrontations, causing distress for both the elderly and their children, and in extreme cases even the neglect or abandonment of aged parents.

It should be emphasized that the few studies that have been carried out by social scientists on the situation of the elderly in India show that by and large the aged continue to find homes with their offspring— usually with sons—or with other close kin. Institutional facilities for the care of the elderly are almost nonexistent in India. Surveys have revealed that only a very small proportion of the elderly live alone, whether in rural or urban areas. And of those who do maintain an independent household (most of them are women), many live very close to one or more of their adult children and/or are supported financially by children who may live elsewhere (Vatuk 1982). However, there is considerable evidence that, for many of the elderly, the material and psychological circumstances of their lives are less than ideal. There are several kinds of social changes that seem particularly detrimental to the elderly and the families in which they live in urban areas. These may indeed point to more serious and widespread problems in the future.

First, because of migration of the young from rural areas and widespread geographical mobility within and between cities, it is increasingly the case that the three-generation families noted by observers as still prevalent in urban India are no longer located in the old person's own home. Rather, the older person, in a growing number of instances, joins the established household of his or her son and son's wife at a late stage in life. Thus, although the household appears to conform to the traditional pattern of the family, in fact the internal dynamics of the group, the distribution of authority and control over resources, is very different. The delayed and voluntary transfer of control from the senior to the junior generation does not occur, since the parent enters the child's home as a dependent from the start. Other kinds of changes in the structure of the urban family are also related to increasing mobility of the population: It is becoming common for parents to choose, or to be forced, to circulate among the households of two or more offspring, rather than establish a permanent home with one. Such arrangements provide a means of sharing the responsibility for the care of aged parents among a set of brothers who do not live together and may even live in different cities. No one brother may be willing or financially able to assume full responsibility on a permanent basis, and none may be in a position to contribute regularly in cash to enable one of their number to keep the parents in his home all year round. Consequently each agrees to take the parents in for a few months at a time. Another novel kind of adaptation is for parents to live with a daughter. In the traditional system, this was considered shameful, in large part because in such a case the daughter's husband and his family would become one's actual source of support, and on these people one had no rightful claim for food and shelter. Even old people with no sons would prefer to make an arrangement with more distant relatives, or to live on their own in their home village, rather than become dependent upon a married daughter. The persistence of cultural ideas such as these about the proper kind of living arrangements in old age continues to present problems of self-respect for those who live with married daughters, and, although increasingly common, they are still regarded as something of an anomaly.

Secondly, the new economic order, in which each individual earns his or her own wages, creates difficulties for the budgetary management of a complex family household. Since the household is no longer a productive unit, but rather only a consumptive one, there is much scope for conflicts over the relative contribution of different earning members to the expenses of the household. And the contributions of those who do not earn cash incomes are likely to be overlooked when their rights of consumption are being assessed. My own research on families of the elderly has shown that in those that are economically relatively well off, it is common for the elderly to be expected to meet all household expenses out of their own resources, whereas earning sons retain their own money, or most of it, for their own needs and those of their wives and children; this practice is tolerated by the elderly because it provides a motive for the young to remain in the family. In poor families, on the other hand, the old find that they must stay in the work force beyond the point that they are really physically able to do so, because their sons are unable or unwilling to assume the burden of their support. When they must finally cease to earn, they have no resources to fall back upon, and their sense of helpless dependency is severe (see, for example, Goldstein et al. 1983).

New ideas disseminated in the urban environment are a third cause of strain for the old person within the family setting. The most direct in their impact upon the role of the elderly are those that relate to parent-child relations. Although most sons still readily acknowledge their duty to support elderly parents and to share their home with them, they no longer feel that it is obligatory for adult children to obey parents in all matters, especially those about which they feel that the older generation is insufficiently informed, because of lack of education or urban experience. At best, young men will consult parents and listen respectively to their opinions but then feel free to act according to their own judgment.

Finally, new standards of behavior, new ways of spending time and money, and the like provide specific sources of conflict between the generations. Disagreement over these frequently results in the kind of confrontation between parents and adult children that generally would not have been openly expressed in the past. Unless the old are prepared to remain silent and suppress their feelings of disapproval before the young, they risk being subjected to verbal argument and contradiction that within their cultural framework constitute the antithesis of appropriate modes of intergenerational communication.

In all of these ways, families of older people are affected by the social transitions taking place in urbanizing India. The impact of changes in economic structure, geographic mobility, education, and cultural values is felt at all social and economic levels. But for the poor, and especially for the poor migrants of recent rural origin, these changes are most threatening to the time-tested system of old-age security, because aged members of these families have no material base of power that can be used to enforce compliance and devotion from their offspring in the face of adverse circumstances.

It is quite evident that the strengths of the Indian family system are considerable and that the family can and does serve to cushion many of the potentially adverse effects of urbanization on the existing social order. But it is a mistake to think that concerns about the future of the family are completely inappropriate in an Indian cultural context, given the material conditions under which millions of urbanites in that country live today. What the solutions might be, it is not easy to say; but promulgating more widespread awareness of what the future may have in store is at least a necessary first step.

NOTES

1. Figures from *Census of India, 1981,* cited in *Statistical Outline of India 1984* (Bombay: Tata Services Limited, 1984), 43–47.

2. The classic statement is that of Louis Wirth, "Urbanism as a Way of Life" (1938).

3. For the United States the work of E. Litwak in the 1950s marked the beginning of questioning by sociologists of the disintegration of the family and kinship ties under industrial urbanization. See his "Extended Kin Relations in an Industrial Democratic Society" (1960).

4. For a discussion of indigenous cultural conceptions about the family in one region of India, see Inden and Nicholas 1977.

5. There is a large literature on Indian family structure; some useful works giving an Indian perspective are Desai 1964; Shah 1974; Madan 1965.

6. As shown by M. Singer's study of business and industrial families in Madras, for example (see Singer 1968).

7. For a discussion of demographic constraints on joint family formation, see Collver 1963. The work of Freed and Freed provides a useful case study of the processes of family formation, partition, and reformation, within a demographic context, and under the pressure of urbanization, in a North Indian village over the past twenty-five years, that is relevant to the present essay. See their "Urbanization and Family Types in a North Indian Village" (1969).

8. Recent studies of slum and shantytown settlements in various Indian cities include Singh and de Souza 1980; Desai and Pillai 1972; Ramachandran 1972; Wiebe 1975.

9. *Census of India, 1981.* For a discussion and data on trends in the growth of the aged population in India, see Mukherjee 1976, and also my "Old Age in India" (1982).

REFERENCES CITED

Bose, Ashish
   1973   *Studies in India's Urbanization: 1901–1971.* Bombay: Tata McGraw-Hill.

Collver, Andrew
   1963   The Family Cycle in India and the United States. *American Sociological Review* 28:89–96.

Connell, John, et al.
   1976   *Migration from Rural Areas: The Evidence from Village Studies.* Delhi: Oxford University Press.

Dandekar, Vishnu Mahadeo, and Nilakantha Rath
   1971   *Poverty in India.* Bombay: Indian School of Political Economy.

Desai, Akshayakumar Ramanlal, and S. D. Pillai
   1972   *A Profile of an Indian Slum.* Bombay: University of Bombay.

Desai, I. P.
   1964   *Some Aspects of Family in Mahuva.* New York: Asia Publishing House.

de Souza, Alfred
   1978   The Challenge of Urban Poverty: An Introduction. In *The Indian City: Poverty, Ecology and Urban Environment,* edited by A. de Souza, xiii–xxix. New Delhi: Manohar.

Freed, Ruth S., and Stanley A. Freed
   1969   Urbanization and Family Types in a North Indian Village. *Southwestern Journal of Anthropology* 25:342–59.

   1982   Changing Family Types in India. *Ethnology* 21:189–202.

Goldschmidt, Walter, and Evalyn Jacobson Kunkel
   1971   The Structure of the Peasant Family. *American Anthropologist* 73:1058–76.

Goldstein, Melvin C., et al.
   1983   Social and Economic Forces Affecting Intergenerational Relations
             in Extended Families in a Third World Country: A Cautionary
             Tale from South Asia. *Journal of Gerontology* 38:716–24.

Goode, William J.
   1963   *World Revolution and Family Patterns*. New York: Free Press.

Inden, Ronald B., and Ralph W. Nicholas
   1977   *Kinship in Bengali Culture*. Chicago: University of Chicago
             Press.

Litwak, Eugene
   1960   Extended Kin Relations in an Industrial Democratic Society. In
             Social Structure and the Family, edited by E. Shanas and G. F.
             Streib, 290–325. Englewood Cliffs, N.J.: Prentice-Hall.

Madan, T. N.
   1965   *Family and Kinship: A Study of the Pandits of Rural Kashmir*.
             Bombay: Asia Publishing House.

Mukherjee, Subhansu Bhusan
   1976   *The Age Distribution of the Indian Population: A Reconstruc-
             tion for the States and Territories*. Honolulu: East-West Center.

Prabhu, Pandharinath Hari
   1963   *Hindu Social Organization*. 4th ed. Bombay: Popular Praka-
             shan, 78–100.

Ramachandran, P.
   1972   *Pavement Dwellers in Bombay City*. Bombay: Tata Institute of
             Social Sciences.

Rowe, William C.
   1973   Caste, Kinship and Association in Urban India. In *Urban An-
             thropology*, edited by A. Southall, 211–50. New York: Oxford
             University Press.

Shah, A. M.
   1974   *The Household Dimension of the Family in India*. Berkeley and
             Los Angeles: University of California Press.

Singer, Milton
   1968   The Indian Joint Family in Modern Industry. In *Structure and
             Change in Indian Society*, edited by M. Singer and Bernard S.
             Cohn, 423–45. Chicago: Aldine.

Singh, Andre M., and Alfred de Souza
    1980   *The Urban Poor: Slum and Pavement Dwellers in the Major Cities of India.* New Delhi: Manohar.

Vatuk, Sylvia
    1972   *Kinship and Urbanization: White Collar Migrants in North India.* Berkeley and Los Angeles: University of California Press.

    1980   Withdrawal and Disengagement as a Cultural Response to Aging in India. In *Aging in Culture and Society,* edited by C. L. Fry, 126–48. New York: J. F. Bergin.

    1982   Old Age in India. In *Old Age in Preindustrial Society,* edited by P. N. Stearns. New York: Holmes and Meier.

Wiebe, Paul D.
    1975   *Social Life in an Indian Slum.* Delhi: Vikas.

Wirth, Louis
    1938   Urbanism as a Way of Life. *American Journal of Sociology* 44:1–24.

Zachariah, K. C.
    1968   *Migrants in Bombay.* Bombay: Demographic and Research Centre.

CHAPTER 13

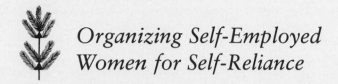

Organizing Self-Employed Women for Self-Reliance

Ela R. Bhatt

Here is a story of people making their headway in the streams of national development while constantly defending their rightful place in the economy and the society. They are the self-employed women of India. I have been involved with their movement from the beginning, and I would like to give you some account of their work and struggles to achieve self-reliance, economically and mentally.

SEWA (Self-Employed Women's Association; also *service* in many Indian languages) is an organization in Ahmedabad, in the state of Gujarat, of 22,745* self-employed women workers. Having grown out of the Women's Wing of the Textile Labour Union in Ahmedabad, it is a registered trade union in its own right. Gandhian thinking is the guiding force for us. We visualize a society in which capital and labor are dispersed, and none is deprived of the capital needed to survive. We operate primarily through joint action of labor unions and cooperatives, and our goals are to organize and create visibility for self-employed women, enabling them to receive higher wages and to have control over their own income. SEWA has spread into six other states as well, and has reached a total of about 40,000* women workers.

---

*Figures apply to 1985.

With this brief background, let me begin with some profiles of the self-employed women and the reality of their situation.*

• A vegetable vendor borrows fifty rupees (four dollars) from a private moneylender early in the morning, buys vegetables, trades in them the whole day, and afterwards returns fifty-five rupees to the moneylender. This goes on day after day. Three generations ago her family had their own land in the village, grew vegetables there, and would make daily trips to the city to sell their produce. The ruler at that time had given a very large market space to the vegetable vendors. But with the coming of textile mills and other industrial units, it gradually was taken over by residential houses and retail shops. Today she and the other vendors are literally pushed into the street.

• A patchworker gets rags of textile-mill waste from a private trader to stitch into quilt covers, using her own sewing machine, thread, and labor. She is paid eight rupees per quilt cover and is able to stitch six of them a day.

• A junksmith buys metal scrap and waste from a scrap dealer to make crude pots, containers, and other household utility items. Working with primitive tools, she must hammer twenty to thirty times just to cut a hole in a metal sheet.

• A farm laborer toils eight to ten hours a day and earns ten rupees. Agricultural work provides income for only a few months of the year, thus making her vulnerable to indebtedness and consequent passive acceptance of low wages to repay loans. Up until the last decade, her family wove cloth for their own consumption and also for sale during the slack season. However, the growth of the textile industry in Ahmedabad and other parts of Gujarat took away much of the handloom weavers' market and their access to yarn for weaving. Most of them have become farm laborers; some migrate to the city and make a living picking wastepaper from the streets.

The list of trades is long, the examples of self-employed are numerous. But these illustrations describe the plight of a vast number of economically active women who are the invisible workers of the nation, and also of the world. They rarely own capital or tools of production, they have no direct link with organized industry and services, and they have no access to modern technology or facilities. All they possess are the skills and knowledge of their trade and their physical labor. They constitute the majority of the enormous population of self-employed workers, normally called the *unorganized sector*. In India, only 6

---

*The monetary figures given are based on 1985 exchange rates, Rs. 12.5 = $1.00.

percent of working women are in organized industry and services; the remaining 94 percent are left to fend for themselves.

SELF-EMPLOYMENT

A major form of work and of earning a livelihood in our country, *self-employment* is usually meant to include individuals who work independently to produce goods and/or services that are sold for a price. (*Employment,* on the other hand, generally defines people who work in regular salaried jobs for somebody else in an employer-employee relationship.)

Historically, the people in our country have been essentially self-employed. In traditional societies, most work is done on a subsistence level, each family having to provide its basic needs—food, clothing, shelter—from its own resources, and also usually by hand. Very few people work for others in an employer-employee relationship, although trading, artisanry, and priestly services, for instance, are performed for the community in a patron-client relationship. Among nomadic and tribal communities particularly, a strong relationship develops with nature and land, be it forest, oasis, or sea, or a pattern of *jhūm* (slash-and-burn) cultivation. This was India until the last century—and even today we find patches of such societies in some parts of the country.

With the industrial revolution, the modes of production shift from work being done by hand to work being done by machines, from work being done in individual homes to work being done in factories. More people, then, are forced into working for others. Concentration of resources increases rapidly in the hands of a few owners, and exploitation becomes rampant. The modern labor movement starts as a response to this rampant exploitation, and the state is influenced to protect those in employment, formulating and enforcing laws, rules, and regulations for them. The employer-employee relationship becomes more and more established, and organized industry, labor, and services become more and more significant in the economy. In India the trade unions, the laws pertaining to employer-employee relationships, and the role of the state in safeguarding the interests of the employees, have all been based on the models of the highly industrialized countries. In these countries, the process of industrialization has continued for over two hundred years and slowly brought most of the working population into regular salaried employment. The rules relating to employment thus ensure the interests of almost the whole working population.

India's traditional economy—only partially commercialized, largely agricultural and tribal, and subsistence based—has now had superimposed on it an industrial economy. The concentration of resources has made a large majority of the subsistence-oriented population resourceless, and the new technologies that are constantly coming into existence displace more and more of them. At the same time, since the economy as a whole has not become industrialized, everybody does not find regular salaried employment, and the labor movement has catered mainly to industrial labor. The situation is that today in our country only 11 percent of the working people are engaged in regular jobs with a recognized employer-employee relationship, the protection of the law, and the benefits of these. Eighty-nine percent must earn their livelihood by creating their own niche in the economy. If the strength of regular employment is security of work and money, this very substantial population has neither.

A subsistence economy gives equal recognition to the work of men and women; with commercialization, the work that can generate cash income becomes more highly valued. In addition, the new skills introduced by industrialization and mechanization have gone primarily to men, forcing the work of women into less and less skilled areas and making it seem less and less important. So women in particular have suffered from the changing economic structure, because they are self-employed workers and because they are women.

CULTURE OF SELF-EMPLOYMENT

Every form of work develops its own culture. In our traditional society, a strong underlying culture that is associated with self-employment has evolved through the ages. Small communities of people engaged in subsistence-oriented work were common, and direct communications with distant places were not possible. As a result, transactions, decisions, payments, and negotiations were accomplished with relatively few known people, face to face, fostering a sense of trust and allowing agreements to be verbal. In such a world there is no real need for the written word. You can live your life comfortably without feeling inadequate or helpless, dependent or exploited because you do not read and write, and our people for this reason have not felt handicapped by illiteracy. This is not to say that the written word was unknown in our traditional system—the scriptures were written, treasury accounts were written, the firmans ("decrees") of kings were written—but writing was only for a few.

Another important characteristic of the culture of self-employment is its sense of time. Fixed schedules, dates, and deadlines do not figure prominently in our traditional work system (although they do in our social life) except for the computation of auspicious hours for performing certain activities, occasions to mark the seasons, and festivals.

This culture of small communities has been affected by the processes of centralization—of larger and larger geographical areas coming under common administration (e.g., the formation of kingdoms and nations) and the establishment of large-scale commercial enterprises during the last fifty to seventy years—of industrialization, of growing employment as described above. What characterizes the new culture of employment is a different discipline with respect to time that is difficult for many to cope with, and written, impersonal dealings with unknown people that follow from the economic units of larger scale.

Although some of the work force have become integrated into this culture, the self-employed—who are mostly poor—are being forced to deal with the unfamiliar world of written transactions. Their illiteracy becomes a major handicap for them. They do not know how to get things done in this system, and they end up exploited. Do we realize the crucial reality of our people? Our SEWA women feel annoyed and sometimes afraid when they receive printed letters at home. "Don't you trust us, that you write letters to us?" they ask. All our programs and schemes for poverty alleviation, for development, for improving the lives of the people are planned assuming that everyone is familiar with the workings of written records, applications, evidence, and authentications. But this assumption is false. Naturally only those who know about and have access to them receive the benefits of the programs, and the people for whom the programs are really intended are at the mercy of the kingpins who are at home in both worlds, written and verbal.

How will we progress as a people, how will we tackle exploitation and the distance between the rich and the poor, unless we recognize the characteristics of our culture? Why do we impose formal structures on it and use them as the measure of our progress? We have to devise ways of making the verbal world valid even in officialdom, ways of keeping illiteracy from enabling our people to improve their lives and situations. We have to develop forums for the illiterate and literate to hold hands without exploitation.

SELF-EMPLOYED WORKERS

These people have been referred to by various names: *unorganized, informal, marginal, unregulated, peripheral, residual.* But such negative terms give them an inferior and insignificant position in the economy, whereas in fact they are in the center of it and contribute a great deal.

To give them positive status and to draw positive attention toward them, we call them *self-employed workers*.

Broadly speaking, there are three categories of self-employed workers: (1) small-scale vendors, petty traders, and hawkers, selling goods such as vegetables, fruits, fish, eggs and other staples, household goods, garments, and similar types of products; (2) home-based producers making such articles as *bidi*s (tobacco leaves rolled into cigarette form), *agarbatti*s (incense sticks), garments, small furniture, footwear, fabric, and handicrafts; and (3) laborers selling various kinds of services, including cleaning, laundering, catering, cooking, helping to care for the sick, or providing labor for construction, transportation, agriculture, or other activities.

The limited amount of data available makes it difficult to assess the size or composition of the self-employed sector. However, over the past several years SEWA has conducted a series of socioeconomic surveys of self-employed women. We have learned that for a great majority (78 percent), capital for initial financing and day-to-day operating costs is their own or comes from relatives, merchants, or private money lenders, not banks. Their daily earnings are minimal and hence many (60 percent) remain in a state of indebtedness. Most (78 percent) rent their means of labor such as *larri*s (handcarts). Despite long workdays, productivity is low because of a broad range of social, economic, and even legal constraints. Many are illiterate, and most (97 percent) live in temporary settlements in city slums. Twenty-one to 33 percent of the women are household heads, and children accompany 70 percent of them to the worksite. They have extremely limited access to raw materials, markets, training, and space for the production and/or sale of goods besides. In sum, the self-employed must work long days under difficult circumstances to eke out a bare minimum living.

The self-employed sector constitutes a substantial proportion of the urban work force (45 percent in Calcutta, 40 percent in Bombay, 55 percent in Ahmedabad). Millions of people then, mainly in the low-income groups (women, children, scheduled castes and tribes, and backward classes), are self-employed. Further, many of the goods and services consumed by the general population are provided by this sector. As such, there is ample justification for focusing on this group in programs aimed at expanding employment opportunities, increasing income, and raising productivity. Any labor movement worth its name must include them and help them share in the fruits of prosperity. And if we want to have a women's movement in India, all of the economically active women, whether they are rural or poor or work at home, should play a role.

We tried to organize self-employed women workers into a trade union, namely, the Self-Employed Women's Association, in 1972.

STRUGGLES FOR SELF-RELIANCE

The first struggle waged by SEWA was for its own registration under the Trade Union Act. "You cannot be a trade union," said the registrar of trade unions, "because you are not workers, you do not have an employer. Against whom are you going to agitate?" We argued, "A worker is not only an employee. A worker is a person who earns his or her living by his or her own effort without exploiting the labor of others." We pointed out as well that "a trade union is not always against an employer, but for the solidarity of the workers, for their own development. A worker is oppressed not only by an employer but by many other sections of society and vested interests." Ultimately the registrar accepted our defense and did register SEWA as a trade union. Today SEWA is affiliated with two internationals, the International Union of Food and Tobacco Workers, Geneva, and the International Farm Plantation Allied Workers, Geneva.

Vendors and Hawkers

Manekchowk is the main vegetable market of Ahmedabad city. Vendors and hawkers have been selling in Manekchowk square for the last three generations, each family in its traditional space. As the city has grown, the square has become more and more crowded, and pedestrians, cars, cycles, rickshaws, handcarts, and vendors jostle each other in the limited area. In January 1980, the city authorities decided to reduce the congestion by removing all of the vendors from the market. Hundreds of women were thus displaced from employment. They approached the authorities, but talks proved futile, as the authorities were determined to throw the vendors out. So the vendor sisters organized a satyagraha, occupying their places in peaceful defiance of the police orders. In spite of the strong opposition from the police, municipality, and large shopkeepers and traders, the vendors sat firmly united. Their defensive action won back their old place in Manekchowk.

But this was not a permanent solution. Three vendor leaders and SEWA had to file a writ petition to the Supreme Court in February 1982 seeking social justice for the vendors of Manekchowk. SEWA's plea was that we are an integral part of the market, having been there far longer than the shops, houses, buildings, and roads, and so we should be given license to vend there. Another demand was to make the market square a pedestrian zone, free of all vehicular traffic. The Supreme Court issued a stay order at the first hearing in 1982 and asked the Municipal Corporation to prepare a suitable scheme to seat the vendors in the market. A proposed model was discussed and mutually agreed upon. The 1984 judgment giving licenses and assuring space to each of the vendors in the existing market has proved a turning point in present urban policy with respect to the status of hawkers in big cities.

"We are giving a useful service to city dwellers," say the vendor sisters. "We are respectable traders, though small. We will not be treated as criminals." However, the negative attitudes toward them are deeply entrenched. The middle-class citizens look down upon the vendors as dirty, loud, and uncultured. The authorities and planners see them as nuisances and traffic obstructions rather than as a necessary part of the city. But the Supreme Court order at least has changed the behavior of the town planners. A new, modern market is being built in consultation with SEWA, in Manekchowk, for the vendors.

Defending Motherhood

Kankuben, twenty-five years old, is an agricultural laborer in a village in Ahmedabad district. She is in the ninth month of pregnancy but must continue to go to work to earn the daily meal for her family. When she feels her labor pains, she comes home and her sister-in-law calls the midwife. Kankuben has neither the time to go to the hospital—because she knows she must be back at work within a week—nor the money. The baby is born in unhygienic conditions and dies of tetanus. Kankuben is ill for many days and unable to work. There is little or sometimes no food in the house, and her children are hungry. When she does return to work she is weak and cannot earn much. Why should Kankuben and others like her be penalized for motherhood? How can they defend their right to have a child under proper medical care without foregoing their daily earnings?

SEWA feels that we as women are providing for the continuity of society, so motherhood should not be seen as a burden to be borne by women alone. With this conviction we went to the insurance companies and asked, "During the time of delivery a mother has to stop working and earning. Can you create a scheme that will protect her motherhood?" The insurance companies tried but in the end replied, "No, women are a high insurance risk and poor women particularly so, since so many of them die. We cannot afford to insure them unless we charge a very high premium." No other agency could help us. SEWA then started its own motherhood defense, the Maternity Benefit Scheme.

Mothers are provided cash for immediate expenditures, lost-work pay, medicines, and nourishment to replenish them after giving birth. The death rate among mothers under the scheme has fallen. The government of Gujarat subsequently adopted the scheme on a pilot scale for agricultural workers. We hope that motherhood defense will reach the working mothers all over the country.

Financial Services

Self-employed women face two most common economic problems: their means of production are hired, and they are short of capital. They are therefore always vulnerable to exploitation. During the early 1970s, our banks were nationalized, and that held out hope for the poor to obtain loans and credit.

But providing finances to the women was not simple. We were inexperienced and so were the banks, at that time lacking the conceptual clarity, technical know-how, and trained personnel to serve the poor. Along with our recommendations, there was continuous pressure from the central government for local banks to give loans to "small" borrowers, and so one of the major banks in Ahmedabad took the first step and made loans to about five hundred SEWA women; then many more banks followed suit. Nevertheless the members still faced a number of practical difficulties. There was the problem of bridging the gap between women in filthy clothes, accompanied by noisy children, and the bank staff, in their neckties and air-conditioned offices, who were used to educated, middle-class clients. Then the women's heavy schedule did not permit them to keep to banking hours. If the bank refused to accept payment at the time of day when the women were free to come, the money was spent—or too often deposited with the very wholesaler or moneylender from whose clutches SEWA was trying to rescue the women, who wanted to protect the loan money from the greedy eyes of their husbands or sons. In short, they had no secure place for their spare cash.

It became quite obvious to us that providing money from the bank was just a beginning. If the self-employed are really to be served, they should have not only credit facilities but also an institutional framework offering various other kinds of services that they sorely lack. The question before us was how to achieve this. At a meeting in December 1973, the members enthusiastically came forward with an answer: "a bank of our own" where they would be accepted in their own right and not made to feel inferior. "We are poor, but we are so many!" they said. With determination, four thousand women contributed share capital of ten rupees each to establish the Shri Mahila SEWA Sahakari Bank (Women's Cooperative SEWA Bank). The SEWA Bank was born against stiff opposition and resistance from the banking system. They thought that a bank for poor, illiterate, self-employed women—who in their view were undependable and not responsible for any financial decisions in their family—was a disastrous and suicidal attempt. "How can women who cannot even sign their name have a bank account?" they objected. We dealt with this by using photographs instead of signatures for identification—that is, a photograph of the borrower was pasted on her passbook and a copy of that photo was kept in the bank records instead of the specimen signature card. Through this device we avoid forgery or cheating and, in Gandhian fashion, also most non-violently eliminate the husband from managing his wife's account. Then, when the members found out that eleven promoters had to sign the registration papers, the illiterate group leaders sat up through a night to learn to write their names without error! In May 1974, the SEWA Bank was registered as a cooperative bank.

Since then we have shattered the existing myths about banking with poor, illiterate women and proved it to be a viable financial venture. At the end of 1984, SEWA Bank had 20,122 savings accounts (99 percent of holders are illiterate) with about one crore rupees as working capital. The loan repayment rate is more than 98 percent. The SEWA Bank and credit fund make available the other supportive services inevitably needed to make the loan productive: training in management of money, counseling in purchase and marketing of goods, legal aid, maternal protection, and life insurance. And most importantly, through their savings accounts, the bank provides the women a secure and exploitation-free way to control their own income.

A COMPLEX OF SEWA COOPERATIVES

The idea for organizing cooperatives originally grew out of our union's involvement in the struggles of women *chindi* (textile rag) workers, hand-block printers, and bamboo workers. After years of being victimized by merchants, over six hundred patchworkers organized in 1977 to pressure for payment of minimum wages. By all rights, this was not an unreasonable demand, and after a long series of negotiations a compromise was reached between the two groups. However, within twenty-four hours, the merchants broke the agreement. Not only did they refuse to pay the women the agreed-upon rate for sewing the *chindi*, they began to harass the workers by giving them bad materials to sew and less work, and in many cases withholding work from them altogether, especially those who were the sole supporters of their family. So with SEWA's backing, these women decided to start a production unit of their own. SEWA's work in organizing hand-block printers brought to light the serious dislocation they were facing due to a declining market for their traditional textile designs. In organizing bamboo workers, SEWA found that although they were highly skilled, the women were not making products and designs for which the modern market was expanding but instead were turning out crude products, which were sold to merchants at low prices. The women had no means to upgrade their skills so that they could produce goods with a high demand in the market and higher returns. Through our experience with these and other trade groups, the need became evident for alternative institutions through which poor, self-employed women can acquire skills, training, and assistance in marketing finished products, purchasing raw materials, securing storage and work space, and acquiring capital.

Sabina Chindi *Cooperative*

For years, Muslim *chindi* workers had been sewing for traders on dilapidated machines to make *khol*s (quilts) that fetched the trader low prices and brought the women low wages. SEWA conducted a survey of these women in the Dariyapur neighborhood in Ahmedabad and subsequently organized them to demand fair wages, with the consequences described above. They formed their own production unit, with just one 50-kilogram bag of *chindi,* in 1978. What began with a survey led to liberation of these Muslim women from vested interests.

Today the Sabina Cooperative has a shop in Dariyapur, right alongside the very merchants against whom they had fought. The shop is mostly managed by *khol* makers themselves.

Because the financial crisis in the textile industry has closed down mills, the cooperative has been facing difficulties in obtaining raw material, and thus in earning income. To overcome this problem, women are being trained in making fancy patchwork and applique items out of textile rags for the urban market. They continue to produce rag *khol*s for rural and urban poor when the raw material is available.

Block-Printers Cooperative, Aabodana

Aabodana consists of Chhipa Muslim women. Prior to the formation of the cooperative, the women were block-printing fabrics for wholesale traders. They worked at home, with the cloth, blocks, and dyes provided by the traders. The women were unaware of how the fabrics they produced were marketed or what price they fetched; they were just laborers paid at meager piece rates—one rupee for three bed covers—and they helplessly accepted this situation since their skills were so limited.

Along with the diminishing consumption of block-printed clothes by tribal men, for example, who switched from printed loincloths to trousers, and middle-class Bania women, who took to wearing plain white saris during mourning periods instead of block-printed saris, the advent of screen printing led to a real crisis for the block printers. The screen-printed fabrics have a far lower sale price because they can be mass produced. The block printers—all of them women—thus were rendered unemployed.

One of the block printers learned that SEWA Bank was offering loans to buy sewing machines. In an effort to find alternative employment, some Chhipa women came to SEWA for help. This prompted SEWA to take a survey of the block printers, and it revealed their appalling socioeconomic conditions. With the assistance of the All India Handicrafts Board, a training program was organized to broaden their skills. Despite resistance not only from the traders and the families of the women but initially the craftsmen, too, who were reluctant to impart the techniques of printing to women, they succeeded through the program in acquiring proficiency in the entire process of producing block-printed material, from mixing of dyes (including the use of vegetable dyes, a long-lost traditional craft) to postprinting processes.

Since the Chhipa women did not want to work again for the middlemen or sit at home unemployed, the next logical step for them was to form a production unit where they could work for insured regular income. The stage was set to convert this production unit into a cooperative.

Aabodana, registered in 1983, is run by a worker-manager aided by a team of cooperative members. They are working hard to get orders and sell directly to consumers also, and are hopeful of becoming financially self-sufficient.

Cane and Bamboo Cooperative, Baansri

A chance meeting with a woman from Bansfodia community (cane and bamboo workers) during a bus journey made by one of our SEWA organizers revealed the grim plight of this community. They were buying raw materials at high prices and getting minimal returns from the sale of their products, only three rupees per day. Home-based workers, they make primitive cane and bamboo articles like baskets and brooms. The bamboo they use is long, and their homes are tiny, so they had to sit on the roadside to work, causing some traffic obstruction and leading to police harassment. Apart from space, their problem is lack of access to raw material, since it is also used for industrial purposes. SEWA organized them to work in a group and created a training program for them in collaboration with the All India Handicrafts Board. They learned to make a variety of articles for the modern market, from pincushions and bangles to pieces of furniture. They have now formed themselves into a cooperative, registered in 1983, and they supply brooms and baskets to all government institutions and offices.

Paper-Pickers Cooperative, Sujata

For hundreds of Harijan women and children paper pickers on the streets, their work is an ordeal. The days are long, the physical strain great, and after it all their collection is bought at a low price by a trader who then makes a profiteering business by selling the wastepaper to large factories for recycling. Women felt they could form themselves into a cooperative with the support of SEWA, and Sujata was registered in 1982.

Although SEWA was successful in petitioning the state government to allow the cooperative to collect wastepaper directly from government offices and institutions, the cooperative still has to face persistent confrontations from vested interests. But the women have not given up. They have bought a place to store their wastepaper and compete with the traders. They will not sell their waste at throwaway prices!

Handloom Cooperative

Some of the paper pickers, who were migrants from villages from Mehsana district, Palanpur, and Banaskantha, were on the lookout for a different way to make a living. They were weavers, but economic circumstances had forced them to give up their traditional craft and become laborers. One of the weaver women made a request for assistance from SEWA Bank to restart her loom. Other women revealed that they also had looms at home, unused for lack of capital to buy raw material, or had had to sell the looms they once owned.

SEWA identified twenty-four women weavers from among the paper pickers, and they have come together to form a cooperative, which was registered in early 1984. As a cooperative, they are entitled to facilities from the state government in the nature of equipment, financial support, and marketing opportunities. A training program was organized at the All India Handicrafts Board Weaver's Service Centre to restore their craft and vocation to them and enhance their skill. SEWA Bank has provided them loans to buy looms and raw materials. The women are enthusiastic and self-confident. They are already looking for a place to build a shed and work collectively, and SEWA is exploring possibilities of getting work space from the Gujarat Industrial Development Corporation. The cooperative also has appealed to the Industries Department to plan for a weavers colony near the city.

Safaikam *(Cleaning) Cooperative, Saundarya Mandali*

When the National Institute of Design asked SEWA for the services of some women to clean their campus, thirty paper-picker women were organized for Saundarya Mandali, to give them a different means of employment as well as bargaining power. Their initial contract for three months was extended to one year.

The cooperative is in its fourth year. Women enter into cleaning contracts with private and public institutes, and by putting in three hours of work a day earn at least two hundred rupees per month. They have gained experience in working together, in different places, and have acquired the skills of systematic work in addition to training in a variety of cleaning processes.

MARKETING AND TRAINING

The cooperatives of the SEWA Economic Self-Reliance Wing are of basically two types: the cooperatives that sell services and the production-oriented cooperatives. For the former, SEWA helps in finding contracts. But for the latter, unless a marketing infrastructure is developed, the objective of finding alternative employment is not fully achieved.

SEWA Dastkari Bazaar, a unique market system, is now a regular feature of SEWA's program. Four times a year in different cities, artisans demonstrate their crafts and sell their products directly to consumers. The appreciation they get from the consumers is in itself unmatched as motivation; the opportunity for direct contact with the consumers also makes the artisans aware of the expectations, tastes, and reactions of their market, to help them modify and diversify their skills and products. SEWA cooperatives participate in this and other such exhibitions held in the country and market their products without the exploitative intervention of middlemen.

SEWA also has two shops in Ahmedabad, in Dariyapur and Ellis Bridge corner, serving as marketing outlets for the cooperatives' artisans.

As a result of several years of persistent efforts, a government of Gujarat resolution was passed in 1980 to the effect that all establishments under the government have to buy their goods and services from women's organizations; only when these organizations submit a certificate that the goods and services are unavailable through them can the government fill its needs from the open market. It has further helped the marketing of the services of cooperatives like Sujata and the products of cooperatives like Baansri. Since the resolution, the Hariayali Vegetable Unit has been supplying fruits and vegetables to all government institutions. This has given a large group of vendors a steady income and also saved them from police harassment in the marketplaces. Efforts are being made to include vegetable growers, who also happen to be women, in the unit. However, because the urban and rural jurisdictions are administered separately, bringing the two together poses technical difficulties for the registrar of cooperatives.

Alongside the marketing facilities, various training programs to upgrade skills, as mentioned above, have been sponsored by SEWA in collaboration with the All India Handicrafts Board Weaver's Service Centre, the National Institute of Design, State Department of Social Defence, and the state government. In addition to traditional areas, women also are learning skills that were hitherto monopolized by men: carpentry, plumbing, domestic wiring, radio repairing, and videotape production.

To keep abreast of modern technology, a team of seventeen, consisting of SEWA organizers and a vegetable vendor, block printer, carpenter, cane and bamboo workers, incense roller, and agricultural worker, were trained in the use of video as a tool of communication. Illiteracy did not interfere with their handling the sophisticated equipment. A number of videotapes have been made on various issues and problems of self-employed women by the participants, who have found video an effective medium to express themselves and make themselves visible. The team of producers call their unit Video SEWA.

Unionizing with SEWA is a process of social awakening and development for the working sisters, the SEWA organizers, the labor officers, and the employers. As most occupations in India are caste based, SEWA's membership similarly reflects the divisions of a caste-ridden society. However, in SEWA the emphasis is on economic activities; there is an unwritten rule that members do not talk about husbands and children, and because SEWA is a labor union, each member should consider herself as a *worker*. With this common self-perception, the SEWA members gradually begin to forget their distances for at least a while and support one another. It has often happened, for example, that when one occupation (caste) has gone on strike, another occupation (caste) has provided food supplies to the strikers and taken care of their children. In this way, SEWA promotes integration and becomes a melting pot of all castes and religions. Joining SEWA, getting together with other sisters, learning the skills of dealing with formal organizations, meeting employers as equals, finding out their legal rights, acting to raise their wages, are usually all entirely new experiences for the women and result in their taking new, assertive leadership roles. At the same time, the process is a molding experience for the organizers. They understand their working sisters better and grow closer to them. They, too, face opposition and resistance and have to show personal qualities of courage and persistence. The labor officers come to realize that there is a whole population of workers who have been left out of the labor laws, or for whom the laws are not being implemented, and after their experience with SEWA they are, in at least some cases, more attentive to the problems of these workers and more helpful in working on solutions. The employers as well are beginning to understand that the working sisters must be treated with respect: Their contribution has to be recognized, as does the fact that each sister is not alone but part of an organization that will defend her.

The SEWA Economic Self-Reliance Wing sees itself as a stepping stone the women can use to become self-sufficient and to break the vicious circle of indebtedness and dependence on middlemen and traders. Through participation in the economic units, the women have gained confidence in entering into nontraditional occupations and activities. Women who have never before sold to the public work in SEWA shops; women go directly to the mills to buy *chindi* and to hospitals, jails, and other institutions to take orders; home-based workers, who are most accustomed to producing for an owner, are introduced to the idea of self-managed production involving all steps of the process, from acquiring raw materials to the final sale. These are small but important steps in enabling women to take more control of their working environments and to strive for improved working conditions and higher earnings. However, the greatest change has come in women's attitudes about their economic role. At first it was difficult for them to define themselves in relation to SEWA as anything but *laborer*. After working for a while they would say, "we are neither owners nor laborers, we are somewhere in between." But now, after time and struggle, they believe, "this is our own production unit." The workers' hope, that the production units become registered cooperatives with the women from the community as the shareholders, directors, managers, and workers, is being realized. Now their efforts and SEWA's are geared to making these cooperatives a viable part of the economy.

So, this is how in SEWA we try to organize ourselves for self-reliance, building on our existing skills, experiences, and capacity. The struggle to claim our rightful economic place and then move forward in the national economy has only just begun. As prices rise, as new technology is introduced, as urbanization increases, more and more working sisters all over the country will come under attack. We hope the sisters will be able to organize, not only to present a united front for defense, but also for social change based on love and justice.

CHAPTER 14

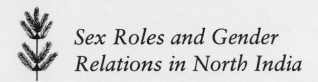

Sex Roles and Gender Relations in North India

David G. Mandelbaum

Jawaharlal Nehru once described his reaction to the staunch uprising of Indian women in 1930 at Gandhi's call for the Civil Disobedience movement. "I think that the most important and significant feature of that movement was the tremendous part that the women of India took in it. It was astounding" (Norman 1965, 1:412–413).

In a 1949 speech, he succinctly stated his views on the status of Indian women. "I am quite convinced that in India today progress can be and should be measured by the progress of the women of India" (Norman 1965, 2:508). Although orthodox Indian Muslims and traditionalist Hindus might disagree with every other aspect of Nehru's ideas about women, most of them would concur that the status of women is of great concern to each man and to all of society.

The focus on women's conduct is particularly strong in those parts of India where the seclusion of women is most stringently practiced. The term *purdah,* "curtain," refers to specific traits of veiling and spatial separation and, more widely, to the values about the proper behavior of women, restrictions on their movements outside the household, and requirements for their respectful demeanor within the home.

Purdah is maintained among peoples over much of the northern sector of the subcontinent. The purdah regions of India include the Indus and Ganges plains from Punjab through eastern Uttar Pradesh, together with the geographically adjoining and culturally close parts of other northern states. Purdah is also practiced in Pakistan and Bangladesh.

A family can observe full purdah only if its income is sufficient to provide separate women's space and to forego women's earnings in field or workshop. But when a formerly poor family of those regions becomes prosperous, its women are usually quite ready to adopt more stringent seclusion, partly because it is a prestigious thing to do and partly because it relieves them from grinding work for wages. And as newly affluent families take on stricter practices, families of established wealth and education commonly relinquish some of the purdah restrictions. Village families are likely to be more scrupulous about women's seclusion than are their class and caste counterparts in cities, though there are a good many urban families whose women do keep to purdah seclusion.

Although the standards for purdah observance vary by regional, caste, and religious groupings, certain features are common to all. Here I propose to sketch these shared fundamentals and note some of the principal variations between Muslim and Hindu versions of purdah. More details and documentation than can be given in this paper appear in my forthcoming book on the subject.

PURDAH OBSERVED

Veiling by women before men—so frequent, commonplace, and reflexive an action that it is scarcely noticed among these peoples unless it is not promptly and properly forthcoming—is but one feature of the mandatory code for a woman's conduct that requires her to behave modestly, restrained in speech, restricted in movement. She must observe, as Sylvia Vatuk put it, "[s]hyness of demeanor, avoidance of eye-contact with males, avoidance of loud speech and laughter (particularly in the presence of or within earshot of males), and the limitation of conversation with non-family males to necessary work-connected topics" (Vatuk 1982, 70). If she is unavoidably in the presence of a conversation among men, she should not actively participate, and if she does speak she should cover her mouth with hand or cloth. Far more than for a man, a woman's conduct is expected to be constrained, and with relatively few exceptions, it is so in practice both inside the home and out.

Within the household, men and women live, for the greater part, in separate places. They sleep in separate rooms or on separate sides of a hut, they relieve themselves in separate fields or locations, they sit apart at all social or religious occasions. Men spend most of their time in their own quarters, which may be a separate structure or platform, an outer room, a veranda or, among the poor, just a cot set outside the house. There the men talk, smoke, work, lounge, entertain, sleep; there a woman rarely sets foot. The women of the household remain apart in the courtyard or inner room, where they carry on domestic and child-rearing tasks and in general spend most of their lives. Into these precincts a man of the family comes to take his meals, to do necessary chores, to exchange communications, and to share a bed briefly and quietly in the still of the night (cf. Minturn and Hitchcock 1966, 21–24; Roy 1979, 20–30; Pettigrew 1975, 48–50).

Over time, a woman modifies some of her respect behavior. When she comes into her husband's parental family as a bride, she must be most diffident, shy, self-effacing, quite unlike her far freer demeanor as daughter in her own parents' house. She keeps her gaze lowered, her voice still, her features covered, her whole presence unobtrusive. She may veil herself even before her mother-in-law and perhaps her husband's brothers' wives. After a period of days or months, she begins to emerge from the bridal shell. Once she has borne a child, she is likely to reduce some of her veiling, such as that before her mother-in-law.

A young wife must appear completely disinterested toward her husband when they are in the presence of others. She should veil before him and should not even look steadily at him. Direct communication between the young couple is to be avoided until they can manage to be alone (cf. Minturn and Hitchcock 1966, 34–35; Aziz 1979, 56; Nath 1981, 23). Only when they become more senior in the family do they relax restraint between them in public.

Outside her household, a woman's movements are restricted in distance, duration, and purpose. She should not venture out alone beyond the immediate vicinity of her home. She should not go beyond the village or town limits except for purposes approved by family elders and preferably accompanied by a male relative. Women who must go out to work in the fields cannot be as closely circumscribed as those who do not, but a woman laborer will be reprimanded if she strays out of the circuit of work and home neighborhood. Even in the fields, she is likely to pull a cloth across her face should she see an elder male approaching. Some household tasks, like shopping, are often done by the men (or by servants in wealthier families) but may also be done by the women of a household. In that event, such tasks should be carried out expeditiously, with as little tarrying as possible.

In religion, women have small part to play in events that are societal, transcendental, public. They do perform domestic rites and conduct those ceremonies that are only for women. In some regions, certain women, usually from the lower-ranking groups, can become possessed and may act as shamans, but there is no claim that these performances have much to do with supernal forces of the high religion (cf. Mandelbaum 1966, 1176–77).

Sanctions on wayward behavior, real or alleged, can be severe. Neighbors' gossip about an unmarried girl may undermine her chances for a worthy marriage. A husband who suspects that his wife's conduct has damaged his and his family's honor may beat her. He may also refuse to allow her to visit her parents' home, a considerable penalty on a young wife. Perhaps worse, he may send her there and refuse to take her back. There she will languish, neither maid nor wife, until her natal kin can negotiate a resolution.

A woman's daily guidance and reproofs come from the senior women of her family, particularly from her mother-in-law. When, in her turn, she becomes a mother-in-law, it is her obligation to see to it that her daughter-in-law maintains the rules and niceties of the kind of purdah that is appropriate to the family's status, wealth, and aspirations.

REASONS: SPOKEN AND UNSPOKEN

Why must a woman send forth, within her own household, an unremitting stream of signals, daylong, lifelong, affirming her subordination, restating her modesty? Why must she curtail her movements beyond her threshold, take care not to be alone abroad, avoid direct eye contact with men or any implication of inviting cordial personal relations?

The answers come readily from the women and men even though this behavior is, for the vast majority of women, part of the given circumstances of their lives, and even though they are aware of challenges to it from various sources: from youngsters who must be properly socialized, from the example of the occasional village woman who, because of personality or circumstance, flouts some of the purdah rules, and from the implicit defy posed by those women, usually well-educated and Western-influenced, who walk freely about the streets with no more shield than a confident air and a pair of sunglasses.

These answers are based on two premises, that there are dangers *to* a woman outside her home, and that there are dangers *from* women inside their households.

Women are not expected to be able to cope with the exigencies of the outside world. The prime threat is from male strangers who, as a category, are presumed to be sexually predatory and always ready to take advantage of an unescorted woman. Some young men (and some not so young) reinforce that notion in town streets and in buses through the common practice known in Indian English as *Eve-teasing*. In the anonymity of the streets, these men—who would spring fiercely to the defense of the women of their own families—pinch and leer, hoot, and make sexually pointed remarks at passing women whom they do not know and who do not know them (cf. Jeffery 1979, 154–55). However, they rarely act that way in their own *mohallā*, or neighborhood.

As for the display of deference and avoidance inside the household, the reasons given are phrased as the need to show respect within the family and as the need to preserve the solidarity of the family. Both explanations imply a certain danger from the women; both have to do with domestic power and politics perhaps more than with concerns about extramarital sex within the joint family.

The myriad face veilings and head coverings before affinal kinsmen are made and received as signs of respect. They are acknowledgments of the right of the receiver to superior status and to priority of consideration. They connote acceptance by the sender of her subordinate role. In the instant of response, a woman does not ponder the meanings of her reflexive reaction when, say, her father-in-law comes into the room. But loud and lengthy excoriations about any lack of proper response will be directed by a mother-in-law to a negligent young daughter-in-law.

Although displays of respect are flashed in many social contexts, they take on particular importance within a joint family—comprising parents, sons, their wives and children, and the unmarried daughters— because family elders tend to view an incoming bride as a potential threat to family solidarity. Each has her own interests and loyalties, such as to her own natal kin, that are not those of her conjugal family. The ideal of a large, harmonious, cooperative joint family is much cherished, but such families are known to be difficult to maintain and destined eventually to disintegrate, either during the waning of the father's command or not many years after his death (cf. Vatuk 1982, 60; Jacobson 1982, 88 and 107; Pettigrew 1975, 51 and 53; Rizvi 1976, 39–41). Blame for the separation is usually put on the wives of the brothers. Commonly enough, relations among the brothers have also become quite brittle, but the male bond seems to be too precious and too tenuous to be so impugned.

To avert such separatist tendencies, a wife is required to keep at some social distance from her husband and children in the presence of others. Among Rajputs of a village in western Uttar Pradesh, "covering the face in the presence of one's husband is also a sign of respect for his mother, another of the customs designed to protect the mother-son relationship from being threatened by a son's attachment to his wife" (Minturn and Hitchcock 1966, 34). Respect avoidance is also supposed to avert improper sexual attraction. "Presumably brothers are less likely to lust after each other's wives if the latter's charms are concealed from them" (Sharma 1978, 219).

Women's fertility produces the blessings of children and the blessed continuity of patriline. But fertility has to be decoupled from sex. A woman's sexuality is suspect because, for one reason, it may be a means by which she can entice her husband away from unswerving allegiance to parents and brothers. The potential of sex to impart shame is abated by such devices as the separateness of wife and husband in public and by the hurried, almost clandestine, visitations for intercourse. Wives are thus seen as both disruptors and guarantors of family and patrilineage.

Although people readily tell that restraints on women serve to protect the women outside the home and to protect family cohesions within it, both functions also protect the men. A man, too, is socially vulnerable. Should a woman of his family be degraded by outsiders, he feels himself disgraced, his honor defiled. Should his joint family come under scorn as an arena of female discord and discredit, he and his close kinsmen feel under contempt, honor diminished. An ambitious man strives to build his honor through industry, loyalty, duty, judgment, and craft. However successful he may be in this, a critical cachet of his achievement is won through the marriage of his daughters into suitably high-ranking families. Conversely, the long building of his honor can come to grief if the women of his family fail him. Honor is the key good for these men, and their honor is balanced on the heads of the women.

MEN'S HONOR AND WOMEN'S SECLUSION

Izzat is the term for which "honor" is the usual translation. It is a word often heard in men's talk, particularly when the talk is about conflict, rivalry, or struggle. It crops up as a kind of final explanation for motivation, whether for acts of aggression or beneficence. Throughout these regions, it expresses a salient theme and includes some of the most highly valued purposes of a person's life: prestige and status, rank and esteem, respect and self-respect. For the Pukhtun of Swat in northern Pakistan, their code of honor "is everything." For the Pirzada of Delhi, it is described as being their central concern (Lindholm 1982, 189; Jeffery 1979, 99–100).

Like any term of strong emotional resonance, it is used in various overlapping meanings and with many nuances. But it always refers to how a person carries out the group's values, how he or she realizes them in actual behavior. For Jat Sikhs in Punjab, Joyce Pettigrew wrote, the concept of *izzat* is a philosophy of life that includes their paramount concerns with power, with reciprocity in giving, equality in vengeance, and nonsubmission to threat. A family's *izzat* must be zealously pursued, preserved at all costs, increased whenever possible. And "if the honor of a family's women is lost, so also is the family's entire public position" (1975, 51 and 58–59).

Public positions are the province of men, and so the primary referents of *izzat* are men. A man's *izzat* is assessed by his kith and kin on several scores, but the conduct of a family's women is always a cardinal consideration. Women are said to bear *izzat* also, as when it was remarked in a Himachal Pradesh village that it is bad for a woman's *izzat* if she does ploughing.

Izzat can be a corporate or a personal attribute or both. Since a person's behavior in the community is commonly seen as a reflection of group traits, rather than the isolable acts of an autonomous individual, *izzat* looms as a group and especially a family quality. Hence each woman's observance or nonobservance of her group's standards of purdah affects the *izzat* of all in her marital family—and not only of them. Should she grossly violate these standards, the *izzat* of her natal family will be hurt as well. A bride may be reminded by her parents that if she does not behave properly in her new home, her notoriety will damage the marriage chances of her still unmarried sisters and so may diminish their whole lives. Conversely, the reputation of both families will be enhanced if her conduct is devoted, dutiful, and irreproachable.

The kind of *izzat* open to a person and family depends on their social position. A family of a generally poor, low-ranking group can scarcely aspire to the *izzat* attainable by a family rich in land and proud of inherited status. But there are families of greater and lesser *izzat* within each set; a family of a lowly group may gain high regard among its peers and more widely in its locality; one of high caste rank may come to be disdained by all.

Izzat and the dangers to it are judged in relative perspective. Zarina Bhatty told of a Muslim family in a village of the Lucknow area, whose elders had long debated whether an unmarried daughter should be allowed to take a post as teacher in the village school. At the same time, however, they were proud that another woman in the family had been elected to the Uttar Pradesh Legislative Assembly and had become a minister in the state cabinet. Her political activities required her to mingle with many kinds of people and to be exposed to public gaze. "Such exposure was tolerated because to be a member of the State Assembly carries high prestige, but similar exposure in the midst of the village folk at the relatively low prestige level of a school teacher was clearly undesirable" (Bhatty 1975, 32).

A person and a family who gain high *izzat* in their community thereby command influence there. Thus *izzat* is a symbolic summary of past achievements and a main element in present power. Power, properly deployed, enhances *izzat*: Izzat legitimizes power.

Although the family is the primary vessel of *izzat,* broader groups are also involved. An individual's serious failing may tarnish, or a notable achievement burnish, the *izzat* of all in the lineage, *jāti,* or village (cf. Naveed-I-Rahat 1981, 75).

Izzat also devolves from distinguished ancestry. But if those who claim ancestral glories are to benefit, they must live up to them. *Izzat* does not keep well; it has to be continually reaffirmed in practice, reinforced in action, defended against challenge, and rewon and advanced in competition.

In India, ancestral memories are predominantly about males, and genealogy is usually reckoned through males only. Yet family *izzat* is pivotally dependent not only on the conduct of the wives; that *izzat* is also inevitably tested when the marriage of a daughter is arranged.

In negotiating a marriage, each side carefully considers the *izzat* of the other family, the amount of the dowry, and other material transactions, as well as the personal qualities of the prospective spouse. Each family ponders on how these ratings will affect their own standing and so influence the prospects of any unmarried daughters and sons. Among Hindus of these regions, the family that gives the bride is the defined inferior in the transaction. A bridegroom can be married to a spouse of somewhat lower standing than his without loss of family face, but not so for the bride and her family. They must, to preserve or increase family *izzat,* secure a bridegroom of as high a personal and family position, within the caste span of possible spouses, as their own resources and reputation can provide.

Izzat is mainly positive in connotation; it embraces what a man should do if he can. Purdah is more negative; it covers what a woman might do but should not. There is some feedback between a family's *izzat* and its purdah practices. The practices, properly done, enhance the *izzat.* The *izzat,* to be properly maintained, requires unfailing purdah observance. So purdah strengthens *izzat* as *izzat* strengthens purdah.

TWO VERSIONS OF PURDAH: MUSLIM AND HINDU

This relation between purdah and *izzat* holds true for both the principal versions of gender relations in these northern regions of the subcontinent: Muslim and Hindu.

Muslims and Hindus there share basic ideas about gender. They agree that a woman should be, and should always take care to appear to be, subordinate to the men closest to her. She must be secluded from easy personal interactions outside her home and excluded from public affairs (except, as we have seen, for those few women who attain prestigious office and so accrue credit to family and group *izzat*). Within the household, a woman should signal her acceptance of the reigning hierarchy by frequent signs of respect. And a man, they also agree, should be zealous about his *izzat,* hold it in constant concern, and be especially vigilant that the conduct of the women closest to him does not demean his honor.

From this common base, Muslim and Hindu gender practices diverge. Muslims are even more concerned than Hindus generally are about protecting their women from outsiders. Hence Muslim women when outdoors wear the tent-like *burkah,* prefer to travel in sight-proofed compartments, and are usually under closer chaperonage when they venture forth. Within the household, a Hindu woman, especially a young wife, seems to be under stricter surveillance than her Muslim counterpart. This is partly because of differences in marriage patterns. These northern Hindus, as we have noted, postulate an inherent inequality between two families related through marriage, the bride givers being inferior to the bride receivers. They also assume antagonism between the two families. It is as though these Hindus, more than do Muslims, fear the disruptive potential of a wife and her natal kin. Hence they have village exogamy: They bar marriage between two from the same village. In some parts, this taboo applies to all caste groups, so that no girl of the village may be given in marriage into a place from which any family of the village has previously taken a bride (Mandelbaum 1970, 102–3). Village exogamy ensures that families related through marriage do not live close to each other and that a young wife does not have ready access to her original family, because when she does visit them, she alters her conduct; she can come out of the connubial closet, can walk about unveiled as she did before her marriage.

Muslims recognize no such inequality or opposition between affinally related families. Indeed, they prefer to arrange marriages between two whose families are already related in kinship or are friendly. The preferred match for a man is with his patrilineal parallel cousin, his father's brother's daughter, a union that is forbidden by Hindu scripture. So a Muslim bride does not necessarily come into her new home as a complete stranger and is likely to be on friendlier, less probationary terms with her new relations.

In explaining purdah, Muslims invoke religious reasons much more than do Hindus. The close seclusion of women, in the popular Muslim belief, is a fundamental precept of Islam, ordained in the Koran, and is a universal hallmark of the true Muslim way of life. Muslim teachers and preachers, *maulvī,* regularly exhort the faithful to safeguard that precious quality of Islam and often admonish their audiences, whether male or female, about derelictions from this essential rule (cf. Vreede-de

Stuers 1968, 61). For Hindus, purdah is not so integral a part of religion, and mandates for purdah in Hindu holy writ are not commonly invoked. Hindu religious teachers tend rather to emphasize, especially when addressing women, the scriptural ideal of *pativrata,* the complete devotion of a wife to her husband.

CONSTRAINED BEHAVIOR, UNCONSTRICTED PERSONALITIES

A woman's personality, whether she is Muslim or Hindu, typically matures and develops within a narrower sphere than does a man's— more restricted in space, activities, social relations, and opportunities for self-assertion. Yet these constraints do not produce generally constricted personalities. Recent reports by women anthropologists who gave long and close study to women in purdah tell of lively, active, interested, alert participation by women rather than a dull uniformity of passive acquiescence by them. Although these reports are only a few samples from a vast and variegated population, they accord with the impressions of other observers.

Thus the village women of Punjab and Himachal Pradesh with whom Ursula Sharma talked do not feel excluded from ownership of land, even though they have no actual legal control over it. They speak of "my land" or "our land" as if it is family property, held in the name of the male head in behalf of all members of the family, female as well as male (Sharma 1980, 53).

Hanna Papanek said of the city women she studied in Pakistan, "Despite the restrictions of the purdah system, at least some women show a greater degree of self-confidence than comparable middle-class men" (1982, 33).

At the end of her account of women in northern and central India, Doranne Jacobson wrote that a woman may undergo much unhappiness and frustration. "But with rare exceptions, she has a clear sense of what she is and what she should be doing. In doing what is expected of her she feels a deep sense of achievement. Every woman complains, for to pride oneself on one's good fortune would be to tempt the fates, but few women would trade places with anyone else" (1977, 107).

Complaints were frequently heard by Sylvia Vatuk when she was studying older women in a village that has been encapsulated in the expansion of New Delhi. But there was a marked discrepancy between the voluble dissatisfactions and "the observed high level of good-humoured and extraordinarily active participation and interest in social, work, and family activities" (1975, 151).

The Pirzada Muslim women in Delhi, with whom Patricia Jeffery talked, poured out to her "a cascade of grievances," but they were about particular injustices and personal abuses rather than about the basic rules; "they press for small changes which would make their position more palatable to them but which cannot be said to strike at the root of the *purdah* system" (1979, 119 and 170).

The dependence of women, Ursula Sharma found, is held by them to be a moral good. "There is a positive celebration of the dependence of women upon men, especially among the high-status groups" (1980, 156). However, these women "often showed great courage and determination in standing up for themselves in difficult circumstances" (1980, 174). Despite their lot as landless laborers, or their problems as housewives trying to make do during rapid inflation, few had any quarrel with traditional women's roles. "Most of the women I know did not experience their position *as women* as being oppressive" (1980, 208).

This is not to say that women's place in society is never a source of dissatisfaction to them, or not an issue in the larger social or political arena. It is to say that these women in purdah have been socialized into a hierarchical order, of which a cardinal principle is the hierarchy of gender. The great majority of them have thoroughly internalized the norms of purdah (cf. Jacobson 1982, 84).

Some insights into characteristic influences in the development of an Indian woman's personality and that of a man are given in Sudhir Kakar's psychological analysis. The cultural devaluation of women, Kakar wrote, is not translated by a girl into a sense of worthlessness or low self-esteem. For one reason, in their infancy, "Indian girls are assured of their worth by whom it really matters: by their mothers." As an Indian girl grows up in a joint family, "there is almost always someone in particular who gives a little girl the kind of admiration and sense of being singled out as special that a male child more often receives from many." The women of the family are her teachers and models and can also be her allies against any abrasions from the outside (Kakar 1978, 60–61).

Up to age four or five, as Kakar has drawn the normative profile, a child enjoys quick, responsive, and reliable care, so that "an Indian generally emerges from infancy into childhood with a staunch belief that the world is benign and that others can be counted on to act in his behalf." Girls and boys both gain that confidence. As a girl approaches puberty and marriage, her training by her mother is "normally leavened with a good deal of compassion" (1978, 63 and 82).

Then comes the event, deliciously and fearfully anticipated, of her marriage. It is expected to be a difficult passage, and often enough it is so experienced and remembered. But it is a testing for which a girl has been prepared by the general ambience of her culture as well as by direct instruction from her family. With motherhood, she comes into her own as a woman, and especially as the mother of sons, she gains a more secure, prideful place in her family and community. "This accounts for her unique sense of maternal obligation and her readiness for practically unlimited emotional investment in her children" (Kakar 1978, 82). It is this investment that helps provide children with the benign environment they typically experience through infancy and early childhood.

Many of the women in purdah are aware that women of other lifestyles, urban or educated or rich or foreign, follow other rules of conduct, but they generally consider those ways irrelevant to the realities of their own lives. Their daughters and granddaughters who get a high school or college education tend to perceive those realities differently, to resent and work to discard some of the strictures; still they typically hold to certain basics of the traditional standards for womanly conduct.

WOMEN AND SOCIAL CHANGE

We can understand now why so many women responded to Gandhi's call and worked effectively in the political arena from which, with few exceptions, they had previously been excluded—and why most Indian men would not be surprised by their participation. The demure, subordinate comportment culturally required of women often enough cloaks a determined and activist spirit, which can be manifested when they choose in certain life situations and at certain historical junctures.

But how can we understand Nehru's statement that the progress of India can be and should be measured by the progress of India's women? Similar ideas that the progress of civilizations could be gauged according to the position of women had been articulated by some nineteenth-century social reformers, including British administrators and missionaries (Leonard 1976, 117). Since sex roles and the patterns of relations between men and women are not only deeply rooted in cultural precepts and individual experiences but are also closely linked to many aspects of the functioning culture and society, they affect and are affected by forces of the economy, polity, religion, and the larger society. They are the stuff of child-rearing and day-to-day human interchange and are not usually susceptible to ready change. So we may take Nehru to mean that a marked improvement in women's status, as he and most educated people in India would define improvement, will denote that comparably great advances have also been made in other sectors of national life.

To be sure, the improvements of the last several decades may be undone by nuclear catastrophe or national calamities, notably the calamities that would ensue if population growth is not effectively mitigated. Greatly increased education for girls and higher standards in that education are among the most feasible, surest ways of population control in India (cf. Mandelbaum 1974, 102–5). If the peoples of the world can avert titanic mishap, and those of India can surmount their particular social and political dangers, the evolutionary course of their cultures and societies seems well set for the kind of changes that have occurred and are going on in more industrialized societies.

Education has been an important vehicle in speeding the systemic social changes that have come about in the wake of the technological, scientific, and political revolutions of recent centuries. Although there have been major improvements in facilities since independence, no one in political authority in India claims that education is now adequate in scope or quality at any level. Yet everyone knows that even the present educational facilities can greatly affect the status and power potentials of individuals and their groups. Educated people (those with a high school education or more) typically differ from those of lesser education in such respects as fertility, health, occupation, life-style, and in their practices concerning gender roles and relations. Still, as we have noted, some elements of purdah are retained among educated urban people. Dowry payments, for one example, show little sign of diminishing in incidence or amount despite decades of vigorous attacks against the practice in the press and legislatures.

In recent years, added impetus to antidowry efforts has come from revelations of the deliberate immolation of young women in order to permit their husbands to gain another bride and dowry. Reports of bride-burning have been broadcast on national and international television and radio and have appeared in newspaper and magazine accounts. The usual story is from New Delhi and other cities; it tells of a husband and mother-in-law who are dissatisfied with a young wife and demand more dowry from her parents. If they do not get it, they see that the young woman is "accidentally" burned to death in her kitchen. They then arrange another marriage for the man and collect another dowry (Lopamudra 1983). Although the incidence of such horrible murders seems to be numerically relatively small, the impact of the reporting of them has been large. It has stimulated activist efforts to alter traditional patterns in many aspects of women's status.

There are feminist organizations in India that have achieved notable successes, especially in getting legislation passed on such matters as divorce, age at marriage, and female inheritance. Their members are largely urban and educated, but these organizations have a growing presence among some village women (cf. Omvedt 1980). However, those like Tara Ali Baig who are in the forefront of the women's movement do not want women's roles in their societies to become the same as those in Western nations. She observed that change in women's status and in Indian society generally "may be taking place at a pace faster than perhaps we realize. The Indian woman is part of this process too. With the wisdom gleaned from centuries of discipline and self-sacrifice, she has something positive to contribute today to the search for a solution to the age-old man/woman relationship" (Baig 1976, 251). Rama Mehta (1970) noted that educated women in India by and large want to retain certain of the traditional values of Indian family life and women's roles. Doing so often entails major personal conflicts in reconciling the ideas gained through their education and the traditional precepts about women's conduct.

In interviews with fifty educated Hindu women, Mehta found that they distinguished modernization from Westernization in their own conduct and the ways of their peers. They were "alarmed by the rapid spread of Western ideas in the elite groups." They were concerned with the problem of adopting the beneficial aspects of Western culture without being "infected by its injurious aspects." The difference between being Indian-modern and Indian-Western is shown in attitudes toward divorce. If a divorce is sought by an educated woman because of extreme provocation and abuses, it is condoned, "but if the separation is for a lesser reason, a woman is condemned" (Mehta 1970, 205).

Muriel Wasi found that the great mass of Indian women are still abysmally backward, and "this indeed is the main reason why India moves so slowly in the total process of modernizing herself" (Wasi 1971, 10). That is all the more true for the peoples of the purdah zone of North India, among whom the traditional standards for women's conduct are so closely bound to central concerns of men's strivings. It may be that with the strong leadership of women activists in India, the status of women in Indian society will be advanced more rapidly. And once significant improvements in women's lot have been made, many other social improvements, as in family planning, will necessarily follow. So an expansion of women's roles and opportunities is both index to and means of implementation for better conditions of health and wealth throughout a society.

REFERENCES CITED

Aziz, K. M. Ashraful
    1979   Kinship in Bangladesh. Dacca: International Centre for Diar-
            rhoeal Disease Research. Monograph Series No. 1.

Baig, Tara Ali
1976   *India's Woman Power.* New Delhi: S. Chand & Co.

Bhatty, Zarina
1975   Women in Uttar Pradesh: Social Mobility and Directions of
         Change. In *Women in Contemporary India,* edited by A. de
         Souza, 25–36. New Delhi: Manohar.

1976   Status of Muslim Women and Social Change. In *Indian Women:*
         From Purdah to Modernity, edited by B. R. Nanda. New
         Delhi: Vikas.

Jacobson, Doranne
1977   The Women of North and Central India: Goddesses and Wives.
         In *Women in India: Two Perspectives,* edited by D. Jacobson and
         S. S. Wadley, 17–112. New Delhi: Manohar.

1982   Purdah and the Hindu Family in Central India. In *Separate*
         Worlds, edited by H. Papanek and G. Minault, 81–107. Delhi:
         Chanakya Publications; Columbia, Mo.: South Asia Books.

Jeffery, Patricia
1979   *Frogs in a Well.* London: Zed Press.

Kakar, Sudhir
1978   *The Inner World. A Psychoanalytic Study of Childhood and*
         Society in India. Delhi: Oxford University Press.

Krygier, Jocelyn
1982   Caste and Female Pollution. In *Women in India and Nepal,*
         edited by M. Allen and S. M. Mukherjee, 76–104. Australian
         National University Monograph on South Asia, No. 8.

Leonard, Karen Isaksen
1976   Women and Social Change in Modern India. *Feminist Studies*
         3:117–30.

Lindholm, Charles
1982   *Generosity and Jealousy: The Swat Pukhtun of Northern*
         Pakistan. New York: Columbia University Press.

Lopamudra
1982   Dowry Death: When Is the End? *Social Affairs* (New Delhi)
         30:4–5.

Mandelbaum, David G.
1966   Transcendental and Pragmatic Aspects of Religion. *American*
         Anthropologist 68:1174–91.

1970   *Society in India.* 2 vols. Berkeley and Los Angeles: University of California Press.

1974   *Human Fertility in India.* Berkeley and Los Angeles: University of California Press.

1988   *Woman's Seclusion and Man's Honor: Sex Roles and Their Consequences in North India, Pakistan and Bangladesh.* Tucson: The University of Arizona Press.

Mehta, Rama
1970   *The Western Educated Hindu Woman.* Bombay: Asia Publishing House.

Minturn, Leigh, and John T. Hitchcock
1966   *The Rajputs of Khalapur, India.* New York: John Wiley and Sons.

Nath, Jharna
1981   Beliefs and Customs Observed by Muslim Rural Women During Their Life Cycle. In *The Endless Day,* edited by F. S. Epstein and R. A. Watts, 13–30. New York: Pergamon Press.

Naveed-I-Rahat
1981   The Role of Women in Reciprocal Relationships in a Punjab Village. In *The Endless Day,* edited by F. S. Epstein and R. A. Watts, 47–84. New York: Pergamon Press.

Norman, Dorothy
1965   *Nehru. The First Sixty Years.* 2 vols. New York: The John Day Company.

Omvedt, Gail
1980   *We Will Smash This Prison: Indian Women in Struggle.* London: Zed Press.

Papanek, Hanna
1982   Purdah: Separate Worlds and Symbolic Shelter. In *Separate Worlds,* edited by H. Papanek and G. Minault, 3–53. Delhi: Chanakya Publications, Columbia, Mo.: South Asia Press.

Pettigrew, Joyce
1975   *Robber Noblemen: A Study of the Political System of the Sikh Jats.* London: Routledge and Kegan Paul.

Rizvi, S. M. Akram
1976   Kinship and Industry among the Muslim Karkhanedars in Delhi. In *Family, Kinship, and Marriages among Muslims in India,* edited by I. Ahmad, 27–48. New Delhi: Manohar.

Roy, Shibani
  1979   *Status of Muslim Women in North India*. Delhi: B. R. Publishing
          Corp.

Sharma, Ursula
  1978   Women and Their Affines: The Veil as a Symbol of Separation.
          Man 13:218–233.

  1980   *Women, Work, and Property in North-West India*. London and
          New York: Tavistock Publications.

Vatuk, Sylvia
  1975   The Aging Woman in India: Self-Perceptions and Changing
          Roles. In *Women in Contemporary India,* edited by A. de Souza,
          142–63. New Delhi: Manohar.

  1982   Purdah Revisited: A Comparison of Hindu and Muslim Inter-
          pretations of the Cultural Meanings of Purdah in South Asia. In
          Separate Worlds, edited by H. Papanek and G. Minault, 54–78.
          Delhi: Chanakya Publications; Columbia, Mo.: South Asia
          Press.

Vreede-de Stuers, Cora
  1968   *Purda: A Study of Muslim Women's Life in Northern India*.
          Assen: Van Gorcum and Co.

Wasi, Muriel
  1971   Who is the Educated Woman of India Today? In *The Educated
          Woman in Indian Society Today,* edited by M. Wasi, 7–17.
          Bombay: Tata McGraw Hill.

CHAPTER 15

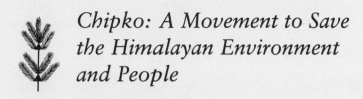

Chipko: A Movement to Save the Himalayan Environment and People

Gerald D. Berreman

INTRODUCTION: SOCIAL MOVEMENTS IN INDIA

It has frequently been remarked in the past few years that grass-roots social movements and action groups are the hope of India, as its formal institutions prove increasingly incapable of coping with the vast problems confronting the people and their nation. Ravi Chopra of the Centre for Science and Environment in New Delhi reported in a lecture at Berkeley in 1984 that he had compiled a directory of no fewer than three thousand formally structured groups, and he estimated that another three thousand are active although only informally organized.[1] Other sources have put the number at fifteen thousand, most of the groups limited to a single issue or a few closely related ones, their membership and activities confined to specific localities or regions (cf. *India Now* 1985).[2]

During 1981–82, I conducted a study in India of perhaps the most widely publicized of the truly grass-roots movements there—Chipko, an environmental movement in the Himalayas. At the same time, I observed an embryonic and primarily elite political movement in the central Himalayas (Uttarakhand) expressing ethnic regionalism and advocating institutions and development programs appropriate to the environment and traditions of the mountain people together with a modest degree of self-governance (Berreman 1983). My inquiry into regional identity and social action grew out of research in the area over a period of twenty-five years, first in a rural village and its surroundings and later in a sub-Himalayan city and its hinterland (Berreman 1963, 1972a, 1972b, 1978, 1979). I have followed the development of both movements, environmental and political, up to the present. Although at this writing the latter movement and its political expression, the Uttarakhand Kranti Dal (Uttarakhand Revolutionary party, UKD), have grown dramatically,[3] it is about the former, the Chipko movement, and its implications that I will write here.

THE CONTEXT: ENVIRONMENT, POLITICS, AND SOCIETY

The Chipko movement began in 1972 among the people of the central Himalayas in India, as an effort utilizing nonviolent direct action to prevent the destruction of their forests and thereby save their environment, their livelihood, their ways of life, and ultimately life itself in their homeland. The characteristic method employed by those participating in the movement to stop the felling of trees is to interpose themselves bodily between tree cutters and the trees—a tactic in the Gandhian tradition. This technique is known by the indigenous term *chipko,* meaning literally "to stick to" or "to hug," and usually translated as "hugging the trees"; hence the movement is *Chipko Andolan,* "the hug-the-trees movement."

The setting for the movement is the northern segment of Uttar Pradesh, an area that has been known historically and reverently as Uttarakhand, the most sacred region of the holy Himalayas, the source and watershed of the Ganges River (Figure 15.1.) Comprising the eight districts of Uttar Pradesh immediately west of Nepal, containing 4 percent of Uttar Pradesh's population, and occupying about 20,000 square miles of precipitous, geologically recent, and fragile mountains, Uttarakhand is a topographically, climatically, and culturally distinct appendage to Uttar Pradesh. In its 16 percent of the state's area are to be found virtually all of the state's forest, mineral, and hydroelectric resources, as well as the state's renowned mountain tourist and pilgrimage attractions.

The 4.5 million people of Uttarakhand include two indigenous ethnic groups: Hindu (and a few Muslim) subsistence farmers, artisans, and other service and specialist castes living in the lower Himalayas (up to about 7,000 feet above sea level), who speak an Indo-Aryan language closely related to the Hindu of the adjacent plains but not mutually intelligible with it. These people and their language are commonly re-

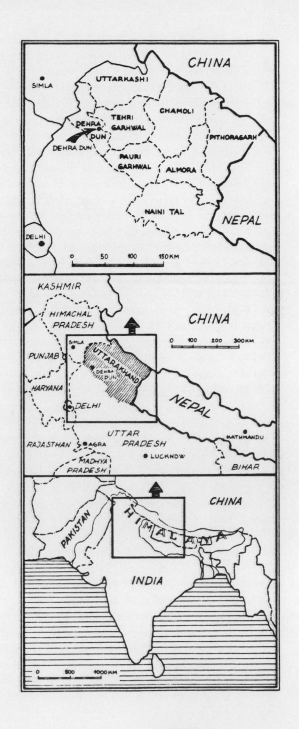

Figure 15.1.
Uttarakhand.

ferred to as *Pahari* ("of the mountains"). Much fewer in number are the Tibetan-speaking Buddhist farmers, herders, and traders who live at higher elevations and generally to the north, called *Bhotiya* ("Tibetan").

Until twenty-five years ago, Uttarakhand was largely inaccessible to outsiders other than hardy foot pilgrims and a few trekkers, except on its southern periphery bordering the plains. Then, following the Indo-Chinese border conflict of 1962, an extensive network of motor roads was constructed throughout the mountains. The motive was strategic, but a major consequence was the opening of this area to traffic of all kinds. Suddenly, Uttarakhand's resources—timber and other forest products ranging from resin to medicinal herbs; minerals ranging from limestone (of which a major stratum of the outer range is composed and which, mixed into cement, is the primary building material of India) and mangesite to potassium and rare metals; hydroelectric sites; and agricultural and pastoral land—were within reach of contractors, corporations, and other entrepreneurs from the distant cities of the plains. The laborers they employ are hired in the plains and transported to the mountains, and the products of their activities are exported to the plains. Bent on profits, they are oblivious to the local populace and its environment.

The road construction for defense purposes wrought dramatic overall environmental degradation in the region and consequently brought social and economic dislocation to the Himalayan people. Such destructive results were then quickly magnified by the extractive industries' rapacious activities (see Bandoypadhyay 1984; Shiva and Bandyopadhyay 1986), leading the authors of *The State of India's Environment, 1982* to note that: "The rate of depletion of forests in the Himalayan ranges, which represent a quarter of India's forest reserves, is so great that this mighty mountain chain could become barren by the first half of the next century" (Agarwal et al. 1982, 35; cf. Agarwal and Narain 1985, 49–98).

The Tehri Dam, under construction in Tehri Garhwal on the Bhagirathi River, one of the two major Himalayan tributaries to the Ganges, is one of more than twenty hydroelectric projects now in Uttarakhand and will be Asia's largest earth-filled dam. Its lake will submerge historic Tehri City in the Himalayas, about one hundred villages (twenty-five of them completely), and 10,000 acres of agricultural land, rendering forty thousand people homeless and separating others by water from their economic resources and social networks. The stress of heavy siltation, the unstable geological makeup of the dam site, the prospects for heavier-than-anticipated inflow of water, and the known seismic activity of the region (combined with the possibility that the dammed water will increase or trigger that activity) pose dangers to life and property downstream. But widespread protests against the dam, backed by research and expert testimony, have been of no avail in the face of the interests that stand to profit from it—none of them local interests (Agarwal et al. 1982, 66).

Because of the roads, lands previously cultivated for subsistence crops or devoted to pasture by local farmers have become attractive to entrepreneurs for growing cold-climate luxury crops, such as apples and apricots, and other commercially valuable crops suited to the environment, such as potatoes, ginger, and (illegal) opium. Industrial giants now vie with lesser capitalists in buying up and exploiting this new-found agricultural bonanza at the expense of local people.

Mass tourism to Himalayan shrines and other sites sacred to Hindus, also made possible by the roads, has taxed the capacity of the environment heavily as well by inundating the pilgrim routes with hotels, restaurants, and shops, with their attendant demands for food to sell to the pilgrims and for wood for building and to fuel the fires that cook their food and warm them.[4] At the same time, and on many of the same routes, secular tourism flourishes, attracting plains people and increasing numbers of foreigners to the vacation spots featuring snow views and wildflowers, touring, trekking, hunting, fishing, and mountain climbing. Tens of thousands annually take advantage of these attractions with little or no attention paid to their impact on the environment or the mountain people.

All of these "development" activities have caused depletion of the forests, erosion of the soil, drying up of the water sources, preemption of the firewood, the fodder, and building materials, and cooptation or destruction of much of the viable agricultural land and pasture. As a result, many of the mountain people thus are unable to make a living. In the past twenty years, there has been accelerated emigration of local men to the plains seeking work, most of them becoming part of the oversupply of urban unskilled and underemployed. Some Uttarakhand villages have been deprived of their able-bodied men to the extent that they have been described by observers as maleless (Rao 1982, 2, citing Rawat). Village life is dangerously impaired, its continuation even jeopardized, under these physical and social conditions.

Throughout the full 1,500-mile length of the Himalayan range, Uttarakhand is the only region without a degree of self-determination: without self-governance as a state, province, or nation. Instead, the government in Lucknow, Uttar Pradesh's capital over 200 miles away, is overwhelmingly made up of plains people unfamiliar with the mountains, their people, and their ways of life, mostly uncaring about them and their problems. In short, one might say that Uttarakhand has become a colony within the state and nation that administer it. It is an internal colony, a domestic colony, but a colony nonetheless, exploited by and for outsiders. Put another way, it is a victim of *fourth world colonialism*, the exploitation of an internal minority by the majority population within a "developing" or "third world" nation. These facts provide an essential context for understanding the Chipko movement.

FORERUNNERS OF CHIPKO

The Trial Forest Settlement in Kumaon, instituted by the British in 1821, represented the first restriction in history on the use of Himalayan forests by their inhabitants (Mishra and Tripathi 1978, 36). Belief that injustice had been done was not limited to the mountain people: In 1907, a British officer, Major General Wheeler, headed a mass meeting in Almora in opposition to his own colonial government's policies vis-à-vis local people's rights of access to the forests and their products, and in so doing he supported those people's own resentment (Dogra 1980, 46; also 1983, 44). But it was not until 1911, when the reserved forest area was greatly expanded to 3,311 square miles and villagers were prohibited from entering it, that overt resistance is reported to have occurred. "People's resentment that had been pent up for almost a hundred years began surfacing in the form of frequent clashes between the villagers and the forest department functionaries" (Mishra and Tripathi 1978, 36; cf. Ramachandra Guha 1985). Resistance and suppression increased over the years until they reached tragic proportions on May 30, 1930. Then the raja of Tehri (beholden for his office to the British, who had awarded it to his ancestors after the latter had supported them in the Anglo-Nepali War of 1814–15) sent his troops to Tilari, in the Rawai region of Tehri Garhwal, on the banks of the Yamuna River, to break up a meeting of local villagers protesting restriction of their rights to forests—restriction patterned on that instituted by the raja's British benefactors. The troops opened fire on villagers gathered in a field, killing seventeen and injuring many more.

Resistance has continued to the present, for the forest policy has remained essentially unchanged from the time of British rule; the Indian Forest Act of 1874, revised in 1927, is still in effect. In 1982 a new bill was circulated for possible adoption and has been widely discussed (cf. Banerjee 1982). Its reforms, however, are minimal. In fact, eighty-one of the eighty-four provisions of the act formulated by the British have been retained intact. One of the few "changes" has to do with the definition of *forest land*. The British had left that term vague, evidently because no definition they could come up with allowed them the freedom to tax and control the wide variety of lands they wanted to tax and control. The new definition is: "any land containing trees and shrubs, pasture lands and any land whatsoever . . . which the State Government declares to be a forest (Section 2 [3])" (Ramachandra Guha 1983, 1942; Banerjee 1982, 63)!

As Guha points out, "the bill is based on the (correct) premise that [forest-dwellers] compete with the mercantile and industrial bourgeoisie for the produce of the forests. . . . To augment the production of industrial wood and the MFP [Minor Forest Produce]—and not to safeguard the environment remains the bill's prime aim" (Ramachandra Guha 1983, 1943). The issue in the Himalayas (and elsewhere) throughout this time span has been cooptation of forests and forest products for taxation and commercial exploitation, while curtailing or prohibiting use of the forests by those who have traditionally lived in and depended upon them. These policies have been rationalized over the decades with the long-standing claim that deforestation results from misuse and overuse of trees by the indigenous agricultural villagers or transhumant herders, or both, who are most often alleged to decimate the forests for firewood, building materials, and fodder. In reality, as anyone who has lived among them in the Himalayas (and presumably most other areas as well) knows, farmers and herders do not cut trees for firewood (they use dead and fallen trees, branches, and brush) or for fodder (they lop branches instead). They fell trees only to satisfy their needs for house construction—which are minimal in view of the fact that houses are made mostly of stone and in any case have a useful life of forty years or more—and the manufacture of utensils and implements. It is true that trees are cleared in order to bring new land under cultivation, but unlike the situation widely reported for Nepal, the opening of new agricultural land in India has long been closely controlled by the government. At the same time, and also unlike the situation in Nepal, road-building programs in India have for some years facilitated access to forests by timber, resin, and charcoal merchants and other profiteers. Therefore, and especially in light of the massive and conspicuous devastation caused in the Himalayas by commercial contractors, to blame the local people for forest destruction, as officials of the Forest Department consistently do, is an egregious and indefensible example of blaming the victim (see, for example, Mathur 1978; contrast Banerjee 1982, 43). The more moderate argument that, whatever the cause, forests are now too depleted to allow their further use by local people might be called "further victimizing the victim" (see, for example, Ashish 1979).

In the early 1960s, local labor cooperatives and small-scale producers' and artisans' cooperatives were established by villagers with the help of volunteer Gandhian *sarvodaya* workers ("those building a just society") in the Himalayan districts of Uttar Pradesh. By organizing to compete for labor and goods contracts, which up to that time had gone only to outsiders via private labor contractors and wholesalers, they hoped to bring to local people whatever benefits might be salvaged from the road-building and other development activities that followed the Indo-Chinese War.

Then, in a series of incidents beginning in 1972, villagers and *sarvodaya* workers militantly confronted both the government's forestry personnal (who were limiting or prohibiting their use of the forests while awarding contracts to timber merchants and overseeing their extensive felling operations) and the contractors and their employees who were engaged in the actual felling. The first, now-famous incident grew out of the fact that near Gopeshwar, headquarters of Chamoli district, the local villagers' cooperative (Dashauli Gram Swarajya Sangh, or DGSS) had been denied permission to cut its usual small annual allotment of ash trees (twelve in this instance) necessary for use in construction and implements. After their appeals had fallen on deaf ears, they were startled and angered when tree cutters arrived in their forest. They discovered that the very trees denied them had been sold at government auction to the Simon Company, a sporting goods manufacturer located in Allahabad, in the plains 350 miles to the southeast, to be made into cricket bats and tennis rackets. Thoroughly exasperated and unwilling to accept a substitute offer of pine trees (which are unusable for their purposes), the villagers and *sarvodaya* workers hit upon the idea of employing Gandhian nonviolent resistance by embracing the trees with their bodies to stop the tree cutters. This they did, to the amazement of their adversaries, so successfully that the felling was stopped, and ultimately, in early 1973, the permit was canceled. The trees had been saved. When the Forest Department then allotted the Simon Company trees in another, more distant forest, members of the DGSS went there, warned nearby villagers, and organized successful opposition of the same sort (Dogra 1980, 46–48). Thus the movement called after their technique, Chipko Andolan, was born.

Chandi Prasad Bhatt, the *sarvodaya* worker in Gopeshwar who organized the DGSS, is generally credited with originating the Chipko method and founding the movement. A native of Uttarakhand, he is a former ticket clerk in a transport company in Gopeshwar. He has worked primarily in Chamoli and Pauri Garhwal districts. Another longtime *sarvodaya* worker and native of the region, Sunderlal Bahuguna, is also credited with a role in founding the movement. His work has been primarily to the north and west, in Tehri Garhwal and Uttarkashi districts.

THE EVOLUTION OF CHIPKO

There have followed approximately a dozen major (and many minor) incidents of Chipko confrontation with contractors, workers, and Forest Department personnel in Uttarakhand since its founding, each exemplifying its nonviolent method and each impressively effective. Whereas the first Chipko action rescued a dozen trees, the third saved twenty-five hundred, and subsequent ones even more. Chipko activists—villagers, *sarvodaya* workers, teachers, and high school and university students—prepare for their confrontations by going from village to village, announcing the plans and encouraging the people's support and participation. Workshops, training sessions, and recruitment drives are accompanied by rallies including informational and inspirational speeches, music, topical songs, and the like. In addition to successes in the forests, Chipko activists have picketed and paralyzed Forest Department auctions of trees held in towns and cities.

Bahuguna has initiated a series of symbolic Chipko marches called *padyātrā*s (evoking the image of religious pilgrimage) throughout the Himalayas to spread the word and gain support. Activists also have participated in research and publication on issues of forest, mineral, soil, and water conservation. Reforestation and afforestation programs have been carried out as well (for an example, see Agarwal and Narain 1985, 183–84). Since 1982, the increasingly diversified environmental actions and education efforts have overshadowed the confrontational activities of the movement, largely because the confrontations have worked so well that they are not as often necessary. In fact, as a result of the activities of Chipko Andolan, in March 1981 an interim ban was placed on all felling of green trees above 1,000 feet above sea level in the Uttar Pradesh Himalayas, that is, in Uttarakhand, and it remains in force at this writing.

The actions and accomplishments of Chipko have received increasing attention throughout India, Asia, and the world. Articles on Chipko have appeared widely in India and abroad in the popular press and in journals of scholarship and environmental advocacy, followed by several books.[5] A British Broadcasting Corporation television special on the movement was first aired on January 24, 1982. The journal

Himalaya, Man and Nature has chronicled the evolution of Chipko, issues and debates surrounding it, and the Himalayan environment in general since 1977 (Gupta). Sources from America and Europe include those by Barthélemy (1982), Berreman (1983), Iliste and Goranson (1980) and Shepard (1981). National and international recognition has come to the leaders of the movement as well. The Government of India's Padma Shri Award was conferred on Bahuguna in 1981, and the National Integration Award was given him by the president of India in 1984. In 1982, in Manila, Bhatt received the Magsaysay Award for public service in Asia, and finally in 1986 he, too, was awarded the Padma Shri.

Meanwhile, the movement in the Himalayas has gradually become divided and is now split, to a significant degree, between the followers of Bhatt and those of Bahuguna (Berreman 1983, 311). Bhatt's group pursues a strategy of pragmatic conservationism with emphasis on ecologically sound use of forests by local people to meet local needs (Bhatt 1985). Their latest undertaking is the "Integrated Watershed Development Project," carried out by the people and *sarvodaya* workers in the vicinity of Chamoli. Assisted by the Planning Commission and the Department of Environment of the Government of India, twenty-seven villages are to work together on a program of conservation and development ranging from forestry to beekeeping, from establishment of child-care centers to promotion of solar cookers and small-scale industries. Their program of cooperative enterprises also includes local sawmills.

Bahuguna and his group deplore these sawmills. Bahuguna sees 1977 as having been a turning point in the history of Chipko. Then, he says, the movement's emphasis shifted from the economic impact of development on the mountain people, and attendant efforts to get jobs and other income for them through cooperatives and local industry, to an almost exclusively ecological program opposing all tree cutting and development. Commenting on this shift, he wrote: "Soil, water and pure air, uniquely offered by forests, are surely more valuable than resin, timber and foreign exchange. Whether the latter even benefits local people is another matter" (Bahuguna 1983a, 7). His adherents have followed a more symbolic, less pragmatic approach employing fasts, the *padyātrā*s mentioned above, and music and songs of traditional genres, often written for the occasion, and in these ways they have invoked Hindu, nationalistic, and Gandhian images.

To generate national and international publicity for their program, Bahuguna often publishes articles and interviews in Indian and foreign newspapers and magazines, frequently in English; Bhatt does so rarely, and most of his appear in local Hindi publications. Bahuguna frequents the offices of newspapers and other media including radio and television and is a familiar participant in international environmental meetings and symposia in such places as Stockholm, Geneva, and New York; Bhatt is a stranger to such events. Thus, their differences are those of style as well as substance. Both kinds of difference, however, have substantial consequences.[6]

Bhatt and his followers consider the Government of India at its highest levels to be the primary culprit in forest destruction. Beholden to timber merchants who profit from tree felling, it sells them the forests with promiscuous abandon in order to curry favor with them and win their support. In his view, the Forest Department is simply an instrument of these governmental policies—a relatively powerless and perhaps even a reluctant one. The Forest Department and its personnel are therefore seen as potential allies in Chipko's conservation efforts.

Bahuguna and his followers tend to perceive the Forest Department as the primary culprit. Its officers sell the trees and profit directly from the bribes and patronage of greedy, unscrupulous contractors, who destroy the trees under their license or their averted eyes. The higher levels of government, then, are well-intentioned allies in the quest for conservation, betrayed by Forest Department underlings.

This schism within Chipko is reflected in responses to the Forest Department's contention (shared by others) that profligate and unscientific use of trees on the part of forest-dwelling villagers constitutes the major threat to the forests and must therefore be stopped. Bhatt's followers dispute this claim, insisting instead that villagers have a traditionally conservationist relationship with their environment including the forests. Rather, they say, it is the alliance of high-level government officials and wealthy, powerful contractors that destroys the environment. Bahuguna's followers lay part of the blame on the villagers and the rest on corrupt low-level Forest Department personnel. Each faction uses its perception of the source of the problem—contractors or villagers—to justify its priorities for achieving conservation of the forests: conservationist use of the trees by and for local people versus a total ban on tree felling.

According to reports, young activists in the sizable towns of Naini Tal and Almora, east of the regions of Bhatt and Bahuguna's work, have come to constitute a third Chipko faction. Although I have little knowledge of this group, it is said to have programs and styles distinct from, competitive with, and possibly more political than those of either Bhatt or Bahuguna.

Chipko's internal division poses a threat to the movement, saddens many of its supporters, and delights its opponents. Yet, on the whole, the Chipko movement has been characterized by dedicated, cooperative, energetic people, determined to save the mountain environment for its people and, as a result, for India. Even those who disagree with one another, including Bhatt and Bahuguna themselves, share this determination. By the very nature of its broad-based, grass-roots support, its realistic goals, its democratic policies and participatory methods, its idealism and its responsiveness to issues formulated in the context of regional traditions, the Chipko movement sustains confidence among the people of the Himalayas and pride in their culture. It helps them to generate apposite analyses of the problems they face and practical proposals toward their solution.

THE DIFFUSION OF CHIPKO

Despite Chipko's accomplishments, widespread public awareness of the movement and its leaders, and continuing efforts to disseminate its message and method at the grass-roots level throughout the Himalayas, the movement there has remained localized, limited mainly to the regions of its origins and early history: that is, around Gopeshwar in Chamoli District and neighboring areas of Pauri Garhwal where Bhatt has focused his work; around Silyara (about 10 air miles northeast of Tehri City) from which Bahuguna carries out his activities in Tehri Garhwal and Uttarkashi Districts; and in the vicinities of Naini Tal and Almora, headquarter cities of the districts of the same names in Kumaon, to which Chipko had spread very early.

On the other hand, Chipko has had an important impact outside of the Himalayas. Recently, it has jumped more than 1,000 miles to the south, to northern Karnataka State (Uttara Karnataka), where it is known as Appiko in Kannada, the language of the region. There, in the rapidly dwindling forests of the Western Ghats, rural farming people are carrying out the mission and method of environmental protection pioneered by Chipko. Their organization, Appiko Chaluvali, began its work in September 1983, in protest against the reckless and illegal logging of local forests (Bahuguna 1983b; Alvares 1984). Appiko encountered the same opposition from timber interests and the same resistance and apathy from Forest Department officials that Chipko had in the Himalayas ten years before. Its activists confront these problems with the same determination and ingenuity as their northern predecessors. But the Appiko workers have found, as did Chipko workers, that in regulating timber cutting the government is immobilized before the combined power of contractors and politicians intent on profiting from the forests at the expense of those who live there. The government in Karnataka, as in Uttar Pradesh, is incapacitated by its own contradictory policies of rapid industrial development and protection of forests, with the latter too often sacrificed to the former (Alvares 1984; cf. Hegde 1985).

In August 1985, the *Overseas Hindustan Times* reported a "threat to launch Chipko" in India's capital by the residents of the Government School Teachers' Housing Cooperative colony. They were protesting the Delhi Development Authority's plan to allow a company to cut eighty to ninety trees in a park in the colony in order to build a gasoline station, despite the fact that the same authority had designated the park a Green Area. The secretary of the colony was quoted as saying, "We will never allow them to build the petrol pump. The trees will be cut over our dead bodies," and the reporter added, "So, in true 'satyagrahi' [nonviolent resistance] spirit, the inspiration for which comes from the famous 'Chipko Andolan' of the Tehri Garhwal hills, the 7,500 residents of this colony are prepared to hug the trees and picket the park they love" (Urfi 1985).

The inspiration of Chipko activism has not been limited to India; it has been felt halfway around the world in California as well. There, on October 7, 1983, in Mendocino County, "about 50 demonstrators who hugged trees marked for cutting and placed themselves in falling paths disrupted the logging of a virgin forest grove" (*San Francisco Chronicle*, 8 Oct. 1983). Two weeks later, as the Georgia Pacific Lumber Company attempted to literally bulldoze its way to resume felling, "five protesters were arrested and a sixth injured by a falling tree" (ibid., 25 Oct. 1983, cf. ibid., 3 Nov. 1983). But the company was foiled in its attempt, as a temporary injuction was issued stopping the chainsaw massacre of Douglas fir and redwood trees (ibid., 16 Nov. 1983).

That injunction stood for a year and a half until, on July 25, 1985, the California State Court of Appeals ruled unanimously against the logging company on the grounds that it violated the California Environmental Quality Act and the Forest Practices Act (Dandero 1985a). The environmentalists' victory was tempered, however, by the fact that the governor of California cut ("axed," in the apt terminology of the reporter) from the state budget the allocation that would have secured the area and its trees as a state park by purchasing it from its willing owners, the timber company (Dandero 1985b).

A year later, in a significant victory for the environmentalists, the Georgia Pacific Corporation reversed itself and turned over 7,000 acres of this timberland, constituting most of the disputed area, to the non-profit Trust for Public Land, which will in turn arrange for it to be added to the adjacent wilderness park (Page 1986). This victory was somewhat dampened by the fact that almost immediately thereafter, in nearby Humboldt County, the Pacific Lumber Company, under new ownership, announced plans to double its timber cutting in the next year, and this in turn triggered another protest, doubtless to be followed by protracted actions aimed at preserving the forests (Champion 1986). The future of these forests therefore remains in doubt—as have so many of Chipko's apparent victories—in the face of timber interests and other monied development interests and their allies in and out of government.

DIVERSITY AND INTEGRATION IN CHIPKO

An impressive feature of Chipko is the social diversity of its support and its integrative social impact. It has consistently cut across social and cultural cleavages that might have been expected to divide it, and which its opponents and many politicians have attempted to exploit for their own ends. Through shared endeavor and meaningful interaction in a common cause, it has united people across often formidable boundaries of sex, age, religion, ethnicity, region, class, and even caste. This is an accomplishment rare indeed in post-Gandhian India.

Women and Men

Chipko has become famous as a movement wherein rural, village women have been prominent as both leaders and participants. Several of the heroes of the movement are women; it has even been described by some commentators as "a women's movement" (Agarwal et al., 1982, 42–43; Bahuguna 1975; Bhatt and Kunwar 1982; Jain 1983; Joshi 1981; Kothari 1981; Mishra and Tripathi 1978; cf. Sharma 1984). What leads many observers to this conclusion is the nature and extent of women's participation, which is unusual and impressive in the context of rural India. It must be understood, however, that men are involved as well as women, in similar ways and to a similar extent.

A combination of factors is no doubt responsible for women playing such a prominent role—equal to that of men—in what might be expected to be a male domain. Significant among them are: (1) Women in this Himalayan area have unusually high status, as contrasted with most of India, along with exceptional freedom of action and movement that accompanies their heavy contribution to the agricultural subsistence economy—a contribution at least as great as that of men (Berreman 1963, 75–77 and 260–62). (2) Because many men are away from their families and villages seeking employment in the plains (a response to the decimation of the environment and the consequent need for supplementary or alternative sources of livelihood), women often remain as the able-bodied adults responsible for their families and villages. These women have become accustomed to leadership in meeting the requirements for community survival. (3) Even when men are present, it is often women who do most of the kinds of work that entail direct, daily use of the forests and water supply and who therefore feel most immediately and acutely the impact of their destruction. Consequently, women are alert to the devastation of the environment and respond readily, knowledgeably, and confidently to the need to protect against it. For these reasons, women's conspicuous and responsible roles in Chipko are not surprising.

Young and Old, Urban and Rural, Literate and Illiterate

The young and old are also more heavily and jointly involved in Chipko than might be expected in a movement seemingly requiring the energy and maturity associated with those in the prime of adult life. In the first place, in the Himalayan region young and old seem to be more thoroughly integrated into the domestic subsistence economy than is the case in most of India. Further, like women, the young and old frequently work daily in the forests and with the water supply, experiencing directly the consequences of their impairment. In addition, under the demanding conditions created by the absence of employable men, young and old of both sexes have joined women in the prime of life to fill economic roles. Therefore they have been motivated and welcomed to active participation in Chipko's efforts to protect the environment.

Other social cleavages that have often divided people in thought and action have been overcome as well in the context of Chipko. Urban and rural youth have worked shoulder to shoulder, as have those from the plains and the mountain districts. Students in high schools and universities have been from the beginning among the most active and militant Chipko workers and supporters, joining their rural, uneducated, or minimally educated compatriots. All of these are categories of people who theretofore knew little of one another beyond the most casual contact and often negative stereotypes.

Ethnicity

But the integrative nature of Chipko involvement goes further still; it also cuts across ancient and powerful ethnic barriers. The two distinct ethnic groups that populate the Himalayas in Uttarakhand, Pahari Hindus and Bhotiya Buddhists, generally occupy different although sometimes contiguous territories defined primarily by altitude and environment, and therefore they usually have little to do with one another. But in some of the Chipko confrontations, they have joined forces to protect their common forests, and throughout Uttarakhand they have recurrently united in support of the Chipko cause. Perhaps the most famous of all Chipko actions was that in the Reni Forest of Chamoli district in 1974, when Gauri Devi, a Bhotiya woman, became the most celebrated of Chipko's heroes. Twenty-five hundred trees in the local forest had been sold on government contract, and the village men and *sarvodaya* workers had been lured away on plausible pretexts by the contractors and Forest Department officials after long and frustrating negotiations on the fate of the trees had failed. During their absence, Gauri Devi saw the contractor's tree cutters skirting the village in hope of avoiding detection en route to the trees. She promptly mobilized village women, both Bhotiya and Pahari, to confront them, and the women's combined courage and energy succeeded in completely thwarting them, even converting some to the Chipko cause—an event immortalized in tales and songs of the movement (cf. Dogra 1980, 48–49; 1983, 45–47; Mishra and Tripathi 1978, 26–30).

An important consequence of Chipko has been that in addition to bringing people together and bridging traditional chasms of ignorance, misunderstanding, tension, and conflict, it also focuses the attention of all of the participants on a wide range of issues and problems otherwise recognized, if at all, only by those particular groups or categories of people immediately affected. Participation in the movement has thereby raised the consciousness and mobilized and directed the energies of enough people to make possible and effective the collective action that Chipko as a social movement represents.

The Difficult Question of Caste

Caste is the most notorious source of conflict in South Asia and remains a uniquely intractable barrier to society-wide, cohesive action of any sort. To be sure, the two elite landowning and farming castes in Uttarakhand, Brahmans and Rajputs, have come together to support Chipko. But it must be noted that these two castes are closely allied and not as much separated in status and life-style as is the case in the plains of India (Berreman 1963, 229–32). The disheartening fact remains that the greatest and most important caste barrier in the region—that between these powerful high castes and the low, Harijan, or Dom castes (artisan and service castes, including all who elsewhere in India would be called Sudra as well as *achut* [untouchable])—has not been significantly breached by Chipko (Berreman 1983, 314; cf. Berreman 1963, 233–58).

Primarily people with no land—or, in the case of a small number who have acquired some through land reform programs, the least productive land—and few livestock, the low castes have little direct stake in the forests and soil. They have almost no voice in community affairs and even less in regional politics. They regard Chipko as a high-caste farmers' concern, an issue only for decision makers and influence wielders, and since they see little opportunity for themselves to benefit from Chipko or to influence it in directions that could benefit them, they have been little involved in it. In the nature of the caste system, the Chipko program excludes these artisans and agricultural servants, who constitute up to 20 percent of the population—an already oppressed and therefore alienated, yet indispensable, segment of society—and this could prove to be the Achilles heel of the Chipko movement. As essential links in the agricultural economy, and as voters in the democratic political process, these people's support of the principles and practices of Chipko is necessary to its long-term success.

To motivate and enable them to participate would require revolutionary social, economic, and political reforms in the direction of a more egalitarian society. High-caste traditions and vested interests make them unlikely to be pursued—but they *must* be, and with tangible results not only in the Himalayas but throughout India, if the environment and ultimately the nation are not to succumb to the poverty and helplessness, the conflict and fear, that the rigidly inegalitarian social, political, and economic structures of caste and class create (cf. Ratcliffe 1978).

In Uttarakhand there would appear to be more hope of overcoming these inequalities and caste tensions than in most regions of the country. That hope, slight as it is, rests on several phenomena. The Himalayan economy, with its subsistence mode of agriculture, is smaller in scale, its villages more independent and self-sufficient, than elsewhere in India, making the population less vulnerable to the vagaries of world and national markets and rendering economic disparities between individuals, households, and castes smaller and competition among them less intense than is usual in the nation (Berreman 1963, 38–79). Castes there also are fewer, the proportion of low-caste people in the population generally smaller, the social barriers between castes (even between high and low) somewhat less rigid and forbidding, and the cultural differences among them less pronounced than in the plains and the rest of the country (Berreman 1960).

It could be argued that to the extent that there is relatively less caste-based inequality and exploitation in the Himalayas than elsewhere, there would be less lost by the high castes here than elsewhere if these disparities were diminished, social justice enhanced, and the low castes assimilated to the local economic, social, and political structure. The advantage to be gained from increased cohesion throughout the society and the possibility of greater collective action for the common good might well outweigh the traditional advantages of the high castes' exclusive hold on power and privilege. The first of these arguments, of course, is only a relative one, and the second is merely a logical one, whereas the problems and their responses are absolute and culturally defined. Perhaps the inequities are too great, and the power of tradition too strong, to allow for the possibility of the arguments' validity being demonstrated in actuality. But if—and this is admittedly a very big "if"—the high castes were to act as these arguments suggest, low castes could be expected to respond positively, greatly increasing the likelihood of constructive change in many spheres, including environmental preservation and consequent enhancement of the quality of life for all, in the Himalayas and in the plains as well.

CONCLUSION

The point being made in this paper is that Chipko is a grass-roots movement responding to the needs of most of the population of Uttarakhand, namely, those people who live in rural villages, close to the soil, forests, and water of the Himalayas. They understand what threatens these resources, what could preserve them, and how crucial they are to human well-being. Their knowledge is far more profound than that of officials and many other outsiders because it is hard earned, daily applied, and therefore deeply ingrained. Two quotations aptly juxtaposed by Dogra (1980, 1; 1983, 5) make this point vividly. First, a senior Forest Department official in 1977 asked Dogra, rhetorically: "What do these villagers know about ecology? What do they know of forestry? They only know how to destroy trees." Dogra followed this with the words of Gauri Devi, the heroine of the Reni village Chipko confrontation of 1974, speaking in remonstrance to the laborers who had come to fell the forest upon which her people depend: "Brother, this forest is our home. From it we satisfy so many of our needs. Do not axe it. If you do, landslides will ruin our homes and fields."

Recognition by the mountain people of the interest they share in solving their common predicament has drawn them together—with the ominous exception of the barriers of caste—into the Chipko movement, across cleavages that in the past have often divided them, cleavages that politicians continue to attempt to exacerbate and employ in their pursuit of power through the age-old technique of divide and rule (Berreman 1983, 301–9 and 314–16). Chipko has frustrated and counteracted these selfish and shortsighted forces, remaining largely uncorrupted and uncorruptible. In the India of today, this is no small or insignificant achievement. And it is, I believe, the hope that Chipko holds for the people of the Himalayas, and as a model for the people of India. Mohandas Gandhi held up such a model in the independence movement, and others have emulated him. But now Chipko is one of the few viable manifestations in India of the Gandhian vision—of a grass-roots, people-oriented movement consistent with the small-scale developmental, appropriate technological, labor intensive, environmentally conservationist, cooperative, socialist, anticolonial, egalitarian, secular, locally self-sufficient and self-determinant, internationally unaligned kind of society with which the origin of the Indian republic is identified—and which has been largely abandoned in the years since independence.

The Chipko movement revives this ideology and hope against tremendous odds. If there is any chance of overcoming these odds, the problems must be clearly identified and confronted. Practical programs for their solution will require agonizing social and economic reforms, forthrightly and courageously implemented. Fortunately, India has its own analysts of these problems and advocates for the requisite programs to alleviate or solve them. If they can acquire a significant audience, the vision of India that motivated the achievement of its independence may yet be realized. I have in mind such spokespersons as economist-journalist Arun Shourie, executive editor of the *Indian Express*; political scientist Rajni Kothari, founder of Lokayan; Ravi Chopra together with his colleagues in the Centre for Science and Environment, including especially his coeditors of the two volumes of *The State of India's Environment*, Kalpana Sharma and Anil Agarwal (now director of CSE); the journalist B. G. Verghese and his compatriots in Citizens for Democracy; the women of *Manushi*; Chipko leaders Chandi Prasad Bhatt and Sunderlal Bahuguna; the young historian of forestry and environment Ramachandra Guha; the editor of *Himalaya, Man and Nature*, Krishna Murti Gupta, and his co-workers; and many others from many walks of life throughout India, all of them people of courage and vision.

POSTSCRIPT

On June 8, 1985, shortly after this paper had been prepared, a small but ominous item from Reuters appeared in the *San Francisco Chronicle*, announcing that "India has issued formal guidelines for foreign academics that bar research into sensitive issues." Puzzled, I sought out an *Indian Express* article that stated, in part: "The Government has put new restrictions on the appointment of foreign nationals in Indian universities, their research programmes and movement into sensitive areas." "Appointments of foreign nationals could be made only under very exceptional circumstances" even for visiting professors, and "exception will not be made even in the case of institutions like the United States Educational Foundation in India." Government clearance will have to be obtained for every foreign participant in international conferences, seminars, and symposia. Moreover, "no foreign scholars will be allowed to conduct research on topics . . . which are politically sensitive or may cause ill-feeling and tension between different groups. . . . Backward tribes, inter-communal or socially sensitive themes or research involving visits to restricted . . . regions . . . have to be excluded." "Foreign scholars have also been debarred from delivering any lecture or talk on topics of a controversial nature." "The universities must monitor the activities and movement of foreign scholars" (*Indian Express*, 8 June 1985).

There is little that is truly new here beyond the fact that now universities are held responsible for obtaining clearances, implementing restrictions, and overseeing the activities of their foreign visitors. What seems significant and disturbing is the fact that the Government of India has felt impelled to issue a pronouncement of such restrictive regulation of foreign scholarship in this severe tone. Although an article in *India-West* (1985) noted that "an education Ministry spokesman told Reuters the new guidelines were to clear up confusion . . . over the status of visiting scholars" and were "routine," one cannot avoid thinking that they may have been issued in response to recent events in India. The *Indian Express* article indicated as much when it remarked that "the Government has reportedly put these restrictions in the wake of recent espionage which had far reaching consequences" (*Indian Express* 1985). One might speculate that the well-known international aspects of recent communal-cum-political conflict in India could be further motivating factors in promulgating these regulations (cf. Singh, Joshi and Singh 1985).

Sixteen years ago, I wrote an article in the *Nation*, deploring colonial attitudes and actions by foreign scholars in India. I said, "The only hope for continued American academic research abroad . . . lies in genuine responsiveness to the needs, desires and demands of host communities. This means not only conformity to explicit requirements when those are set forth, but evidence of full respect for the intellect, judgment and responsibility of scholars and citizens of the other society" (Berreman 1969, 508). I concluded: "If deference to indigenous values and scientific priorities is the price to be paid for research in newly emancipated societies, it should be remembered that this price has always been exacted by uncolonized societies. It is neither exorbitant nor dishonorable. . . . [If this is not recognized and acted upon] Americans face a long period of enforced academic isolationism" (ibid.).

I still believe that. But the costs are paid by both sides. I would simply point out that research such as I have reported above might well be prohibited under the new guidelines. So might most of the research that has been carried out in India by foreign social scientists. That would be India's loss as much as ours—probably more so.

The imposition of sensitivity as a criterion for scholarly research is a step back from an open society, whose policies are derived from and tested against full information and open public debate. What is deemed "sensitive" will likely prove to be what is uncomfortable or inexpedient for those in power to hear or allow their public to hear.

Such guidelines suggest a move toward obscurantism and therefore a retreat from *"the politics of truth,"* whose essential role in social science and social justice the great sociologist C. Wright Mills taught us (Mills 1963, 611; 1959, 178–79), and they also constitute a retreat from *"experiments with truth,"* whose essential role in defining India's promise and achieving its greatness the revered Mohandas Gandhi taught us (Gandhi 1957).[7]

NOTES

1. Perhaps the most extensive, readily available listing of these activist groups is to be found in the Centre for Science and Environment's second major volume, *The State of India's Environment, 1984–85* (New Delhi 1985), iv–x, et passim.

2. The scholarly and political periodical literature in India has produced numerous recent articles on this subject. In one, entitled "Toward a People's Science Movement," Anwar Jaffry and his coauthors (1983) discuss some twenty major voluntary work groups addressing issues at "the interface of science and society" in such fields as the environment, the impact of development schemes, appropriate technology, health and housing. In another, "Undeclared Civil War: A Critique of the Forest Policy," the People's Union for Democratic Rights describes and discusses a number of movements in opposition to infringements of forest rights in several regions of India (S. Banerjee, "Critique of Forest Policy," 1982:55–59). One of the best documented historical accounts of movements based on issues of class, caste, and ethnicity is Kathleen Gough's "Indian Peasant Uprisings" (1974). A spate of scholarly books on historical and contemporary social movements of protest, resistance, and advocacy in India also have appeared during the past decade. Some of the best known are those edited or authored by: D. N. Danagere (1983), A. R. Desai (1979), Ranajit Guha (1983, 1983–85), S. C. Malik (1977), K. N. Panikkar (1980), M. S. A. Rao (1978, 1979), N. Sengupta (1982). And there are more, many of them devoted to specific movements, as is Sengupta's.

3. In July 1987 *India Today* described the UKD as "an almost unknown organization till recently" which emerged on March 9 with a rally drawing ten thousand people in the hill town of Pauri, Garhwal, followed by another on June 9 in Dehra Dun drawing eight thousand, one on June 20 in Pithoragarh drawing one thousand, and more to follow in Tehri, Chamoli, Uttarkashi, and Naini Tal. "The highlight of the string of rallies will be an Uttarakhand Bandh [strike] on August 9" (Awasthi 1987).

4. Whereas a few hundred people per year arrived on foot in Badrinath, a Himalayan shrine, twenty-five years ago, now 250,000 people per year reportedly motor there (Agarwal et al. 1982, 43).

5. The most useful published descriptions of Chipko are no doubt those by Dogra (1980; 1983) and by Mishra and Tripathi (1979). The most incisive accounts of the historical context for the movement are by Ramachandra Guha (1983 and 1985).

6. Virtually every published account of Chipko focuses principally on one or the other of these two leaders as the source and model for its rendering of the nature of the movement and its accomplishments. Two partial exceptions are Dogra (1980; 1983), who, though leaning toward the Bahuguna camp, gives substantial attention to Bhatt as well, and Mishra and Tripathi (1978), who, though favoring Bhatt, also give Bahuguna his due. Foreign accounts have generally relied on Bahuguna's group for their information and interpretations.

7. Unhappily, in the two years that have elapsed since this paper was presented, these concerns have proven to be all too justified. Substantial social science research by foreign scholars has been drastically curtailed in India. One can only hope, for India and for scholarship, that this is a temporary side effect of troubled times.

REFERENCES CITED

Agarwal, Anil
    1984   Beyond Pretty Trees and Tigers: The Role of Ecological Destruction in the Emerging Patterns of Poverty and People's Protests. *ICSSR Newsletter* (Indian Council of Social Science Research, New Delhi), 15 (April–September):1–27.

Agarwal, Anil, Ravi Chopra, and Kalpana Sharma (eds.)
    1982   *The State of India's Environment, 1982: A Citizens' Report.* New Delhi: Centre for Science and Environment.

Agarwal, Anil, and Sunita Narain (eds.)
    1985   *The State of India's Environment, 1984–85: The Second Citizens' Report.* New Delhi: Centre for Science and Environment.

Alvares, Claude
  1984   From Chipko to Appiko. *Express Magazine* (*Indian Express*),
            9 Sept.:1.

Ashish, Sri Mahadeva
  1979   Agricultural Economy of Kumaon Hills: Threat of Ecological
            Disaster. *Economic and Political Weekly* 14:1058–64.

Awasthi, Dilip
  1987   Uttar Pradesh: A Hill Demand. *India Today,* 15 July:61.

Bahugana, Sunderlal
  1983a   What Man Does to Mountain, and to Man. *Future* (First
            Quarter):6–11.

  1983b   Chipko Movement Comes South. *The Hindu* (International
            Edition), 3 Dec.:9.

  1984   Women's Non-Violent Power in the Chipko Movement. In *In
            Search of Answers: Indian Voices from Manushi,* edited by
            Madhu Kishwar and Ruth Vanita, 129–30. London: Zed Press.

Bahuguna, Vimla
  1975   Contribution of Women to Chipko Movement. *Indian Farming*
            25:69–71.

Bandyopadhyay, Jayanta, et al.
  1984   *The Doon Valley Ecosystem.* New Delhi: Department of
            Environment, Government of India.

Banerjee, Sumata
  1982   A Report: A Critique of the Forest Policy. *Philosophy and Social
            Action* 8(2):41–72.
            This also appeared as: P.U.D.R. (People's Union for Democratic
            Rights) pamphlet: Undeclared Civil War: A Critique of the
            Forest Policy. New Delhi (April 1982).

Barthélemy, Guy
  1982   *Chipko: Sauver les Forêts de l'Himalaya.* Paris: Éditions
            l'Harmattan.

Berreman, Gerald D.
  1960   Cultural Variability and Drift in the Himalayan Hills.
            American Anthropologist 62:774–94.

  1963   *Hindus of the Himalayas.* Berkeley and Los Angeles: University
            of California Press. (2d, expanded edition, 1972. Citations of
            1963 ed. are accurate for 1972 ed. as well.)

1969   Academic Colonialism: Not So Innocent Abroad. *Nation,* 10 Nov.:505–08.

1972a   Social Categories and Social Interaction in Urban India. *American Anthropologist* 74:567–86.

1972b   *Hindus of the Himalayas: Ethnography and Change* (2d, expanded edition). Berkeley and Los Angeles: University of California Press.

1978   Ecology, Demography and Domestic Strategies in the Western Himalayas. *Journal of Anthropological Research* 34:326–68.

1979   *Himachal: Science, People and "Progress."* IWGIA Document 36. Copenhagen: International Work Group on Indigenous Affairs.

1983   Identity Definition, Assertion and Politicization in the Central Himalayas. In *Identity: Personal and Socio-Cultural* (Uppsala Studies in Cultural Anthropology 5), edited by A. Jacobson-Widding, 289–319. Stockholm: Almqvist and Wiksell International, and Atlantic Highlands, New Jersey: Humanities Press.

Bhatt, Chandi Prasad
1985   Voluntary Agencies: A Movement to Conserve Forest Wealth. *Indian and Foreign Review* 22(7):9–10, 29.

Bhatt, Chandi Prasad, and S. S. Kunwar
1982   "Hill Women and Their Involvement in Forestry." In *Hugging the Himalayas: The Chipko Experience,* edited by S. S. Kunwar, 84–89. Gopeshwar, Chamoli: Dasholi Gram Swarajya Mandal.

Centre for Science and Environment (See: Agarwal, et al.)

Champion, Dale
1986   Redwood Cutting Plan Provokes a Protest. *San Francisco Chronicle,* 23 Oct.:24.

Danagere, D. N.
1983   *Peasant Movements in India, 1920–1950.* Delhi: Oxford University Press.

Dandero, Mark
1985a   Courts Spare Sally Bell. *Redwood Record* (Garberville, California), 1 Aug.:1.

1985b   Sinkyone Funds Slashed. *Redwood Record* (Garberville, California), 4 July:1.

Desai, A. R. (ed.)
  1979   *Peasant Struggles in India.* Bombay: Oxford University Press.

Dogra, Bharat
  1980   *Forests and People: The Efforts in Western Himalayas to Re-Establish a Long-Lost Relationship.* Rishikesh: Himalaya Darshan Prakashan.

  1983   *Forests and People: A Report on the Himalayas.* (2d, revised ed.
  [1980]   of Dogra 1980). New Delhi: Bharat Dogra.

Gandhi, Mohandas K.
  1957   *An Autobiography: The Story of My Experiments with Truth.* Boston: Beacon Press. (First published in 1927 and 1929, 2 vols., in Gujarati.)

Gough, Kathleen
  1974   Indian Peasant Uprisings. *Economic and Political Weekly* 9(32–34):1391–1412.

Guha, Ramachandra
  1983   Forestry in British and Post-British India: A Historical Analysis. *Economic and Political Weekly* 18(44 and 45–46):1822–96 and 1940–47.

  1985   Forestry and Social Protest in British Kumaon, c. 1893–1921. In *Subaltern Studies IV: Writings in South Asian History and Society,* edited by Ranajit Guha, 54–100. Delhi: Oxford University Press.

Guha, Ranajit
  1983   *Elementary Aspects of Peasant Insurgency in Colonial India.* Delhi: Oxford University Press.

Guha, Ranajit (ed.)
  1983–85 *Subaltern Studies: Writings in South Asian History and Society.* 4 vols. Delhi: Oxford University Press.

Gupta, Krishna Murti (ed.)
  1977   *Himalaya, Man and Nature* (a journal). Delhi: Himalaya Seva Sangh.

Hegde, Pandurang
  1985   Wanton Felling and Damaging of Trees. *Himalaya, Man and Nature* 9(1–2):2–4.

Iliste, Ivo, and Birgitta Goranson
  1980   Crisis in the Himalayas, 1980. *Inside-Outside* (India) March:37–51.

India Now
1985   Human Rights Movement, A Part of Peace Movement: Mary
        Kaldor Interviews Kothari. *India Now* 8, no. 10:11.

India-West (Emeryville, California)
    14 June
    1985   Foreign Scholars Restricted by New India Guidelines, 35.

Indian Express (New Delhi)
    8 June
    1985   New Curbs on Postings of Foreigners in Varsities.

Jaffrey, Anwar, Mahesh Rangarajan, B. Ekbal, and K. P. Kannan
    1983   Toward a People's Science Movement. *Economic and Political
            Weekly* 18:372–76.

Jain, Shobita
    1983   Women and "People's Ecological Movement": A Case Study of
            Women's Role in the Chipko Movement in the Garhwal Region
            of Uttar Pradesh, India. Paper presented at the Eleventh Interna-
            tional Congress of Anthropological and Ethnological Sciences,
            Vancouver, British Columbia, Aug. 23.

Joshi, Gopa
    1981   Protecting the Sources of Community Life: Slandered by the
            Community in Return. *Manushi: A Journal about Women and
            Society* (Delhi) 7:22–24. (Reprinted in M. Kishwar and R. Va-
            nita, eds., *In Search of Answers: Indian Voices from Manushi*,
            125–29. London: Zed Press.)

Kothari, Ashish
    1981   Chipko Andolan: Women Fight for Trees and Justice. *Himmat*
            (15 April):37–40.

Malik, S. C. (ed.)
    1977   *Dissent, Protest and Reform in Indian Civilization*. Simla: Indian
            Institute of Advanced Study.

    1978   *Indian Movements*. Simla: Indian Institute of Advanced Study.

Mathur, H. N.
    1978   Chipko Needs a New Direction. *Himalaya, Man and
            Nature* 2(5):1–7.

Mills, C. Wright
    1959   *The Sociological Imagination*. New York: Oxford University
            Press.

1963   On Knowledge and Power. In *Power, Politics and People: The Collected Essays of C. Wright Mills,* edited by I. L. Horowitz, 599–613. New York: Ballantine Books. (First published 1955.)

Mishra, Anupam, and S. Tripathi
    1978   *Chipko Movement: Uttarakhand Women's Bid to Save Forest Wealth.* New Delhi: People's Action for Peace and Justice.

Overseas Hindustan Times
    26 Nov.
    1983   Half of H. P. Forest Area Denuded in Eight Years, 11.

Page, Peter
    1986   Environmentalists' Timberland Victory. *San Francisco Chronicle,* 27 Sept. 27:10.

Panikkar, K. N. (ed.)
    1980   *National and Left Movements in India.* New Delhi: Vikas Publishers.

People's Union for Democratic Rights (P.U.D.R.) (See: Banerjee)

Rao, M. S. A. (ed.)
    1978 and   *Social Movements in India.* Vol. 1 (1978) *Peasant and Backward*
    1979   *Classes Movements;* Vol. 2 (1979) *Sectarian and Women's Movements.* New Delhi: Manohar Publications.

    1980   "Some Aspects of Sociology of Migration." Unpublished paper presented to the Sub-Panel on Migration, Fifteenth All India Sociological Conference, Meerut, Uttar Pradesh, 2 April.

Ratcliffe, John
    1978   Social Justice and the Demographic Transition: Lessons from India's Kerala State. *International Journal of Health Services* 8(1):123–44.

San Francisco Chronicle
    8 Oct.
    1983   Protesters Prevent Cutting of Old Trees, 6.

    25 Oct.
    1983   Mendocino Logging Protesters Jailed, 2.

    3 Nov.
    1983   Mighty Struggle Over Ancient Redwoods, 4.

    16 Nov.
    1983   Court Appeals Spare Redwoods, 4.

8 June

1985   Guidelines for Scholars, 3.

10 Dec.

1985   American, Canadian Win "Alternative Nobel Prizes," 15.

Sengupta, Nirmal (ed.)

1982   *Fourth World Dynamics, Jarkhand.* Delhi: Guild Publications.

Sharma, Kumud

1984   Women in Struggle: A Case Study of the Chipko Movement. *Samya Shakti* 1(2):55–62.

Shepard, Mark

1981   Chipko: North India's Tree Huggers. *Co-EVOLUTION Quarterly* (Fall):62–70.

Shiva, Vandana, and J. Bandyopadhyay

1986   The Evolution, Structure, and Impact of the Chipko Movement. *Mountain Research and Development* 6(2):133–42.

Singh, Ralph, Barbara Joshi, and Surjit Singh (eds.)

1985   *The Turning Point: India's Future Direction?* Syracuse: Committee on Human Rights.

Urfi, Abdul Jamil

1985   Battle for the Woods. *Overseas Hindustan Times,* 3 Aug.:8.

PART 4

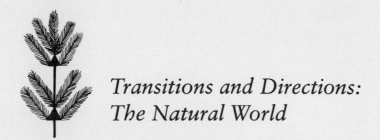

Transitions and Directions:
The Natural World

CHAPTER 16

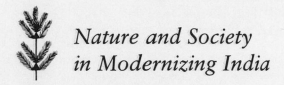

Nature and Society in Modernizing India

Anil Agarwal

In traditional Indian cultures, as in other cultures of the world, there has been a great understanding of the way the natural environment functions and how people ought to live within it. In fact, the cultural diversity that emerged in the world was not a historical accident; it was a direct response to the biological diversity in the world, to people's struggles to develop life-styles harmonious with their environments.

My mother once told me a famous myth about the descent of the Goddess Ganga from the heavens, the ecological implications of which I have only come to appreciate recently. King Bhagiratha wanted the goddess to come down to earth to wash off the sins of his forebears. After much prayer to her, Ganga agreed, but only on condition that somebody be prepared to tie her down. "If I am not," she told Bhagiratha, "I will not be the life-giving source that you expect me to be, but I will create enormous chaos and destruction on earth." So Bhagiratha searched and searched and finally found the only one who could restrain the mighty Ganga, the powerful God Siva. He went into another period of prayer, this time to Lord Siva. Siva eventually granted his prayer, and Ganga descended into Siva's hair locks, from there running out as a trickle (the Ganga, or Ganges River) to give life to the vast plains of northern India.

But look at the myth in another way. The monsoon, a life-giving system for the Indian subcontinent, is nothing but the descent of Ganga every year. Siva in many ways is synonymous with the Himalayas, and if you accept that, then Siva's locks are the forests of the Himalayas. Over the last 150 years, as human beings have acquired the temerity to cut down the forests, it is not surprising that the Ganges is now turning into the fury that the myth had said it would become, bringing more floods and more droughts.

Human beings have watched the universe over the centuries and have come to formulate such myths—or metaphors—behind which there is much empirical knowledge that all of us must understand. Unfortunately, the processes of modernization have tended to neglect traditional knowledge systems. (Modern scholars are usually full of disdain for traditional knowledge.) The result of such neglect is environmental destruction and associated human misery. And what we find in India today is not only a threat to the country's biological diversity and environmental integrity but also a threat to its cultural diversity. This is hardly just an Indian problem, either; it affects the entire globe. If we have the multinational corporation and its multinational technology, we also have the multinationalization of culture.

The environment, at least, is an idea whose time has come in India. Newspapers give prominent display to environmental horror stories. Government statements on the need to preserve the environment are commonplace. There are massive schemes for afforestation; in the last four years, some one thousand crore seedlings have been distributed or planted. There are new laws for control of air and water pollution and for the conservation of forests. India has received plaudits all over the world for what it has done to protect tigers. Planning documents and party manifestos both are careful to mention the importance of the environment.

But there is a major problem with this entire range of activities and concerns: It does not reflect a holistic understanding of the relationship between the environment and the development process taking place in the country. The programs are ad hoc, without any sharp priority. They seem to be based on the belief that concern for the environment essentially means protecting and conserving it partly from development programs but mainly from the people themselves. In this case, there is little effort to modify the development process itself in a manner that will bring it into greater harmony with the needs of the people and with the need to maintain ecological balance, while increasing the productivity of our land, water, and forest resources.

The environment is not just pretty trees and tigers, threatened plants and ecosystems. It is literally the entity on which we all subsist, and on which our entire agricultural and industrial development depends. Development can take place at the cost of the environment only up to a point; beyond that point, it will be like the foolish person trying to cut the very branch on which he is sitting.

Among the hundreds of voluntary groups working at the field level within the country, there has been a remarkably rapid growth of interest in environmental problems—so rapid, in fact, that sometimes we even loosely tend to describe it as the beginnings of an environmental movement. During the last four years, the Centre for Science and Environment has been involved in producing two citizens' reports on the state of India's environment, and we have had the fortune and opportunity to interact with many of these groups in the process.

The groups' experiences and goals are extremely diverse. Some want to prevent deforestation, whereas others are only interested in afforestation; many want to prevent the construction of one dam or another, and others are trying to prevent water pollution.

The famous Chipko movement in the Uttar Pradesh Himalayas, probably the oldest and most famous of all the groups, has played a major role in bringing the issue of deforestation to the fore of public opinion. Plans for dams like those in the Silent Valley and Bedthi have already been stopped because of strong peoples' protests, and now the well-known social worker Baba Amte is leading a major campaign against the proposed Bhopalapatnam and Inchampalli dams on the borders of Madhya Pradesh, Andhra Pradesh, and Maharashtra. The Kerala Sastra Sahitya Parishad has waged a long battle over the pollution of the Chaliyar River in Kerala by a rayon mill. The India Development Service finds itself embroiled in another case of river pollution by a rayon mill in Karnataka. Meanwhile, the Shahdol Group has been working against the pollution of a river in the Shahdol district by a paper mill. And the Mitti Bachao Abhiyan organizes farmers against the waterlogging caused by faulty irrigation systems.

Although environmental protection per se may not even be the highest priority of some groups, including Chipko, one thing that binds most of them is their concern for a more equitable and sustainable use of the environment and for putting the environment at the service and in the control of the people, the local communities who live within that environment. It is the groups' understanding of the relationship between the people and their environment that is probably the most fascinating development for a reporter of events like me.

To appreciate the nature of environmental problems in India, it may be useful to compare and contrast certain environmental trends and issues in India with those in the West, especially since the current concern for the environment first arose in the West and since many groups in India, including political parties, have long dismissed it as a petty Western concern—as well as arguing that worrying too much about the environment can only retard economic and industrial development.

The Third World today faces both an environment crisis and a development crisis, and both these crises seem to be intensifying and interacting to reinforce each other. On the one hand, there does not seem to be any end to the crucial problems of inequality, poverty, and unemployment that the development process is meant to solve. On the other hand, environmental destruction has proceeded rapidly. But what is noteworthy is that although many environmental problems, especially those related to air and water pollution, have tended to become less severe in many parts of the industrialized world because of the introduction of pollution-control technologies, they have continued to grow to alarming limits in many parts of the developing world.

Very simply speaking, the major environmental problems in the West are those arising out of waste disposal—air and water pollution and disposal of highly toxic industrial and nuclear wastes. Although problems of acid rain have definitely increased and there does not yet seem to be any solution for disposing of toxic wastes, it is true that some cities and rivers do look cleaner.

In the Third World, as its own industrialization proceeds, waste disposal problems, which are getting worse day by day, are still not the major or only environmental problems: These arise out of the misuse of the natural resource base—soils, forests, and water—to supply raw materials for its own industries, as well as for the industries of the West.

For instance, the Japanese and Western timber industries have been the biggest cause of forest destruction in Southeast Asia. Having turned countries like Thailand from net exporters of wood into net importers of wood, Japanese companies are now casting greedy eyes toward the last great wooded frontier of the world, the Amazon Basin. The food needs of the Western world have played havoc with the lands of the Third World, too. No statistics on this are available, but if someone did collect them, I am sure we would find that many times more land is being used today in the developing world to meet the food needs of Western countries than in the 1940s, before the process of decolonization began.

In our own country, the first major attack on the forests of the northeast came with the establishment of tea plantations by the British. The current overfishing on India's coasts, as on the coasts of almost all Southeast Asian countries, is taking place because of the heavy demand for prawns in Western and Japanese markets, and it is leading to considerable tensions and violent encounters between traditional fisherfolk and trawler owners. Recently, Indonesia completely banned the operation of trawlers from its coastal waters, and several countries, including India, have set up regulations to prevent trawler operators from fishing in the first few kilometers from the coast, reserving this zone for the traditional fisherfolk. But policing trawlers over such an extensive coastline is an expensive proposition, and the regulations are, therefore, seldom observed or enforced. The export of frogs' legs to cater to the palates of Western consumers and its impact on the agricultural pest population in affected areas is now a well-known story (see *The State of the Environment, 1984–85,* Centre for Science and Environment, New Delhi).

The pattern of environmental exploitation that we see on a global scale reproduces itself on a national scale. Exactly what Western industry does to the Third World environment, Indian industry does to the Indian environment. To give an idea of how heavily dependent modern industry is on the natural environment, let me point out that nearly half the industrial output in India is accounted for by industries that can be called biomass based: that is, industries like cotton textiles, rayon, paper, plywood, rubber, soap, sugar, tobacco, jute, chocolate, food processing and packaging, and so on. Each of these industries exerts enormous pressure on the country's cultivated and forest lands, energy, and water resources.

The Indian paper industry has ruthlessly destroyed the forests of India. Paper companies in Karnataka, having gone through all the bamboo forests, are now getting their raw materials from the last major forested region of India, the northeast. The Andhra Pradesh government has meanwhile set its sights on the forests of the Andaman and Nicobar Islands for a paper mill it wants to build in Kakinada, on the Andhra coast. The shortage of raw materials for wood pulp has already forced the government to liberalize import of pulp for the country's paper industry, thus adding to the pressure on the forests of other Third World countries.

The first lesson is, therefore, clear: The main source of environmental destruction in the world is the demand for natural resources generated by the consumption of the rich (whether they are rich nations or rich individuals and groups within nations), and because of their gargantuan appetite, the wastes generated by satisfying them contribute substantially to the global pollution load.

The second lesson, however, is that it is the poor who are affected the most by environmental destruction. The field experience of voluntary groups shows clearly that the eradication of poverty in a country like India is not possible without the rational management of our environment and that, conversely, environmental destruction will only intensify poverty. The reason is simple though seldom recognized.

The vast majority of rural households meet their daily household needs through biomass or biomass-related products, which are mostly collected freely from the immediate environment. In short, they live within nothing other than a biomass-based, subsistence economy. Food, fuel (firewood, cowdung, crop wastes), fodder, fertilizer (organic manure, forest litter, leaf mulch), building materials (poles, thatch), herbs, and clothing are all biomass products. Water is another crucial product for survival; although it is not biomass itself, its availability is closely related to the level of biomass in the surrounding environment. Once the forest disappears, the local pond silts up, the village well dries up, and the perennial stream gets reduced to a seasonal one. The water balance becomes totally upset with the destruction of vegetation; in a monsoonal climate like ours, with highly uneven rainfall over the year, this means greatly increased runoff and floods during the peak water season and greatly increased drought and water scarcity in the lean, dry season.

The magnitude of India's dependence on biomass for meeting crucial household needs can be appreciated by looking at the energy situation. We love to point out that India has the world's fifteenth largest industrial output. But even then, over 50 percent of our fuel consumption is for such a fundamental survival activity as cooking. In developed countries, cooking consumes less than 10 percent of the total national fuel consumption. On top of that, over 90 percent of the cooking fuel in India is biomass: that is, firewood, cowdung, and crop wastes. Even urban households rely extensively on firewood as fuel.

Biomass resources also provide a range of raw materials for traditional occupations. Firewood and cowdung are important sources of fuel for potters; bullock carts, catamarans, and agricultural implements are made from wood; bamboo is a vital raw material for basket weavers. Traditional crafts are being threatened not just by the introduction of modern products but also by the acute shortage of biomass-based raw materials. A study from the Indian Institute of Science, the first in India on the changing market for bullock carts, reports that people in the village Ungra in Karnataka can now no longer afford to buy new bullock carts with the traditional wooden wheel because wood has become so expensive. The Murugappa Chettiar Research Centre in Madras reveals that traditional fisherfolk find it very difficult to make new catamarans because of the scarcity and high price of the special wood they use. Social activists in Saharanpur in Uttar Pradesh have pointed out the travails of *bān** makers: The Uttar Pradesh Forest Development Corporation discriminates in favor of paper mills, depriving the *bān* workers of their sources of *bhabhar* grass, and this policy has turned thousands of these workers into destitutes, landless laborers, and urban migrants.

Several reports from around the country—from Madhya Pradesh, Maharashtra, Tamil Nadu—describe the severe problems hundreds of thousands of basket weavers have in eking out a bare existence because of the acute shortage of bamboo. In the Bhandara and Chandrapur Districts of Maharashtra, nearly seventy thousand mat and basket weavers have been protesting the small quota of bamboo given to them, while large bamboo forests have been leased to big paper mills. In Karnataka, Madhav Gadgil undertook a study of the use of the state's bamboo forests by paper mills, after a series of protests by basket weavers. He found that whereas bamboo could be obtained by paper mills at fifteen rupees per ton, it was offered to basket weavers and other small bamboo users in the market at twelve hundred rupees per ton.**

Thatch has become so scarce that people can hardly maintain and repair their mud and thatch huts. A government report from Bastar, still one of the heavily forested districts in the country, identifies a village where no new hut has been built over the last two decades because the entire area around the village has been deforested. Traditional mud roofs have almost disappeared from many parts of the country since so much timber is needed for them. They are being replaced by tiled roofs, but baking of tiles still requires large quantities of firewood.

Fodder is another vital resource that is in acute shortage. With only 2.45 percent of the world's land mass, India supports 15 percent of its cattle and goats, and 52 percent of its buffalos. These animals play a very important role in the integrated system of agriculture and animal husbandry that Indian farmers practice. As a study from the tribal areas of Gujarat shows, shortage of fodder, especially from public lands, means that poor landless households and marginal farmers cannot benefit much from the milk cooperatives and animal improvement schemes in the region.

In such a situation, the destruction of the environment by any

---

*A kind of rope commonly used in charpoys in northern India.
**Based on 1985 exchange rates, Rs. 12.5 = $1.00.

policy that reduces access to biomass resources by those whose survival is based on them has an extremely adverse impact.

THE TRANSFORMATION OF NATURE

There are two major pressures operating on the country's natural resources today. The first, created by population growth and thus increased household demand for biomass resources, has been widely discussed. But the second set of pressures, generated by modernization, industrialization, and the general penetration of the cash economy, is seldom talked about, at least in policy-making circles.

Modernization affects nature in two ways. It is extremely destructive of the environment in its search for cheap, biomass-based raw materials and cheap opportunities for waste disposal. Unless there are strong laws that are equally strongly implemented, both public and private industrialists will pass environmental costs on to society rather than absorb them. State governments are also happy to give away large tracts of forests for a pittance and throw water pollution control laws to the winds if they can attract a few more factories.

In addition, modernization steadily transforms the very character of nature. In physical terms, the tendency is to reduce the diversity in nature, disregarding its ecological importance, in favor of high-yielding monocultures. In social terms, the movement is generally away from a nature that has traditionally come to support household and community needs and toward a nature that is geared to meet urban and industrial needs, a nature that is essentially cash generating. Excellent examples of such changes are the replacement of old oak forests by pine forests in the Himalayas, of sal forests by teak forests in the Chotanagpur Plateau, of natural forests by eucalyptus plantations in the Western Ghats—and now there are proposals to grow oil palms in place of the tropical forests in the Great Nicobar Island. Both of these phenomena—the destruction of the environment and the creation of a new, commercially oriented nature—have been taking place simultaneously in the Indian environment and on a massive scale.

The effect of this extensive environmental transformation has been disastrous for the people, especially when we realize that in a country like India, where we have an extremely high level of poverty and a reasonably high level of population density, there is hardly any ecological space left in the physical environment that is not occupied by one human group or another for its sustenance. Therefore, if, in the name of economic development, any human activity results in the destruction of an ecological space or in its transformation to benefit the more powerful groups in society, then inevitably those who were earlier dependent on that space will suffer. Development in this case leads to displacement and dispossession and will inevitably raise questions of social injustice and conflict. The experience of microlevel groups shows clearly again that it is rare to find a case in which environmental destruction does not go hand in hand with social injustice, almost like two sides of the same coin.

The destruction of grazing lands has meant enormous hardships for poor people, especially for the nomadic groups. In India, nearly two hundred castes—almost 6 percent of the population—are engaged in pastoral nomadism. India is unique in the world in the diversity of animals associated with pastoral nomadism. There are herders of camels in Rajasthan and Gujarat, of donkeys in Maharashtra, of yaks in Ladakh, of pigs in Andhra Pradesh, and even of ducks in southern India. Sheep, goats, and cattle are, of course, the main animals involved.

A number of factors, including land reforms and development programs that have promoted expansion of agriculture on to marginal lands, have led to the erosion of grazing lands. The Rajasthan Canal, a government project, has transformed extensive grazing lands into agricultural lands. No effort was made by the government to ensure that the nomads who had used these grazing lands would benefit from the canal on a priority basis. In almost every village, the panchayat (community) lands, traditionally used as *gauchar* (pasture) lands, have been encroached upon by powerful interest groups and have been privatized. Nomadic groups have grown increasingly impoverished over the last thirty years, and more and more of them are being forced to give up their traditional occupations, to become landless laborers or migrants to cities.

Although little data are available on their plight, riverine fisherfolk constitute another group that has suffered immensely from environmental destruction. Riverine fisheries are being seriously affected by increasing water pollution. Large-scale fish deaths are regularly reported, and in the 158-kilometer stretch of the Hooghly River, the average yield of fish in the polluted zones is just about a sixth of that in the unpolluted zones. Rivers have now become cheap dumps for urban and industrial India to use for their wastes—and all this is sanctioned in the name of economic development.

The planting of eucalyptus on farmers' fields and even on so-called barren fields also illustrates the adverse biomass conversion—adverse to the people—promoted by modernization. In Punjab, for example, a rich farmer (and former governor) with over 100 hectares of land has stopped growing cotton and has switched to eucalyptus. Because of the shortage of firewood, crop wastes from the landlords' fields are the major and almost only source of fuel for poor landless villagers, and so as long as this owner grew cotton, enormous quantities of cotton sticks were available for the village laborers. Now these people are in a precarious position. This is a case in which afforestation has actually created a fuel famine for the neediest community.

Thus what we see in India today is growing conflict over the use of natural resources, and over biomass in particular, between the two sectors of the country's economy: the cash economy, or the modern sector; and the nonmonetized, biomass-based subsistence economy, the traditional sector.

As the growing stock of biomass goes down, the demand for biomass from the cash economy goes up, demand begins to exceed supply, and pressure to exploit the remaining biomass increases dramatically. Biomass prices rise, and destructive processes accelerate because of sheer market forces. Stealing a few dozen trucks of illegally cut timber is the surest and easiest way to become rich.

ENVIRONMENT AND WOMEN

The destruction of the environment clearly poses the greatest threat to marginal cultures and occupations like those of tribals, nomads, and fisherfolk, who have always been dependent on their immediate environment for their survival. But the maximum impact of the destruction of biomass sources is on women. Women in all rural cultures are affected, especially women from poor landless, marginal, and small farming families. Given the existing, culturally accepted division of labor within the family, the collection of household necessities like fuel, fodder, and water is left to women. As the environment degrades and these become increasingly difficult to obtain, women have to spend an extraordinary amount of time foraging for them in addition to doing household work, agricultural work, and caring for animals. The data that are already available on women's current work burden are downright shocking. In many parts of India, women spend fourteen to sixteen hours working every day, and it does not matter whether they are young, old, or pregnant. Day after weary day, the routine repeats itself, and year after weary year fuel- and fodder-collection time increases. In many areas, the women may have literally reached their "carrying capacities."

The worst situation is in the arid and semiarid parts of the country and in the hill and mountain villages, where trees and forests have been steadily destroyed. Because of a number of factors—soil and climatic conditions, very small land holdings, lack of irrigation—the green revolution, which could enormously increase biomass from crop lands, has not reached these areas. As a result, there is now a severe biomass famine in these areas. Women can spend as much as five to six hours every day, in some households as much as ten hours, just collecting fuel and fodder.

The increasing work burden deforestation causes women is affecting everything else in their lives. A study from the Indian Institute of Management in Ahmedabad shows that five times more men than women seek treatment at primary health centers; women do not have time to seek health care, even when they are ill. Another study from rural Punjab recently described the problems faced by poor women from agricultural labor households after tubectomy operations. Nine out of ten of them complained about postoperative pains, and all of them wanted to rest, but none of them could. Collecting fodder alone took three hours of digging grass and other weeds from between wheat plants in a number of fields; gathering firewood meant still more work and another journey. The bending and stretching increased the pain. If the women tried to pass on their work to others, especially their children, they ran into conflicts with their husbands and their children who preferred to play. One woman kicked and punched her daughter so hard for not working with her that she died. Such viciousness may be rare, but increased family tensions are commonplace.

The penetration of the cash economy is affecting the relationship between men and women in a peculiar way and is creating a real dichotomy in their respective relationships with nature. Men have become more involved with the cash economy than women; women continue to deal with the nonmonetized, biomass-based subsistence economy of the household. Even within the same household, we can find instances of men glad to destroy nature to earn cash, even though it would create greater hardships for the women in meeting the daily fuel and fodder needs.

The Chipko movement has provided us numerous examples of this divergence in male–female interests, and the role of women in preventing deforestation and in ecological regeneration has been paramount in the movement. Even though many basic household needs could be met by rehabilitating the local village ecosystem—by planting fuel and fodder trees, for instance—the men do not show any interest in doing so. It is women who are carrying out all the afforestation work organized by the Chipko movement.

It is not surprising that eucalyptus-based "social forestry," trotted out to be such a great success by the World Bank and the forest departments, is all in the hands of men, planting trees with the cash motive. Other than employing women as cheap labor in nurseries, these agencies have nothing to show in terms of involvement of women—the very people who deal with fuel and fodder. But then making a fast buck, even at the expense of society and ecology, is probably the most social thing we can do in a cash economy.

The new culture created by the penetration of the cash economy has slowly but steadily alienated the men psychologically from their ecosystem. Employment for them means work that can put cash in their hands. Such employment can be found mainly in the city and, hence, there is mass male migration. This kind of migration, a major phenomenon in modern society, also increases the work burden of women, as they then have to devote more time to the family's agricultural fields as well as take care of household needs. But as the time it takes to collect fuel and fodder grows, and firewood becomes scarcer, agriculture must be neglected. A study of three villages in the Kumaon region of Uttar Pradesh, for instance, shows that already 2.5 times more human energy is spent in collecting fuel and fodder than is spent on agriculture. Abandonment of the traditional practice of manuring fields seems imminent. Cowdung will be used as fuel instead, as in the plains, but with the lack of manuring, fragile soils will soon be exhausted. It will be a disastrous situation, both for the local people and for the environment.

Because of the increasing intensity of floods, there has been considerable talk in recent years about integrated watershed management in the Himalayas and in the Ghats. The Himalayas, an ecosystem that determines the fate of several hundred million people in the Indo-Gangetic plains, are being described as one of the most threatened ecosystems in the world. But if any action for ecological reconstruction has to be taken in the hills, it cannot be done without the involvement of women. The census data of 1981 show that all the districts in the country having a high proportion of adult female workers are situated in the Himalayas or in the Ghats. In the Himalayas, most women workers are also classified as cultivators. Therefore, any program that aims at ecological rehabilitation in these areas will have to involve heavily overworked women—unless, of course, labor is brought into these areas from outside, which will create tensions with the local labor force.

Fortunately, the experience of the Chipko movement shows that women in these regions, despite their backbreaking schedule, work with great eagerness, especially in tree planting, and they fight any obstacles that may be created by men, so that we get as a result some of the highest tree survival rates found in afforestation efforts. It has also been learned that when women participate in afforestation, they tend to demand fuel and fodder trees, trees that can meet household needs. The greatest ally in the demand for an ecologically and socially sound nature is, therefore, womankind.

As identical experiences have been noted in East and West Africa, in Kenya and in the Sahelian countries, there is every reason to believe that this differential interest in nature between men and women is cross-cultural in character. The designation of trees as *male* trees and *female* trees is now even becoming common jargon among those interested in involving communities in afforestation.

If we take a head count at this stage, we will find that the destruction of the environment and its transformation are already affecting, on an immediate and daily basis, at least the following groups: artisans, nomads, tribals, fisherfolk, and women from landless, marginal, and small farming households. These groups add up to no less than one-half to three-quarters of the country's rural population. And unlike the situation in the West, the question of environmental destruction is not an issue related to the quality of life; it is a question of survival.

IMPROVING THE COUNTRY'S *GROSS NATURE PRODUCT*

Nothing could be more important for planners and politicans today than to rebuild nature. But this can only be done if we reestablish a healthy relationship between the people and their environment. Regardless of how much we may want to catch up with the West in the name of modernization—with its electronics revolution, biotechnology inventions, communications satellites, and its efforts to mine the oceans and to build solar cells and windmills—rebuilding nature and harnessing the power of the people to the power of the land will remain the only way to solve the problem of poverty and possibly even unemployment.

Even if enough biomass were available, poverty—that is, lack of cash, as defined by economists and by modern civilization—would not disappear. But the growing rigors of poverty and the increasing susceptibility to natural emergencies like floods and droughts definitely would be arrested by creating more biomass. In fact, conventional measurements of poverty based on income or on food calories are clearly inadequate in a situation where the other biomass needs are becoming ever more difficult to meet. And not only are these calculations inadequate; they also reflect a strong gender bias, dealing as they do mainly with those aspects of poverty (lack of cash) that the male is generally concerned with, not with those aspects of poverty (lack of fuel, fodder, water, etc.) that affect the woman.

An indicator like a *gross nature product* would be many times more important for the poor than the conventional gross national product (GNP), because they do not get much from the GNP and are the ones who are most critically dependent on the gross nature product. GNP calculations do not reflect the growing stock of biomass, and most economists, not surprisingly, have no clue what happens to a subsistence economy when its biomass resources are affected, nor do they care whether the growing stock lives or dies, exists or disappears. Only in studies of political economy are increasing hardships and conflicts over land, forests, grazing lands, and water sources considered. Unfortunately we do not know as yet how to construct such an indicator. But I am sure that if we did, we would find that while the GNP has gone up, the gross nature product has steadily gone down, the former acting as a parasite on the latter, and that understanding of the gross nature product and how it behaves within the national ecological space (or shall we say national economy) would probably tell us far more—and far more accurately—about the changing reality in the subsistence sector of a country like India.

Just as the economists worry about the structure of the GNP, it is equally important, if they have their poor in mind, that they worry about the structure of the gross nature product. Not only is the quantity of biomass important for meeting basic household needs but so is its diversity: Sources of biomass within any village ecosystem must be used for fuel, fodder, building materials, artisans' materials, and so forth. The diversity in nature has also acted as insurance during periods of emergency by reducing societal vulnerability. When there have been droughts and resulting crop failures, which are recurring phenomena in many parts of India, roots, leaves, and wild animals in the forests became alternative sources of nutrition. In 1983, the tribals of Chotanagpur survived a drought not because of government assistance, but despite government callousness. It is the forests that gave them their nutrition. A study from Africa found that in times of drought, traditional societies had nearly 150 responses; they even fed the thatch of their huts to their goats. But in a modern village, there were only two responses: pray to God (which even the Tamil Nadu government recommended during the Madras water crisis) or migrate to the towns. The combination of trees, grasses, crops, animals, and ponds, which we found in almost every village, was an extraordinarily interactive system, resilient to emergencies. Instead of destroying this complex and interrelated system, science must be used to build on it.

In other words, it is not enough to preserve biological diversity only in those areas of our country where the flora and fauna are genetically rich by setting up biosphere reserves and national parks; that biological diversity must be preserved and/or recreated in every village ecosystem. Concentrating on the production of a few commodities (cereals, for instance) is totally inadequate in a society that is only partly monetized and where the vast majority still has to depend on access to few biomass resources from the immediate environment. Every village has to become a biosphere reserve.

The answer to India's immediate problem of poverty lies in increasing the biomass available in nature and increasing it in such a way that access to it is ensured on an equitable basis. But giving a *green cover* to the country—the real green revolution—would probably require the most holistic thinking that planners, economists, and scientists have ever known. The conflicts and complementarities in the existing land-use patterns have to be extremely well understood, or these patterns will remain as chaotic as they are today. Poorer peasants will continue to oppose planting trees on community lands under so-called social forestry programs because they are afraid they will lose their grazing lands. Forest departments and richer peasants will only plant those trees which animals cannot touch (like eucalyptus), even though there is a stark fodder crisis all around. Nothing could take us closer to Gandhiji's concept of *grām svarājya** than striving to create village ecosystems that are biologically diverse and self-reliant in their local biomass needs to the maximum extent possible. This will clearly demand an intensive use of our natural resources, like land and water, to generate a huge and diverse growing stock of biomass. Any science that teaches how to do this will truly have the right to be called a people's science—and indeed it will have to begin with the knowledge of the people.

An even bigger challenge is before social workers and politicians who have to play a crucial role in ensuring that people can participate in this biomass-based development process. No biomass-based strategy can succeed without the involvement of the people, especially women.

If we fail to recreate nature on a massive scale in a manner that generates employment and equity, not only our villages but also our cities will become unlivable. Many people prefer to call the urban migrants economic refugees from the countryside; to my mind, many of them are really ecological refugees, displaced by dams, by mines, by deforestation, by destruction of grazing lands, by floods, by droughts. Managing our huge urban population—today the world's fourth largest, and before the end of the century the largest—will call for extraordinary political and administrative sagacity, something we cannot learn from the rest of the world. But one thing is certain: unless the process of urbanization ceases to make the same demands on our rural environment, it will only accelerate the destruction of the rural environment and in turn create an impossible urban environment. India cannot survive without a low-energy, low-resource-input urbanization. Only a holistic approach to our problems will work.

---

*Village self-rule.

CHAPTER 17

The Greening and Cleaning of India: An Overview of Environmental Challenges and Prospects

B. B. Vohra

The environmental movement in India may, for all practical purposes, be said to have begun in 1972, the year in which Mrs. Indira Gandhi attended the Stockholm Conference and set up the National Environmental Committee to act as a nodal point in the Government of India for the consideration of environmental issues. With the passage of time and the growth of popular awareness in this field, there came a demand that government should take a more direct interest in the environment, and in response to this the Department of Environment was constituted in 1980 and placed under the charge of the prime minister.

To begin with, environmental thinking took its cue from the developed countries and perceived the control of industrial pollution and the protection of wildlife as the country's major environmental goals. During recent years two other objectives, which have great relevance for India and indeed for most other developing countries, also have been clearly identified. These relate to the need to prevent any further degradation and depletion of the country's basic natural resources and life-support systems of land, water, and vegetation and to provide all human settlements with at least clean drinking water and a minimum level of sanitation. Today there is a fairly broad consensus that these four objectives must constitute the core of any environmental plan the country adopts for itself.

The reasons for including the management of natural resources and the provision of sanitation are obvious but can nevertheless bear repetition. Saddled as India already is with a population of over 750 million—which threatens to increase to 1 billion by the year 2000 and not stop growing till it has more than doubled—its only hope of combating poverty lies in making optimum use of its basic resources and in stabilizing its population as quickly as possible. However, the latter objective can hardly be achieved unless the nexus that exists between the lack of sanitation and population growth is recognized and given due attention. On this point, one cannot do better than to quote Barbara Ward: "In some third world countries two out of every five children die before they reach the end of childhood and a prime factor in this mortality is polluted water. So long as parents experience the death of their first children they will continue to bring more into the world—not out of folly or ignorance, but as an insurance for today's workload and tomorrow's old age."[1]

Popular awareness about environmental issues steadily continues to increase. Although consciousness regarding the need to save threatened species dates from the early 1970s, when Project Tiger was taken up as part of a World Wildlife Fund program, the dangers of industrial pollution were forcefully brought home to the people by the Bhopal tragedy of December 1984. A great deal of credit must go to the present prime minister for the manner in which he has generated greater awareness regarding the other two concerns. In his first broadcast to the nation, in January 1985, Shri Rajiv Gandhi called for a massive effort to combat what he described as the "major ecological and socio-economic crisis" created by continued deforestation and simultaneously announced his government's resolve to cleanse the Ganges and restore it to a state of pristine purity.

It is impossible to overestimate the far-reaching effects of the prime minister's policy pronouncements, particularly as he quickly followed them up with bold decisions at the operational level. The separate new Department of Forests was created from out of the Ministry of Agriculture and made responsible to him directly. He established a high-powered body—which includes all state chief ministers as its members and functions under his own chairmanship—to oversee the new national afforestation program in particular, and, in general, to ensure better use of the country's total land resources. He also has set up the strong Central Ganga Authority, once again serving as chairman himself, to rid this river of pollution.

These decisions certainly have given an extremely powerful impetus to the environmental movement in the country. The adoption of a very ambitious target—the afforestation of 5 million hectares of land every year—has jolted state forest departments out of their complacency and forced state governments to look beyond them in seeking the help of the people and voluntary organizations. Forestry has undergone a sudden transformation, and a lively national debate is taking place today regarding ways to combat continuing deforestation and denudation. In the process, one hears for the first time of seedlings being raised by schoolchildren and private farmers. There is also an acceptance of the concept that the people must be allowed to grow fruit, fodder, and other kinds of trees according to their own needs and liking—and not merely the eucalyptus and pine species traditionally favored by forestry establishments. Another idea that has found favor is giving farmers wastelands on nominal lease for the purpose of tree cropping, in much the same way as is being done in China.

The project for cleaning the Ganges has had a similar catalytic effect on sanitation. It has forced public health engineers and municipal authorities of the twenty-seven riverside towns covered by it to grapple energetically and on a time-bound basis with problems of sewage treatment and pollution control that had been neglected for decades. New technologies—often the very best—are being considered and adopted for recycling city wastes to generate energy as well as to produce organic fertilizers. It is clear that as the project progresses, it will have a powerful fallout effect on towns and cities besides those being tackled just now. Demands have in fact already begun to be made that other rivers should also be cleaned in the same way as the Ganges—for in India, all rivers are considered holy, even though the Ganges is believed to be the holiest. We can be sure that as consciousness about better sanitation spreads, there will be increasing pressure on government as well as on municipal bodies to devote more attention to this subject. The filth and open defecation that disfigure many Indian towns and villages are indeed so disgraceful in themselves and constitute such a threat to public health that they must not be tolerated any longer. It is important to note that a major proportion of all morbidity in the country is now caused by contaminated food and water and insanitary conditions of living.

Although Indian environmentalists certainly draw comfort from the fact that their major concerns are beginning to be understood by a wider public, and even shared by the government, they are under no illusion whatsoever that effective steps can be taken to meet the situation on anything like the scale and with anything like the speed that it demands. This is so because of the awesome dimensions and complexity of these problems on the one hand and, on the other, our present lack of preparedness to deal with them.

The gap between what needs to be done and what we are in a position to do is particularly wide in the management of the country's natural resources—a field that presents the greatest challenge to the country's environment and, indeed, to its very survival. According to official statistics, out of our total land resources of 266 million hectares that possess any potential for biotic production, as many as 175 million or fully two-thirds are degraded to a greater or lesser extent. What is more, around 90 million out of these 175 million are so badly degraded—mostly on account of denudation and continuing loss of topsoil but partly also on account of waterlogging and salinization—that they are almost completely unproductive. The remaining 85 million hectares, which are partially productive, constitute the bulk of the 143 million under cultivation. No wonder the country suffers from recurring floods, droughts, and chronic poverty.

The causes of this sorry state of affairs are not difficult to find. In their preoccupation with the need to achieve self-sufficiency in food, Indian planners have placed great faith in big irrigation projects in the belief that these offer the quickest means to increase agricultural production. The country accordingly has invested heavily in this sector and, in the process, allowed other aspects of land management, including afforestation, to suffer from comparative neglect. For a number of reasons, which need not be gone into here, this strategy has failed to produce the results expected from it.[2] Thus, although around 50 million hectares of our total agricultural area of 143 million are today classified as *irrigated,* the production of foodgrains in the country is still only approximately 150 million tons per annum. By contrast, China claims to have achieved a production of over 400 million tons from only about 100 million hectares of agricultural land and today boasts a per capita availability of foodgrains that is about twice as much as India's.

In this scenario, nobody will dispute that the restoration of permanent vegetal cover to a third of the country's total land area deserves the highest priority. Still, it would be a great mistake to get so preoccupied with this formidable problem as to overlook certain other, almost equally urgent aspects of land management:

(1) It is vitally necessary that the 30-odd million hectares of good natural forests—all that we are left with—should not be allowed to be depleted any further (the going rate is 1.5 million hectares per annum). This task calls for great vigilance to prevent illegal fellings, which today represent one of the easiest ways of making quick money. It also calls for the vigorous substitution for timber of other materials for various uses and for the conservation of firewood on the widest possible scale through the introduction of more fuel-efficient stoves.

(2) In order to make the country really self-sufficient in food, the productivity of surface-irrigated lands—which represent about 50 percent of the total irrigated area—must be increased substantially,

from the present level of around 1,700 hectares to at least 4,000–5,000 hectares, however difficult, expensive, and laborious doing so may be.

(3) Surface-irrigated lands must be provided with adequate drainage and saved from the threat of waterlogging and salinization, even as lands that have been already lost for these reasons are reclaimed.

(4) The present highly infructuous policy of *controlling* floods through engineering works executed by irrigation departments must be replaced by a policy of *preventing* floods through appropriate land managment and afforestation in watersheds.

(5) Groundwater resources, which today serve nearly half the total irrigated area, should no longer be taken for granted and given second-class treatment by irrigation departments. Effective steps must be taken to regulate groundwater extraction in order to prevent water tables from falling disastrously. It needs to be mentioned in this connection that the overexploitation of groundwater has already resulted in saline intrusion into sweet-water aquifers in many areas along the coast of Saurashtra. The replenishment of groundwater must also be deliberately undertaken by natural means, such as reducing monsoon runoff to the minimum, as well as artificially.

(6) The 90-odd million hectares of rain-fed agricultural lands must be given more attention and their productivity improved by proper soil and water conservation measures like contour terracing and contour bunding. In the long term, such rain-fed areas as have soils too shallow or too steep for sustained agriculture must be reverted from marginal cultivation and placed under permanent vegetation for economic as well as ecological reasons.

(7) Except when absolutely unavoidable, good agricultural lands must not be permitted to be diverted to urban uses. Stringent land-use planning for all present and future urban centers will be necessary to maintain such lands.

Each of these tasks will require the exercise of an extraordinary degree of political understanding and will, coupled with large financial and administrative inputs. How long it will take us to respond adequately to these challenges is anybody's guess; if one is to go by the obstacles already encountered in the execution of the massive afforestation program announced by the prime minister in 1985, the prospects are not especially encouraging.

It would be worthwhile to consider these obstacles in some detail. Although it had been foreseen, even before the program was launched, that it could not be executed through forest departments, because of their traditionally adversarial relationship with local populations and the excessively high costs associated with barbed-wire fencing and the provision of guards to protect afforested areas, the alternative of involving local populations in afforestation activities has not proved to be easy. Setting up large numbers of new nurseries on a localized basis to produce billions of saplings of various kinds of trees every year (at the rate of two thousand saplings per hectare) has posed numerous challenges. Further, it has been found that even if saplings become available in the required numbers, it is a very difficult job to distribute denuded lands for tree growing among individuals or cooperatives without coming into conflict with powerful vested interests, who do not want to see any changes take place in the rural social structures and who have often encroached upon common lands. Local administrations are quite often too lethargic to permit any major departures from existing practices to be carried out easily. In many cases, impediments are caused by existing laws, which need to be amended.

The authorities in charge are also beginning to realize that for large-scale afforestation to be achieved, we must make use of the regenerative forces of nature in a big way. To reclothe the vast open spaces beyond the immediate environs of villages, the first prerequisite is that the damage caused to young vegetation by large numbers of freely grazing cattle, sheep, and goats must become a thing of the past. Experiments have demonstrated that—thanks to bird droppings and seeds carried by the wind—denuded lands situated in even the most inhospitable areas like the Rajasthan desert acquire a mantle of grasses and young trees within a season or two, provided they are protected against all human and animal interference. Once natural regeneration has taken place, such lands can permanently support substantial animal populations at a satisfactory level of nutrition, as long as they are exploited with care, either through the hand cutting of grasses or a closely regulated system of rotational grazing.

However, such regeneration can be accomplished only if entire village communities can be persuaded to work together in saving the land from further abuse and enabling it to produce more for the common good. This, in turn, can be done only if these communities can be made much more egalitarian, much more cohesive, and much more self-governing than they are today. Seen in this light, the key to the problem of reforestation lies in breaking the hold of the feudal elements and muscle-men who still rule the roost in our villages (in collaboration, of course, with unscrupulous political and bureaucratic forces) and in carrying out far-reaching changes in the social, economic, and administrative structures of rural India. If such a transformation can take place, the problems of ridding common lands of encroachments and leasing them out to the poor and landless for tree growing will also become easier to solve.

It is necessary to point out here that, with respect to afforestation programs, financial constraints are not nearly as important as they are sometimes made out to be. Huge sums of money are already being poured into the countryside through a number of schemes aimed at poverty alleviation, employment creation, and rural development. The problem is that, because of the serious leakages that take place in a corrupt, politicized, and inefficient bureaucratic system and because the schemes themselves are poorly conceived and taken up in a fragmentary and uncoordinated manner by a multiplicity of agencies, which often work at cross-purposes, a large proportion of such investments have proved to be unproductive. If only all the monies being spent on such schemes could be pooled at the district level and utilized basically for better resource managment in close consultation with, if not actually through, well-run village communities, the results achieved would be dramatic and would place the country firmly on the road to economic recovery.

Enough has been said to show how enormously difficult the regeneration of denuded lands is going to be. And the other essential tasks of natural resources management, to which reference has been made, will also pose challenges of an almost equally formidable nature. But these challenges must be faced with determination, for, if they are big, so will be the rewards of meeting them successfully. We have indeed no option in this matter, if the country is to survive as a viable and self-respecting nation and not remain forever condemned to chronic poverty.

Fortunately, the other three environmental objectives are, by comparison, far easier to attain. The protection of wildlife—both fauna and flora—can be ensured in the short run by paying greater attention to the policing and management of existing sanctuaries and reserves and by establishing new ones wherever necessary. In the long run, though, the preservation of threatened species will hinge on the success we can achieve in conserving our existing forests, in creating new ones, and in protecting our rivers and lakes against pollution. The people must also be educated to the fact that the conservation of species is not something to be taken up solely for aesthetic and cultural reasons, important enough though these are, but also because the preservation of genetic diversity is necessary on strictly practical grounds. For the present generation has no right to destroy genes that may prove to be of incalculable value in solving problems of human health and biotic production that cannot even be imagined today.

As far as the provision of clean drinking water is concerned, 81 percent of the country's urban and 54 percent of its rural population already are claimed to have been covered, and plans exist to extend this basic amenity to the entire population by 1990. Given the necessary funds, it should be entirely possible to execute this program, as the work involved is essentially engineering in nature. So also is the provision of sanitary facilities, which already have been extended to 33 percent of the urban and 1 percent of the rural population and should reach 80 and 25 percent respectively by the end of the decade. Investments in this field will be meaningful only if city wastes are properly disposed of and not merely dumped into rivers or landfills as is happening only too often today. They would also yield better results if the usual leakages of funds are prevented, greater care is given to the maintenance of the facilities created, and the people are made conscious of the benefits of keeping their surroundings clean. Perhaps a national cleanliness drive should be launched (as was done in Mao's China) and special attention given to the provision of large numbers of public toilets in slum areas and to the need for keeping scrupulously clean the pilgrim centers and other places regularly visited by large numbers of people. The beginnings of such a movement are indeed already discernible in the Ganges project.

The control of industrial pollution is beset with many difficulties but is still a fairly manageable proposition. A sound strategy in this field would demand that no new industrial units be allowed to come up unless they have built-in arrangements for pollution abatement, and existing units should be brought into line through an appropriate system of incentives and disincentives. Thus, whereas liberal financial and technical assistance may be given to units that are prepared to install pollution-control devices within a specified time period, those which drag their feet should be penalized on a progressive scale till they comply. In certain circumstances, the industries also may have to be relocated. The control of air pollution caused by automotive engines in crowded cities is a relatively simple matter, provided the necessary political will is there.

As should be evident by now, we still are far from even formulating clear-cut and time-bound plans for combating environmental degradation, let alone implementing them. Nevertheless mention may be made here of certain suggestions for how we should proceed:

(1) In the Indian federal set-up, the constitutional responsibility for dealing with the environment rests with the states, and not with the central government. The central government does, however, have a large say in the country's planning process and in the formulation of state plans and is also directly responsible for all aspects of administration in the union territories. In a new and comparatively uncharted field like the environment, the traditional method of exhorting state governments to take up suitable programs by giving them advice and making appropriate financial provisions in their annual plans may not prove to

be effective, particularly because of serious resource constraints. In these circumstances, perhaps the soundest possible start for national environmental programs—and one that would also carry the greatest conviction with the states—would be for the center to formulate and carry out such programs in all union territories. To illustrate, the cities of Delhi and Chandigarh could be made models of good sanitation, waste disposal, and pollution control, and the union territories of Pondicherry and the Andaman Islands could be made models of natural resource management and wildlife protection. Such an approach would not only establish the central government's credibility in the environmental field but also equip it with the expertise and insights necessary for providing appropriate leadership to the states.

(2) The central government has another direct responsibility in the environmental field, which arises out of the fact that it owns and runs a large number of industrial enterprises in products such as steel, coal, power, textiles, cement, and petrochemicals. It would be eminently desirable for the central government to ensure that such industries do not contribute in any way to pollution and environmental degradation, before it can acquire the moral authority to advise state governments to take suitable action in respect to their own public-sector and private-sector industries.

(3) There is a real danger that the existence of the Department of Environment may serve as an alibi for other departments of the Government of India to take only a nominal or even no interest in the improvement of the environment. It must be appreciated that, by the very nature of things, it is not realistic for the fledgling Department of Environment to shoulder responsibility by itself for all aspects of the environment. Such responsibility must indeed be borne, to the fullest extent possible, by the concerned ministries of the Indian government. To illustrate, responsibility for the control of industrial pollution must rest with the Ministry of Industry, and for the control of air pollution caused by automotive engines with the Ministry of Transport. By the same logic, it is the Ministries of Health and Urban Development that must accept responsibility for drinking water and sanitation programs, as well as for preventing the diversion of good agricultural lands to urban uses; the Ministry of Human Resources Development that must be made responsible for creating greater awareness of environmental problems among students; and the Ministry of Information and Broadcasting, for creating a similar awareness among the public at large. In this view of the matter, the exact role of the Department of Environment must be thought out afresh and clearly defined.

(4) Responsibility for planning programs for the management of land, water, and forest resources rests with a number of central minis-

tries—Forest, Agriculture, Water Resources, and Rural Development—
each of which functions independently of the others. Since these resources are inextricably linked with one another, it is today difficult for
these ministries to provide the desired results. The Ministry of Water
Resources, for example, cannot ensure either the replenishment of
groundwater or the prevention of floods because both are a function of
good watershed management, and this in turn cannot be achieved either
by the Department of Forests or the Ministry of Agriculture or the
Ministry of Rural Development acting by itself, but only by all of them
working closely together at the field level. Only a holistic administrative
approach can meet the needs of this situation, and in the long run such
an approach can be best ensured through the creation of an integrated
ministry of natural resources, which can take an overall and synoptic
view of interrelated problems, determine priorities, and redeploy scarce
resources to the best advantage.

That the environmental movement in the country has come as far as it
has is in no insignificant measure due to the efforts of a comparatively
small number of dedicated environmentalists. Such people must be encouraged in every possible way to keep on doing the good work they are
engaged in: the creation of greater environmental awareness and an
informed public opinion, which alone can generate the political will on
the part of the government to pay greater attention to environmental
problems. May their tribe increase.

   However, when all is said and done, the future of the environmental movement in India will depend to a very great extent on the kind
of money the country can practically afford to spare for environmental
purposes. Environmentalists throughout the world bemoan the fact
that although the international community spends something like one
trillion dollars every year on armaments, environmental programs
languish for want of funds. Developing countries like India, which already face acute resource problems, have particular reason to complain
that regional tensions, caused primarily by rivalry among the super-
powers, compel them to spend disproportionately large amounts on
defense. On this concern, it is worth quoting from the message that
Mrs. Indira Gandhi sent to the Governing Council of the United Nations at its 1982 session:

> The problems of peace, development and conservation are interre-
> lated. We must curb the growing sense of fear and doubt in human-
> ity's ability to solve problems. The only way is for people of faith and
> vision to get together and reiterate their views. In all countries the
> voices for Peace are now more numerous and louder. They want to

check the arms race and advocate greater cooperation among nations to reduce economic disparity. The environment movement will gain by allying itself with these related causes.

NOTES

1. Ward in Erik Eckholm, *Down to Earth* (New York: W. W. Norton, 1982), xiv.

2. For a detailed treatment of this subject, reference is invited to the author's "The Greening of India," vol. 1 (New Delhi: The INTACH Environmental Series, Indian National Trust for Art and Cultural Heritage, 1985), and "Land and Water: Towards a Policy for Life-Support Systems," vol. 2 (New Delhi: The INTACH Environmental Series, Indian National Trust for Art and Cultural Heritage, 1985).

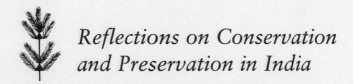

CHAPTER 18

Reflections on Conservation and Preservation in India

S. Dillon Ripley

The need for a coherent program of conservation and preservation in India is a subject in which I have been interested for many years. Beginning in the 1950s, when I was a biologist working at Yale University, I began to realize that it was folly not to pay particular attention to the deterioration of the world environment. Conservation in those days was thought to be a monopoly of "strident hysterics" and "little old ladies in tennis shoes," to use two hackneyed comparisons, but today it has become a highly accepted component of biological theory and environmental planning.

It is never appropriate to let governments go it alone in regard to the question of environmental preservation, however. The professional administrators who tend to become heads of governments' departments of the environment may neglect biological principles, too often depending on companies or groups who can perform environmental assessment studies on contract—a "quick-fix" job, when trained ecologists might need fifteen years for a proper study.

Anyone concerned with the environment today should realize that it is an international subject which knows no boundaries. The *Gita* tells us that people must show respect for the essential elements on which we are dependent—the land, the air, and water—and such basic premises do not change. It is no one's divine right to overlook ecological principles.

Beyond this I have always thought that conservation is a dual subject: conservation both of nature and the environment in which we live, as well as of ethnicity and the environmental associations of those who live on the land. There should be an international union not only for the conservation of nature, but also an international union for the conservation of ethnicity. It seems to me, as I have lectured in the past in India, that the work in saving local customs, folklife, and folkways pioneered in recent years by people like the late Verrier Elwin and the recent work of Robin Hanbury-Tenison is in essence just as important as much of the work of conserving nature. The Smithsonian happily has reinforced my concerns with numerous research projects dealing with the interdependence of biological and cultural diversity—basic research on tropical, arid zone, arctic, and temperate zone environments, and at least two major symposia, "The Fitness of Man's Environment" (1967) and "How Humans Adapt: A Biocultural Odyssey" (1981). In 1970 another symposium, published as *The Cultural Drama*, focused on ethnic and cultural pluralism. The Festival of American Folklife on the National Mall also presents a rich diversity of ways of life, documents them, and encourages cultural conservation.

Of course, I do not recommend a static society frozen in time, with innovation suppressed in the name of keeping people in living museums of the past. Ethnic cultures evolve in their own environment. They are in great danger of being lost in the rush toward a kind of homogenized technological milieu. We cannot survive by just overlooking the innate adaptations of indigenous people to live in their own specific environments. We cannot survive or afford the cost in resource use by simply increasing techniques and methods for yet more green revolutions and yet more development with its potential waste and degradation of the land itself.

Some years ago I recommended to members of the Planning Commission in India that a mapping project be undertaken for the whole of the subcontinent, using landsat photography as well as older forest and land-use maps to determine the optimal original environment of the land, whether in mountains, arid zones, tropical zones, or open savanna plains. The idea would be to set aside reserves in each of these areas, inspired by the analysis of Champion (1936) and later Champion and Seth (1968) of forest types in India, so that typical plots of standard environments could be preserved like miniparks.

Much too often planners overlook the native plant species, which obviously were preadapted over many generations to optimal survival in any particular one of these zones. The present rush to establish 5 million hectares of replanted trees in India is not really the answer to conservation and land-use planning for the future. The environment will not be restored in a hurry.

Environmental issues often are compartmentalized and pigeon-holed with resulting long-range dislocations. Not enough attention is paid to the whole composite of problems, which should be studied thoroughly. Instead people tend to take a short-term point of view, reflected in diagnoses such as "the monsoon failed last year," "we do not have sufficient water in the tanks because of the growth of water weeds," or "lack of cattle to graze in the ponds has encouraged the silting up of the ponds themselves." Add these factors to the decline in rainfall (by half in Andhra Pradesh since the 1940s, for instance) and the destruction of forest cover (by nearly 20 percent in the same area), and consider also the evidence around the coastal towns of increasing settlement, sprawling shacks, and an uncontrolled destruction of brush and hillside cover, and the situation becomes very clear. The technological and industrial development by required cyclical plans is seen as a substitute for long-term land studies.

America itself provides splendid examples of destructive development, which Indian environmental planners should be encouraged to examine. We are guilty of every environmental fault in today's lexicon. Far be it from me to criticize such examples of lack of long-term planning. They are inherent in every interaction between government and the environment in every country of the world in which I have studied them. The political pressures for modernization, advanced technology, and industrialization and the amelioration through medical and other welfare programs of the day-to-day stress on the human population continually blind us to long-term results.

Ecologists and environmentalists tend to sound like Cassandras today. They are constantly reminding other people of things they do not wish to hear. Since the Stockholm Conference of 1972, so many books have been written, so many television programs have been made, so many conventions of thinkers and planners have been held that it is hard to comprehend that this Tower of Babel is really worth listening to.

How then can one provide advice that is cogent if not optimistic for the future? As my friend the Yale biologist Evelyn Hutchinson has pointed out (quoted in my book *The Paradox of the Human Condition*), eroding the diversity of species and habitats is economically prodigal. It closes off people's options and removes tools a scientist may well need to serve humanity. If endangered species and their habitats, like the air we breathe and the water we drink, can be thought of as common resources of humankind, then they, too, can serve to illuminate other dimensions of the complexities of common property resources. Such species represent the conflict between personal advantage and community loss, the difference, for example, between exploitation and conservation of presently international ecosystems like the oceans or the Antarctic continent. There must be a willingness in the future to codify international property rights in the name of the heritage of species that are in danger. This heritage could promote a sense of dignity and standing among all the nations.

The sadness of museums of anthropology is that most of them are legacies of cultural extinction. Zoos and natural history museums may become similar symbols of human irresponsibility to our fellow beings. But these museums also are scientific data banks. Their collections put the whole panorama of ecological change into perspective and should be used to encourage monitoring of the rates of this change. Otherwise, in the same way that desertification is spreading over the lowlands of India, some changes will occur without our really being aware of their taking place.

I know that what has been undone in life can be redone. I would urge us to recognize that the tapestry of cultural change through evolution, which stretches across the continents, is one that contains within it tales from the past, actions of the present, and thoughts for the future. It is up to us to make sure that all is in sequence and that scientific understanding will triumph over environmental loss.

CHAPTER 19

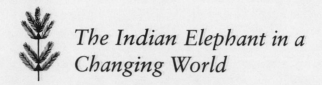

The Indian Elephant in a Changing World

D. K. Lahiri Choudhury

It is difficult to imagine India without elephants; they are so much a part of India's myths, history, and cultural heritage. The mount (*vāhana*) of Indra, the king of the gods, the counterpart of Zeus in the Hindu pantheon, is the celestial elephant Airavata (in Indian languages the standard simile for anything huge is "Airavata-like," and every child in India believes that rains are water poured out of Airavata's trunk). Of all gifts, the gift of an elephant has the highest sanctity and indemnifies the donor against the danger of Hell. Eight celestial elephants (*diggaja*) guard the eight points of the Hindu firmament, and sculptured elephants adorn the walls of Hindu temples. The Goddess Lakshmi, the presiding deity of wealth, is iconographically represented with two elephants, one on each side of her. And who does not know of Ganesa, the elephant-headed god of wisdom and success?

The elephant also plays an important part in the Jataka stories of the lives of Buddha in different incarnations. In one of his incarnations, it is said, Buddha was born as a king-elephant. The mother of Prince Gautama (later to become the Buddha) one night dreamed that a white elephant was descending toward her, a symbolic vision of the great birth of which she was to be the vehicle. A white elephant, thus, is even now an object of worship in Buddhist Southeast Asia, and elephant tusks are a coveted ornament in Buddhist monasteries throughout the Himalayas, from Towang to Leh. Both Buddhist and Hindu legends say

Figure 19.1. The Descent of the Ganges/Arjuna's Penance *(detail), relief, Pallava Dynasty, seventh century* A.D. *Mahabalipuram, Tamil Nadu.*

that when a king died without an heir, the royal elephant would be let loose to, literally, pick up the right person for the august position.

The standard Sanskrit word for elephant, *hastī*, has at least fifty-six synonyms. Women are divided into three types in Vatsyayana's *Kamasutra*; one of them is *hastinī* ("female elephant," which in this context has the same connotation as the modern English slang "cow"). On the other hand, a woman with a graceful walk, hips swaying, is commonly called *gajendragāminī*, "one who walks like an elephant," in Sanskrit poetry. One could cite countless other examples of elephants in folklore, in art, in design (Figure 19.1).

Kautilya's *Arthasastra,* the world's first treatise on public administration (variously dated between c. 300 B.C. and A.D. 300), includes a chapter on the duties of public officials in charge of the management of elephants, and is considered to be the beginning of Indian elephantology.[1] An independent *śāstra* or "lore" of elephants started with Palakapya's *Hastyayurveda* ("Treatise on the Treatment of Elephants"), the date of which is uncertain.[2]

The war elephants of Porus meeting Alexander's cavalry changed the course of India's history. In medieval India as well, war elephants were used regularly, with evidence of this still to be found in many medieval forts, in the spikes that survive on the door-leaves of the main

D. K. Lahiri Choudhury

gate meant to prevent elephants from battering down the door with their heads.

Abu'l-Fazl Allami (1551–1602), the famous court historian of Akbar (1542–1605), the greatest of the Great Mughals, devotes nine complete sections and several subsections in his *A'in-i Akbari* (1596–97) to elephant lore and the elaborate system of elephant management in the imperial stables. Akbar, says Abu'l-Fazl, was the first to encourage and establish the practice of captive breeding of elephants.[3]

Emperor Jahangir (1569–1637), Akbar's son, claimed to have 12,000 largest-size elephants in active army service and another 1,000 to supply fodder to these animals. (Elephants spend most of their waking hours eating; when they are employed in strenuous work throughout the day and cannot collect fodder for their consumption at night, large quantities must be provided for them in camp on their return from duty.) (Figure 19.2) Additionally, so it is claimed, there were 100,000 elephants to carry male courtiers, officials, and their attendants, and—both apparently given the same status—court ladies and baggage.[4] Even allowing for a certain high-minded imperial exaggeration in these figures, particularly in the figure of 100,000 (the editors of Jahangir's memoirs, finding the figure too high to be credible, tend to attribute it to scribal error), there can hardly be any doubt that the elephant arm of the imperial Mughal fighting forces must have been truly formidable.

Figure 19.2. Domesticated animals after a day's grazing in the forest bringing back fodder for feeding in the stall at night. The Mughal emperors had to keep a vast number of elephants to feed their war elephants, as engaged in active service during the day they would not have time to collect and carry their own fodder for later consumption.

According to Jahangir, Akbar had 12,000 fighting elephants of the largest class and another 20,000 of lesser size to provide fodder and provender to them.[5] On the death of his brother Sultan Danial, who apparently had a passion for collecting fine elephants and belles,[6] among other assets of the deceased 1,500 elephants and three hundred women devolved on Jahangir.[7]

When the British took over from the Mughals, they accepted the place of the elephant in state pomp, the army, and the civil administration and tried to codify the existing practices of elephant management.[8] District officers in outlying areas were regularly allotted elephants for their use, a practice that died out only after the advent of the jeep in the post–World War II period. (Until then one read announcements of vacancies in the "elephant cadre" in north Bengal.) The status of Indian princes and the land-holding gentry (zamindars) was often signaled by the number and quality of elephants they kept. Even late in this century, a cavalcade of Rolls Royces never has had the magic and glamour of a procession of elephants on Dussehra Day.

Big-game shooting from elephantback became the favorite pastime of the nouveaux nabobs of India in the nineteenth and early twentieth centuries. The fashion, actually an inheritance from the Mughals, caught on, and spectacular shikar "meets," often organized by the native princes and big landlords as much for their own sport as for the entertainment of their new masters, mark the last years of the Raj. A tiger for the viceroy could cover up a multitude of sins.

Most of these animals in domestic service were taken from the wild, Akbar's early attempts at captive breeding notwithstanding, as they continue to be today.

Yet when some of us started our field investigations in 1975, or later in 1977, when elephants were included in Schedule I (rare and endangered species) of India's Wildlife (Protection) Act of 1972, following the inclusion of the Asian elephant in Appendix I of the Convention on International Trade in Endangered Species (CITES), and the Asian Elephant Specialist Group of the Species Survival Commission (SSC) of the International Union for Conservation of Nature and Natural Resources (IUCN) was formally constituted, little was known of the actual geographical distribution, estimated number, and status of wild elephants in India. The Asian Elephant Specialist Group qua group, and some members of the group in their personal capacity, have been able to piece together an elephant distribution map for the whole country and identify some of the more vulnerable areas and populations. The brief description below of the status and distribution of the species in India is based mainly on data available up to December 1983.[9]

Already by 1977, it had been determined that wild elephants in India were distributed in four broad, widely separate geographical zones: southern, central, northern, and northeastern India. The major vegetation types constituting their habitat were dry and moist deciduous, semievergreen, and evergreen forests, swamps, and grasslands, both high and low (Figure 19.3). It was soon noticed that within each of these broad zones, there were wide discontinuities of habitat permanently separating individual populations into pockets, and that existing

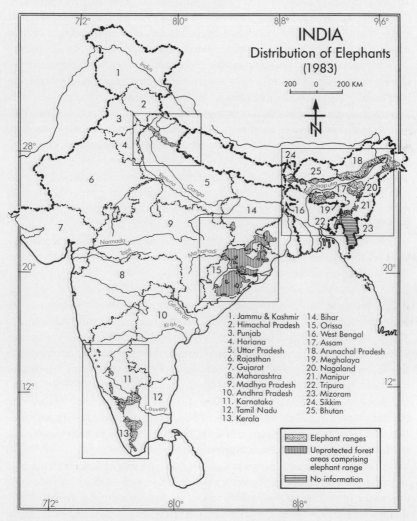

Figure 19.3. India: Distribution of Elephants (1983).

fissures in the habitat were widening even within the home range of these already separated populations, threatening to fragment them further.

In southern India, the Palghat gap has long divided the elephant zone into two halves. Discontinuities within each half now appear to be becoming permanent.[10]

In central India, except in Simlipal National Park in the state of Orissa, which has the additional status of a tiger reserve and holds a population of 300–400 elephants, the forests that constitute the existing elephant ranges enjoy legal protection as government reserve forest only in patches. Thus about 75 percent of the total estimated number of elephants in Orissa, the key elephant-bearing state in the region—with, according to one official guesstimate, about 2,000 elephants in the wild—have no proper legal protection of their habitat.

In northern India, elephants are found only in the sub-Himalayan government reserve forests. Here again the elephant zone is divided into two widely separate blocks. The smaller eastern range only recently has acquired elephants, which are probably temporary migrants from adjacent Nepal. The larger western range, where most of Uttar Pradesh's 400-odd elephants are, faces the threat of further fragmentation due to a development project at a place called Chilha.[11]

The situation is more complicated in northeastern India, which has the largest wild elephant population in the country. On the north bank of the Brahmaputra River the habitat is continuous, and a considerable area with an estimated population of about 1,400 enjoys sanctuary (tiger reserve) status. In the remaining sub-Himalayan tract, the situation is less satisfactory.

On the south bank of the Brahmaputra, however, the picture is grim. The estimated number here in round figures is between 5,800 and 8,600. Of these, only about 2,000–3,000 can be said to have some kind of legal protection of their habitat; the rest, particularly those 2,500–3,500 animals in the hilly state of Meghalaya, are homeless, vagrant creatures, facing the threat of extermination in the course of the next twenty years or so.

Our present estimate of the elephant population for the whole of India as calculated in November 1985 is between 16,500 and 21,500, not taking into account the official census figures for southern India. Details of the estimate are given in Table 19.1. Of these, about 4,000–5,000 on the south bank of the Brahmaputra in northeastern India are critically endangered, and another 1,500 or so are in an only marginally more secure position in Orissa in central India. As things are, in the years to come there seems to be a viable future in India for only around 10,000–12,000 elephants. (This can be contrasted, perhaps not quite fairly, with the figures we have for the Mughal imperial stables alone:

32,000 in Akbar's time, 113,000 in Jahangir's.) That is, about 25–30 percent of the present estimated number of elephants in India face elimination unless drastic legal and constitutional measures can be taken to protect their habitat. It is clear that we can no longer take the continued existence of these magnificent animals for granted (Figure 19.4).

TABLE 19.1

Wild Elephants in India
All-India Distribution and Population Estimates (November 1985)

Geographical zone	Estimated number	States
Southern India	5,750–7,050	Kerala, Karnataka, Tamil Nadu
Central India	± 1,635	Orissa, Bihar, southwest part of West Bengal
Northern India	445	Uttar Pradesh (1976 census—an average of three counts plus one lone tusker at Dudhwa)
Northeastern India	8,705–12,231	Arunachal Pradesh, Assam, Manipur, Meghalaya, Mizoram, Nagaland, northern part of West Bengal
Total	16,535–21,361	

Note: These figures reflect the latest estimates presented at the meeting of the Asian Elephant Specialist Group, IUCN/SSC, held in Bandipur National Park, Karnataka, India, in November 1985.[15] The official 1983 census figure for southern India as a whole was 8,623, higher than the group's findings. The considerable variation in the two estimates for northeastern India is explained by the Arunachal Pradesh Forest Department's two widely varying 1981 guesstimates—2,000–4,300—which have been retained here in place of the subsequent official census figure of c. 2,400 (1983–84 and 1984–85), and by the persisting uncertainty about the actual number of elephants in Meghalaya despite a second estimate attempted by the Meghalaya Forest Department in December 1984. In April 1986, the West Bengal Forest Department carried out an enumeration of wild elephants in the forests of northern Bengal. The number they arrived at, 152, has been incorporated in this table. In the estimate for Assam, which forms a part of the total estimate for northeastern India, the figures for Darrang (East and West) and North Lakhimpur civil districts are of the two counts taken in 1981, and not of the count in 1982.

Figure 19.4. A wild tusker in tropical, moist, deciduous sub-Himalayan forest ideally suited as habitat to the Indian elephant.

Elephants are wide-ranging animals, and in Indian conditions reserves cannot be demarcated for them everywhere to protect their entire range. Since, being at the top of the food chain, they depend upon their habitat for survival, the main threat to elephants comes from threat to their habitat. And it is in habitat where things have changed most in recent years under pressure of increasing human population. The National Forest Policy of 1952 prescribed that one-third of the land area in the plains and two-thirds in the hills should be under forest cover. Although officially only about 23 percent of the country's land area is under the control of the forest departments, by 1980–82, according to satellite data, the total forest cover in India had been reduced to 14.1 percent, and the loss in the country's forest cover between 1972–75 and 1980–82 was 16.25 percent or one-sixth. During this period, closed-canopy forests, which occupy a crucial position in the mosaic of vegetation types constituting an elephant range, dropped from 14.12 percent to 10.96 percent; in absolute terms, India lost 10.4 million hectares of closed-canopy forests, and an additional 1.29 million hectares of such forests were converted into degraded forests. The rate of loss was 1.3 million hectares of natural forest every year (Figure 19.5), a loss that cannot be compensated for fully by afforestation programs because of the impossibility of achieving the genetic diversity of tropical natural forests in a man-made forest, however well made. Besides, these plantations aim at production of timber and thus tend to rely on quick-growing species, often exotics. One informed guess is that the natural forest cover in India today, the elephants' preferred habitat, would not exceed 6–7 percent of the total land area.[12] It should be noted that much of this meager 6–7 percent would be in the hills in the temperate and higher regions, and thus beyond the normal range of elephants. Saving the Indian elephant is largely a matter of saving the scant residue of natural tropical and subtropical forest cover.

The loss of forests has been going on since the days of the Indus Valley civilization (c. 2500–1500 B.C.). If an elephant distribution map for ancient India were made, it would probably cover all of India: from the present Thar Desert in the west to the evergreen forests of northeastern India, from the Himalayan foothills in the north to Cape Comorin in the south, with scattered patches of human settlements along the fertile river valleys.

The Aryan invasion that came from the northwest and spread along the Ganges Valley caused what was probably the first major crack in the compact elephant habitat, which eventually permanently separated the southern from the northern population. In the course of time, elephants gradually retreated along with the forest from the west, away from the human population and land that no longer sustained them. By

Figure 19.5. Desert in the highest rainfall area in the world (Mawsingram) in West Khasi Hills, Meghalaya, a soil no longer any good to human or beast.

the middle of the nineteenth century, if not earlier, elephants had retreated eastward from the forests of the central Indian highlands as well, possibly because of excessive capture by the Mughal court. As prime elephant country, Abu'l-Fazl mentions what is now western Uttar Pradesh (Agra Suba), large areas of what is now Madhya Pradesh, and territories extending as far south as Berar. He also records that elephants from Panna (Madhya Pradesh) were the best. None of these areas now holds elephants.[13]

Figures 19.6 and 19.7. Shifting cultivation of slash-and-burn type is one of the major causes of degradation of forest, soil, and environment in northeastern Indian hill states. After the initial burning, the slopes await sowing by a low-yield variety of paddy.

D. K. Lahiri Choudhury

The process of deforestation accelerated dramatically after independence in 1947. In this investigator's own lifetime, the once-compact elephant habitat of northeastern India has become disjointed beyond any hope of repair or restoration (Figures 19.6, 19.7). The resultant picture is the same everywhere: loss and degradation of habitat leading to increasing, and increasingly direct, human–elephant confrontation, an unequal conflict in which the elephant is bound to come out the loser.

Despite the special esteem in which the elephant has been held in India historically, in the last twenty years or so the relation between humans and elephants in India has undergone a drastic change; contraction and loss of habitat have made it antagonistic. People encroach on the elephants' land; elephants eat the crops on the occupied land or ravage property; people strike out at elephants for doing this; elephants retaliate (Figures 19.8, 19.9). More than 100 people were killed by elephants in the small state of West Bengal alone between 1975 and 1982, and between 1979 and 1984, 211 people in Assam. The value of crops and property damaged or destroyed by elephants would come to millions of rupees. In such areas, the elephant has become the people's enemy, the symbol not of wisdom but of destruction. Few stop to think that this reversal of role is the result of human folly and greed, and that destruction of forests is ultimately working against long-term human interests. Deforestation has now reached such a level that, causing soil erosion and affecting the water regime, it has become the root cause of major

Figure 19.8. A group of huts destroyed by a herd of elephants in northern Bengal. Three persons were killed and one seriously injured. The huts had been set up illegally on forest land.

Figure 19.9. Rogue makna *(tuskless male elephant) liquidated. The axe gives the scale. Note the huge burn mark on its back and a few smaller ones on its withers. Burnt engine-oil is supplied to tea-garden laborers for making torches to scare away nighttime marauding elephants. Rags soaked in this oil are lighted and thrown on the elephant; they stick on the body and burn. A marauder quickly turns into a killer rogue.*

environmental disaster in many regions. A typical case in point is the way the slash-and-burn type of shifting cultivation in northeastern India is not only despoiling prime elephant habitat but also degrading land to the state of being useless to human and beast alike.

The human–elephant confrontation in many parts of northeastern India has become so critical that it is often a political issue of the first magnitude. Thus one of the main efforts of the Asian Elephant Specialist Group has been directed toward devising ways of reducing this confrontation. Apart from the question of preserving and protecting elephant habitat by suitably persuading the authorities that be, this means devising management techniques for containing and preventing elephant depredation. Numerous and varied experiments with anti-elephant depredation measures have been carried out. Energized fences are now in use at a number of places in India. The first pulser set ever in this country, a gracious present from a friend of India's wildlife in the United States, was introduced by the group experimentally in northern Bengal in 1979. The traditional elephant-proof ditch is expensive but still useful (Figures 19.10, 19.11). Among the more exotic experiments carried out recently were one with tiger urine and tape-recorded tiger calls, and one with tear gas.

Figures 19.10 and 19.11. Masonry-sided elephant-proof ditches, though expensive, are still useful to protect small areas especially vulnerable to elephant depredation. The drawbridge across the ditch is taken up at night or when wild elephants are heard or seen close by.

This account of the Indian elephant in a changing world, a story of the degradation of the status of this great animal in the subcontinent, is an expression of a deep concern for the future of the species in our ancient land, as our population approaches the one billion mark, and we the twenty-first century. Humans' present relation with elephants in the wild is just one half of this story. The other half concerns the elephant in captivity, the story of the elephant as people's friend, and how it is being affected by the altered status of the animal in the wild.

Nothing symbolizes this change better than the great annual animal fair (melā) at Sonepur on the north bank of the Ganges in the state of Bihar, which opens for a fortnight on the full-moon day in the month of Kartik (usually November; the exact date shifts around a bit because the calculation is by lunar month). Nobody knows how old the fair is, except that it is "very, very old" (it is generally believed that Chinese travelers to India referred to it fifteen hundred years ago). It is the season's first, and the greatest of the four important animal fairs of northern Bihar, all taking place in the cool dry season (see Table 19.2). And elephants have always been its chief glory, though all kinds of animals are bought and sold here—horses and ponies in hundreds, cattle and buffalo in thousands, camels, goats, asses, and so on. Before the enactment of India's Wildlife (Protection) Act in 1972, this was also the main selling ground for wild animals and birds.[14] In India it is a place of pilgrimage for anyone who has anything to do with elephants (Figure 19.12, Plate 15).

Before independence one could see well over 1,000 elephants at Sonepur in some years. Even the war could not stop the melā, nor could this government a few years ago by scattering pamphlets from the air and resorting to ban and warnings when there was a threat of an encephalitis epidemic spreading.

TABLE 19.2

Elephants and Humans: The Great Animal Fairs of North Bihar

Locale	Time	Remarks
Sonepur, north of Patna	Full-moon day in the month of Kartik (November)	The greatest of them all; number of elephants brought for sale is sharply dwindling (frequently more than 1,000 in pre-independence days; c. 600 in 1976; c. 380 in 1983; 350 in 1984; 225 in 1985; and 215+ in 1986).

D. K. Lahiri Choudhury

TABLE 19.2 *(cont.)*

Locale	Time	Remarks
Sitamari, about 60 miles from Sonepur	Full-moon day following the full moon in Kartik (Sonepur)	Traditionally, the elephants that do not get sold at Sonepur are marched off to Sitamari. There is no up-to-date information regarding its present status with this investigator.
Khagra, near Kishenganje	Sometime in January; date is announced by the local landlord according to his convenience.	Never very remarkable for elephants. In 1980 only about 20 were brought there for sale. No elephant has been put up for sale since 1982.
Singheswar, about 60 miles north of Katihar	Sivaratri Day in February (New Moon Day)	With the date coming at the close of the elephant-catching season (November–March), this *melā* was the place where most of the freshly captured animals of the season used to be brought for sale. To find 200 animals, even 300, was not uncommon. In 1982, however, there were only about 30 animals, in 1984 around 30 elephants as well, mostly belonging to local owners, in 1985 fewer than 10, and in 1986 only one. End of Singheswar.

Figure 19.12. Elephants at their morning bath at Sonepur being washed and scrubbed before being taken back to their stalls for display.

The elephant ground of the *melā* is now divided into two parts: *zamindārī paṭṭī*, or the private owners' ground, and *saudāgarī paṭṭī*, or the traders' ground. The separation, however, is not rigid. *Saudāgarī paṭṭi* traditionally does not go in much for display. Dealing in freshly captured animals bought directly from the capture depots in the forests of northeastern India has always been the traders' main area of operation. On the other hand, "show" is a big thing in *zamindārī paṭṭī*. Many large tuskers are brought here more for parading the pride of possession of the owner than for sale. This is the ground for the grander, more mature animals, and the gorgeously caparisoned elephants are the chief attraction for the half-a-million people who gather there on the day of the ceremonial opening of the *melā*. Some of these magnificent creatures are notorious killers, and traditional herbal drugs are regularly used to keep them under sedation during the period of the *melā*.

Elephants are valued according to their points. Fewer than eighteen nails altogether in an animal's feet would sharply decrease its market price, for, as is common knowledge, such animals bring bad luck to their owners. The same applies to tusks of the wrong shape and size. The color of the palate should be a rosy pink without any black spot. The brush of the tail should be full; its length should not be such that it touches or sweeps the ground (very unlucky, that, too!). The ears should be large; the head massive with a prominent frontal bump; the eyes a dark, limpid brown; the back straight or sloping; the skin thick, loose, and wrinkled; the feet without any crack. Then there is the question of age, a difficult thing to estimate in adult animals, and temper. Buying an elephant at Sonepur is no job for a novice; the unwary are likely to have fobbed off on them an animal long past its prime or diseased, or even a vicious killer temporarily under sedation.

Over the years the character and composition of the buyers have changed. Formerly, the main demand was from the landed gentry and the feudal order. Even earlier, Sonepur must have supplied war elephants to mighty rulers and powerful warlike chieftains. Now most of the buyers are the forest and tourism departments of various state governments, and circus companies. Next come the timber companies, who are finding elephant labor increasingly more attractive in an era of steadily rising labor and automobile fuel and maintenance costs. Besides, elephants have the singular virtue of not forming trade unions—a very attractive quality in any labor force. In 1983, an elephant in Assam earned for its owner Rs. 1.50* per cubic foot of timber hauled, whereas the daily wage of an unskilled laborer employed for such work was Rs. 8.50.* By 1986 the rate of timber-hauling by elephant was Rs. 8 per cubic foot. Understandably enough, from Sonepur there is an increasing flow of elephants, once captured as young animals in northeastern India, *back* to northeastern India, where as adult animals now they are being taken to work in the logging industry. The demand for large tuskers from southern India, mainly for temples, continues. Smaller landed gentry from northern Bihar and eastern Uttar Pradesh still seek to buy elephants as status symbols.

Yet the changes at Sonepur extand far beyond buyers. The *melā*'s elephant sector itself is dying out; no fresh animal is coming to the market. Only three years after the ban on commercial capture in 1981, the number dwindled from about 600 in 1976 to around 300 in 1984, and further to only 225 in 1985, most of them decrepit, blind, or lame animals, with no takers. Expectedly, prices have shot up. A good mature cow in 1983 fetched about sixty thousand rupees (in 1986 the asking price for such an animal was around ninety thousand rupees); even in 1981 such an animal was worth only twelve thousand rupees or so. Of the three other *melā*s, two do not attract elephants any longer, and the third one was still valiantly trying to keep up its end with about 30 animals or so in 1984, mostly belonging to local owners, but had only one animal to show in 1986. The simple fact of the matter is, elephants are no longer available for domestic use.

This brings us to several important issues concerning the management of the species. It has already been pointed out that about one-third

---

*Based on 1985 exchange rates, Rs. 12.5 = $1.00.

of the present population of wild elephants in the country face the prospect of elimination in not too distant a future. Should we then try to save these animals? Is that a feasible proposition? Or should we accept things as they are, acknowledge the reality of drastically reduced forest areas as change irreversible, and reconcile ourselves to the idea of a population of about 12,000, kept stable by judicious culling by capture, in place of the present 19,000–21,000? Loss and degradation of habitat have pushed the human–elephant confrontation to such a level that we can no longer afford to let matters drift; the unpleasant reality does not go away if we just close our eyes to it. If the habitat of the identified critically endangered populations cannot be legally secured and effectively protected, there is no alternative to large-scale culling by capture. This concerns the elephants on the south bank of the Brahmaputra most; forests there are private or community property, open to unrestricted human use and exploitation, including, alas, slash-and-burn shifting cultivation. In some parts of Arunachal Pradesh, most of Nagaland and Meghalaya, and much of Mizoram and Tripura, forests do not even enjoy legal protection under the Indian Forests Act. In the case that culling is the choice, CITES notwithstanding, we have to think of the most rational way of disposing of these unwanted animals. And, to ensure the survival of the species, is it absolutely necessary to sever the special millennia-old tie between people and domesticated elephants in India, and treat elephants as just another wild species that is best left wild? Is there no alternative to killing off a three-thousand-year-old tradition and a whole way of life? The Sonepur situation helps to bring that problem into sharp focus.

We have already lost too much of our forests and are just beginning to realize that people need them quite as much as the animals. The persecuted state of our elephant population reflects the present status of our tropical and subtropical forests. If we can protect and manage, conserve, what we have even now, perhaps Sonepur and all it stands for can still live; and from the rapacious plunder of some of our richest natural resources—and the elephant stands at the head of the list—as in the past, we can move to an era of scientifically managed sustainable yield. Then the elephant can continue to occupy the very special niche it has always occupied in India's history, coming from the wild and yet becoming a friend of humankind.

NOTES

The author's grateful thanks are due to Prof. Sukumari Bhattacharyya for her comments and suggestions on the opening passages of this article dealing with the subject of the elephant in Indian mythology.

1. On the content, form, and date of Kauṭilya's *Arthaśāstra*, see A. B. Keith, *A History of Sanskrit Literature* (1920; reprint, Delhi etc.: Oxford University Press, 1973), 452–62; F. Edgerton, *The Elephant Lore of the Hindus* (New Haven: Yale University Press, 1931), xi. *Arthaśāstra* (book II, chaps. XXXI–XXXII) also mentions "castes" of elephants, thereby setting the trend for the later works, and has observations on care and feeding of elephants. For a review of old Sanskrit literature on elephants, see Keith, *History of Sanskrit Literature*, 465; Edgerton, *Elephant Lore of the Hindus*, x–xi and 1–5. The treatment of the subject in both Keith and Edgerton is cursory, and there is scope for more comprehensive coverage taking in all elephant literature in Indian languages up to the end of the eighteenth century.

2. Keith, *History of Sanskrit Literature*, 465; Edgerton, *Elephant Lore of the Hindus*, viii–ix, 1 n.1, 2.

3. Abū'l-Faẓl Allāmī, *Ā'in-i Akbarī*, trans. H. Blockmann (Calcutta: Asiatic Society of Bengal, Series Bibliotheca Indica, 1873). 2d ed. revised by D. C. Phillott (Calcutta: Royal Asiatic Society of Bengal, Bibliotheca Indica, work no. 61, vol. 1, issue no. 1492, New Series, 1939), secs. 41, 126. The original 1873 translation was revised by Phillott in 1927, but was actually published in 1939. (Incidentally, the Asiatic Society of Bengal never went "Royal," though asked to do so as a branch of the London-based Royal Asiatic Society. The offer was declined on the ground that the Asiatic Society of Bengal had been founded long before the London Society came into existence. The author is grateful to Prof. Ashin Das Gupta, Director, National Library, Calcutta, for this information. However, despite this haughty refusal to become "Royal," "Royal" kept on intruding in the Asiatic Society of Bengal's publications from time to time. In the present case, the title page reads "Asiatic Society of Bengal," whereas the cover reads "Royal Asiatic Society of Bengal.")

4. David Price, trans., *Autobiographical Memoirs of the Emperor Jahangueir* (1829; reprint, Calcutta: Editions Indian, 1972), 18–19.

5. Ibid., 52.

6. Ibid., 55.

7. Ibid., 71.

8. Apart from such standard later works as G. H. Evans, *Elephants and*

Their Diseases (Rangoon: Superintendent, Government Printing, Burma, 1910), and G. W. Milroy, *A Short Treatise on the Management of Elephants* (Shillong: Government Press, Assam, 1922), see J. Emerson Tennent, *The Wild Elephant and the Method of Capturing and Training in Ceylon* (London: Longmans, 1867) (a very unreliable work, chiefly of historical interest now); G. P. Sanderson, *Thirteen Years Among the Wild Beasts of India* (London: William Blackwood & Sons, 1878); G. P. Sanderson, *Pack-gear for Elephants* (Calcutta: Superintendent of Government Printing, India, 1883); J. H. Steel, *A Manual of the Diseases of the Elephant and His Management and Uses* (Madras; printed at the Lawrence Asylum Press by W. H. Moore, 1885); Captain H. Wilberforce Clarke, *Note by Captain Wilberforce Clarke, Deputy Consultant Engineer, Government of India, for the Guaranteed Railways, On Elephants* (Calcutta: Government Central Press, 1878); F. X. Mascarenhas, *A Few Hints on the Management and Treatment of Elephants and Bullocks* (Madras: no publisher, 1906).

9. The 1983 assessment was updated at the meeting of the Asian Elephant Specialist Group, IUCN/SSC, held in Bandipur Wildlife Sanctuary, Karnataka, in November 1985. The earlier Orissa estimate of c. 2,000 was modified here to 1,300. The group's earlier estimate for southern India (5,775–6,300) was also revised here. A clearer picture of the status of the species in these two regions has emerged from the recent reports (see n. 14 infra). In December 1984, the Meghalaya Forest Department (northeastern India) carried out an estimate of the number of wild elephants in the state. The Arunachal Pradesh Forest Department (northeastern India) carried out an enumeration of elephants on the north bank of the Brahmaputra in the dry season of 1983–84, and on the south bank in 1984–85. However, a full discussion with the department is necessary before their figures are accepted. The Assam Forest Department carried out a census of elephants in Darrang (East and West) and North Lakhimpur civil districts on the north bank of the Brahmaputra in November–December 1982, the third such operation in the same area in two years. The report was circulated among a selected few in August–September 1985. The West Bengal Forest Department carried out an enumeration of elephants in northern Bengal in the second half of April 1986. For the latest estimate of the population in different geographical zones, see Table 19.1.

10. S. S. C. Nair, P. V. Nair, S. C. Saratchandra, M. Gadgil, "An Ecological Reconnaissance of the Proposed Jawahar National Park," *Journal of the Bombay Natural History Society* 74, iii (1977):401–35.

11. V. B. Sing, "Elephant in N.W. India (Uttar Pradesh)," *The Asian Elephant in the Indian Sub-continent* (Bombay: J. C. Daniel, Chairman, Asian Elephant Specialist Group, IUCN/SSC, c/o Bombay Natural History Society, 1980).

12. *The State of India's Environment, 1984–85: The Second Citizens' Report* (New Delhi: Centre for Science and Environment, 1980), 80.

13. Abū'l-Fazl Allāmī, *Ā'īn-i-Akbarī*, sec. 41, 129–30.

14. Because of the late inclusion (1977) of the species *Elephas maximus* in Schedule I of India's Wildlife (Protection) Act, 1972 (schedule of rare and endangered animals), certain anomalies with respect to elephants remain in the act. Domesticated animals continue to be defined as *cattle* and are thereby kept outside the purview of the act. In the case of buffalo and pigs, for example, wild and domesticated strains, though zoologically identical, have been distinguished from one another legally in the act through the use of the qualifier *wild*; elephants, however, do not receive such treatment. Furthermore, legal capture of Schedule I animals, which comes under the definition of *hunting,* can be done only if there is a threat to life, for scientific purpose, and for population management. This provision does not take into account the fact that elephants, unlike other domesticated animals, are culled from the wild for domestic use and not bred for the purpose.

15. *WWF Monthly Report* (Gland, Switzerland), January 1986.

CHAPTER 20

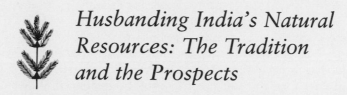

Husbanding India's Natural Resources: The Tradition and the Prospects

Madhav Gadgil

SACRED GROVES

The hill ranges of the Western Ghats, dotted with the forts of Shivaji, the founder of the Maratha empire, are close to the heart of every Maharashtrian. So my thoughts naturally turned to fieldwork on the forests of these hills when I returned from six years of theorizing at Harvard. As a school boy, I had read of Shivaji's edicts that the woods on the slopes of his hill forts should not be destroyed on any account. The edicts were promulgated in 1672; in 1972 I discovered barren hills, eroded, laterized. But every once in a while one came across a patch of pristine forest, a relict of a quarter or a half a hectare, or, in rare instances, ten or twenty hectares. These were sacred groves, dedicated to village deities and spared the axe by religious sentiments.

After three months of wanderings on the Western Ghats I received a remarkable letter. It was from a tiny village, Gani, located in a remote area of Konkan. The villagers had learned, the letter said, of my interest in sacred groves. Their particular village had one of the best, and it had recently been marked for felling by the Forest Department. Could I come over and help them save it from this fate? Intrigued, I promptly took a bus to Srivardhan and then trekked over 8 kilometers of barren hills to Gani, a hamlet of forty huts. It was occupied solely by women, children, and a few old men; all the able-bodied males were working in the metropolitan city of Bombay, and their families subsisted on money orders from them and by selling firewood in the market at Srivardhan, along with a little cultivation of hill millets. Above the settlement was a beautiful patch of rain forest, some 25 hectares in extent, in the catchment of the stream that ran past the village. The villagers had witnessed other streams drying up as tree cover had been lost over the last half century and were determined to save their catchment forest.

Fortunately, I was able to persuade the Forest Department to abandon plans to fell this sacred grove. In the process I discovered that many foresters thought of it as a stand of overmature timber. For the villagers, though, it evidently was something more. In fact, they were aware of its value not only for water conservation, but also as a gene bank. For they showed me a specimen of the magnificent leguminous climber *Entada pursaetha* in another grove and explained that its seeds were of great use in treating snake-bite among cattle. People came from as far as 40 kilometers away to collect the seeds from that grove (Gadgil and Vartak 1975).

These groves had been preserved over time not because of any such economic or practical arguments but rather, as mentioned earlier, on the basis of religious beliefs. It is of course possible that the benefits obviously flowing out of such religious practices are fortuitous. But it is more likely that they are not. The benefits of sacred groves accrue to the social group on a long-term basis; the individuals often would be better off in the short run by violating the grove. It then seems probable that cultures have cast prescriptions that lay in the long-term interest of the group, and against the short-term interest of individuals, in the form of religious sanctions (Rappaport 1971).

SIDDHARTHA

The sacred grove is undoubtedly an ancient tradition. We learn from the story of the Buddha's life that he was born in one in the sixth century B.C. (Kosambi 1962). When the time came for Siddhartha's birth, his mother, Mahamaya, wished to go to her parents' home for delivery. On her way she passed through a grove of sal trees dedicated to the Goddess Lumbini. From roots to the tips of branches, the trees were loaded with fruits, flowers, and countless bees of fine color. In them were flocks of different birds singing sweet melodies. Witnessing this heavenly scene, there arose a desire in the heart of Mahamaya to halt and sport for a while. Alighting from her palanquin, she walked up to the foot of a magnificent sal tree. A pleasant breeze was blowing, and Mahamaya rose on her toes and caught a bough that had swung down with the wind. At once she was lifted up in the air and, being shaken, felt the pangs of childbirth. She delivered Siddhartha while holding on to that sal tree bough. He, who then exhibited a sense of compassion toward all forms of life from his earliest years, as a young man achieved enlightenment during the course of a long meditation under a great pipal tree outside of Gaya and thenceforth was called the Buddha.

THE KHANDAVA FOREST

The Buddha condemned the tremendous slaughter of animals and burning of great quantities of wood at the *yajñas*, fire sacrifices that were a hallmark of the Brahmanical religion then in ascendance. He also insisted on the ethical equality of all social groups. His preachings represented a major revolt against a tradition that is perhaps symbolized most aptly by the burning of the Khandava forest.

It is narrated in the *Mahabharata* that Krishna and Arjuna once went for a picnic in this forest on the banks of the Yamuna River (c. 1100 B.C.). While they were there, a poor Brahman approached them for alms. On being granted his request for something to quench his hunger, he revealed himself as Agni, the fire god, and begged to be allowed to consume the entire forest, including every creature living therein. Krishna and Arjuna agreed to this; Agni provided them with a splendid chariot and a bow and arrows and set the forest on fire, and Krishna and Arjuna patrolled its periphery driving back any creature that attempted to escape the furious blaze—including Nagas, presumably the hunting-gathering tribals of the forest. Only one Naga escaped death, because he had gone out of the forest on that day, and he wreaked vengeance on Arjuna's descendants two generations later (Karve 1967).

This episode evidently illustrates the conflict between the indigenous hunting-gathering forest dwellers and the agricultural-pastoral invaders on the Gangetic plain. Ultimately the former were vanquished, their habitat burnt and put to plough, and they themselves reduced to the lowest of the social groups, the Sudras and Chandalas, who came to constitute the peasantry and menial laborers of the new society.

HUNTING PRESERVES

The rulers in this society had their own priorities for the conservation of nature. The *Mahabharata* recounts that the Pandavas camped in the forest and hunted day in and day out. Appearing in the dream of Yudhishthira, the eldest of the brothers, the animals pleaded for a respite from the hunting pressure lest their populations be totally wiped out. The Pandavas acceded and moved on (Karve 1967).

Some thousand years later, we learn from Kautilya's *Arthasastra,* the ancient Indian manual of statecraft, that the princes maintained hunting preserves near their capitals (Kangle 1969). The tradition of princely hunting preserves continued unbroken through the ages, the Mughals, too, being fond of the chase (Ali 1928). In British times, the Asiatic lion was saved from total extermination in the Gir hunting preserve of the nawab of Junagarh; the nawab, it is believed, pretended that the lion had been wiped out altogether to resist the pressure from every visiting British duke and general to add this prestigious trophy to his bag (Seshadri 1969). With independence these hunting preserves provided the nucleus of the nature reserves—Ranathambhor, Bharatpur, Gir, Radhanagari, and Bandipur, to name just a few (Gadgil 1984).

DIVERSIFICATION OF ECOLOGICAL NICHES

Nature has been preserved in the country not merely through princely hunting preserves and modern wildlife sanctuaries but also because of a rich tradition of the people. Indian society is an agglomeration of thousands of endogamous groups, the castes. Among these, the lower castes, close to the earth, have followed hereditary professions at least since the time of Megasthenes, the Greek ambassador to the court of Chandragupta Maurya in 302 B.C. (Thapar 1984). While looking closely at how various communities make use of natural resources, my anthropologist friend Kailash Malhotra and I discovered a remarkable diversification of their ecological niches.

In Maharashtra we have two groups of nomadic basket weavers, Kaikadis and Makadwallas. Traditionally, Kaikadis only use bamboo as raw material for basket weaving, and Makadwallas palm leaves. In coastal Karnataka, there are two sedentary castes that weave mats, the Halakkis and the Patgars. Whereas the Halakkis use only *Pandanus* for their mats, the Patgars use only reeds. Or consider the three major communities of nomadic hunters in the dry tracts of Maharashtra, the Phasepardhis, Nandiwallas, and Vaidus. The Phasepardhis are specialist hunter-gatherers who snare antelopes and deer with the help of cows: The Phasepardhi creeps quietly behind the cow, which has been trained to move slowly toward antelope and deer herds, and lays snares; then once the herd is surrounded, it is flushed and some of the animals trapped. The Phasepardhis also snare partridges, quails, and peafowl. In addition to performing and prophesying with the aid of a sacred bull, the Nandiwallas hunt, too, but primarily using dogs, and their quarry includes wild pigs, porcupines, and monitor lizards. The Vaidus, who dispense herbal medicine, do much hunting of smaller carnivores—mainly civets, mongooses, and cats—with traps baited with a dead squirrel. They are also good at hunting river turtles and hunted crocodiles as well until a few decades ago.

This group of three sympatric hunters has culturally diversified their niches to avoid excessive overlap with potential competitors, a phenomenon quite familiar to the student of ecology (MacArthur 1971). The result has been that each community has exclusive rights over certain resources of certain localities. For example, the antelopes of Ahmednagar district were traditionally hunted by only the Phasepardhis. They married among themselves and regulated their own caste affairs, enabling the persistence of a number of traditions of ecological prudence. They would have never killed a fawn or a pregnant doe caught in their snares but would have released it instead, for the maintenance of the antelope populations of that tract was going to benefit members of the Phasepardhi community itself in days ahead. The trapping of antelopes was considered a service as well by the farming community, with whom the Phasepardhis had a good rapport, although they did not hesitate to do a little thieving on the side when an opportunity offered itself (Gadgil and Malhotra 1983).

MOUNTING CONFLICTS

The British, equipped with their guns, went on a great hunting spree, decimating the enormous antelope herds of the dry plains of Maharashtra—a mission the Indian elite completed after the British left. The Phasepardhis, who were one of the groups officially designated criminal tribes during the British Raj, also have contributed to the demise of the antelopes, for when they found others hunting what was once their exclusive resource, they began to forsake their own traditions of prudence and kill fawns and pregnant does. With the resource base for their subsistence depleted, they have taken increasingly to theft and today live in a state of great tension with the settled rural populations in their territory. In fact, a number of modern-day communal conflicts in India are traceable to the twin causes of the depletion of resource bases and the abandonment of the earlier traditions of ecological prudence.

A COMPLEX CULTURE

Indian society and culture are amazingly heterogeneous. They are a juxtaposition of many elements, both supportive of and inimical to the conservation and good husbandry of the country's natural resources.

We cannot point to the culture of one particular social class or *varṇa* as opposing and that of another class or *varṇa* as conducive to ecological prudence. Nor were there ever some periods when conservation held sway and others when profligacy ruled supreme. It is therefore not possible to build on our tradition now by simplistically invoking a few lines from the *Rg Veda* or the edicts of Asoka or appealing to our spiritual heritage. We cannot point to sacred groves or the few well-managed village forests in remote Himalayan hamlets and claim that our rural people in all their traditional wisdom will take good care of natural resources. Nor can we look for solutions in so-called modern scientific resource management alone. For all management must be geared toward some objectives, and so-called modern scientific management is flawed by its insistence that the only legitimate demands on our natural resources are those of the urban-industrial sector, and that the subsistence needs of the rural population are a burden to be done away with the sooner the better. This approach also suffers from a great deficiency in the empirical information base necessary for deciding the levels at which a resource can be utilized in a sustainable fashion (Gadgil, Prasad, and Ali 1983).

What is therefore needed is an open-minded, eclectic approach. Such an approach should draw on elements conducive to good husbandry of our natural resources and reject those inimical to it, regardless of whether they are a part of our own tradition or of the modern, scientific, technical culture primarily based in the West. The various elements must, of course, stick together and the approach be workable on the ground. I am entirely optimistic that this is possible, and my optimism derives from an experiment I have had the privilege of participating in over the last three years in the Uttara Kannada District of the Western Ghats of Karnataka, just to the south of the Maharashtra Western Ghats with which I began.

GREEN HILLS OF UTTARA KANNADA

I became involved in this experiment because of my interest in bamboos, the fastest-growing group of plants on the surface of the earth. The deciduous forests of Uttara Kannada are rich in bamboos, and I have spent much of the last ten years working in the field on these fascinating plants. While thus engaged, I naturally came to be acquainted with the peasants of the tract. I met many perceptive, intelligent, wise people, some of them totally illiterate. One of the remarkable communities of the tract is the Haviks, whose traditional occupation is cultivation of spice gardens. These gardens present a striking parallel to the natural multistoried forest of the hills, having cardamom as the ground layer, plantains or cocoa as the middle layer, and betelnut trees as the upper layer. Each betelnut tree has a pepper vine coiling around it, and the periphery of the spice garden is lined by tall mango, jackfruit, and coconut trees. The gardens are located in valleys, and the hill slopes supply vital leaf manure and mulch for them. Traditionally the gardeners had rights over the hill forests; Buchanan, writing in 1802, mentions that some of the green hill forests are extremely well maintained by the gardeners to whom they belong. Indeed these hills are called *soppinabeṭṭa*s, literally "hills of leaves," here referred to as the green hills.

Over the years, however, the situation has changed. The green hills have been overused, especially in the last four decades when better prices for betelnuts have enabled the gardeners to engage the local landless peasants to collect the leaf material for the gardens. Since the laborers only care about collecting the most leaves as quickly as possible, the trees are brutally lopped, and many of the hills are a very sorry spectacle today (Mani 1984).

THE HULGOL COOPERATIVE

But the spice gardeners, whom Buchanan found to be as "cunning as foxes," are an exceptionally well-educated farming community. In their tract is a region known as *tōṭada sīme*, "the finest garden country," with Hulgol as a central village. At Hulgol is one of the best run of the farmers' cooperatives, primarily serving the spice gardeners. It has built upon the base of its rich tradition of gardening, but without shirking modernization. These gardeners were the first to introduce cocoa as a shade-tolerant understory shrub to take the place of plantain, which dies as the betelnut trees close their canopy. They also introduced *Glyrecedia* as a hedge plant to provide leaf manure, and installed biogas plants based on cowdung fully twenty-five years ago. To celebrate the silver jubilee of their cooperative, they arranged a model-farm demonstration project in collaboration with the state's agricultural university and published a manual of farm practices particularly appropriate for the local conditions, in the local language.

The members of the Hulgol Cooperative had come to realize that modernizing the spice garden was not enough; the green hills, too, must be well tended. It was with this in view that they interrupted my bamboo watching and asked me to think of better management of their green hills. I was intrigued by the people and their initiative and readily agreed to work with them. Obviously, we had to tackle the problem on many fronts. The green hills provided not only leaves but also fuel and fodder. The fuel was being burnt wastefully, especially to heat water for bathing, and the fodder was being used wastefully as well, as large numbers of undernourished cattle ranged all over the countryside to graze.

The resources of interest to us—soil, water, fuel, and fodder—had been largely neglected. The foresters tended to concentrate on a few species, like teak and eucalyptus, of little relevance to the farmers, and the water resource managers only thought of building large dams, not of the overall health of the watershed.

Even more arduous than the challenging scientific problems were the managerial ones. The success of any revegetation effort depended on controlling grazing of all of the cattle—for the noncooperation of even a single individual can have disastrous consequences. While considering replanting, we had to think of the operation of raising seedlings. How many tree nurseries should there be, where should they be located, who should run them, what species should we grow?

Solving these problems is a matter of achieving cooperation on a wide front, from the landowners and the landless, and from the government agencies as well. The managerial solutions do not come easily, either from the peasantry or the bureaucracy on its own. Each of them has its own ways of pursuing narrow interests. They have to be brought together, cajoled. The teacher, the scientist—the modern incarnations of ancient priests—can play a useful role in this context as a neutral, disinterested party. What we have ended up doing is organizing a network of interacting farmers, government officials, and technical experts to look at and work on a variety of issues.

The problems being tackled typically include revegetation of barren hill slopes with trees, grasses, and legumes. This calls for organizing nurseries to raise seedlings. We have found decentralized nurseries to be an excellent solution. They are best raised by local schools and youth clubs, with government financing. The nurseries require seed supply. Many of the species of interest are indigenous forest trees, so we have to learn a great deal about their seed biology and identify the so-called plus trees as seed sources (Prasad et al. 1985).

Much of this has to draw in an interesting fashion on traditional practices and knowledge. The functioning of the Hulgol Cooperative itself has its origins in the tradition of the caste council of the spice gardeners. But now the cooperative needs to readapt itself to include the participation of peasants and landless who belong to other castes. The selection of plant species is rooted in the traditional knowledge of the ecology and utilization of the indigenous flora, as is the selection of good seed sources.

Finally, the farmers we are working with have, on their own, come to the conclusion that they must also strive to preserve the biological diversity of their land. And one of the devices they have rediscovered is the sacred grove. All the larger sacred groves of the tract are gone; what remains are fragments of a few hectares or less. So they are now working with the Forest Department to establish a series of groves of a few hundred hectares each, near the five major temples of the district representing the various ecological zones of the region. I am delighted to add that three of these were planted in the monsoon of 1985, just after the meeting in Washington.

REFERENCES CITED

Ali, Salim
    1928   The Moghul Emperors of India as Naturalists and Sportsmen. Parts I to III. *Journal of the Bombay Natural History Society* 31 and 32.

Buchanan, Francis
    1802   *Journey through the Northern Parts of Kanara.* Karwar: Nagarika Printers.

Gadgil, Madhav
    1984   Conserving Biological Diversity: The Indian Experience. In *Ecology in Practice, Part I: Ecosystem Management,* edited by F. Di Castri, F. W. G. Baker, and M. Hadley. Dublin: Tycooly International Publishing Limited, 485–91.

Gadgil, Madhav, and Kailash C. Malhotra
    1983   Adaptive Significance of the Indian Caste System: An Ecological Perspective. *Annals of Human Biology* 10:465–78.

Gadgil, Madhav, S. Narendra Prasad, and Rauf Ali
    1983   Forest Management in India: A Critical Review. *Social Action* 33:127–55.

Gadgil, Madhav, and V. D. Vartak
    1975   Sacred Groves of India: A Plea for Continued Conservation. *Journal of the Bombay Natural History Society* 72:314–20.

Kangle, R. P.
    1969   *The Kauṭilīya Arthaśāstra: An English Translation with Critical Notes* (two parts). 2d ed. Bombay: University of Bombay.

Karve, Irawati
    1967   *Yugānta.* Pune: Deshmukh.

Kosambi, D. D.
    1962   *Myth and Reality*. Bombay: Popular Press.

MacArthur, Robert H.
    1972   *Geographical Ecology: Patterns in the Distribution of Species*.
            New York: Harper and Row.

Mani, A.
    1984   Agrarian Technology and Eco-degradation of Betta Forests in
            Salkani Village in North Kanara District, Karnataka. Bangalore:
            Centre for Ecological Sciences, Indian Institute of Science, Tech-
            nical Report No. 1:57.

Prasad, S. Narendra, M. S. Hegde, Madhav Gadgil, and K. M. Hegde
    1985   An Experiment in Eco-Development in Uttara Kannada District
            of Karnataka. *South Asian Anthropologist* 6:73–84.

Rappaport, Roy A.
    1971   The Sacred in Human Evolution. *Annual Review of Systematics
            and Ecology* 2:23–44.

Seshadri, Balakrishna
    1969   *The Twilight of India's Wildlife*. London: John Baker.

Thapar, Romila
    1984   *From Lineage to State*. Bombay: Oxford University Press.

PART 5

Building a Heritage

CHAPTER 21

Between Notion and Reality

Balkrishna V. Doshi

Talking about architecture is always a difficult proposition. Architecture is an extremely complex phenomenon, neither purely physical, purely intellectual, nor purely psychic but a comprehensive manifestation of the three and capable of influencing the lives of individuals and communities. It is not often that in an architectural creation the physical, intellectual, and psychic aspects all are understood, translated into a design concept, and carried through in the built form. When that does happen, though, the result rises above the mundane level to be sanctified and revered by generations.

Treating physical needs alone in a built form produces an experience that is body oriented and a response that is direct. The built form itself is characterized by its emphasis on textural modulations, voluptuous forms, and silhouettes, attributes one finds in folk art (Plate 16). Satisfying only rational demands generates a measure-oriented experience and responses connected to answering specific functional requirements. Many of the socioeconomic considerations in architectural design are interpreted in measurable terms. Architecturally speaking, the approach is toward efficient planning, but designs that are based on mere logic tend to be sterile.

Both of these aspects of architectural design do serve basic needs of the community and the individual. Although emphasis on just one eventually will necessitate changes in the built form as gradually the awareness of the others is felt, together they can lead to a cohesive response. However, the built forms that reflect only the physical and the rational do not necessarily form a sense of unity with the community, and without this they do not become worthy of an emerging heritage. The present reaction against contemporary architecture, with its intellectual and function-oriented styles, clearly indicates its failure in this important respect. Architecture calls for an attempt to address the fundamental need of human beings to be in central relation with themselves and to be in subtle touch with the built form.

In my opinion, supreme among architectural experiences are those which occur along routes of movement and in spaces that could be characterized as *pause* or *ambiguous plural* spaces. These spaces activate the human psyche and induce it to sink toward the center, the mythical world of human's primordial being. Time and space become internalized, and a deeply rooted personal identity with the built form gets established. Several of these space-psyche experiences over a period of time generate a set of *spandana* (vibrations), so that the qualitative aspect of the experiences becomes memorable, cherished by the community at large as well as by individual members and passed on to subsequent generations as part of their heritage. Here rituals play a significant role in elevating the psychic response to a built form. Rituals invite considerations of environment, of society, and of humankind, and they

Figure 21.1. Architecture born out of rituals (Sun Temple at Modhera).

Balkrishna V. Doshi

Figure 21.2. Lingaraj Temple at Bhubaneshwar.

endure longer than individuals, society, or even the environment. So when space is a place for observance of rituals or is associated with rituals, it becomes sacred (Figure 21.1). At this point, I think, architecture emerges. The built form becomes timeless and has a quality that goes beyond the obvious, a meaning and profoundness that transcend the particular person or action. It enriches the entire living order.

Hindu temples are classic examples of architecture that fulfills these purposes. An elaborate sequencing of spaces starts with the open space at the entrance and culminates at the *garbhagṛha,* the "sanctum sanctorum," a dark and totally enclosed area except for the doorway through the *nṛtyamaṇḍapa,* the dance pavilion, open on its other three sides (Figure 21.2). Of different sizes and with varied ceiling heights as well as degrees of enclosure, the spaces are in tune with the nature of the rituals assigned to each one of them—from the more festive in character at the entrance to the meditative in the *garbhagṛha.*

Most of us, irrespective of personal beliefs, are moved when we pay a visit to a temple. And I have been trying to understand this "moving" experience in architectural terms with the objective that it could be applied to create new built forms of lasting value. It seems to me that the pauses, transitional spaces, and thresholds act as catalytic agents for the built forms and the individual or the community to enter into a dialogue at their level of comprehension—a dialogue that gives direction to the community at large in the realization of goals for the self and

Figure 21.3. A typical house, Jaipur.

Figure 21.4. A typical street entrance to a house, Jaipur.

338   Balkrishna V. Doshi

society. As a result of the holistic experience they generate, they finally become institutions. And it is within the framework of the values these institutions then establish that an individual's freedom of expression is encouraged. In the effort to emulate the spiritual experience of being in constant contact with the center and the periphery, each individual strives for excellence.

No insignificant part of our architectural heritage was achieved in this special way. For example, it is said that during the execution of the rock-cut temple complex at Ellora, the master architect would come to the site only once every few years, to set broad guidelines, and left much of the detail to the individuals working there. The exercise of creative freedom by each architect-sculptor within an overall framework, across the centuries, produced an extremely rich architectural experience. Long corridors flanked by myriad sculptured columns, varied ceiling heights, courtyards, and especially sensitive modulation of light and rhythm have for all these years allowed visitors to Ellora a pause to regain personal faith and identity.

Similar concepts to enhance the psychic experience were adopted in the larger urban fabric, through the organization of a hierarchical network of interior and open spaces, large and small, public and domestic, that serve to bring people together (Figures 21.3, 21.4). Buildings associated with rituals, such as shrines, became the active centers of the community—routes leading to them became sanctified places of cultural and ritual performances—and evolved into temple cities like Srirangam. At the domestic level, porches and balconies became the outward physical expression of the family and its contact with the community, and the open court (atrium) within the dwelling acted as the communication center for the family. The court in a house and the central open space in an urban structure are, according to traditional Indian tenets of planning, presided over by Lord Brahma. Being open to the sky, these spaces infuse in individuals and the community the consciousness of nature, as well as bringing the occupants into daily contact with the supernatural and the mythical, and giving them a sense of humility.

The realization that the psychic experiences in architecture are central and that physical and intellectual experiences are to be developed around them is what fascinates me. It has led me to a critical viewing of the traditional architecture of my environment where a holistic experience is strongly felt, as well as to an effort to identify the spatial characteristics and architectural tools that made it possible, in order to recreate such an experience in my work. The urge to design a built form rooted in all its aspects to the land where it stands also has preoccupied my thinking for several years. Below I describe a few of the

Figure 21.5. Plan of
Fatehpur Sikri.

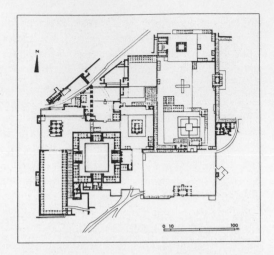

institutional projects in which I have attempted to incorporate the elements of pause and ambiguity and to emphasize the kinds of routes of movement I observed and studied. If nothing else, it certainly is such spatial characteristics that set these projects apart from much contemporary design practice, including my own of a few years ago.

INDIAN INSTITUTE OF MANAGEMENT, BANGALORE (1978)

Emperor Akbar established his well-known capital at Fatehpur Sikri in the sixteenth century. Although it remained unoccupied except for a few years, it is appreciated universally for its scale, clarity, architectural style, and most significant of all, its spatial organization (Figure 21.5). Here one discovers solutions to the now familiar problem of how to extend or add buildings and yet relate them to the whole, how to ensure that all the individual, constituent parts of the complex evoke a sense of belonging to the larger fabric. And it is not surprising that the tools employed at Fatehpur Sikri to simultaneously functionally divide and unite the various buildings in a complex are the same as those used in planning temples in South India.

The response is achieved by adopting a system of major corridors for movement along which activity areas are disposed. The corridors themselves are very much like an umbilical cord in an extended family, separating the individual members and yet connecting them, even though tenuously. Within the network of corridors, the spaces between the activity areas become courts having the sanctity of Brahman, into

340   Balkrishna V. Doshi

Figure 21.6. View of model showing courts and classrooms, Indian
Institute of Management, Bangalore.

Figure 21.7. Linking corridor in Tirupati Temple complex.

*Figure 21.8. Corridor,
Indian Institute of Man-
agement, Bangalore.*

which the activities can extend and related ones take place (Figure 21.6). These courts regenerate the primordial sense of continuity, growth, and relation to the environment.

Also of great interest to me at Fatehpur Sikri is that the presence of the buildings is felt very strongly, in spite of their being relatively small. This is made possible by the well-conceived relation of the building to the ground and sky, and the backdrop of the linking corridor (Figure 21.7).

With an extensive academic program that stretches and changes over the years, the institute similarly required a design that would attend to continuity and growth and give the buildings an individual and common identity. Bangalore's climate is comfortable, and the city is full of lush green lawns and trees. Incorporating the characteristics of the local environment into the design, the "building" in this project includes the outside spaces, where academic exchange also can take place. Functional and physical attributes of the design were attuned to the local traditions of pavilionlike spaces, courtyards, and ample provision for grass and plants.

Because these local elements by themselves do not necessarily touch everyone, the design also included long and unusually high (three-storied) corridors with numerous vistas or focal points for generating a

Figure 21.9. Corridor, Indian Institute of Management, Bangalore.

dialogue with one's self. The corridors sometimes seem open, through the use of pergolas and skylights (Figures 21.8, 21.9). To further activate the spatial experience, the width of the corridors was modulated in many places to allow casual sitting and interaction. They generate constant activity, as they provide access to classrooms and administrative offices as well. Owing to the varying rhythm of solids and voids, that is, walls and openings, coupled with direct or indirect light, the links change in character at different times of day and seasons, offering students, faculty, and others occasions to feel the presence of nature while they are inside the structure and enriching the activities pursued within the building because they become one with the larger, total world. Architecturally, the links appear and disappear, and this gives a sense of being and not being wherein the actual becomes notional. In the morning and evening, the sun's golden rays are reflected in the glazed windows, and the long corridors with the main central court surrounded by classroom walls give a feeling of presence in a place not unknown to one's inner being.

SANGATH, AHMEDABAD (1979)

This program envisioned a complex that would encourage activities in the areas of fine and technological arts related to architecture, planning, and crafts. Spaces were needed for long- and short-term workshops and seminars, and to accommodate a professional architectural firm and an office for the Vastu-Shilpa Foundation—in other words, for many functions.

In the initial stages of planning, a flow pattern of activities and their volumetric space requirements were determined; this generated not only the spatial but also the structural dimensions of the complex. Conditions in the hot, dry climate of Ahmedabad and various energy-efficient designs, primarily based on passive response, were evaluated for the control of interior heat. The sum total of these rational needs was then studied volumetrically, and the building-site relationship was established. Since, at a sensuous level, it was felt essential that form, light, and space should be integrated, a design combining these with functional climatic and technological considerations was evolved. Somehow, though, the model still did not express the vitality of the activities planned for the complex; it seemed capable of allowing only the measurable functions.

In order for the built form to match the dynamic concept of *sangath* (in the vernacular it stands for moving together to a goal), it appeared that equally dynamic articulating methods had to be discovered, to give another dimension to the transitional spaces and to continually generate experiences of the ambiguous. One way of doing this was to incorporate into the built form a series of contrasts, such as spaces that push below ground (Figure 21.10) and surge above ground (Figure 21.11), or high spaces, flooded with light, and low spaces, dimly lit.

The entire building has three different, closely interlinked structural systems. One comprises load-bearing brick walls carrying the vaulted roof; the second, with a retaining wall and brick column structure of irregular shape, supports a flat roof; the third employs load-bearing walls combined with post-and-beam structure to carry heavier loads. Each system has been optimally used to create the variety of spaces described earlier. Likewise, three means of allowing light into the interior were devised: one through normal windows punctured in the wall, another through a skylight, the third through direct penetration from the flat roof through the glass brick. Such spaces, articulated by particular structural systems, make the built form specific.

However, all these methods of articulation remained technical, only marginally moving beyond the physical, falling short of touching the psyche. At this juncture efforts turned to building the surprises in a certain rhythm, or sequence. If a building stretches, is cut into many parts, is seen as fragments, direct confrontation with it is replaced by a sense of gradual transformation that diverts the mind. The long double structures and unexpected unassigned spaces heighten and accentuate the experience of surprise (Plate 17).

Figure 21.10. Pataleshwar Temple, Pune.

Figure 21.11. Shikhara Temple at Khajuraho.

Figures 21.12 and 21.13. Sangath, views from across the garden and steps.

Balkrishna V. Doshi

Finally, to bring the individual into focus, it was decided to underplay the overall scale of the built form. This has been accomplished through a practice that, although widely used in traditional temple architecture, is rather unusual in the contemporary context, relating to the treatment of the plinth (base). The articulation of the interior spaces as described earlier led to sinking certain areas and elevating others. Articulating the plinth in several ways that one notices as one approaches the building has mitigated the external massing of the building. The approach walkway gradually becomes steps for gathering and, through a series of platforms, culminates at the terrace where the upper-level entrance is situated. This low base and the high roof vaults may evoke in an Indian mind the proportions of the deity's face and the tall *śikhara* (crown) of a temple with its low base. The sunken floor level at the lower entrance summons the experience of entering the ancient caves. The roundly articulated edges of the vaults and other surfaces accessible from the low terraces generate a firm relationship with the ground, like that found in a Buddhist stupa (Figures 21.12 and 21.13, and Plate 18).

The ambiguous, open-ended character of the built form starts to reveal itself right at the entrance, which makes one wonder about where to move and how to reach the sanctum. In achieving a destination, there are many ways to go. You can find your own space, in your own time, through your own movement. And the space has to be something beyond just a structure; it has to be like a book, to reach different people and give them the kind of information they need at certain points of time and space. Sangath has two entrances, one at $+6'$ and the other at $-3'$ levels. Both finally reach the same place but through different paths.

Many visitors, learned or otherwise, architects and laypeople, have felt an unusual experience at Sangath. Since one is touched at some center of one's being, I feel that I have succeeded in activating the psychic aspect of the relationship between architecture and the community.

GANDHI LABOUR INSTITUTE, AHMEDABAD (1979)

I have observed over the years that architecture in a hot, dry climate has evolved a dual system of structuring: There is one main system to support the activity areas and another to support an envelope that protects the inside from the harsh weather conditions (Figure 21.14). This building within a building with a central court corresponds to the body and the soul, with the house representing the body and the open court its soul, symbolizing Brahman. Most often this court evidences a

Figure 21.14. Havelī (large residence) in Jaisalmer, showing a separate skin for openings to the exterior and shading the main structure.

Figure 21.15. Plan of havelī, *Jaisalmer.*

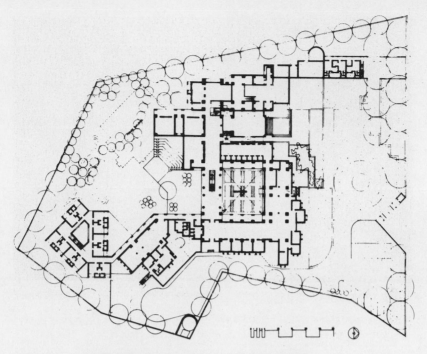

Figure 21.16. Site plan of ground floor, Gandhi Labour Institute, Ahmedabad.

formal geometric character, whereas the external edge of the building responds to the configuration of the site (Figures 21.15, 21.16).

A second characteristic I have observed and incorporated into this design, as well as that of Sangath, is the way sacred buildings relate to the ground and articulate the plinth. Raising a plinth makes a building seem no longer ordinary but important (Figures 21.17, 21.18). Access with reverence is also made possible by breaking surfaces to avoid solidity; the silhouette thus achieved establishes a strong relation with the earth and the sky.

The qualities of the village square also provided inspiration for this design. Usually featuring a large tree under which a platform is raised, the square is essentially a court surrounded by buildings, but the scale and modulation of the buildings somehow efface social disparities, create a cohesive community, and give the place a sense of belonging (Figures 21.19, 21.20). These three varied aspects of an accessible yet respectful place, within a small-scale urban setting and responding to the local climate, constitute the main theme of the Gandhi Labour Institute.

Figure 21.17. Temple at Vadtal.

Figure 21.18. View of entrance, Gandhi Labour Institute, Ahmedabad.

Figure 21.19. Central court, Gandhi Labour Institute, Ahmedabad.

Figure 21.20. Corridor around the central court, Gandhi Labour Institute, Ahmedabad.

Figure 21.21. Exhibition Hall, Gandhi Labour Institute, Ahmedabad.

Figure 21.22. Gandhi Labour Institute, Ahmedabad.

352   Balkrishna V. Doshi

This state-owned institute, which conducts research, training, seminars, and workshops in labor management and welfare, is relatively small but has the potential to grow. The functional demands are similar to those of any such institute: a library, classrooms, seminar rooms, administration, trainees' accommodations, a canteen. In order to generate a design comprehending the functional, symbolic, and notional levels, I referred to and adopted the models of an inner court of a large *haveli* in Jaisalmer and a temple at Vadtal, as well as a typical village square, and I employed a series of thresholds and linkages of varied scales to accentuate the meaning of these images.

The Gandhi Labour Institute's front plaza with a long, wide flight of approach steps allows sufficient time for the visitor to absorb the experience of this otherwise imposing building. The long linkages, with their high exhibition space (Figure 21.21) and narrow movement areas between the internal and external courtyards, connect all the functional areas of the complex, through visual or actual contacts (Figure 21.22). In the central inner court, with its linkage to the outer court, amphitheater, dining area, and the terraces of the dormitories, one has the feeling of being in a village square, as an individual or as a member of the community, and its small pool captures for the observer sun, moon, and sky reflected in it.

The counterbalancing of different structural systems, along with constantly changing floor configurations and the skewing of the dormitory block from the right-angle geometry of the institute's building, are natural reflexes much like our constant inhaling and exhaling. It is through all these elements that an attempt is made to relate an individual's center to the physical and intellectual world (Plate 19).

Architecture is not a temporary affair. If we can make space that can exalt itself, it will take root, have meaning, and last a long time.

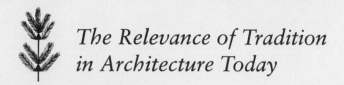

CHAPTER 22

The Relevance of Tradition
in Architecture Today

Raj Rewal

The vast range of traditional Indian architecture can be understood in different ways. Architectural historians have divided it into periods: Hindu, Buddhist, Islamic, and colonial. There is a secular trend in Indian architecture, too, underlying monuments, civic complexes, and vernacular buildings, although it has been largely ignored in the literature. And certain themes recur at various stages of its development, emerging in contemporary form. Architects may look to the past for inspiration, or even try to prove themselves by contradicting the older models.

Building methodology, social conditions, and climate shaped Indian architecture. Building techniques are changing quickly, and the pattern of living is in the process of evolution, but the factor of climate remains constant. The traditional elements of design based on the warm Indian climate definitely have relevance in terms of our work today.

One of my first major buildings was a permanent exhibition complex for trade fairs, built in 1972 in New Delhi. The space-frame structural system follows the mainstream of modern architecture for covering large halls, and its construction was adapted to labor-intensive Indian industry.

The plan is composed of one large hall of 256 square feet connected

---

Unless otherwise noted, photographs are by Raj Rewal or Hélène Rewal.

Figure 22.1. Exhibition complex.

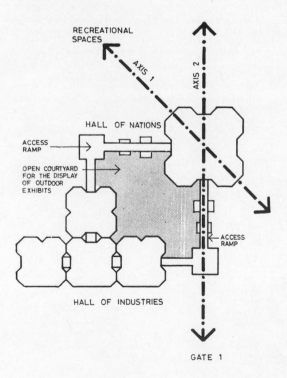

RECREATIONAL SPACES

AXIS 1

AXIS 2

HALL OF NATIONS

ACCESS RAMP

OPEN COURTYARD FOR THE DISPLAY OF OUTDOOR EXHIBITS

ACCESS RAMP

HALL OF INDUSTRIES

GATE 1

Figure 22.2. Plan of exhibition complex.

with four smaller halls of 144 square feet by means of ramps enclosing a central courtyard for outdoor displays and meetings. As in the traditional Indian pattern of public spaces, the courtyard emerges as the focal point of the scheme.

An art historian compared the spatial geometry of the plan to the Mughal structure of Humayun's Tomb. Personally I was surprised by the observation, as I had never consciously thought of that particular reference. But I realize that formal Indian structures of all periods have a certain affinity in the manner of ordering spaces or modulating enclosures, though their external appearance may be different.

The depth of the structural system of the exhibition complex was utilized as a sun breaker and conceived in terms of the traditional Indian *jālī*, a geometrical pattern of perforations forming a major element of design on the facade that serves to obstruct direct rays of the harsh sun while permitting air circulation.

In 1972 I designed the Nehru Pavilion, a museum to exhibit objects and photographic panels on Nehru's life and times. While working on the design, I kept in mind the personality of Nehru, a sensitive intellectual and democrat who would have hated any manifestation of pomposity to honor him.

How could a pavilion allow one to symbolize Nehru's life? There were no relevant contemporary prototypes; I began to search deliberately for older models. I had seen Buddhist grass mounds in Nepal that contained relics of the Buddha. Inspired by these, I came upon the idea of grassy embankments enclosing exhibition space at two levels. The circulation system for the exhibition was based on *parikrama*, the circumambulatory movement around the central shrine of temples, and the plan began to resemble Tantric *yantra*s!

Figure 22.3. Plan of Humayun's tomb.

Figure 22.4. Traditional jālī.

Figure 22.5. Detail, Hall of Nations, exhibition complex.

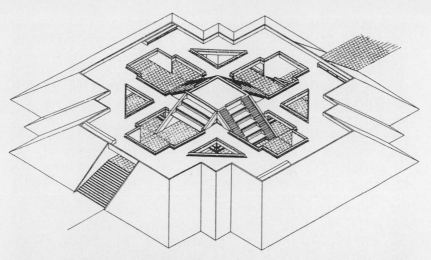

Figure 22.6. View of Nehru Pavilion.

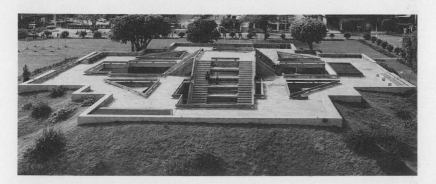

Figure 22.7. Nehru Pavilion.

But Nehru was a secular person, and I had to reinterpret these elements so as not to confuse his personality with "sacred" connotations. The children of India refer to Nehru as a loving uncle, "Chacha Nehru"; the grass embankments and the central steps to the roof were designed for children to run up and down, before settling down to see the exhibits on two lower floors. The search for symbolic values that fulfill contemporary aspirations but carry relevant echoes of the past assumes importance in the Nehru Pavilion.

In the realm of practical climatic considerations, the traditional morphology of Rajasthan cities has important lessons to teach for today's low-rise, high-density housing developments, and it directly influenced my design for the Asian Games Village of five hundred housing units in New Delhi (1982).

The institutional and sterile pattern of housing favored by departmental engineers for public and municipal works, based on an endless repetition of a design, is rejected here. Instead, an attempt has been made to create urban norms from a network of pedestrian streets and squares. The peripheral road provides motor access from two ends to the parking squares, which in turn give way to pedestrian paths or to the garages of individual housing units. The village reinterprets several salient elements of vernacular design that have stood the test of time.

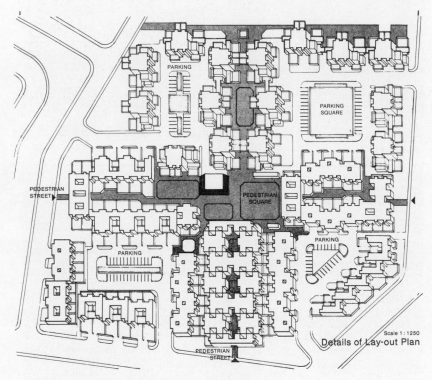

Figure 22.8. Plan of Asian Games Village.

Figure 22.9. The alternation between solids and voids in the densely formed city of Jaisalmer is the archetype of the Indian urban fabric. The entire city is built within very well defined parameters.

Figure 22.10. The Asian Games Village creates a new urban pattern from these basic values. The development is different from plotted residential colonies or terrace housing, and the common factors that create group identity are retained by means of the total environmental design.

Figure 22.11. The narrow pedestrian street, shaded and vitally alive, constitutes an important feature of the vernacular tradition. This street is in Jaisalmer.

Figure 22.12. The plan of the Asian Games Village is based on similar narrow streets linking a variety of clusters. The streets are consciously broken up into visually comprehensible units, so there are pauses, points of rest, and changing vistas.

CLUSTER

Figure 22.13. The cluster is the outcome of a traditional manner of forming an assembly of housing units. The identity of the individual unit is partially submerged. Photograph is of Jaisalmer.

Figure 22.14. The design solution for the Asian Games Village reflects the belief that it is possible to develop kinds of units—individual houses or apartments—that can be linked together to form a cluster. Different types of apartments generate a variety of clusters, avoiding the monotony of large-scale public housing schemes.

Figure 22.15. The traditional function of the gateway was to define the territory of a community. The darwāzas *were an imposing element of design to keep intruders out. Photograph is of Jaipur.*

Figure 22.16. Entrance gates punctuate the sequence of spaces around communal courtyards and define neighborhood zones in the Asian Games Village. In this case, the gateways are formed by linking overhead functional roof terraces.

Figure 22.17. Sequential views along the movement path are formed by a succession of gateways in Adalaj, Gujarat.

Figure 22.18. The Asian Games Village utilizes a similar system of repetitive gateways to enclose a variety of open spaces around a pedestrian spine.

366   Raj Rewal

Figure 22.19. Roof terraces are essential to the life-style of the traditional cities of North India. In the hot, dry climate they provide welcome space for sleeping on summer nights; the inner chambers emit the heat absorbed during the scorching day and in winter are used as outdoor living areas when the inner rooms are cold. Photograph taken in Rajasthan.

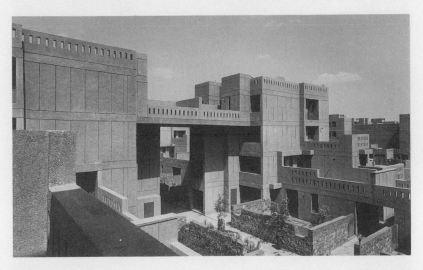

Figure 22.20. Private roof terraces and courtyards are an integral part of the design of the Asian Games Village. The high parapets offer privacy and are pierced with jālīs to allow air circulation. The roof terraces form extensions of the living room or bedrooms.

Figure 22.21. The community space, or mohallā, is a significant design feature of North Indian cities, such as Jaipur. The public courtyards accommodate multiple activities ranging from marriage ceremonies to the celebration of festivals.

Figure 22.22. In the design of the Asian Games Village, the hierarchy of open spaces is also an important consideration; the semipublic courtyards are the focus of common activities and promote social interaction. Weaving through them is a network of pedestrian paths giving access to the individual units.

The last project I shall discuss, the National Institute of Immunology, New Delhi, is influenced by the *havelī*s (large residences) and civic complexes of the Rajasthan cities. I carefully studied the manner in which they counter the intense heat during the day by building around courtyards and then incorporated it within the framework of current functional requirements.

The design is based on the creation of three separate clusters (for senior scientists, junior scientists, and scholars) with their own internal courtyards of discernible character. It is the organization of these internal spaces that distinguishes the scheme.

The courtyard for senior scientists can be approached from four corners, as the building is laid out on a diagonal axis to the main road. This space not only functions as the entrance hall for all twelve apartments but also provides the focus for community interaction. The roof terraces of the upper units overlook the central court, which is in shadow during most of the day and is an appropriate place for small children to play.

Figure 22.23. Havelī.

The cluster for junior scientists is placed on a central axis, in alignment with the planned auditorium. Its internal courtyard is of an intimate scale and forms a focal point for the flight of steps connecting the lower road to the upper-level ridge. The twelve apartments of approximately 70 square meters are grouped around two staircases at three levels overlooking the internal court. Each apartment has a roof terrace, and the cluster follows the form of the land in its stepped section.

The hostel for scholars consists of individual rooms around an octagonal court, built as a small amphitheater corresponding to the contours of the site. The plan is symmetrical on both axes and affords an orderly solution for providing roof terraces on successive upper stories. The one side of the octagon along the diagonal axis frames distant views of the hills.

In none of these housing programs, and the earlier works I have described, has there been any effort to embellish the designs with false oriental arches, domes, or carvings. The inspiration from the past is reinterpreted in terms of rational structures, modern techniques, and new building materials, to meet practical realities.

Figure 22.24. Residence, National Institute of Immunology.

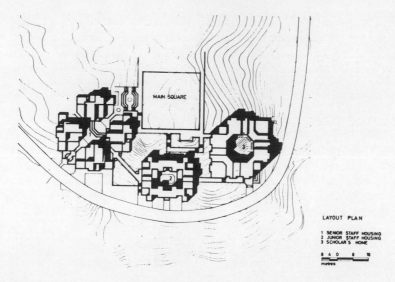

LAYOUT PLAN

1 SENIOR STAFF HOUSING
2 JUNIOR STAFF HOUSING
3 SCHOLAR'S HOME

0 4 0 8 16
metres

Figure 22.25. Plan, National Institute of Immunology.

Figure 22.26. Senior Scientists Cluster, National Institute of Immunology.

372   Raj Rewal

Figure 22.27. Junior Scientists Cluster, National Institute of Immunology.

Figure 22.28. National Institute of Immunology.

Tradition in Architecture   373

Figure 22.29. Amphitheater, National Institute of Immunology.

Figure 22.30. National Institute of Immunology complex.

CHAPTER 23

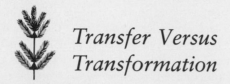

Transfer Versus Transformation

Charles Correa

Mythic images exercise a primordial—and sometimes irrational—power over us. If you are an architect who puts up a glass building in the heat of Saudi Arabia, you may have ten different reasons to "justify" your design, but the operative one, which you may not even recognize at a conscious level, is that you are building an image of the quintessential city: in this case, probably Houston, Texas.

Architecture always deals with mythic images. But merely *transferring* them—and it doesn't matter whether they come from overseas or from your own past—can lead to deplorable consequences. Not only may buildings become unusable and totally inappropriate for the local context, but they can have a destructive effect on the life fabric of the society itself. Instead, as the myths and images surface, their underlying values have to be understood. These must be absorbed and redefined, *transformed* as opposed to transferred. There is a crucial and basic difference between the two processes.

Today we are in grave danger of using the past as mere pastiche. An architecture that disregards the fact that technology and materials change is dishonest; and it also threatens to falsify—*devalue*—the past. Soon we find ourselves making Elizabethan houses out of steel and plastic. We must carefully distinguish between a superficial scan of a mythic architectural image and what might be called its deep structure.

Consider the way we treat space in different parts of the world. In northern Europe, the house becomes of necessity a sealable box inside which you're safe, protected from the cold weather. In fact, there is always a precise moment of entry, though the door; the peripheral skin creates a very clear, dualistic relationship between outside and inside. In a warm climate, though, you get another experience entirely. Once you're through a doorway there, you move into a series of spaces that are highly ambiguous, indoors and outdoors not clearly demarcated. Aside from the rooms, you also have verandahs and platforms, court-yards and terraces. Such ambiguity of spaces is evident in Fatehpur Sikri (Figure 23.1). Even when there are enclosing elements, they usually take the form of porous screens, so the skin is not only visually transparent, but air and breezes can move through.

From experiences like these are generated mythic images and val-ues. Thus whereas in America the enclosed "little red schoolhouse" is the symbol of education, in India it is the guru sitting under the tree. (And believe me, you're more likely to achieve enlightenment sitting under a tree than in a claustrophobic room! *Ākāśa,* open sky, is tremen-dously important to humanity.)

In the holy city of Srirangam in South India, which is based on a mandala diagram, the pilgrim passageways and spaces used for the great rituals are open to the sky. You find this also in Indonesia, in Borobudur (Figure 23.2), probably the most perfect mandala of all. And

Figure 23.1. Fatehpur Sikri.

376   Charles Correa

Figure 23.2. Borobudur.

why does the Alhambra, actually a decadent building (at least structurally, as far as I'm concerned), knock you out? Because it deals with centrality, with water channels and fountains, and with God's sky above. Courtyards have always had a decisive value in warm climates, almost regardless of proportion or material. They seem to convey to us something fundamental that we cannot explain—like the tribal memory of a lost paradise. To see the effects of covering them over, visit the air-conditioned atrium of a new hotel. Everything seems artificial and plastic: the plants, the food, even the people.

Climate influences architecture in other, more direct ways as well. For instance, the famous windcatcher houses in Hyderabad, Sind, have scoops on the roof to catch air and take it down and over water, humidifying and cooling the whole house. And in Jaipur, the stone *jālīs* around the windows of the Hawa Mahal can be sprinkled with water during the dry, hot season, so that there's a cool breeze through the whole palace.

Responses to climate can involve not only these kinds of ingenious contrivances but one's whole life-style. In the Meena Bazaar in the Red Fort at Agra, hooks were provided along the periphery of the courtyard so that early in the morning in the hot weather a curtain could be strung across it to trap the cold overnight air inside. This allowed the lower level of rooms to be used during the day. When the heat had subsided in the evening, the Mughal emperor and his court would occupy the upper level of terrace pavilions (Figure 23.3). During the cold but sunny winter months, they would reverse the procedure. In other words, to deal with climate the Mughals invented a kind of nomadic life-style. Coming from Kabul, and before that from Uzbekistan, in moving to Delhi they transformed their traditions. They used what they wanted to use and changed what needed to be changed.

We can, and do, mishandle the deep-structure values. To me, the essence of the Parthenon in Athens is the movement upward along a sacred pathway. Of course it has marble columns, and it represents many, many other layers of architectonic decisions, but the basic mechanism—in human terms—is the upward, open-to-sky pathway. Now what is the result when you try to transfer (not transform, but transfer) this architecture? In Figure 23.4, see the same Parthenon on its way to becoming the Bank of England. This is accomplished by taking superficially what is really just one aspect of it, namely the marble columns, and making them into wallpaper, into tattooing, in order to create some "meaning." I took this photograph in 1962, in Leningrad. The building on the right was built in 1929 by a contemporary of Le Corbusier; the structure on the left with the fake classical columns had just been finished. I thought this was hilariously funny. Today, of course, the joke is on us. This kind of facile eclecticism is being practiced everywhere.

I would now like to describe a project in Goa, south of Bombay, the part of India my family comes from. Goa has many beaches and little towns, kind of village towns, with colorfully painted buildings. When we were

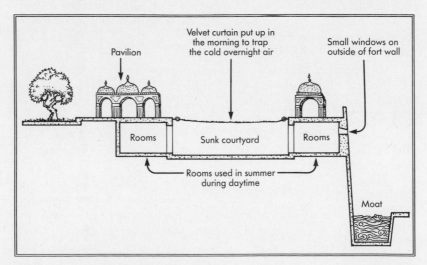

Figure 23.3. Section of Red Fort, Agra.

Figure 23.4. Two buildings in Leningrad.

asked to build a hotel there, I thought we'd use the evocative name of one of the towns, Cidade (City) de Goa, for it.

The project begins as a city of virtual imagery. Plate 21 shows the entrance. You can see that many of the images are three-dimensional built form, but some are just painted signs and symbols of a city—done by ordinary sign painters, as a matter of fact, who in India can be very, very good.

There is much ambiguity in the plan; we keep breaking the axis and unhinging it to give an episodic quality. And as you walk through, you encounter slices of Goa's history, from the pre-Portuguese time, through the Portuguese, and so on, right up to the present. Then as you get further into the hotel, it becomes a *real* city, a city of rooms and balconies and terraces. It is a kind of highly intensified, exaggerated, surrealistic version of what happens in Goa's villages and small towns, in the vernacular.

But art for art's sake is not the whole truth, by any means. While we architects are busy on projects such as Cidade de Goa, another set of events is overtaking Bombay. Like many other Third World cities, Bombay has grown phenomenally since World War II. It is not just that the national population is increasing, but also that the urban sector is growing twice as fast. Today almost half of Bombay's population, more than four million people, are illegal squatters. The question I want to address in this context is, how can we transform the past, specifically the way of building in the past, so as to make it relevant to *them*. For if we don't do that, then we haven't really achieved very much.

If you examine the concentration of jobs in Bombay and the land values, you will see that they are both highest on the southern tip of the island. This means that the poor cannot afford to live there except in the crevices—the pavements, staircases, parks—and even these are filling up. The planning models of the West are really not applicable in our situation. What we have to do is restructure the city by generating more urban land that will be serviced by public transportation and related to work opportunities. And so we developed the concept of New Bombay, a growth center across the harbor for two million people. But how would we proceed to plan housing there for people with very low incomes?

Looking at old towns and cities—or villages for that matter— shows that people live in a whole hierarchy of spaces, from the private to the public: the private area for family use, the doorstep between the units where people can converse with neighbors, the neighborhood meeting places (e.g., the community tap or the village well), and finally the biggest space, which is usually near the temple. What we call housing is not the room itself; that is only *one* element in the spatial system. If we do not recognize the system, then we make the wrong definitions, and we ask the wrong question, which is: How can we pile these rooms one on top of the other? Since only about one-third of any city's area is used for housing, actually we are not saving much land by piling up these boxes anyway, and we end up with inhuman, unlivable environments.

In the low-income housing we have constructed in New Bombay, individual houses are very tightly packed, and rather than linear streets we have used a metaphor of the old courtyard. Seven houses surround every courtyard, and each house relates to that space (Figure 23.5). Repeating the pattern three times forms a larger courtyard. Then if you repeat *that* all over again, you get a larger community square— and so forth, forming an organic hierarchy of spaces. The typology of houses ranges from those that cost about twenty thousand rupees (about eighteen hundred dollars—three hundred down and the rest loaned by the government) all the way up to sophisticated multilevel little townhouses.

But the important thing here is not the design of the houses; it is the site planning. In fact, we designed the houses in a simple, direct way, using the traditional vernacular. For I firmly believe that it is not necessary for architects to design houses; people already have a rich heritage of constructing them. In Rajasthan, for example, we find an extraordi-

Figure 23.5. Belapur Housing, New Bombay.

nary layering, using color and pattern. First of all, there is the architectural space; and then there is an overlay of painterly space (Figure 23.6). The painterly work is quite different from the architectural, and the interaction of the two gives you the final product, which is something else again. Were there not such a heritage and wealth of knowledge for people to draw on, ugliness rather than beauty would be the more likely result (it's the principle of Miami Beach). Unfortunately, too many of the architects who do work for the poor are avisual, or even antivisual—this despite the fact that all over the Third World there exist such wonderfully inventive design solutions, of color, form, and building. What doesn't exist, of course, is the urban context in which those solutions are viable. So that is what our real responsibility is: to create that urban context. We have to understand our past well enough to value it, but at the same time know why, and how, it needs to be changed.

I would like to end with two revealing illustrations. One shows people living in pipes, sections of water mains left lying around along the main roads of Bombay (Figure 23.7). In a sense, they are like birds building nests. The man in the pipe is having a cup of tea with his friend. It is a social occasion. Far from being vicious and desperate, they still possess a great humanity. And that fact gives me enormous hope for the Third World. The people, as human beings, are still intact. They are not

Figure 23.6. Mud house, Rajasthan.

Figure 23.7. People in pipe.

Figure 23.8. Mythic city.

mugging you. It takes centuries, I think, to make people so decent, so humane; I suppose that is what you call civilization. But under such conditions, how long will it last?

The other image is also of the very poor, the construction workers (who are really a kind of squatters). Behind them is the modern city of Bombay (Figure 23.8). Those incredibly ugly buildings are, for these people, the new myths. For we do not live in societies that are absolutely static; no, we are witness to an era of constant and mind-boggling change. The urbanization, the distress migration to cities all over the Third World, is going to be the central issue of the next twenty-five years. How well we transform the old values, patterns, and symbols to meet the migrants' rising aspirations could well determine our survival. The architect, instead of reinforcing the status quo, must be an agent who helps to invent the future.

Appendixes

Biographies of Contributors

ANIL AGARWAL, director and founder, Centre for Science and Environment. Holds B. Tech. from Indian Institute of Technology, Kanpur. Concerned with science and development, energy and environment policies. Science correspondent, *Hindustan Times, Indian Express*. Education director, Earthscan, London. Articles, six books include *Mud, Mud: The Role of Earth-Based Materials in Third World Housing*; coeditor, *State of India's Environment 1982* and *1984–85*. Chairperson, board of directors, Environment Liaison Center, Nairobi. Delivered World Conservation Lecture, London, 1985. Received first A. H. Boerma Award, Food and Agriculture Organization, Rome, 1979; Vikram Sarabhai Memorial Award, 1984; Padma Shri (Award), 1986. Born in Kanpur, 1947.

ARJUN APPADURAI, professor of anthropology, University of Pennsylvania. Received B.A., Brandeis University, 1970; M.A., University of Chicago, 1973; Ph.D., Chicago, 1976. Research interests in religion, public culture, and agriculture in India; articles and books published on these topics include *Worship and Conflict under Colonial Rule: A South Indian Case* (1981), an edited collection, *The Social Life of Things: Commodities in Cultural Perspective* (1986), and a book of essays entitled *Improvisation and Experience in an Agricultural Society* (in preparation), based on fieldwork in Maharashtra, 1980–81. Member, executive committee and board of trustees, American Institute of Indian Studies (AIIS); Joint Committee on South Asia; American Council of Learned Societies; and Social Science Research Council. Honorary Andrew Mellon Faculty Fellow, University of Pennsylvania, 1978–79; Janice and Julian Bers Assistant Professor of Social Sciences, Pennsylvania, 1978–80; fellow, Center for Advanced Study in the Behavioral Sciences, Stanford, 1984–85. Research grants from Social Science Research Council, National Science Foundation, AIIS. Born in Bombay, 1949.

GERALD D. BERREMAN, professor of anthropology, University of California, Berkeley. Educated at University of Oregon (B.A. 1952, M.A. 1953) and Cornell University (Ph.D. 1959). Research conducted in India on Himalayan village society, culture, and change (1957–58); urban social organization and interaction (1968–69); regional politics and environmental movement in Himalayas (1981–82). Other work focuses on comparative social inequality, interaction theory, ecology, research methods, and professional ethics. Articles published on those topics. Books include *Hindus of the Himalayas, Caste and Other Inequities, The Politics of Truth: Essays in Critical Anthropology, Social Inequality: Comparative and Developmental Approaches* (editor). Awarded honorary doctorates by University of Stockholm (1978) and Garhwal University, India (1979). Born in Portland, Oregon, 1930.

ELA R. BHATT, founder and general secretary, Self-Employed Women's Association (SEWA), Ahmedabad; appointed in 1986 to Rajya Sabha (upper house of Indian Parliament). Educated at Gujarat University (B.A., LL.B.). Chairperson, Co-operative Bank of SEWA. Member of board of directors, Women's World Banking, New York; of governing council, Gandhi Labour Institute, Ahmedabad; and of advisory boards of numerous labor organizations. International consultant on women, employment, and banking. Received Magsaysay Award for Community Leadership (1977), Susan B. Anthony Award for National Integration (1983), Right Livelihood Award, Sweden (1984), Padma Shri (Award) (1985), and Padma Bhushan (Award) (1986). Born in Ahmedabad, 1933.

CARLA M. BORDEN, associate director, Office of Interdisciplinary Studies, Smithsonian Institution. Received B.A. from Barnard College (1970), M.A. from Columbia University (1974). Interests in contemporary Indian culture, comparative sociology, sociology of knowledge, language, literature, ethnicity, folklore. Fieldwork in Yugoslavia on traditional music and dance and in Yugoslav-American communities on the role of music in ethnic identity. Came to Smithsonian in 1973, to be field research coordinator for "Old Ways in the New World" program of the

Festival of American Folklife. Has written a number of book reviews; coeditor, *The Muses Flee Hitler: Cultural Transfer and Adaptation, 1930–1945* (1983), a collection of essays on intellectual refugees from Nazi Europe. Born in Brookline, Massachusetts, 1948.

CHARLES CORREA, architect and planner. Educated at University of Michigan (B.Arch. 1953) and Massachusetts Institute of Technology (M.Arch. 1955). Chairperson, Government of India National Commission on Urbanization. Has planned cities, townships, and buildings, including Mahatma Gandhi Memorial Museum, Sabarmati Ashram, Ahmedabad; Kanchangunja Apartments, Bombay; Bharat Bhavan Museum, Bhopal; Cidade de Goa, Panjim; and low-income housing, Belapur, New Bombay. Chief architect for New Bombay, 1971–74; member, governing council, National Institute of Design, Ahmedabad, 1974–77. Work published in various journals, as well as in books by Mimar (Singapore, 1984) and Pidgeon Audio-Visual (London, 1980). Member, steering committee, Aga Khan Award for Architecture, 1977–present. Was awarded Padma Shri, 1972; honorary doctorate, University of Michigan, 1980; Sir Robert Mathew Prize, Union of International Architects, 1984; Gold Medal, Royal Institute of British Architects, 1984; 1986 Chicago Architecture Award, American Institute of Architects. Nehru Professor, Cambridge University, 1985–86. Born in Hyderabad, 1930.

VEENA DAS, professor of sociology, University of Delhi. Received Ph.D., Delhi, 1970. Interested in symbolic systems, religion, kinship and marriage, and the analysis of texts. Author, *Structure and Cognition: Aspects of Hindu Caste and Ritual,* and articles in professional and popular journals. Received Ghurye Award, 1977; elected to Henry Myers Lectureship, Royal Anthropological Institute, London, 1982; was Luce Professor, Amherst College, 1985–86. Born in Lahore, 1944.

BALKRISHNA V. DOSHI, architect; senior partner, Stein Doshi & Bhalla; director, Vastu-Shilpa Foundation for Studies and Research in Environmental Design. Educated at Sir J. J. College of Arts, Bombay. Senior designer, Le Corbusier Studio, Paris, and representative for Le Corbusier in Ahmedabad for his major buildings in Chandigarh and Ahmedabad, 1951–57. Founding member and first honorary director, School of Architecture, Centre for Environmental Planning and Technology (CEPT), Ahmedabad, 1962–72; founding member and honorary director, School of Planning, CEPT, Ahmedabad, 1972–78; visiting professor, CEPT, 1962–present. Visiting critic/professor, University of Pennsylvania, 1962–present. Paul Cret Adjunct Professor, University of

Pennsylvania, 1984. Contributor to numerous magazines and journals. Major works include industrial complexes, cultural, educational, and health institutions (e.g., Indian Institute of Management, Ahmedabad, with Louis I. Kahn), and new township in Indore. Fellow, Indian Institute of Architects; honorary fellow, American Institute of Architects; associate member, Royal Institute of British Architects. Recipient of Padma Shri (Award), 1976. Born in Pune, 1927.

MADHAV GADGIL, professor of ecological sciences and of theoretical studies, Indian Institute of Science (IIS), Bangalore. Holds Ph.D. in biology from Harvard University. Scientific interests include plant, animal, and human ecology and behavior, sociobiology, and the environment; has also been intimately involved in practical problems of conservation and ecodevelopment. Lecturer in biology at Harvard, 1969–71; at IIS since 1973. Has published over sixty research papers and written and broadcast extensively on science and environment in English, Marathi, Hindi, and Kannada. Works with villagers in Uttara Kannada District, Karnataka, in action program for better management of natural living resources. Fellow, Indian National Science Academy and Indian Academy of Sciences. Member, Science Advisory Council to the Prime Minister. Received Harvard Computing Center IBM Fellowship (1969), Government of India National Environment Fellowship (1979–81), Padma Shri (Award) (1981), Government of Karnataka Rajyotsava Award (1983), and Rathindranath Award, Visvabharati University (1985). Born in Pune, 1942.

RAMCHANDRA GANDHI, philosopher; holds Haridas Chaudhuri Chair of South Asian and Comparative Philosophy, California Institute of Integral Studies. Ph.D.'s from Universities of Oxford, Delhi. United Nations University Fellowship at Centre for the Study of Developing Societies, New Delhi, for work on peace and survival from the standpoint of Indian philosophy and spirituality (1985–86). Formerly professor of comparative religion, Visvabharati University; professor of philosophy, University of Hyderabad; taught philosophy in Great Britain. Has published four books, most recent being *I am Thou: Meditations on the Truth of India* (1984). Born in Madras, 1937.

GIRISH KARNAD, playwright, filmmaker, and actor. Educated at Karnatak University, Dharwad, and then Rhodes scholar at Oxford University, 1960–63. Original plays and filmscripts draw on myths, legends, and history. Editor with Oxford University Press, 1963–70. Director, Film and Television Institute of India, 1974 and 1975. Fulbright scholar in residence and visiting professor, University of Chicago, 1987–88. Plays in Kannada are *Yayati* (1961), *Tughlaq* (1964), *Hayavadana* (1970), which received Sangeet Natak Akademi Award and Kamaladevi Award of Bharatiya Natya Sangha for best play of 1971, *Anjumallige* (1978), and *Hittina Hunja* (1980). *Tughlaq* and *Hayavadana* also translated and performed in other Indian as well as in European languages and published in English by Oxford University Press. Film career started with *Samskara* (1969); wrote script and dialogue as well as playing lead role. Apart from scripting and acting in films for others, has directed *Vamsha Vriksha* (1972) and *Godhuli* (1977)—both with B. V. Karanth—and *Kaadu* (1973), *Ondanondu Kaaladalli* (1978), and *Ustav* (1984). Films have won several national awards and represented India at international film festivals. Homi Bhabha Fellow, 1970–72. Awarded Padma Shri, 1974. Born in Matheran, 1938.

DHRITI KANTA LAHIRI CHOUDHURY, professor and head, Department of English, Rabindra Bharati University, Calcutta. Educated at University of Calcutta (M.A.) and University of Leeds (Ph.D.). Professional research interest in medieval English and tragedy; passional interest in management of large mammals in the wild, particularly elephants, and conservation in general. Coordinator, North-East India Task Force, Asian Elephant Group, International Union for Conservation of Nature (IUCN)/Species Survival Commission, 1978–84. Principal investigator, IUCN/World Wildlife Fund project 3031, "Status Survey of Elephants in North-East India." Consultant to Government of India for Wildlife Action Plan. Author of articles and reports on wildlife. Member, Eastern Region Committee, World Wildlife Fund-India; steering committee, West Bengal State Wildlife Advisory Board; board of directors, West Bengal Forest Development Corp. Ltd. Visiting associate fellow, Clare Hall, Cambridge, England. Born in Calcutta, 1931.

DAVID G. MANDELBAUM, professor emeritus of anthropology, University of California, Berkeley, at the time of his death in April 1987. Educated at Northwestern University (B.A. 1932), Yale University (Ph.D. 1936). Field studies of American Indians, 1933–36, and in India periodically from 1937. Other research interests included anthropological theory, applied anthropology. Taught at University of Minnesota and Cambridge University. Author of *The Plains Cree* (1940, second enlarged edition 1979), *Soldier Groups and Negro Soldiers* (1952), *Society in India*, vols. 1 and 2 (1970), *Human Fertility in India* (1974), *Woman's Seclusion and Man's Honor* (1988). Editor, *Selected Writings of Edward Sapir* (1949, new edition 1985). Principal investigator and coeditor, *The*

Teaching of Anthropology (1963). Among last articles is "Anthropology for the Nuclear Age," *Bulletin of the Atomic Scientists,* June 1984. Born in Chicago, 1911.

C. M. NAIM, chairperson, Department of South Asian Languages and Civilizations, and associate professor of Urdu, University of Chicago; publisher and editor, *Annual of Urdu Studies.* In 1963 cofounded *Mahfil: A Quarterly of South Asian Literature* (now known as *Journal of South Asian Literature*) and was coeditor until 1978. Has published on Urdu language and literature and the cultural history of the Muslims of South Asia. Born in Bara Banki, 1936.

WENDY DONIGER O'FLAHERTY, Mircea Eliade Professor of the History of Religions, Divinity School, and professor of Indian Studies, Department of South Asian Languages and Civilizations, University of Chicago. Educated at Radcliffe College (B.A. 1962), Harvard University (Ph.D. 1968), Oxford University (D.Phil. 1973). Work has centered on Hindu mythology, particularly the mythologies of sexuality, evil, and dreams. Translated selections from the *Rig Veda* (Penguin Classics) and a source-book of Hindu myths, from Sanskrit. Most recent publications include *Women, Androgynes, and Other Mythical Beasts; Dreams, Illusion, and Other Realities*; and *Tales of Sex and Violence* (all from University of Chicago Press). Studied in India under a grant from the American Institute of Indian Studies, in Ireland under a National Endowment for the Humanities grant and a Guggenheim Fellowship, and in Moscow. President, American Academy of Religion, 1985. Born in New York City, 1940.

GIEVE PATEL, painter and writer. Graduated as general medical practitioner from Bombay University, 1965; in charge of a primary health centre in Gujarat, 1968–70; at present has private medical clinic in central Bombay. Artistic work has been influenced by experiences as a doctor in rural and urban India. Paintings in museums and private collections and displayed in exhibitions in India, England, the United States, France, Italy, Yugoslavia, Bulgaria, and Belgium. Three plays performed in Bombay, *Princes* (1970), *Savaksa* (1982), and *Mister Behram* (1987). Two books of poetry published, *Poems* (1966) and *How Do You Withstand, Body* (1976); poems also represented in anthologies. Fellow, Woodrow Wilson International Center for Scholars, 1984. Born in Bombay, 1940.

AROON PURIE, founding editor, *India Today.* Studied at London School of Economics. Member, Editors Guild. Born in Lahore, 1944.

A. K. RAMANUJAN, poet; professor, Department of South Asian Languages and Civilizations, Committee on Social Thought, and Department of Linguistics, University of Chicago. Received B.A., M.A. in English literature, Mysore University; Ph.D. in linguistics, Indiana University. Publications include poetry in Kannada and English (*The Striders, Relations*) and translations from Tamil and Kannada (*The Interior Landscape, Speaking of Siva*). Currently finishing volume of Kannada folktales. Awarded MacArthur Fellowship, 1983, and Padma Shri, 1976. Born in Mysore, 1929.

RAJ REWAL, architect and urban design consultant. Educated in Delhi and London. Worked in Paris before starting architectural practice in Delhi. Professor, School of Planning and Architecture, Delhi, 1963–72, teaching theory of design and history of Indian architecture. Lectured on traditions of Indian architecture and space-frame structures at Columbia University, University of Pennsylvania, Yale School of Architecture, and McGill University. Awarded first prize in major Indian architectural competitions including Bhikaiji Cama Bazaar, Engineers India Building, Television Centre for Delhi, North Eastern Hill University, Asian Games Village, stadium for five thousand persons for Asiad, SCOPE office complex in Delhi. Other works include Permanent Exhibition Complex in Delhi, staff quarters for French Embassy, National Institute of Immunology in Delhi, Nehru Pavilion in Delhi. Works widely published and exhibited in Autumn Festival, Paris, 1983; also featured in "Search for Identity," Pratt Institute, New York. Organized architectural exhibition for Festival of India in France, 1985, on traditional Indian architecture. Associate, Royal Institute of British Architects, Indian Institute of Architects. Born in Tanda, 1934.

S. DILLON RIPLEY, Secretary Emeritus, Smithsonian Institution; ornithologist and ecologist. Educated at Yale University (B.A. 1936) and Harvard University (Ph.D. 1943). Research specialization in the distribution and ecology of birds of the Old World, especially the Indian subcontinent. Director, Peabody Museum of Natural History, 1959–64; Secretary, Smithsonian Institution, 1964–84. Author of ten books and more than two hundred scholarly articles; recent publications include the monograph *Rails of the World* and *Compact Edition of the Handbook of Birds of India and Pakistan* (with Salim Ali). Fellow, American Association for the Advancement of Science; member, National Academy of Sciences. Awarded the Medal of Freedom, 1985; Padma Bhushan, 1986. Born in New York City, 1913.

RAJEEV SETHI, design and art projects consultant. Received B.A. in history, University of Delhi, 1968, and subsequently French government scholarship to study graphics with S. W. Hayter. Worked on industrial and clothing design (with Pierre Cardin), interior and environment design, theater and film production, educational workshops on communications, population, and development. Directed and designed international exhibitions, including "Forum of People" for United Nations World Population Conference in Bucharest, "Aditi" for Festival of India in Britain and the United States, "The Golden Eye" to develop crafts with international collaboration. Involved in establishment and management of arts and cultural cooperatives, in design of habitat and shelter for groups of rural artisans and families of itinerant performers. Member, All India Handicrafts Board; standing committee, National Crafts Museum; board of directors, Central Cottage Industries Corporation, Nehru Bal Bhavan Society of India, and National Children's Museum. Received Sanskriti Award, 1980, for outstanding social and cultural achievement, and Padma Bhushan (Award), 1986. Born in New Delhi, 1949.

GULAM MOHAMMED SHEIKH, painter; professor and head, Department of Painting, Faculty of Fine Arts, M. S. University of Baroda. Received M.A., Baroda, and A.R.C.A., Royal College of Art, London. Has taught Eastern and Western art and Indian aesthetics, Department of Art History, Baroda. Artist in residence, School of the Art Institute of Chicago, during 1987. Work has been exhibited at five one-man shows in Bombay and New Delhi, internationally in Tokyo, Paris, Washington, and London. Published articles on art in Gujarati, Hindi, and English, and book of poems in Gujarati, *Athawa*; coedited journal *Vrishchik*, 1969–73. Member, governing council, National Institute of Design. National Award, Lalit Kala Akademi for Painting, 1982, and Padma Shri (Award), 1983. Born in Surendranganar, 1937.

MILTON SINGER, professor emeritus, Department of Anthropology, and Paul Klapper Professor of the Social Sciences, University of Chicago. Received B.A. (1934), M.A. (1936), University of Texas at Austin; Ph.D. (1940), University of Chicago. Postdoctoral studies of Indian civilization and South Asian anthropology at University of Pennsylvania and University of California, Berkeley; field research in Madras. Associate director with Robert Redfield and later director of an interdisciplinary project at Chicago on the comparative study of cultures and civilizations (1951–61). Helped organize Committee on Southern Asian Studies, Chicago, and develop its teaching and research programs (1958–70). Coeditor with Robert Redfield of *Comparative Studies in Cultures and Civilizations* (1953–58), with Gerhart Piers of *Shame and Guilt: A Psy-*

choanalytic and Cultural Study (1953), with Bernard S. Cohn of *Structure and Change in Indian Society* (1968); editor, *Introducing India in Liberal Education* (1957), *Traditional India: Structure and Change* (1959), *Krishna: Myths, Rites, and Attitudes* (1966), *Entrepreneurship and Modernization of Occupational Cultures in South Asia* (1973); author, *When a Great Tradition Modernizes: An Anthropological Approach to Indian Civilization* (1972), *Man's Glassy Essence: Explorations in Semiotic Anthropology* (1984). Fellow, American Anthropological Association; fellow emeritus, American Academy of Arts and Sciences. Recipient, 1984 Distinguished Scholar Award, Association for Asian Studies.

SYLVIA VATUK, professor of anthropology, University of Illinois at Chicago. Educated at Cornell University (B.A. 1955), University of London (M.A. 1958), Harvard University (Ph.D. 1970). Research has focused on contemporary India, particularly family and kinship organization, women's roles, and the roles of the elderly in the urbanization process. Publications include *Kinship and Urbanization: White Collar Migrants in North India* (1972) and numerous scholarly articles. Fieldwork in India funded by research grants from American Institute of Indian Studies, National Institute of Mental Health. Board of directors, Association for Asian Studies. Born in Providence, 1934.

BAL BIR VOHRA, chairman, Advisory Board on Energy, Government of India. Educated at University of Punjab, Lahore (M.A. 1943). Joined Indian Administrative Service, 1948. Chief administrator, Chandigarh Project, and head, Punjab Government Agriculture Ministry, 1958–66. Served Government of India in various capacities in Department of Agriculture between 1967 and 1975; as head, Ministry of Petroleum, 1976–81. Appointed chairman, National Committee on Environmental Planning, 1981. Led Indian delegation at ninth and tenth sessions of UNEP Governing Council, 1981 and 1982, and first Indian Environmental Delegation to China, 1981. Has written many papers on management of land, water resources, and the environment. Delivered Sardar Patel Memorial Lectures, 1980. Born in Lyallpur, 1923.

Symposium Program

*"The Canvas of Culture: Rediscovery of the
Past As Adaptation for the Future"*

Smithsonian Institution, Washington, D.C.,
June 21–23, 1985

Chairpersons: Pupul Jayakar, Cultural Advisor to the Prime Minister
     of India
     S. Dillon Ripley, Smithsonian Institution

June 21
Opening Ceremonies
Auditorium, Freer Gallery of Art,
10:30 A.M.–noon

Presiding: Wilton S. Dillon, Smithsonian Institution

Recognition of Sponsors
Introduction of Special Guests
Greetings and Messages
    Rajiv Gandhi, Prime Minister of India (read by
     Mr. Ripley)
    J. William Fulbright, Washington, D.C. (read by
     Mr. Ripley)

John McTague, Office of Science and Technology
Policy, the White House

Speakers: Pupul Jayakar, "Culture and the Creative Mind"
              S. Dillon Ripley, "The Conservation of Nature and
              Culture in India"

Being and Meaning
Baird Auditorium, National Museum of
Natural History, 2:15–5:00 P.M.

Chairperson: Stella Kramrisch, Philadelphia Museum of Art

Speakers: Kapila Vatsyayan, Indira Gandhi National Centre for
              Arts, New Delhi, "Canvas or Body Organism"
              Veena Das, University of Delhi, "Difference and
              Division As Designs for Human Society"
              Wendy Doniger O'Flaherty, University of Chicago,
              "Impermanence and Eternity in Indian Literature
              and Art"
              Jyotindra Jain, Crafts Museum, New Delhi,
              "Significance of Regional Myths, Rituals, and Art
              Forms"
              C. M. Naim, University of Chicago, "Being a Muslim
              in India: Opportunities and Challenges"
              Ramchandra Gandhi, New Delhi, "*Advaita:*
              Meditations on the Truth of India"

India on Film
Baird Auditorium, 8:00–10:00 P.M.
Premiere of "Pleasing God," a 1985 trilogy by Robert Gardner, Akos
Östör, and Allen Moore, Film Study Center, Harvard University.

June 22
The Environment
Baird Auditorium, 9:15 A.M.–noon

Chairperson: B. B. Vohra, Government of India Advisory Board on
              Energy, New Delhi

Speakers: S. Dillon Ripley, Smithsonian Institution, "The Need
             for a Coherent Program of Conservation and Pres-
             ervation in India"
             Madhav Gadgil, Indian Institute of Science, Bangalore,
             "Husbanding India's Natural Resources: The Tra-
             dition and the Prospects"
             D. K. Lahiri Choudhury, North-East India Task Force,
             IUCN/SSC Asian Elephant Group, Calcutta, "The
             Indian Elephant in the Wild and Domesticity: An
             Overview"
             Gerald D. Berreman, University of California, Berke-
             ley, "Chipko: A Grass-roots Movement to Save
             the Himalayas"
             Anil Agarwal, Centre for Science and Environment,
             New Delhi, "Awareness, Education, and Action"
             B. B. Vohra, "The Greening of India: Challenges and
             Opportunities"

"Reclaiming the Desert,"
a 1984 film by Ishwar Pandey

Baird Auditorium, 1:00–1:30 P.M.

Artists Speak
Baird Auditorium, 2:00–6:00 P.M.

Chairperson: Ashok Vajpeyi, Department of Culture, Government of
                Madhya Pradesh

Speakers: A. K. Ramanujan, University of Chicago, "Classics
             Lost and Found"
             Gieve Patel, Bombay, "Daruwalla's Asoka Poem and
             Patwardhan's Drawings in Time: Two Studies"
             Gulam Mohammed Sheikh, University of Baroda,
             "Among Several Cultures and Times"
             Girish Karnad, Bombay, "In Search of a New
             Theater"
             Haku Shah, Tribal Arts Museum, Ahmedabad,
             "Creativity Inborn"
             Rajeev Sethi, New Delhi, "Dialogues on Continuity
             and Change" (followed by a special visit to the
             exhibition "Aditi: A Celebration of Life")

Contemporary Reinterpretation
of Traditional Architecture

Auditorium, Hirshhorn Museum and
Sculpture Garden, 8:00–11:00 P.M.

Chairperson: Sylvia Gottwald-Thapar, Washington, D.C.

Speakers: Raj Rewal, New Delhi
Balkrishna V. Doshi, Ahmedabad
Charles Correa, Bombay

June 23
Social Transitions
Baird Auditorium, 10:00–12:45 P.M.

Chairperson: Bernard S. Cohn, University of Chicago

Speakers: Surajit C. Sinha, Centre for Studies in Social Sciences,
Calcutta, "Tribes in Modern India: Scope for Con-
servation and Restructuring"
David G. Mandelbaum, University of California,
Berkeley, "Women and Men in India: Sex Roles
and Gender Relations in the Purdah Regions"
Ela R. Bhatt, Self-Employed Women's Association,
Ahmedabad, "Organizing Self-Employed Women
for Self-Reliance"
Sylvia Vatuk, University of Illinois at Chicago,
"Making New Homes in the City: Urbanization
and the Contemporary Indian Family"
Aroon Purie, *India Today,* New Delhi, "The Changing
Social Role of Journalism"
Arjun Appadurai, University of Pennsylvania,
"Changes in the Culture of Agriculture"

The Interplay of Science,
Technology, and Culture
Baird Auditorium, 3:00–5:45 P.M.

Chairperson: Nathan Glazer, Harvard University

Speakers: David E. Pingree, Brown University, "Innovation and
               Stagnation in Medieval Indian Astronomy"
               Robert S. Anderson, Simon Fraser University, "Forest,
               Field, and Heaven: Three Perspectives on Science
               in Modern India"
               Kartikeya V. Sarabhai, Nehru Foundation for Develop-
               ment, Ahmedabad, "Technology for Development:
               The Cultural Context"
               Sudhir Kakar, Centre for the Study of Developing So-
               cieties, New Delhi, "Models of Psychological
               Healing: Indian and Western"
               E. C. G. Sudarshan, University of Texas, Austin,
               "Global Aspects of Indian Culture"

A Final Look Back—and Forward
Auditorium, Hirshhorn Museum, 8:30–10:00 P.M.

Introduction: K. Shankar Bajpai, Ambassador of India to the United
                States

Speaker: F. Champion Ward, Cos Cob, Connecticut, "Toward a
                Congenial Progress"

June 24

Intellectual Cooperation with India:
Some Next Steps
Library, Woodrow Wilson
International Center for Scholars,
Smithsonian Institution Building,
10:00 A.M.–noon

Presiding: John E. Reinhardt, Smithsonian Institution

Panelists: Ted M. G. Tanen, Indo-U.S. Subcommission on Educa-
                tion and Culture
                Deborah Wince, Office of Science and Technology
                Policy, the White House
                Ahmed Meer, American Embassy, New Delhi
                David Challinor, Smithsonian Institution
                Ludwig Rudel, India International, Inc.
                Scott DeLisi, U.S. Department of State
                Francine Berkowitz, Smithsonian Institution

COMMENTATORS

Joseph W. Elder, professor, Departments of Sociology and South Asian Studies, University of Wisconsin

McKim Marriott, professor, Department of Anthropology and Social Sciences Collegiate Division, University of Chicago

Ahmed Meer, counselor for scientific and technological affairs, American Embassy, New Delhi

Deba P. Patnaik, director, Third World House, and Faculty Professor of Humanities, Oberlin College (subsequently moved to University of Michigan)

Karl Potter, professor, Department of Philosophy and South Asian Program, University of Washington

V. Narayana Rao, professor, Department of South Asian Studies, University of Wisconsin

Roger Revelle, professor, Program in Science, Technology, and Public Policy, University of California, San Diego

Sunil K. Roy, member, National Commission for Environment Planning, New Delhi

Mildred Talbot, New York City

Phillips Talbot, president emeritus, The Asia Society

Index

Art, 5–6, 20–21, 22, 28, 36–37, 151; contemporary, 38–39; education, 109–11; fluidity in, 83–84; forms of, 107–8, 119n.6; permanency of, 83; realism in, 115, 127; sacred, 84–85; traditional, 150–52, pls. 13, 14; variety in, 108–9
Arthasastra (Kautilya), 302, 326
Arunachal Pradesh, elephants in, 307(table), 318, 320n.9
Arya Samaj, 48
Asian Elephant Specialist Group, 304, 312
Asian Games Village, traditional design in, 360–69
Asoka, Emperor, in poetry, 122–25
Assam, 4; elephant distribution in, 307(table), 311, 320n.9
Assassination of Indira Gandhi (Chitrakar), pl.7
Astronomy, 34

Baansri, 214–15, 217
Bahuguna, Sunderlal, 247, 257, 260n.6; activity, 248–49
Baig, Tara Ali, 233
Bamboo cooperatives, 212, 214–15
Bandipur, 326
Bangalore, 341(fig.), 342–43
Bangladesh, 59, 222
Banking, for self-employed, 211–12
Bansfodia community, 214
Bastar district, 275
Bayalata drama, 105
Belapur housing, 381(fig.)
Bengal, 311
Bengalis, 114
Berar, 310
Bhagavadgita, 14, 95, 297
Bharati, Dharma Vir: *Andha Yug*, 94–95
Bharatpur, 326
Bhatt, Chandi Prasad, 246, 248, 249, 257, 260n.6
Bhima, 54
Bhindranwale, (Sant) Jarnail Singh, 104, 170
Bhotiyas, 242, 253–54
Bhubaneshwar, 337(fig.)
Bihar, 307(table); animal fairs, 314–17
Biomass, 274–75, 277, 281; depletion of, 278–79, 280; increasing availability of, 282–83
Block-printing cooperatives, 212, 213–14
Bombay, low-income housing in, 379–83; theater, 95, 96
Bombay Beggary Act (1954), 152
Borobudur, 377(fig.)
Bose, Subhas Chandra, 163
Brahma, 339, 340, 347
Brahmanism, 325

Brahmans, 6, 48, 83, 254
Brahmaputra River: elephant population on, 306, 318, 320n.9
British Raj, 163, 304, 326–27
Buddha, 301, 325
Buddhism, 84, 122, 133; elephant lore in, 301–302. *See also* Buddhists
Buddhists, 242, 253–54

Calcutta, 95
Cane cooperatives, 214–15
Castes, 4, 8, 31, 36, 45–47, 97, 98, 99–101, 194, 277, 325, 330; in Chipko, 254–56; ecological niches of, 326–27; employment of, 153, 217–18; ideology, 51–53; in SEWA, 217–18; violence against, 50–51. *See also various castes*
Central Ganga Authority, 286
Centre for Science and Environment, 257, 271
Ceremonies, 182. *See also* Rituals
Chamoli district, 246, 248, 250, 254
Chandalas, 325
Chandimangal stories, 114, 119n.11
Chhipas: block-printing cooperatives, 213, 214
Chilha, 306
China, 159–60, 164, 165, 287, 288, 292
Chindi cooperative, 212, 213, 218
Chipko Andolan, 8, 10, 31, 239, 256–57, 271, 279; actions of, 247–49; castes in, 254–56; diffusion of, 250–52; divisiveness in, 249–50; leadership of, 252–53, 260n.6; origins of, 240, 246–47; social diversity in, 252–56
Chitrakar, Ajit: *Assassination of Indira Gandhi*, pl.7
Chopra, Ravi, 257
Chotanagpur Plateau, 276
Christianity, 5, 48, 49, 55; *advaitin* philosophy and, 71–72
Cidade de Goa, 379, pl.21
Cilappatikaram, 133
CITES. *See* Convention on International Trade in Endangered Species
Cities. *See* Urban sector; *various cities*
Citizens for Democracy, 257
City for Sale (Sheikh), 118
Civakacintamani, 134, 135, 136
Classics: fluidity of truth in, 82–85; Indian, 79–82; Western, 77–79. *See also* Tamil texts
Colonialism, 21, 97, 244; forest policy, 244–45; legacy of, 33, 47–48, 51, 95. *See also* British Raj; Great Britain
Comics, 87
Communalism, 4, 60, 95, 118, 157, 170, 327

See also *Advaita*

Illiteracy, 82, 158, 159, 206, 207, 208, 212, 217

Income, 208, 222. *See also* Employment; Self-employment

Independence, 21, 93, 97, 99, 163, 256–57; of press, 163–64

Indian Development Service, 271

Indian Express (newspaper), 167

Indian Forest Act, 244–45, 318

Indian Institute of Management, Bangalore, 341(fig.), 342–43

India Today (magazine), 168

Indo-Aryans, 84

Indo-Chinese border war, 242

Indology, 134

Indra, 301

Industrialization, 9, 152, 155, 205–6, 207, 272–73. *See also* Pollution: industrial

Indus Valley civilization, 309

"Integrated Watershed Development Project," 248

International Farm Plantation Allied Workers (Geneva), 209

International Union for Conservation of Nature and Natural Resources (IUCN), 304

International Union of Food and Tobacco Workers (Geneva), 209

Irrigation, 288–89

Islam, 27, 48, 49, 60, 63n.3, 64n.6, 108, 114; community organization of, 57–58; fundamentalism, 5, 55; poetic imagery of, 121–22. *See also* Muslims

Isvara, 48

IUCN. *See* International Union for Conservation of Nature and Natural Resources

Izzat, and women's seclusion, 226–28

Jahangir, Emperor, 303–4

Jain, Jyotindra, 35–36

Jains, 83; Tamil texts of, 134–35

Jaipur, traditional architecture in, 338(figs.), 364(fig.), 368(fig.), 377

Jaisalmer, traditional architecture in, 348(figs.), 360(fig.), 362(fig.), 363(fig.)

Jama'at-i-Islami, 59

Jayakar, Pupul, 12, 24

Jokumara, 105

Jokumaraswamy (Kambar), 105

Journalism, 157, 170; changes in, 163, 164–65; magazine, 167–68; role of, 161–62, 168–69

Journals, 163

Kaikadis, 326

Kakar, Sudhir, 7–8, 9, 32–33, 86, 99, 231–32

Kakinada, 273

Kali, 47, 74, 102

Kama, 86

Kamasutra (Vatsyayana), 302

Kambar, Chandrasekhar, 105

Kangra painting, 112, 119n.9

Karanth, B. V., 102

Karanth, Shivaram, 102

Karnad, Girish, 132

Karnataka state, 102, 271, 275, 307(table), 326; forest development in, 250–51

Kathakali, 102

Kathasaritsagara, 102, 118, 120n.15

Kautilya: *Arthasastra*, 302, 326

Kedarnath, 54

Kerala, 271, 307(table)

Kerala Sastra Sahitya Parishad, 271

Kesari (newspaper), 163

Khagra, 315(table)

Khajuraho, 345(fig.)

Khandava forest, 325

Khilafat movement, 59

Kin (Sheikh), 117–18, pl.9

"The King Speaks to the Scribe" (Daruwalla), 122–25

Knowledge, forms of, 48, 136, 174–82, 270, 283, 328, 330

Kota painting, 112, 119n.8

Kothari, Rajni, 257

Krishna, 53, 54–55, 86, 95, 325

Kshatriyas, 47

Kumaon, 244, 280

Kumbakonam, 134

Kurukshetra War, 94–95

Labor, agricultural, 175, 184n.1. *See also* Employment; Self-employment; Trade unions

Ladakh, 277

Lakshmi, 301

Land ownership. *See* Property

Land reform, 277

Land use: agricultural, 288–89; village, 289–90

Language, 4, 5, 39–40n.5, 94, 96, 101, 131, 134, 137, 170, 180, 240; and agricultural knowledge, 180–81. *See also* Sanskrit

Law, 51; and morality, 52–53; of nation-state, 52

Lions, 326

Literature, 5, 6, 22, 86, 88, 131; immortality of, 83–84. *See also* Classics; Tamil texts

Livestock. *See* Animal husbandry

Madhya Pradesh, 275, 310

Madras, 95

Magazines. *See* Press
Magic, 149
Magsaysay Award, 248
Mahabharata, 70, 79, 83, 118, 325; oral tradition of, 80–81; in plays, 94, 95; in written texts, 81–82
Mahamaya, 324–25
Maharashtra, 97, 275, 277; agricultural changes in, 182–83; castes in, 326–27; traditional agriculture in, 177, 178–79, 180–82
Maharshi, Ramana, 68–69
Mahdavis, persecution of, 58, 63n.1
Mahishasura, 54
Makadwallas, 326
Malabar, 49
Manasa stories, 114, 119n.11
Manekchowk, 209
Manimekalai, 133
Manipur, 307(table)
Manushi (journal), 170, 257
Markets: city, 209–10; SEWA, 216–17
Marriage, 182, 228, 229, 233
Marxism, 97, 98
Mass media, craft production and, 153–54
Materialism, 72, 73
Maternity Benefit Scheme, 210
Mathematics, Indian, 34, 35
Maudoodi, Maulana, 59, 64n.8
Mazes, symbolism in, 149–50
Media, 158, 160, 247. *See also* Press
Meena Bazaar, 377–78
Meghalaya State, elephant distribution in, 306, 307(table), 318, 320n.9
Mehta, Vijaya, 101
Menon, V. K. Krishna, 165
Migration, 243, 282; and family structure, 188, 191–93, 194, 196–97; to urban centers, 9, 187–88
Ministry of Agriculture, 286, 294
Ministry of Health, 293
Ministry of Human Resources Development, 293
Ministry of Industry, 293
Ministry of Information and Broadcasting, 293
Ministry of Rural Development, 294
Ministry of Transport, 293
Ministry of Urban Development, 293
Ministry of Water Resources, 294
Mitti Bachao Abhiyan, 271
Mizoram state, 307(table), 318
Modernism, 5, 11–12, 46, 51, 55, 60, 371
Modernity, 8, 39, 39n.4, 95, 136, 328
Modernization, 8–9, 36, 45–46, 88, 134, 180–81, 183, 270, 299, 281; distinguished from Westernization, 234; and environ-

mental degradation, 276–78
Modhera, 336(fig.)
Mohenjo-Daro, 14
Monotheism, 48, 71
Morality, and law, 52–53
Mrcchakatika, 101
Mr. Sampath (Narayan), 86–87
Mudaliyar, Ramasami, 134
Mughals, 151, 310, 326; architectural design, 357, 377–78; art, 112–14, 113(fig.), 118, 127, pl.14; fighting elephants, 303–4
Murals, in Shekhawati, 112, 113–14
Murugan, 137; poems about, 138–45
Music, 105, 112, 114
Muslim Personal Law, 64n.5
Muslims, 4, 5, 27, 63n.4, 64n.5, n.7; community organization of, 57–59; and purdah, 222, 228, 229–30; sacred sites of, 46, 55; South Asian, 61–62, 63n.3
Mythology, 6, 35–36, 46, 60, 67, 83, 94–95, 100, 135–36; in architecture, 375–76; in children's literature, 88; creation, 46–47; elephants in, 301–2; in environment, 269–70; preservation of, 86–87, 88; survival of, 85–87

Naccinarkkiniyar, 135, 136
Nagaland, elephant distribution in, 302(table), 318
Nagas, 325
Naini Tal, 249, 250
Nandiwallas, 326
Nandy, Ashis, 60, 97
Narayan, R. K.: *Mr. Sampath,* 86–87
Nathdwara, 108
National Environmental Committee, 285
National Forest Policy (1952), 308
National Institute of Design, 217
National Institute of Immunology, pl.20; design of, 370–74
National Integration Award, 248
Nationalism, 21, 46, 63n.3, 163; and language, 39–40n.5
Nation-state, 5; concept of, 45–46; legitimacy of, 51–53
Nature. *See* Environment
Nature reserves, 326
Nehru, Jawaharlal, 4, 221; *The Discovery of India,* 21; press and, 163, 164–65
Nehru Pavilion, design for, 357–59
New Bombay, low-income housing in, 380–83
New Delhi: Asian Games Village, 360–69; exhibition complex, 355–57, 358(fig.); National Institute of Immunology, 370–74
Newspapers. *See* Press
Nicobar Islands, 273

Nilgiri Hills, 132
Nonduality. *See Advaita*

Oral tradition, 5, 6, 35–36, 68, 77, 87; fluidity of truth in, 82–85; *Mahabharata*, 80–81; *Rg Veda*, 79–80
Orissa state, elephant distribution in, 306, 307(table), 320n.9

Pabuji ka Phad, pl.6
Padma Shri Awards, 248
Paharis, 242, 253–54
Painting, 84, 107, 119n.4; contemporary, 116–18, 127; folk, 153; Indian style, 111–14; idea sources for, 108, 115–18; ritual, 85, 149; of stories, 114–15, 118
Pakistan, 59, 222
Palakapya: *Hastyayurveda*, 302
Palgat gap, 306
Pandavas, 325–26
Panicker, K. N., 101
Panna, 310
Paper industry, 273, 275
Paper-pickers' cooperative, 215
Parliament, parties in, 160–61
Parsi theater, 96–97
Past, 11, 13, 46, 78, 94, 134, 140, 151, 318, 359, 371, 375; "amnesia," 95; dangers of, 31, 60–62, 132; multiplicity of, 6, 20, 27, 60–61, 135; rediscovery of, 3, 6, 19, 20–22, 25, 35, 46, 60, 62, 131, 184, 331; relationship with present, 7, 12, 20, 26, 102, 105, 107, 116, 125, 129, 131–33, 136–37, 151, 355, 380
Pastoral nomadism, 276
Pataleshwar temple, 345(fig.)
*Pata*s, 114
Patel, Jabbar, 104–5
Patgars, 326
Patwardhan, Sudhir, 121, pls. 13, 14; drawings, 127–29
Pauri Garhwal district: Chipko, 246, 250
Phasepardhis, 326, 327
Physics, 35, 73
Pilgrimages, 182; environmental impact of, 243, 260n.4; integration through, 53–55
Pillai, Minakshisundaram, 136
Pingree, David, 13, 34
Planning Commission, 248, 298
Plays, 94; historical, 97–98; modern, 102–3; mythology in, 94–95; Parsi, 97–98; production of, 104–5
Pluralism, 4, 5–6, 7, 28, 46–47, 55–56, 83, 108
Poetry, 22; Daruwalla's, 121–27; imagery in, 122–25; religious, 133, 140–45; Tamil, 132–34, 137–40

Pollution, 271, 273; industrial, 285, 286, 292, 293; water, 271, 273, 277
Polytheism, 47–48, 49, 71
Population growth, 233, 276, 286
Porus, 302
Poverty, 194, 281; in Bombay, 379–83; and environment, 274–76
"Prayers to Lord Murugan" (Ramanujan), 140–45
Press, 158; censorship of, 160, 166–67; and environmental movements, 247–48; freedom of, 162–63, 170; and government, 160–61, 165–66; and independence, 163–64; magazines, 167–68; post-independence, 164–65; responsibility of, 159, 160; role of, 159–60, 164, 168–69, 170–71
Press Commission, 164
Progress, 48, 173, 183, 221, 232
Project Tiger, 286
Property, 51, 230; family ownership of, 189, 190
Psychotherapy, 7–8, 32–33
Pune, 345(fig.)
Punjab, 4, 169, 221
Purdah, 9–10, 221–22, 232; Hindu, 228, 229, 230; Muslim, 228, 229–30; observing, 222–24, 233; as protection, 225–26
Purusha, 47, 50

Radhanagari, 326
Radio, 160
Ragamala paintings, 112
Raj. *See* British Raj; Colonialism
Rajasthan, 277; architecture, 367(fig.), 380–81, 382(fig.)
Rajasthan Canal, 277
Rajputs, 225, 254
Ramanujan, A. K.: "Prayers to Lord Murugan," 140–45
Ramayana, 82
Ranathambhor, 326
Red Fort (Agra), 377–78
Redfield, Robert, 3–4, 13
Reforestation. *See* Afforestation
Regionalism, 62; in Himalayas, 239–40
Religion, 4, 46, 50; aboriginal, 73–74; *advaita* in, 68, 69; art and, 84–85; fundamentalism in, 55–56; monotheism in, 48, 71; polytheism in, 47–48, 49, 71; purdah and, 229–30; reform in, 47–48; women's roles in, 223–24. *See also* Rituals; *various religions*
Renaissance, 78, 111, 119n.6; Tamil, 136
Reni Forest, 254
Research, foreign, 257–58, 260n.7
Resources, 242; cultural diversity and, 326–28; exploitation of, 272–76; manage-

ment of, 285–86, 287–89, 328. *See also*
Biomass; Environment; Forests
Returning Home after a Long Absence
(Sheikh), 116(fig.)
Revolving Routes (Sheikh), 118, pl.11
Rg Veda, 79–80, 84–85
Rituals, 5, 8, 49, 182; and architecture,
336–37; continuation of, 150–51
Roads, in Uttarakhand, 242, 243
Roy, Raja Rammohun, 48
Rural sector, 31, 170, 194, 195, 230, 283;
afforestation programs in, 289–90; agri-
cultural knowledge in, 179–80; emigration
from, 187, 188; environmental movement
in, 253, 256–57; environmental use,
274–76, 277–78; land use, 289–90; lower
castes in, 254–55; resource management
in, 328–29; Uttarakhand, 243, 249;
women in, 184, 278–80. *See also* Forests;
Urban sector

Sabina cooperative, 213
Sacred groves, 20; protection of, 323–24
Safaikam cooperative, 216
Sakuntala, 101
Sangath, 343–44, 346–47, pls.17, 18
Sanitation, 286, 287, 292, 293
Sanskrit, 140, 302; oral tradition of, 6, 7; in
theater, 101–2; written texts, 6, 79–82
Santoshi Ma (film), 86
Sarabhai, Kartikeya, 12, 33–34
Saraswati, Dayanand, 47–48, 50
Sarvoyada workers, in environmental move-
ments, 246–47, 254
Satta Pir, 114
Satyartha Prakash, 48
Saundarya Mandali, 216
Science, 13, 32–35, 45, 73, 179, 282–83,
297, 328
Scroll paintings, 114
Second Press Commission, 170
Secularism, in art, 84; in polity, 27, 45–46,
73, 179; in texts, 48; in theater, 96–97
Self-Employed Women's Association
(SEWA), 28, 203, 207; castes in, 217–18;
cooperatives of, 212–16; financial services
for, 208, 211–12; functions of, 216–19;
markets for, 209–10; maternity benefits
for, 210–11
Self-employment, 10, 28; categories of,
207–9; cooperatives for, 212–16; culture
of, 206–7; financial services for, 211–12;
maternity issues in, 210–11; in traditional
society, 205–6; women's, 203, 204–5. *See
also* Self-Employed Women's Association
Separatism, 4, 46

SEWA. *See* Self-Employed Women's Associa-
tion
SEWA Bank. *See* Shri Mahila SEWA Sahakari
Bank
SEWA Dastkari Bazaar, 216
SEWA Economic Self-Reliance Wing, 216,
218
Shah, Haku, 36–37
Shahdol district, 271
Shahdol Group, 271
Sharma, Kalpana, 257
Shasti, 149
Sheikh, Gulam Mohammed: *About Waiting
and Wandering,* 117(fig.), 118; *City for
Sale,* 118(fig.); *Kin,* 117–18, pl.9;
Returning Home after a Long Absence,
116(fig.), 117; *Revolving Routes,* 118,
pl.11; *Speaking Street,* 118, pl.10; *Summer
Diary,* pl.12
Shekhawati, murals in, 112, 113–14, 119n.10
Shikhara temple, 345(fig.)
Shilpa Sagar, 155
Shitala Mata, 150
Shivaji, 323
Shourie, Arun, 257
Shri Mahila SEWA Sahakari Bank, 212, 214,
215–16
Siddhartha, 324–25
Sikhism, 5, 55
Sikhs, 4, 46
Silyara, 250
Simlipal National Park, 306
Simon Company, 246
Singheswar, 315(table)
Sinha, Surajit, 4, 6, 35–36
Sitamari, 315(table)
Siva, 54, 86, 103, 269–70
Social movements, 239–40, 254. *See also*
Chipko Andolan; Environmental move-
ments
Sonepur: animal fair, 314, 316–17, 318, pl.15
Songs, 150
Speaking Street (Sheikh), 118, pl.10
Species Survival Commission (SSC), 304
Spice gardens, 328–29
Squatters, architecture for, 379–83
SSC. *See* Species Survival Commission
State Department of Social Defence, 217
Statesman (newspaper), 166, 167
Stories, illustrating, 114–15, 118
Sudarshan, E.C.G., 13, 34–35
Sudras, 47, 325
Sufi cults, 55
Sujata, 215, 217
Summer Diary (Sheikh), pl.12
Sunday (magazine), 168
Syrian Christians, 49

financial services for, 211–12; illiteracy among, 207, 208; and *izzat,* 226–28; maternity benefits for, 210–11, 232; and purdah, 221–24, 232; self-employment of, 28, 203, 204–5, 208. *See also* Self-Employed Women's Association

Women's Cooperative SEWA Bank. *See* Shri Mahila SEWA Sahakari Bank

Work. *See* Employment; Labor, agricultural; Self-employment

Yakshagana, 102
Yayati (Karnad), 94
Young India (journal), 163
Yudhishthira, 325–26

This stimulating collection of essays explores the dynamics of tradition in contemporary Indian life. From a variety of perspectives and disciplines, twenty-three leading intellectuals energetically address questions that are central to them personally and to Indian society as a whole. Multiple pasts and presents coexist, interact, and collide, as do Western and indigenous systems of knowledge, belief, and practice. How to construct out of these diverse influences an authentic, vital culture, supported by a sustainable natural resource base, is one of the fundamental tasks facing postcolonial societies worldwide. India's experience with such a challenge, as the world's largest democracy and heir to one of its oldest civilizations, is particularly compelling.

The contributors to this volume are a remarkable group, drawn mainly from the generation that came of age as India was realizing its independence. The presence here of playwrights, poets, painters, environmentalists, philosophers, architects, designers, union organizers, and journalists, as well as American and Indian scholars, nourishes a rich interplay of ideas and insights about the nature of Indian civilization and also about alternative models for modernization. As the essays show, the mere transfer of values and practices from other eras or societies often leads to distortion, displacement, and conflict. Instead, these values and practices must be understood in their essence, then reinterpreted in ways appropriate to the contemporary context. Through the contributors' engaging anal-